LAW AND THE LAWLESS

LAW AND THE LAWLESS

A READER IN CRIMINOLOGY

Gresham M. Sykes
College of Law, University of Denver

Thomas E. Drabek
Department of Sociology, University of Denver

RANDOM HOUSE
New York

FIRST PRINTING

Library of Congress Catalog Card Number: 69–10776

Manufactured in the United States of America by American Book–Stratford Press, Inc.

Designed by Richard-Gabriel Rummonds.

PREFACE

There are few social problems that arouse greater public concern than the problem of crime. Whether the crime be murder or embezzlement, assault or the peddling of drugs, violations of criminal law evoke a strong demand for corrective action. Theories about the nature of crime, its causes, its prevention, and its cure clamor for our attention.

In an area so charged with emotion, the need for clear vision is imperative. The definition of crime itself is often filled with ambiguities and frequently involves a clash of values that is quite ignored in the haste to find a solution to the problem. The cause of crime is still an intricate puzzle in social behavior, and no easy explanation will fit the observed facts. The rehabilitation of the offender may be a worthy goal, but society lacks a proven means; and society is always faced with the difficult task of weighing individual liberties against the protection of its members from harm.

We make no pretense in this collection of readings of covering the subject of crime in depth. The topic is too complex and the literature too vast. Instead, our intention is to expose as many of the main issues as possible, and each selection should be viewed as no more than a small window opening onto an extensive and complicated area of debate.

Our choice was between a relatively limited number of readings presented in full and a larger number of selections cut down and shaped to reveal the major points. We have followed the latter course, with all its dangers, in the belief that an understanding of crime and its control must be based on an awareness of the total system of behavior that is involved. (We have eliminated all footnotes to the readings in the interest of brevity.)

What people are willing to call a crime depends in part on what they think they can do about the behavior in question. The effectiveness of facilities for the rehabilitation of offenders depends in part on the number of offenders recognized and arrested by the police. The type of criminals placed on probation influences the composition of the prison population. The stigma of being labeled a criminal, by conviction in a court, may be both a consequence of criminal behavior in the past and a cause of criminal behavior in the future. If we focus on only a small portion of the crime problem, without any knowledge of the larger system in which it is embedded, we are all too likely to arrive at a distorted or misleading interpretation.

War, it has been said, is too important to be left to the generals. If the readers of this collection, in the same spirit, finish with the feeling that the problem of crime is too important to be placed in the hands of a few experts and then ignored, then they will be in agreement with us. The definition of crime and the handling of crime are the proper concern of society at large. It is a concern, however, that carries with it the need to be informed, taking into account opposing viewpoints—and the need to keep our minds fixed on the concept of justice as we attempt to enforce the law.

One further point should be made. We could well have called this collection of readings an anthology, rather than a reader, with the idea of underlining the element of personal choice that is involved in such a collection. An *anthologia* is, after all, a gathering of flowers, the work of other men, and our contribution must be largely in our choice. Other social scientists would undoubtedly come up with a different set of readings, but that is as it should be. We have often gone outside the traditional boundaries of the literature in criminology, for crime shows an odd reluctance to fit itself neatly into any particular academic discipline.

We would like to thank the American Foundation for Continuing Education for providing financial support for our project.*

We would also like to express our great appreciation for the efforts of Boyd Littrell and Charles Cortese. It was their work, to a large extent, that made this collection possible.

Gresham M. Sykes and Thomas E. Drabek

* The AFCE is a nonprofit educational organization devoted to the development of study programs in a variety of disciplines, focusing on the issues of our times. A catalog of materials is available upon request from the American Foundation for Continuing Education, 437 Madison Avenue, New York, N.Y. 10022.

CONTENTS

PART II: WHAT CAUSES CRIME?

PART III: WHAT CAN BE DONE?

PART I

WHAT IS A CRIME ?

INTRODUCTION

Lawrence P. Tiffany

The Meaning of Crime

The most important point to remember when addressing the question "What is a crime?" is simply this: What the legal system chooses to label a crime depends to a great extent on the context in which the question is raised. The same conduct will often be treated as criminal for some purposes but not for others, and the word "crime" has no single, consistent meaning.

Consider, for example, the common occurrence of speeding. Is speeding a crime? The answer will often depend upon why the question was asked, as two cases arising in the state of New York illustrate.

In the first case, a woman convicted of speeding applied for a court order setting aside the revocation of her license. One of the arguments she used was that she had not been advised of her right to have a lawyer, and the court replied:

There is no substance to her contention. . . . The New York Constitution and sections of the Code of Criminal Procedure deal with the right of a defendant to the aid of counsel in a criminal action. It will be noted that the Constitution and these sections of the code speak of crimes *and* criminal actions. *However, in this case the defendant was not accused and convicted of a crime. Speeding is a* traffic infraction *and not a crime . . .*[1]

In the second case a man was convicted of speeding but sued the officer who arrested him on the grounds that the arrest was illegal. He claimed that the officer failed to inform him of the reason for his arrest. In this case the appellate court held that speeding is a crime when the question is what procedures must be followed in making an arrest. Since the man was caught in the act of speeding, he did not have to be informed of the reason for the arrest. Therefore the false arrest suit was dismissed.[2]

If speeding is a crime for some purposes but not for others, we might therefore conclude that the speeder is sometimes a criminal. But the law avoids this logical implication; the Vehicle and Traffic Code of New York states that "the penalty or punishment imposed (for violation of the Code) shall not be deemed for any purpose a penal or criminal penalty or punishment . . ."[3]

Another aspect of the problem of definition deserves mention. Although the word "crime" generally refers to conduct made punishable by law, it is sometimes given a much more narrow meaning. Walter Reckless, in his book *The Crime Problem,* states that "the best test is to say that crime exists when it is brought forward to an official source, usually reported to the police . . . The non-reported offenses (which are either invisible or not brought forward) according to this test are not crimes. They remain unreported violations."[4] This situation, of course, places a severe restriction on the meaning of "crime." In effect, the statement quoted above equates crime with *reported* crime or *known* crime. All that is unusual about this statement, however, is that the author is careful to make his meaning explicit rather than implicit, for this equation is often the implicit definition of crime in much of the current public debate about the "crime problem." If a commentator asserts that statutory rape increased 10 percent in one year, he almost always means that 10 percent more statutory rapes were reported in that year than were reported in the previous year. Nothing is said about the frequency of the conduct proscribed by criminal law. It may, in fact, have decreased. Although it is certainly accurate to conclude that some of the behavior that violates a criminal statute does come to the attention of the authorities, it is another matter to assume that what is not reported does not exist. Failure to recognize this fact has serious effects on our perception of crime.

The Defining Process

A basic principle of the law requires that no behavior be treated as criminal unless it previously has been defined as criminal by a public body having the authority to do so. Complexity arises, however, out of the overlapping power of various public bodies that have the authority to define crimes.

In the first place, the overlapping jurisdictions of the federal, state, and local governments can lead to a considerable duplication of efforts. For example, the robbing of a federally insured bank involves two different crimes because it violates both a federal and a state law.[5] The offender may be convicted and punished by both federal and state authorities. Similarly, overlapping can occur between state and local governments, as in the case of an assault that violates both state and local law. In some cases, such as the possession of drugs, the offense may involve all three levels of government. In addition to the problems of duplication, of course, there are the problems of conflicting definitions in the area of crime, particularly with regard to criminal procedures.

In the second place, there are difficulties posed by the multiplicity of "crime-defining" agencies within any one level of government, because legislative, judicial, and executive branches of government all have a part to play in the process of attaching the label of crime to a particular piece of behavior—and they are not always in agreement. In general, the state legislatures are supposed to have the bulk of the responsibility for defining crimes, but by and large they have not been subjected to a comprehensive and systematic examination since they were first adopted in an earlier time in our history; and the changes that have been made consist largely of ad hoc additions in erratic response to immediate problems. The language, content, and underlying principles of many of our state criminal codes are remarkably antiquated.

The judicial branch of each level of government also has a significant role to play in the crime-defining process. It is their task to make the final decision as to whether or not the particular behavior involved in a criminal case falls within criminal law. This process of judicial interpretation may best be illustrated by the case of *People of Illinois v. Menagas.*[6] The Illinois legislature had enacted a criminal code, but as is true of most states their definitions of crimes were derived largely from the criminal law developed by English judges prior to the time of the American Revolution, and they had rather uncritically written this body of law into legislation. The legislature had, by this process, substantially adopted the common law definition of larceny: the trespassory taking and carrying away of the personal property of another with the intent to permanently deprive the owner of its use.

In the case of *People of Illinois v. Menagas,*[7] there was no factual dispute about what the defendant had done. He had wired the meter on his house so that the local power company could not measure how much electricity he had used. He was convicted of larceny and appealed his conviction to the Illinois Supreme Court. The legal question thus posed to that court was whether or not his conduct constituted larceny, and the court had to solve two problems. First, the court had to decide if electricity was "personal property" that could be "taken and carried away," as called for by the definition of larceny. On the basis of rather questionable premises about the nature of electricity, the court held that it was. Second, the definition of larceny required that it be shown that the owner had been deprived of the use of his property. But it is clear that the owner—in this case, the power company—wanted Menagas to use the electricity. It is true that the owner was deprived of the opportunity to measure how much electricity Menagas had used, but that may have been more a matter of fraud than of larceny; and larceny was the basis of the charge against him. In any event, the court avoided the problem and the conviction was upheld.

By this type of interpretative method, judges play their part in the crime-defining process. As a result of the Menagas case, larceny now meant something different than what the Illinois legislature had meant, because they obviously had not anticipated the question.

The aftermath of this case also illustrates what has been the dominant pattern of legislative function in defining crimes. The case publicized a problem and legislatures were quick to react: they could not rely on the strained interpretation of the Illinois Supreme Court. The conduct engaged in by the defendant in that case was quickly and specifically defined by legislation as a crime in most states. It is in this fashion that crimes are often added to the existing criminal codes.

The Enforcement Process

The role of the administrative branch of government in the process of defining crimes is somewhat more complicated. Administrative officials are sometimes delegated authority to exercise legislative authority. For example, federal legislation has placed restrictions on the use of dangerous drugs, and violation of these restrictions may subject the violator to criminal penalties. The Food and Drug Administration has been delegated authority to change from time to time the list of drugs that are considered dangerous. The FDA, by adding a new drug to the list, in effect creates a new set of crimes.[8]

Administrative enforcement authorities, however, have another and perhaps more significant function. Whereas legislatures and courts set the outer limits on what conduct *may* be treated as criminal, administrative officials set the outer limits on what conduct actually *will* result in prosecution. Although it is clear that behavior that falls outside the definition of crime may not be treated as criminal, it should not be assumed that behavior that falls within the literal limits of criminal law will, in fact, be treated as criminal. In short, police and prosecutors engage in what is called selective enforcement.[9]

Selective enforcement occurs in two general ways. In the first, the officials may desire full enforcement of criminal law but are unable to achieve it. In the second, even if the officials are able to fully enforce the law, they frequently decline to do so. Because of its importance to the question of what is a crime, we will need to discuss selective enforcement in some detail.

One of the most obvious conclusions to be drawn from observation of the current system of the administration of criminal justice is the fact that those responsible for the enforcement of criminal laws do not have sufficient resources to accomplish anything approaching full enforcement. It is extremely unlikely that when a legislature extends the catalog of crimes, it will make an appropriation to provide the additional resources necessary to enforce the new law. Thus, behind every decision in the system there lies the fact that if one offender is fully proceeded against, another cannot be. With limited resources, administrators must choose which crimes and which offenders will be given the most attention and will be viewed as the most serious.

Less than full enforcement may also be due to the conflict of goals within the system. The problems involved in the area of narcotics can serve as an example. The police concerned with narcotic law enforcement are very likely to regard the apprehension and conviction of major distributors of narcotics as an important task. That goal, however, may conflict with the goal of prosecuting the users of narcotics if the police have come to believe that it is essential to maintan a system of narcotic users as informers. Many detectives argue that a system of informers is essential, that minor criminals—including addicts—must be protected so that they will provide information about more serious offenders. When these minor criminals commit an offense they may be charged with a lesser crime, or may be released outright, in exchange for their having given information in the past and in the expectation that they will provide information in the future. Persons who otherwise would be charged with possession of narcotics may be set free if they will participate in a supervised sale of narcotics with a suspect higher up in the distributive chain.

In each of these situations, police, prosecutors, and judges are under pressures not to enforce the laws fully. But it should not be concluded from this discussion that administrators would fully enforce criminal laws if these pressures caused by limited resources and goal conflicts did not exist. The system of law enforcement maintains a considerable level of tolerance of rule breaking for reasons quite apart from pressures within the system itself, and several illustrations will make the point clear.[10] Administrators, for example, may not believe that the legislature actually meant for the law to be strictly or literally enforced—a typical situation with regard to gambling statutes. Such criminal laws frequently are drafted in a way that would, if read literally, make a crime of Saturday night poker games and bingo games held for charitable purposes. Thus, full enforcement of gambling statutes would quickly lead to substantial public criticism.

Other laws seem to be designed only to state what ought to be considered immoral conduct, but without any expectation that violators of the moral code will actually be subjected to prosecution. The crime of adultery is an outstanding example.

There are other important factors that contribute to less than full enforcement. These factors include the feeling of the authorities that it would be unfair to enforce the law in certain situations, that the objectives underlying the existence of criminal statutes may be achieved in ways not involving formal charging and conviction, and that criminal prosecution either would serve no legitimate end in the particular situation or, indeed, might exacerbate the problem rather than ameliorate it. One common situation involves aspects of all of these. Suppose a middle-aged, respected member of the community is identified as a Peeping Tom whose behavior has caused some concern in the neighborhood. Voyeurism of this type may be attributable to a psychiatric disturbance not severe enough to amount to a legal defense. When interviewed by the police and prosecutor, the suspect admits awareness of his problem and promises to seek private psychiatric assistance in an attempt to control it. In this situation, what could be accomplished by prosecution? The suspect's behavior could become widely known and his reputation ruined in the community. The loss of his job is likely. He may even be imprisoned and thus make effective psychiatric assistance an unlikely part of his rehabilitative efforts.

In many communities, a common disposition would be an agreement that the suspect is to refrain from such conduct in the future, that he is to seek psychiatric assistance, and that the privately retained psychiatrist is to remain in communication with the authorities to make sure that the conditions of the agreement continue to be met.

To the extent that administrative officials—police or prosecutors—do not attempt to enforce the criminal statutes fully, the defining function of those statutes is significantly changed: the statutes do not define who *will* be prosecuted, only who *may* be prosecuted. It is to this extent that administrators share in the crime-defining process. Recognition of that fact has precipitated what may be the most significant current discussion among those concerned with criminal justice administration. The basic question is: Should administrative officials have authority to decline to enforce criminal statutes when enforcement is possible? The question is far from being resolved.

Trends in the Definition of Crime

The definition of what constitutes a crime is not static. Although it is probably historically true that the dominant trend has been toward expanding the scope of criminal law, it is also true that there has been increasing attention paid to the question of what behavior should not be considered a crime.

Appellate courts, in addition to their function as interpreters of criminal law, have played an important role in placing limitations on what conduct legislatures have authority to declare criminal. These courts derive authority from their status as interpreters of constitutional limitations on governmental power; and from time to time, the courts have said that constitutional requirements, both state and federal, have placed limitations on otherwise unrestricted legislative power to define crimes. The legal doctrines are as yet murky and insufficiently developed to ensure the accuracy of any general statements about them, but some examples may be cited.

Courts have said that such involuntary conduct as behavior caused by a physical disease may not be the subject of punishment.[11] Recently, for example, some courts have said that it would be "cruel and unusual" to punish an alcoholic for being drunk in public.[12] The United States Supreme Court has said that states, for the same reason, could not define the status of being a narcotic addict as a crime, although they may still outlaw the use, sale, possession, and transportation of narcotics and related conduct.[13] In very limited circumstances, a few courts have said that it violates due process of law to punish a person as a criminal when he had no adequate way of ascertaining that his conduct might be criminal and thus was unable to conform to the law.[14] There is an extremely ambiguous doctrine that the legislature has no power to define crimes unless it has a "legitimate" end in view and the means adopted (punishment) is reasonably related to that end. Finally, crimes may not be defined in terms of impermissible categories. For example, state legislature may not prohibit interracial marriages, because such a statute is necessarily based on racial classification and penal legislation that discriminates on the basis of race is held to violate the equal protection clause of the Constitution.[15] Courts by this process have undertaken the task of placing limitations on the power of the legislative branch to define the nature of crimes. Courts have, however, used this power with great caution, and its present extent and future development are unclear. They have consistently been urged to declare void those statutes that are antiquated in the sense that no one has any expectation of enforcement despite open and frequent violation. The courts of this country have, with equal consistency, refused to acknowledge the existence of such judicial authority.[16]

Courts are also being urged to reexamine other questionable areas, such as (1) enforcement of morality by criminal laws; (2) criminal laws that exist to authorize techniques of police investigation otherwise prohibited; (3) use of criminal laws to remove nuisances from society; and (4) use of criminal laws to fill gaps in social welfare services.

The use of criminal laws to enforce the morals of the community, or at least assumed morals, occurs largely in that group of crimes that are in a sense without victims. In these crimes if there actually is an identifiable victim, he is a willing one,[17] such as a gambler, a narcotics offender, a prostitute, or a homosexual. These crimes often share several characteristics: (1) they usually consist of transactional acts, the trading of money for goods or services; (2) there is considerable public ambivalence about whether or not the laws should be enforced; (3) the lack of complainants makes enforcement extremely difficult if limitations on police powers are to be observed; and (4) the goal generally seems to be to protect the "victim" from his own immoral conduct.

Another questionable area involves vagrancy laws, which are frequently drafted in such broad terms that their function becomes doubtful. It is often made a crime to "wander from place to place without apparent means of support." These laws date from the labor shortages in feudal England resulting from the Black Death, and they have demonstrated remarkable resistance to change.[18] Such laws may be used when police desire to investigate a person they suspect of a more serious crime but who cannot be arrested because of existing limitations on police power. Thus, the suspect may be arrested and convicted of vagrancy, giving the police more time to investigate the case while the suspect is in custody. It has also been charged that these laws are used to justify periodic attempts by municipal authorities to "clean up the city" by arresting for vagrancy unkempt persons who loiter in view of the presumably offended public. They may serve the further purpose of providing a person with institutional care and treatment of sorts when he is no longer able to care for himself.

The utilization of criminal laws to fill gaps in existing public services, to conceal the distasteful, or to diminish the public's notion of the enormity of a problem is a dubious enterprise. But more is involved.

The utilization of the criminal justice system for such purposes also probably adversely affects the crime control function of law enforcement agencies. It is a major drain on existing police, prosecution, court, and detention resources. The identification, apprehension, and conviction of dangerous offenders is hampered by this misallocation of resources to the social services field. And few are willing to argue that the quality of the service is very good.[19]

This use of law enforcement agencies for purposes other than the protection of the public from criminal activity has served to confuse the purposes for the existence of criminal law. Traditionally, the aims of criminal law have been rehabilitation, punishment, and deterrence. But alcoholics, for example, are generally not rehabilitated, because the necessary resources and knowledge are not available. To punish them for conduct that is often beyond their control seems pointless. They are not generally deterred by our existing procedures.

Despite what appears to be a growing concern for reappraisal of the goals and limits of the system of criminal justice, it remains true that the dominant trend—as we pointed out earlier—has been to expand the reach of criminal law. The largest expansion has probably been the creation of a vast number of so-called public welfare offenses.[20] These have developed as concomitants to the ever larger role played by government in regulating the affairs of businesses and individuals in such matters as health, fire, food, and transportation.

Summary

This essay is really less an answer to the question "What is a crime?" than it is an attempt to provide some appreciation of the complexities arising out of the question. The difficulties that will be encountered by anyone who seriously concerns himself with a study of crime have been succinctly stated by the President's Commission on Law Enforcement and Administration of Justice:

The most understandable mood into which many Americans have been plunged by crime is one of frustration and bewilderment. For "crime" is not a single simple phenomenon that can be examined, analyzed and described in one piece. It occurs in every part of the country and in every stratum of society. Its practitioners and its victims are people of all ages, incomes and backgrounds. Its trends are difficult to ascertain. Its causes are legion. Its cures are speculative and controversial. An examination of any single kind of crime, let alone of "crime in America," raises a myriad of issues of the utmost complexity.[21]

The readings that follow deal with selected aspects of this complicated and little understood phenomenon. They are designed not to simplify but to place the problem of crime in a broad historical and cultural perspective and to provide some insights into the recurrent themes and issues important today.

Notes

1. Lea v. MacDuff, 126 N.Y.S. 2d 646 (1954).
2. Squadrito v. Griebsch, 154 N.Y.S. 2d 37, 136 N.E. 2d 37 (1957).
3. *The Consolidated Laws of New York Annotated: Vehicle and Traffic Law,* Book 62A, sec. 155 (Brooklyn: Edward Thompson, 1960), p. 33.
4. Walter Reckless, *The Crime Problem,* 3rd ed. (New York: Appleton-Century-Crofts, 1961), p. 27.
5. For example, see Bartkus v. Illinois, 359 U.S. 121, 79 SC 676 (1959). Here the United States Supreme Court upheld the power of Illinois to try the defendant and convict him after he had been acquitted in federal court on charges arising out of the same robbery.
6. People of Illinois v. Menagas, 367 Ill. 330, 11 N.E. 2d 403 (1937).
7. Rollin M. Perkins, *Criminal Law* (Brooklyn: Foundation Press, 1957), p. 190.
8. The process is actually much more complicated than this. See authorities cited in Kenneth Culp Davis, *Administrative Law Treatise* (St. Paul, Minn.: West, 1958), I, 306.
9. An excellent collection of the legal literature on the problem of selective enforcement by police may be found in Joseph Goldstein, "Police Discretion Not to Invoke the Criminal Process: Low Visibility Decisions in the Administration of Justice," *Yale Law Journal,* 69, No. 4 (March 1960), 543–594.
10. Some of these are discussed more fully in Wayne R. LaFave, *Arrest: The Decision to Take a Suspect into Custody* (Boston: Little, Brown, 1965).
11. The requirement of a voluntary act is discussed in *Model Penal Code,* Article 2, sec. 01 (Philadelphia: The American Law Institute, 1959), p. 9.
12. Driver v. Hinnant, 356 F. 2d 761, s243 F. Supp. 95 (1966). See also Easter v. District of Columbia, 361 F. 2d 50, s209 A. 2d 625 (1966).
13. Robinson v. California, 370 U.S. 660, 82 S. Ct. 1417 (1957).
14. For example, see Lambert v. California 355 U.S. 225, 78 S. Ct. 240 (1957).
15. Loving v. Virginia, 388 U.S. 1, 87 S. Ct. 1817 (1967).
16. For example, see Arthur E. Bonfield, "Abrogation of Penal Statutes by Nonenforcement," *Iowa Law Review,* 49, No. 2 (Winter 1964), 389–440.
17. Edwin Schur, *Crimes Without Victims* (Englewood Cliffs, N.J.: Prentice-Hall, 1965).
18. These statutes are increasingly coming under constitutional attack. See for example: Murtagh, "Status Offense and Due Process of Law," 36 *Fordham Law Review,* 51 (1967).
19. An excellent article on this problem is contained in the President's Commission on Law Enforcement and Administration of Justice, "Substantive Law Reform and the Limits of Effective Law Enforcement," *Task Force Report: The Courts* (Washington, D.C.: U.S. Government Printing Office, 1967), pp. 97–107.

20. Francis B. Sayre, "Public Welfare Offenses," *Columbia Law Review*, 33, No. 1 (January 1933), 55–58.
21. The President's Commission on Law Enforcement and Administration of Justice, *The Challenge of Crime in a Free Society* (Washington, D.C.: U.S. Government Printing Office, 1967), p. 1.

Suggestions for Further Reading

Allen, Francis A. *The Borderland of Criminal Justice.* Chicago: University of Chicago Press, 1964.

Breitel, Charles D. "Controls in Criminal Law Enforcement," *University of Chicago Law Review,* 27 (Spring 1960), 427–435.

Donnelly, Richard C., Joseph Goldstein, and Richard D. Schwartz. *Criminal Law: Problems for Decision in the Promulgation, Invocation and Administration of a Law of Crimes.* New York: Free Press, 1962.

Goldstein, Joseph. "Police Discretion Not to Invoke the Criminal Process: Low Visibility Decisions in the Administration of Justice," *Yale Law Journal,* 69, No. 4 (March 1960), 543–594.

Hall, Jerome, and Gerhard O. W. Mueller. *Cases and Readings on Criminal Law and Procedure.* 2nd. ed. Indianapolis: Bobbs-Merrill, 1965.

Kadish, Sanford H. "The Crisis of Overcriminalization," *The Annals of the American Academy of Political and Social Science,* 374 (November 1967), 157–170.

Kalven, Harry, Jr., and Hans Zeisel. *The American Jury.* Boston: Little, Brown, 1966.

LaFave, Wayne R. *Arrest: The Decision to Take a Suspect into Custody.* Ed. Frank J. Remington. Boston: Little, Brown, 1965.

Miller, Frank W., and Frank J. Remington. "Procedures Before Trial," *The Annals of the American Academy of Political and Social Science,* 339 (January 1962), 111–116.

Newman, Donald J. *Conviction: The Determination of Guilt or Innocence Without Trial.* Boston: Little, Brown, 1966.

Paulsen, Monrad G., and Sanford H. Kadish. *Criminal Law and Its Processes: Cases and Materials.* Boston: Little, Brown, 1962.

Perkins, Rollin M. *Criminal Law.* Brooklyn: Foundation Press, 1957.

President's Commission on Law Enforcement and Administration of Justice. *The Challenge of Crime in a Free Society.* Washington, D.C.: U.S. Government Printing Office, 1967.

———. "Substantive Law Reform and the Limits of Effective Law Enforcement," *The Courts.* Washington, D.C.: U.S. Government Printing Office, 1957. Pp. 97–107.

Remington, Frank J., and Victor G. Rosenblum. "The Criminal Law and the Legislative Process," *University of Illinois Law Forum,* 1960 (Winter 1960), pp. 481–499.

Scott, Austin. "Constitutional Limitations on Substantive Criminal Law," *Rocky Mountain Law Review,* 29 (April 1957), 275–295.

Tiffany, Lawrence P., Donald M. McIntyre, and Daniel L. Rotenberg. *Detection of Crime: Stopping and Questioning, Search and Seizure, Encouragement and Entrapment*. Ed. Frank. J. Remington. Boston: Little, Brown, 1967.

Williams, Glanville. *Criminal Law: The General Part*. London: Stevens, 1961.

1 OTHER TIMES, OTHER PLACES

The ideas and customs of diverse cultures far back in history have helped to shape our present legal system. Many of our definitions of crime and our concepts of justice come to us wearing the patina of centuries; and the law's respect for the past is made manifest in its doctrine of stare decisis et non quieta movere—*that is, let the decision stand and do not move that which has been settled.*

The substance of our law, then, as well as the procedure of our law, sometimes gives the appearance of great inertia. Yet the law does change, as do other elements of the social order, and our legal system exists in a curious compromise of constancy and flux as it seeks to adapt itself to the changing necessities of the time. Each generation, whether it knows it or not, is confronted with fundamental questions: What is lawful or unlawful? What are the grounds for our choice? What means shall we use to secure lawful behavior?

This questioning of the law may sometimes become sharply critical, challenging the most fundamental assumptions. But it is only through such questioning that we can begin to understand the law as a means to an end, an instrument to achieve a just social order, rather than an end in itself.

1. The Argument Begins

The Socratic method of teaching is an illuminating device in many forms of education because, despite some faults, there is nothing like it to force a person to articulate the logic of his thoughts. When Thrasymachus answered the questions of Socrates, his easy confidence in the idea that might makes right began to waver—and to this day we continue to look for a better basis for our laws.

Listen then, Thrasymachus began. What I say is that "just" or "right" means nothing but what is to the interest of the stronger party. Well, where is your applause? You don't mean to give it me.

I will, as soon as I understand, I said. I don't see yet what you mean by right being the interest of the stronger party. For instance, Polydamas, the athlete, is stronger than we are, and it is to his interest to eat beef for the sake of his muscles; but surely you don't mean that the same diet would be good for weaker men and therefore be right for us?

You are trying to be funny, Socrates. It's a low trick to take my words in the sense you think will be most damaging.

No, no, I protested; but you must explain.

Don't you know, then, that a state may be ruled by a despot, or a democracy, or an aristocracy?

Of course.

And that the ruling element is always the strongest?

Yes.

Well then, in every case the laws are made by the ruling party in its own interest; a democracy makes democratic laws, a despot autocratic ones, and so on. By making these laws they define as "right" for their subjects whatever is for their own interest, and they call anyone who breaks them a "wrongdoer" and punish him accordingly. That is what I mean: in all states alike "right" has the same meaning, namely what is for the interest of the party established in power, and that is the strongest. So the sound conclusion is that what is "right" is the same everywhere: the interest of the stronger party.

Now I see what you mean, said I; whether it is true or not, I must try to make out. When you define right in terms of interest, you are yourself

From **The Republic of Plato,** translated by F. M. Cornford. Oxford University Press, 1941. Reprinted by permission.

giving one of those answers you forbade to me; though, to be sure, you add "to the stronger party."

An insignificant addition, perhaps!

Its importance is not clear yet; what is clear is that we must find out whether your definition is true. I agree myself that right is in a sense a matter of interest; but when you add "to the stronger party," I don't know about that. I must consider.

Go ahead, then.

I will. Tell me this. No doubt you also think it is right to obey the men in power?

I do.

Are they infallible in every type of state, or can they sometimes make a mistake?

Of course they can make a mistake.

In framing laws, then, they may do their work well or badly?

No doubt.

Well, that is to say, when the laws they make are to their own interest; badly, when they are not?

Yes.

But the subjects are to obey any law they lay down, and they will then be doing right?

Of course.

If so, by your account, it will be right to do what is not to the interest of the stronger party, as well as what is so.

What's that you are saying?

Just what you said, I believe; but let us look again. Haven't you admitted that the rulers, when they enjoin certain acts on their subjects, sometimes mistake their own best interests, and at the same time that it is right for the subjects to obey, whatever they may enjoin?

Yes, I suppose so.

Well, that amounts to admitting that it is right to do what is not to the interest of the rulers or the stronger party. They may unwittingly enjoin what is to their own disadvantage; and you say it is right for the others to do as they are told. In that case, their duty must be the opposite of what you said, because the weaker will have been ordered to do what is against the interest of the stronger. You with your intelligence must see how that follows.

Yes, Socrates . . . that is undeniable.

2. The Need for Law

Why have any law at all? What justification is there for the state with its authority to make rules and enforce them? The answer given by Thomas Hobbes is still accepted by many people in spite of the fact that it provides a singularly unflattering view of man and his nature. Oppressive as government and law might appear, he argued, there was no other alternative to a war of all against all, given mankind's tendency to resort to force and fraud. We must live with the massive governmental power that he labeled Leviathan.

In the nature of man, we find three principall causes of quarrell. First, Competition, Secondly, Diffidence; Thirdly, Glory.

The first, maketh men invade for Gain, the second for Safety; and the third, for Reputation. The first use Violence, to make themselves Masters of other men's persons, wives, children, and cattell; the second, to defend them; the third, for trifles, as a word, a smile, a different opinion, and any other signe of undervalue, either direct in their Persons, or by reflexion in their Kindred, their Friends, their Nation, their Profession, or their Name.

Hereby it is manifest, that during the time men live without a common Power to keep them all in awe, they are in that condition which is called Warre; and such a warre, as is of every man, against every man. For Warre, consisteth not in Battell onely, or the act of fighting; but in a tract of time, wherein the Will to contend by Battell is sufficiently known: and therefore the notion of *Time,* is to be considered in the nature of Warre, as it is in the nature of Weather. For as the nature of Foule weather, lyeth not in a showre or two of rain; but in an inclination thereto of many dayes together: So the nature of War, consisteth not in actual fighting; but in the known disposition thereto, during all the time there is no assurance to the contrary. All other time is Peace.

Whatsoever therefore is consequent to a time of Warre, where every man is Enemy to every man; the same is consequent to the time, wherein men live without other security, than what their own strength, and their own invention shall furnish them withall. In such condition, there is no place for Industry; because the fruit thereof is uncertain: and consequently no Culture of the Earth; no Navigation, nor use of the commodities that may be imported by Sea; no commodious Building; no Instruments of moving, and removing such things as require much force, no Knowledge of the face of the Earth; no account of Time; no Arts; no Letters; no Society; and which is worst of all continuall feare, and danger of violent death; And the life of man, solitary, poore, nasty, brutish, and short.

3. The Force of Custom

We might agree that law is a necessity, but it also must be recognized that the sanctions of the state are only one of the many forces at work to control man's behavior. If we think that a decent, orderly society can only be achieved by constantly calling upon the punishing power of the government, it is possible that we will destroy the very thing we are seeking, and Leviathan will swallow us all.

In those primitive societies where the organized machinery of government is lacking, as described in the following account of Eskimo life by E. Adamson Hoebel, we may be able to see more clearly the intricate forces that underlie conformity to the rules—and the various conceptions of right and wrong that exist in different cultures.

Senilicide, invalidicide, and suicide are expressions of the same postulate that underlies infanticide—life is hard and the margin of safety small. Those who cannot carry their full share of the productive load forfeit the right to live.

Although others may decide that the days of an aged one are done, the request for death usually comes from the old person. The actual killing should be performed by a relative to preclude the possibility of vengeance. Infanticide is casually accepted, but not so senilicide and invalidicide. Emotional bonds are not easily severed that have been built up through the years and not infrequently the aged one has to insist upon his demand-right to be killed; the kinsman is forced into performance of his duty.

Weyer records a poignant example:

A hunter living on the Diomede Islands related to the writer how he killed his own father, at the latter's request. The old Eskimo was failing, he could no longer contribute what he thought should be his share as a member of the group; so he asked his son, then a lad about twelve years old, to sharpen the big hunting knife. Then he indicated the vulnerable spot over his heart where his son should stab him. The boy plunged the knife deep, but the stroke failed to take effect. The old father suggested with dignity and resignation, "Try it a little higher, my son." The second stab was effective, and the patriarch passed into the realm of the ancestral shades.

From E. Adamson Hoebel, **The Law of Primitive Man** (Cambridge, Mass.: Harvard University Press, 1954). Reprinted by permission.

Stabbing is but one form of Eskimo senilicide. Hanging, strangulation, blocking up in a snow house to freeze to death, and abandonment in the open wastes by a traveling group are all used by various Eskimos. The mental conflict entailed in these practices is revealed in Eskimo mythology, however. There may be no overt social onus toward those who destroy their aged, but the myths of the Iglulik in which the infirm or aged are abandoned, "generally provide some miraculous form of rescue . . . with a cruel and ignominious death for those who abandoned them."

Between suicide and senilicide and invalidicide stands suicide-with-assistance. At Chesterfield Inlet a son-in-law helped his wife's mother, who was sick with tuberculosis, to hang herself. "She felt that she was old, and having begun to spit up blood, she wished to die quickly, and I agreed. I only made the line fast to the roof, the rest she did herself."

In East Greenland, a woman who led a blind neighbor to the local suicide cliff so that she could jump off to her end, virtuously told Holm how she had refused pay for her services. She was not a relative, but after all, she was a friend.

A really nice sophism in the reconciliation of two conflicting systems of values was that of the wife of Qalaseq, an old man of Chesterfield Inlet. After a year's illness he hanged himself with the assistance of his wife. It was not, however, she pointedly explained to Rasmussen, a real hanging. Both she and her husband were mission-converted Catholics and they had taken to heart the teaching that taking a human life was for God alone. Therefore, at her husband's request she stood by with a crucifix while he strung himself up, and just before he expired—this can be paralleled from Inquisition practice—she released him and held up the cross. Hence, as she saw it, he died a natural death. They had "only hurried death up a little, as it is apt to be so very slow at times."

Outright suicide seems to be practiced on rare occasions because of "mental anguish." In the two such cases reported by Rasmussen a pattern of freezing to death, naked, is indicated for self-destruction motivated by such reasons. An Iglulik old woman accidentally froze to death, whereupon her son deliberately went out naked and did likewise.

An irritable foster-father declared to his adopted son, "I wish you were dead! You are not worth the food you eat." The youth then declared he would never eat again. That night he went out naked into the snow, to lie down and freeze to death.

Hunters in extreme danger or about to drown may slit their own throats. Among the Iglulik the Moon Spirit calls gently, "Come, come to me! It is not painful to die. It is only a brief moment of dizziness. It does not hurt to kill yourself."

. . .

Revenge killing does not evoke a display of bravery, for it is generally exacted by stealth while the murderer is busily engaged at some task and not aware of what is about to happen. Only in West Greenland does the avenger give preliminary warning by announcing the offense for which the victim is about to die. In this connection, H. König calls attention to the fact that old Scandinavian law demanded the verbal pronouncement of the death warrant before the slaying of an outlaw and suggests that the practice was transmitted from the Scanindavians to the Greenland Eskimos.

A killer who murders several persons at once may enhance, not injure, his prestige in the community. Not so, the homicidal recidivist. He becomes a social menace liable at any time to strike down another victim. As a general menace, he becomes a public enemy. As a public enemy, he becomes the object of public action. The action is legal execution: a privilege-right of the executioner. The single murder is a private wrong redressed by the kinsmen of the victim. Repeated murder becomes a public crime punishable by death at the hands of an agent of the community.

The classic case has been given by Boas, who wrote:

The fact that the custom is found among tribes so widely separated will justify a description of those events which came under my own observation. There was a native of Padli by the name of Padlu. He had induced the wife of a native of Cumberland Sound to desert her husband and follow him. The deserted husband, meditating revenge . . . visited his friends in Padli, but before he could accomplish his intention of killing Padlu, the latter shot him . . . A brother of the murdered man went to Padli to avenge the death of his brother; but he also was killed by Padlu. A third native of Cumberland Sound, who wished to avenge the death of his relatives was also murdered by him.

On account of all these outrages the natives wanted to get rid of Padlu, but yet they did not dare to attack him. When the pimain (*headman*) *of the Akudmirmiut learned of these events he started southward and* asked every man in Padli whether Padlu should be killed. All agreed; *so he went with the latter deer hunting . . . and . . . shot Padlu in the back.*

Similar practices exist among all the Eskimos on whom we have reports, save the East Greenlanders. The important element is that the executioner, who undertakes the slaying, seeks and obtains, in advance, community approval for his act of riddance. When such approval is obtained no blood revenge may be taken on the executioner, for his act is not murder. It is the execution of a public sentence in the name of the people, and the responsibility is theirs. Furthermore, revenge is precluded for the simple reason that unanimous consent involves also the consent of the murderer's relatives, if any be in the community.

As a double safeguard against blood revenge on the executioner, close kinsmen may be themselves called upon to carry out the community will. In 1921, for instance, the headman of the Arviligjuarmiut was deputed by his fifty-four co-villagers to execute his own brother, who occasionally went berserk, having killed one man and wounded others in his fits. The headman went reluctantly to his brother and explaining his position, asked how he chose to die—by steel, thong, or shot? The brother chose the latter, and was killed on the spot.

4. The Birth of Law

The idea that the definitions of crime and the methods for its control are not fixed but change as social conditions change, building on existing traditions, is perhaps best seen by looking at the development of our legal system in early English history. As Alan Harding points out, the concept of crime as a wrong against the community rather than as a wrong against a particular individual did not come into being all at once but emerged in a process of slow growth. The consequences for breaking the law and the responsibility for ensuring peace and order changed over time as society abandoned individual revenge or legal self-help as a remedy.

The beginnings of the Common Law are often placed in the twelfth century, but English society is of course much older, and as early as the seventh century the laws on which that society rested were remarkable for their vigour.

In the year 597, missionaries from Rome arrived in Kent; and the local kings of England began to issue laws, as Bede said, "in the Roman style," but in the English language:

The property of God and the Church is to be paid for with a twelve-fold compensation; a bishop's property with an eleven-fold compensation . . . a deacon's property with a six-fold compensation . . . the peace of the Church with a two-fold compensation. . . .

If the king calls his people to him, and anyone does them injury there, he is to pay a two-fold compensation and 50 shillings to the king. . . .

The breach of the king's protection, 50 shillings. . . .

The breach of a ceorl's *protection: six shillings. . . .*

If anyone kills a man, he is to pay as ordinary wergild 100 shillings. . . .

If hair-pulling occur, 50 sceattas [= *2½ Kentish shillings*] *are to be paid as compensation. . . .*

The reason for making this "law" is clear enough. The foreign clergy, venturing into a rough and pagan society, had to be given an appropriate status and protection for the property they would acquire from noble patrons. There was a ready way of calculating worth and position: each level in that rigidly hierarchical society had its particular *wergild,* the sum of money which had to be paid as compensation to the lord or the kin of a

From Alan Harding's book, **A Social History of English Law** published by Penguin Books 1966.

murdered man. So King Ethelbert wrote down the customary worth of his subjects, as well as the sums, proportional to the victim's wergild and the nature of the wrong, to be paid for injuries less than homicide; and he put the clergy at the top of the hierarchy of worth.

Ethelbert's decree is no more than a tariff of the compensation which has to be paid for violent attacks on other people. It says nothing of courts or judges, because there are none, save perhaps the community itself in its "folk-moots." The "judicial system" can cope with nothing more subtle than the outright violence to which most private disputes would come. But Ethelbert is not really making law at all: he is writing down the custom of the people in all its weird and inflexible detail.

The tariff of compensation presupposes the existence of the blood-feud, a factor in the development of most societies (from it stems the theme of tragic necessity in both ancient Greek and German literature). This does not mean that the Anglo-Saxons were in the anarchical "state of nature" imagined by Thomas Hobbes. There was a sort of "peace in the feud." Men knew that killing brought vengeance, that there was a large group of kinsmen, extending to sixth cousins, whose duty it was to avenge a murdered man. For lesser wrongs the victim himself could take revenge. The "king" or "kin-representative," and the Church with its notion of an avenging God, intervened first of all to see that the duty of vengeance was fulfilled.

But sixth cousins include almost everyone in the community, who are thus related to both murderer and victim. Consequently there is always tension between the loyalty of the kin and their desire for a quiet life, and every effort will be made to end the feud by honourable compensation. In Iceland there were regular assemblies of the whole people at which the arbitration of disputes was the main business, but there seems to have been no comparable system in England. *Njal's Saga,* which describes the Icelandic practice, refers to a time four centuries after Ethelbert, but to a warrior society in a recently settled land. Ethelbert's laws suggest that Kentish society had passed beyond the stage of arbitration under the eye of the whole community: the detailed tariff implies that disputes are normally and almost automatically settled by payments or by the enslavement to the plaintiffs of the malefactors who cannot pay.

A self-respecting Anglo-Saxon king would always try to bring order and tranquillity to his people, and in Ethelbert's laws there was already one principle by which kings could extend their influence. That was the principle of the *peace*. England was not a land of a single peace but of many, one belonging to each great lord and one to the church. Peace was something precious and almost tangible which went along with a priest or a lord, and which great lords could give to their followers to take with them: in that case peace was often called *protection.* There could be different values of peace. Long after the idea had grown up that the high roads and then the whole country were in some sense automatically within the king's peace, it remained more heinous to infringe the king's "hand-given" peace, the peace which the king had explicitly declared. Just as one could injure a man himself, one could injure his peace, by committing a crime in his house, or in his presence, or against his protected servant; and there was a traditional compensation for the breach of his peace.

It took many centuries for the king's peace to swallow up all the rest. Yet Ethelbert himself possessed two rights which marked him out as the special guardian of the law. Firstly, whenever a freeman was killed, fifty shillings had to be paid to the king, in addition to the compensation to the victim's kin. Secondly, the king held assemblies of the whole people, and an injury committed in one of them involved double compensation to the victim and again a fine of fifty shillings to the king. The king's court was already acquiring special authority.

Some late-seventh-century Kentish laws set out the quite elaborate procedure which had become customary for arbitration in the folk-moots. When a man had a claim against another, he took surety from him to submit to arbitration: in other words he forced someone to be responsible for the defendant's appearance. The defendant had then to do "such right as the judges of the people of Kent should prescribe." There was no attempt to sift evidence. The judges or doomsmen were merely guardians of a ritual performance, who at the most decided by which of a number of mechanical means the defendant should try to clear himself. Normally the defendant could avoid paying compensation only by bringing a set number of "oath-helpers" to swear to the reliability of his oath that he was innocent.

In the majority of cases violence must have originated in disagreements over commercial transactions. Buying and selling were essential to the Anglo-Saxons as to any other society: so a great mass of customary rules appeared to prevent fraudulent selling. Here were special opportunities for the king to intervene and refine the procedure by his edict. Goods had to be bought in open market ("market overt," as the legal phrase still goes), and it was decreed that a man who bought in the great market at London had to have the transaction witnessed by "two or three honest ceorls, or the king's town-reeve." If he did not do this and the bartered goods were subsequently claimed as stolen property, the defendant had to produce "at the king's hall" the man who had sold them to him, or else return them to the plaintiff.

The first surviving laws of Wessex, the kingdom to the west of Kent, are those of King Ine. The seriousness of the problem of keeping order is shown by Ine's classification of robber gangs. "We call up to seven men 'thieves,'" says his law; "from seven to thirty-five a 'band'; above that it is an army." An extension of the system of fines to the king is evident in Ine's law, another clause of which runs: "If anyone within the boundaries of our kingdom commit robbery and rapine, he is to give back the plunder and give 60/–as a fine." The king has to be compensated too, because he is wronged as guardian of the peace. The idea of compensation to the private plaintiff and the idea of compensation to the king are both present, but they do not lead to a distinction between "civil" and "criminal" cases, "private" and "public" law, for the same wrongs are very often subject to both payments at once.

King Alfred's laws, made between 871 and 899, declared that for treachery to a lord there could be no compensation and no mercy, "because Almighty God adjudged none for those who scorned him, nor did Christ, the Son of God, adjudge any for him who gave him over to death; and he [Christ] charged [everyone] to love his lord as himself." Treason is treachery to one's lord or patron, with whom one has sacred ties. High treason is already present in Alfred's laws: "if anyone plots against the king's life, directly or by harbouring his exiles or his man, he is liable to forfeit his life and all that he owns." The existence of these "bootless" wrongs, not to be satisfied by compensation or *bot*—by the eleventh century they were house-breaking, arson, obvious theft, manifest murder and betrayal of a lord—may suggest that some real crimes were recognized. But they were punished by death rather as sins against the laws of God than as crimes against the king's laws.

. . .

The consistent aim of the Wessex dynasty was to do away with the blood-feud as the basis of private law. Alfred's laws forbade a plaintiff to attack an opponent in his home until he had besieged him for thirty days and sought justice from the king. Athelstan's laws provided that if anyone failed to answer a summons by a plaintiff to three successive borough courts it was for the leading men of the borough (not the plaintiff) to ride to him "and take all that he owns and put him under surety." Already one of its essential elements, delay, was entering legal procedure; delay, while the peaceful settlement that civil law seeks was arrived at, if possible "out of court." Private or "civil" law arbitrates between the parties, and on the other hand a criminal offence is one for which the state will allow no settlement, even if the wronged person desires it. From Canute's reign we have the earliest record of a civil law-suit, settled by the shire-court of Herefordshire.

The mitigation of the disastrous effects of "self-help" was attained by the extension of the idea of the king's peace and the responsibility of all, not just of the parties to a quarrel, to see that it was observed. Athelstan thought of his laws as "enacting a peace" and ordered his bishops, aldermen and reeves over all his dominions to observe it. Canute's laws imposed a fine on anyone who came across a thief and did not raise the hue and cry, and upon anyone who refused to ride in pursuit of the thief. Yet there was still no assumption of a single and general and permanent peace which a crime automatically broke. For a long time after the Norman Conquest peace "died with the king" and had to be proclaimed anew by his successor, licence reigning in the interlude.

The eleventh-century kings tried to keep order by putting the whole community in the place of the kin, responsible for a man's behaviour. According to Canute, everyone over twelve years of age who wanted the rights of a free man in legal proceedings had to be in a hundred and a tithing. The *tithing* was a group of ten men, who were automatically obliged to stand surety or give pledge for one of their number: thus the system was called by the Normans the "frankpledge system." The tithing eventually became a new territorial division coinciding with the village, and its head, the tithing-man, became the village constable. Its origins must be connected with those of the hundred. The hundred may originally have been an area obliged to produce so many men for the *fyrd,* the Anglo-Saxon militia, and throughout the middle ages men were required to maintain weapons both for service in war and to keep the peace at home. Thus from the beginning the tithing was probably a sub-unit of the police. As early as the reign of Athelstan, the men of London organized a voluntary "peace-guild," and resolved "that we always are to reckon ten men together—and the senior is to have charge of the nine . . . and afterwards a hundred of them together, and one hundred-man"; and they were to turn out as required to ride along the trail of stolen cattle.

The opinion of neighbours always prevailed, and a trial was a test of character: the question was, "can the oath of the defendant be relied upon?" Notoriety in England, as in many primitive societies, was for long as good a reason for condemning a man as proof of a particular crime: a man "regarded with suspicion by all the people," said Canute, was to be put under surety by the king's reeve to answer any charges brought against him, and if he had no surety he was to be slain and to lie in unconsecrated ground.

Lords were still required to be responsible for their retainers, but the creation of the new administrative areas and moots of the tenth century kept the folk system alive alongside the aristocratic one. The shire and hundred moots were also the king's courts, and justice never fell into the hands of the nobles in England as it did in France. But the legacy of the folk system was not entirely beneficial. The king's aldermen in the shire courts and his bailiffs in the hundred courts were not judges in our sense, capable of applying general principles to specific cases. They were rather the mere presidents of moots where the customary law was "found" by the leading men of the area. Such law was necessarily enshrined in simple, unsophisticated and unrelated maxims, which had to provide specifically for every likely situation.

The law extended little by little into "private" matters, even reinforcing the mutual responsibilities of members of the family. At a marriage, the bridegroom was to announce what he granted to his bride "if she should live longer than he"; that is, what dower she should have. Perhaps this was an example of the general tendency of law, posited by Sir Henry Maine, to advance from the protection of status within communities to the enforcement of contracts between individuals.

Towards the end, the Anglo-Saxons knew several sorts of contract. When a man was summoned to appear in court, or an agreement was made to pay compensation which a man could not immediately raise; or when a couple were betrothed (at a "wedding"); then a contract would be made by the surrender of a *wed* (which the Normans called a *gage*) as security for performance. The *wed* may once have been valuable, but soon became a token only. More serious was the surety which had to be found in a legal action, for the surety (the "pledge" of Anglo-Norman times) was a man—hostage, bound "body for body" to the accused, as the man who goes bail in modern criminal cases is still deemed to be. Gage and pledge played an essential part in the development of the concept of liability for contract.

The law was at its most mechanical in the actual trial of the accused. Primitive law is so complicated because the issues are too serious to be left to the discretion of judges, indeed of any human person. Law is "unchangeable" custom; verdicts are for God who searches the hearts of men. The oath was really an appeal to God, since a perjured oath was expected to bring its own punishment. But increasing reliance was placed upon the ordeal, as a less equivocal way of discovering the verdict of heaven. The more notorious a criminal, the greater was his ordeal. He must fast, go to Mass and swear to his innocence; then he holds the hot iron (if the burn festers, he is guilty); or is lowered into water (he is guilty if he floats, for the water rejects him); or, if he is a clerk, swallows the sacred morsel which has been adjured to choke the guilty man.

Occasionally a more modern attitude creeps in. One of Canute's laws says that "it does not seem right to us that any man should make good his claim to goods where there is a witness and where it can be shown that there has been fraud." Several stages of legal reasoning existed side by side in pre-Conquest law. Beside the barbarity of Canute's decree that the oft-convicted man should have his eyes "put out and his nose and ears and upper lip cut off, or his scalp removed" must be set the same king's astonishingly modern statements on criminal liability. "In many a deed," he said, "when a man acts under compulsion, he is then the more entitled to clemency in that he did what he did out of necessity; and if anyone acts unintentionally, he is not entirely like one who does it intentionally." Even though these ideas were taken (by Archbishop Wulfstan, who composed Canute's laws) from the penitentials of the Church, where quite sophisticated psychology was applied to prescribing penances for sins, it is obvious that the "tariff" mentality was losing its strength.

5. A Satirical Barb

There are many people, of course, who believe that our ideas about crime are not changing fast enough and that we are still dominated by a harshly punitive attitude better suited to an earlier and more savage era. Almost one hundred years ago, Samuel Butler attempted to expose what he considered to be the irrationalities of his time. In the imaginary country described in his novel Erewhon, *he attacked the harsh system of criminal law of the Victorian era, but his contemporaries were reluctant to look into the mirror he held before them.*

But I shall perhaps best convey to the reader an idea of the entire perversion of thought which exists among this extraordinary people, by describing the public trial of a man who was accused of pulmonary consumption—an offense which was punished with death until quite recently. It did not occur till I had been some months in the country, and I am deviating from chronological order in giving it here; but I had perhaps better do so in order that I may exhaust this subject before proceeding to others. Moreover, I should never come to an end were I to keep to a strictly narrative form, and detail the infinite absurdities with which I daily came in contact.

The prisoner was placed in the dock, and the jury were sworn much as in Europe; almost all our own modes of procedure were reproduced, even to the requiring the prisoner to plead guilty or not guilty. He pleaded not guilty, and the case proceeded. The evidence for the prosecution was very strong; but I must do the court the justice to observe that the trial was absolutely impartial. Counsel for the prisoner was allowed to urge everything that could be said in his defense: the line taken was that the prisoner was simulating consumption in order to defraud an insurance company, from which he was about to buy an annuity, and that he hoped thus to obtain it on more advantageous terms. If this could have been shown to be the case he would have escaped a criminal prosecution, and been sent to a hospital as for a moral ailment. The view, however, was one which could not be reasonably sustained, in spite of all the ingenuity and eloquence of one of the most celebrated advocates of the country. The case was only too clear, for the prisoner was almost at the point of death, and it was astonishing that he had not been tried and convicted long previously. His coughing

From Samuel Butler, **Erewhon and Erewhon Revisited** (New York: Modern Library, 1927). Reprinted by permission.

was incessant during the whole trial, and it was all that the two jailors in charge of him could do to keep him on his legs until it was over.

The summing up of the judge was admirable. He dwelt upon every point that could be construed in favor of the prisoner, but as he proceeded it became clear that the evidence was too convincing to admit of doubt, and there was but one opinion in the court as to the impending verdict when the jury retired from the box. They were absent for about ten minutes, and on their return the foreman pronounced the prisoner guilty. There was a faint murmur of applause, but it was instantly repressed. The judge then proceeded to pronounce sentence in words which I can never forget, and which I copied out into a note-book next day from the report that was published in the leading newspaper. I must condense it somewhat, and nothing which I could say would give more than a faint idea of the solemn, not to say majestic, severity with which it was delivered. The sentence was as follows:—

"Prisoner at the bar, you have been accused of the great crime of laboring under pulmonary consumption, and after an impartial trial before a jury of your countrymen, you have been found guilty. Against the justice of the verdict I can say nothing: the evidence against you was conclusive, and it only remains for me to pass such a sentence upon you, as shall satisfy the ends of the law. That sentence must be a very severe one. It pains me much to see one who is yet so young, and whose prospects in life were otherwise so excellent, brought to this distressing condition by a constitution which I can only regard as radically vicious; but yours is no case for compassion: this is not your first offense: you have led a career of crime, and have only profited by the leniency shown you upon past occasions, to offend yet more seriously against the laws and institutions of your country. You were convicted of aggravated bronchitis last year: and I find that though you are now only twenty-three years old, you have been imprisoned on no less than fourteen occasions for illnesses of a more or less hateful character; in fact, it is not too much to say that you have spent the greater part of your life in a jail.

"It is all very well for you to say that you came of unhealthy parents, and had a severe accident in your childhood which permanently undermined your constitution; excuses such as these are the ordinary refuge of the criminal; but they cannot for one moment be listened to by the ear of justice. I am not here to enter upon curious metaphysical questions as to the origin of this or that—questions to which there would be no end were their introduction once tolerated, and which would result in throwing the only guilt on the tissues of the primordial cell, or on the elementary gases. There is no question of how you came to be wicked, but only this—namely, are you wicked or not? This has been decided in the affirmative, neither can I hesitate for a single moment to say that it has been decided justly. You are a bad and dangerous person, and stand branded in the eyes of your fellow-countrymen with one of the most heinous known offenses.

"It is not my business to justify the law: the law may in some cases have its inevitable hardships, and I may feel regret at times that I have not the option of passing a less severe sentence than I am compelled to do. But yours is no such case; on the contrary, had not the capital punishment for consumption been abolished, I should certainly inflict it now.

"It is intolerable that an example of such terrible enormity should be allowed to go at large unpunished. Your presence in the society of respectable people would lead the less able-bodied to think more lightly of all forms of illness; neither can it be permitted that you should have the chance of corrupting unborn beings who might hereafter pester you. The unborn must not be allowed to come near you: and this not so much for their protection (for they are our natural enemies), as for our own; for since they will not be utterly gainsaid, it must be seen to that they shall be quartered upon those who are least likely to corrupt them.

. . .

"I do not hesitate therefore to sentence you to imprisonment, with hard labor, for the rest of your miserable existence. During that period I would earnestly entreat you to repent of the wrongs you have done already, and to entirely reform the constitution of your whole body. I entertain but little hope that you will pay attention to my advice; you are already far too abandoned. Did it rest with myself, I should add nothing in mitigation of the sentence which I have passed, but it is the merciful provision of the law that even the most hardened criminal shall be allowed some one of the three official remedies, which is to be prescribed at the time of his conviction. I shall therefore order that you receive two tablespoonfuls of castor oil daily, until the pleasure of the court be further known."

When the sentence was concluded the prisoner acknowledged in a few scarcely audible words that he was justly punished, and that he had had a fair trial. He was then removed to the prison from which he was never to return. There was a second attempt at applause when the judge had finished speaking, but as before it was at once repressed; and though the feeling of the court was strongly against the prisoner, there was no show of any violence against him, if one may except a little hooting from the bystanders when he was being removed in the prisoners' van. Indeed, nothing struck me more during my whole sojourn in the country, than the general respect for law and order.

2 THE LAWLESS SOCIETY

When the American colonists transplanted and modified the law of England, they changed not only the formal legal system but many of their attitudes toward law as well. As the new nation, founded in the overthrow of authority, grew into a sprawling country with few courts and few lawyers and with violence a familiar companion, the people of the United States established a reputation for lawlessness in the eyes of many observers.

The image of a lawless society is probably most often evoked by accounts of life on the American frontier—the source of many of our ideals and enduring myths. It seems quite possible that the place of Jesse James, Billy the Kid, and Wild Bill Hickock is as secure in the pantheon of American folk heroes as that of Bat Masterson and Wyatt Earp. We seem to remember our sheriffs and our outlaws with equal pleasure.

The frontier undoubtedly has had an influence on our attitudes toward the nature of wrongdoing, yet other forces have been at work as well. It is possible that in most societies there is a hidden fascination with lawlessness as modern man plays out his repressed impulses in fantasy. In any event, when we speak of defining crime it is more than a matter of formal rules. It also involves a society's beliefs, attitudes, and emotions concerning criminal behavior.

1. The Outlaw: Twain Meets Slade

What is lawful or unlawful? What are the grounds for our choice? What means shall we use to secure lawful behavior?

There are those who argue that Americans have always been very uncertain about answers to these questions and exhibit a profound ambivalence about the wrongfulness of many crimes. It is certainly true that the man who breaks the law holds an abiding interest for many people, as Mark Twain shows in his account of Joseph Slade. If we admire the criminal as well as condemn him—and we sometimes do—what shall we say about his crimes?

Really and truly, two-thirds of the talk of drivers and conductors had been about this man Slade, ever since the day before we reached Julesburg. In order that the Eastern reader may have a clear conception of what a Rocky Mountain desperado is, in his highest state of development, I will reduce all this mass of overland gossip to one straightforward narrative, and present it in the following shape:

Slade was born in Illinois, of good parentage. At about twenty-six years of age he killed a man in a quarrel and fled the country. At St. Joseph, Missouri, he joined one of the early California-bound emigrant trains, and was given the post of train master. One day on the plains he had an angry dispute with one of his wagon drivers, and both drew their revolvers. But the driver was the quicker artist, and had his weapon cocked first. So Slade said it was a pity to waste life on so small a matter, and proposed that the pistols be thrown on the ground and the quarrel settled by a fist fight. The unsuspecting driver agreed, and threw down his pistol—whereupon Slade laughed at his simplicity, and shot him dead!

He made his escape, and lived a wild life for a while, dividing his time between fighting Indians and avoiding an Illinois sheriff, who had been sent to arrest him for his first murder. It is said that in one Indian battle he killed three savages with his own hand, and afterward cut their ears off and sent them, with his compliments, to the chief of the tribe.

Slade soon gained a name for fearless resolution, and this was sufficient merit to procure for him the important post of overland division agent at

Julesburg, in place of Mr. Jules, removed. For some time previously, the company's horses had been frequently stolen, and the coaches delayed, by gangs of outlaws, who were wont to laugh at the idea of any man's having the temerity to resent such outrages. Slade resented them promptly. The outlaws soon found that the new agent was a man who did not fear anything that breathed the breath of life. He made short work of all offenders. The result was that delays ceased, the company's property was let alone, and no matter what happened or who suffered, Slade's coaches went through, every time! True, in order to bring about this wholesome change, Slade had to kill several men—some say three, others say four, and others six—but the world was the richer for their loss. The first prominent difficulty he had was with the ex-agent Jules, who bore the reputation of being a reckless and desperate man himself. Jules hated Slade for supplanting him, and a good fair occasion for a fight was all he was waiting for. By and by Slade dared to employ a man whom Jules had once discharged. Next, Slade seized a team of stage horses which he accused Jules of having driven off and hidden somewhere for his own use. War was declared, and for a day or two the two men walked warily about the streets, seeking each other, Jules armed with a double-barreled shotgun, and Slade with his history-creating revolver. Finally, as Slade stepped into a store, Jules poured the contents of his gun into him from behind the door. Slade was plucky, and Jules got several bad pistol wounds in return. Then both men fell, and were carried to their respective lodgings, both swearing that better aim should do deadlier work next time. Both were bedridden a long time, but Jules got on his feet first, and gathering his possessions together, packed them on a couple of mules, and fled to the Rocky Mountains to gather strength in safety against the day of reckoning. For many months he was not seen or heard of, and was gradually dropped out of the remembrance of all save Slade himself. But Slade was not the man to forget him. On the contrary, common report said that Slade kept a reward standing for his capture, dead or alive!

After a while, seeing that Slade's energetic administration had restored peace and order to one of the worst divisions of the road, the overland stage company transferred him to the Rocky Ridge division in the Rocky Mountains, to see if he could perform a like miracle there. It was the very paradise of outlaws and desperadoes. There was absolutely no semblance of law there. Violence was the rule. Force was the only recognized authority. The commonest misunderstandings were settled on the spot with the revolver or the knife. Murders were done in open day, and with sparkling frequency, and nobody thought of inquiring into them. It was considered that the parties who did the killing had their private reasons for it; for other people to meddle would have been looked upon as indelicate. After a murder, all that Rocky Mountain etiquette required of a spectator was, that he should help the gentleman bury his game—otherwise his churlishness would surely be remembered against him the first time he killed a man himself and needed a neighborly turn in interring him.

Slade took up his residence sweetly and peacefully in the midst of this hive of horse thieves and assassins, and the very first time one of them aired his insolent swaggerings in his presence he shot him dead! He began a raid on the outlaws, and in a singularly short space of time he had completely stopped their depredations on the stage stock, recovered a large number of stolen horses, killed several of the worst desperadoes of the district, and gained such a dread ascendancy over the rest that they respected him, admired him, feared him, obeyed him! He wrought the same marvelous change in the ways of the community that had marked his administration at Overland City. He captured two men who had stolen overland stock, and with his own hands he hanged them. He was supreme judge in his district, and he was jury and executioner likewise—and not only in the case of offenses against his employers, but against passing emigrants as well. On one occasion some emigrants had their stock lost or stolen, and told Slade, who chanced to visit their camp. With a single companion he rode to a ranch, the owners of which he suspected, and opening the door, commenced firing, killing three, and wounding the fourth.

From a bloodthirstily interesting little Montana book [*The Vigilantes of Montana,* by Thomas J. Dimsdale] I take this paragraph:

While on the road, Slade held absolute sway. He would ride down to a station, get into a quarrel, turn the house out of windows, and maltreat the occupants most cruelly. The unfortunates had no means of redress, and were compelled to recuperate as best they could. On one of these occasions, it is said he killed the father of the fine little half-breed boy Jemmy, whom he adopted, and who lived with his widow after his execution. Stories of Slade's hanging men, and of innumerable assaults, shootings, stabbings, and beatings, in which he was a principal actor, form part of the legends of the stage line. As for minor quarrels and shootings, it is absolutely certain that a minute history of Slade's life would be one long record of such practices.

Slade was a matchless marksman with a navy revolver. The legends say that one morning at Rocky Ridge, when he was feeling comfortable, he saw a man approaching who had offended him some days before—observe the fine memory he had for matters like that—and, "Gentlemen," said Slade, drawing, "it is a good twenty-yard shot—I'll clip the third button on his coat!" Which he did. The bystanders all admired it. And they all attended the funeral, too.

On one occasion a man who kept a little whiskey shelf at the station did something which angered Slade—and went and made his will. A day or two afterward Slade came in and called for some brandy. The man reached under the counter (ostensibly to get a bottle—possibly to get something else), but Slade smiled upon him that peculiarly bland and satisfied smile of his which the neighbors had long ago learned to recognize as a death warrant in disguise, and told him to "none of that!—pass out the high-priced article." So the poor barkeeper had to turn his back and get the high-priced brandy from the shelf; and when he faced around again he was looking into the muzzle of Slade's pistol. "And the next instant," added my informant, impressively, "he was one of the deadest men that ever lived."

The stage drivers and conductors told us that sometimes Slade would leave a hated enemy wholly unmolested, unnoticed, and unmentioned, for weeks together—had done it once or twice at any rate. And some said they believed he did it in order to lull the victims into unwatchfulness, so that he could get the advantage of them, and others said they believed he saved up an enemy that way, just as a schoolboy saves up a cake, and made the pleasure go as far as it would by gloating over the anticipation. One of these cases was that of a Frenchman who had offended Slade. To the surprise of everybody Slade did not kill him on the spot, but let him alone for a considerable time. Finally, however, he went to the Frenchman's house very late one night, knocked, and when his enemy opened the door, shot him dead—pushed the corpse inside the door with his foot, set the house on fire, and burned up the dead man, his widow and three children! I heard this story from several different people, and they evidently believed what they were saying. It may be true, and it may not. "Give a dog a bad name," etc.

Slade was captured, once, by a party of men who intended to lynch him. They disarmed him, and shut him up in a strong log house, and placed a guard over him. He prevailed on his captors to send for his wife, so that he might have a last interview with her. She was a brave, loving, spirited woman. She jumped on a horse and rode for life and death. When she arrived they let her in without searching her, and before the door could be closed she whipped out a couple of revolvers, and she and her lord marched forth defying the party. And then, under a brisk fire, they mounted double and galloped away unharmed!

In the fullness of time Slade's myrmidons captured his ancient enemy Jules, whom they found in a well-chosen hiding-place in the remote fastnesses of the mountains, gaining a precarious livelihood with his rifle. They brought him to Rocky Ridge, bound hand and foot, and deposited him in the middle of the cattle yard with his back against a post. It is said that the pleasure that lit Slade's face when he heard of it was something fearful to contemplate. He examined his enemy to see that he was securely tied, and then went to bed, content to wait till morning before enjoying the luxury of killing him. Jules spent the night in the cattle yard, and it is a region where warm nights are never known. In the morning Slade practiced on him with his revolver, nipping the flesh here and there, and occasionally clipping off a finger, while Jules begged him to kill him outright and put him out of his misery. Finally Slade reloaded, and walking up close to his victim, made some characteristic remarks and then dispatched him. The body lay there half a day, nobody venturing to touch it without orders, and then Slade detailed a party and assisted at the burial himself. But he first cut off the dead man's ears and put them in his vest pocket, where he carried them for some time with great satisfaction. That is the story as I have frequently heard it told and seen it in print in California newspapers. It is doubtless correct in all essential particulars.

In due time we rattled up to a stage station, and sat down to breakfast with a half-savage, half-civilized company of armed and bearded mountaineers, ranchmen, and station employees. The most gentlemanly-appearing, quiet, and affable officer we had yet found along the road in the Overland Company's service was the person who sat at the head of the table, at my elbow. Never youth stared and shivered as I did when I heard them call him SLADE!

2. The Lawman: Myth in Embryo

Perhaps some of our uncertainty about the meaning of crime comes from the methods we use to control it; for here, often enough, violence meets violence. The sheriff and the outlaw walking toward a confrontation on a dusty street are a basic part of our folklore, the theme of countless motion picture and television Westerns. But who is the outlaw and who is the lawman? Stuart Lake, in his retelling of Wyatt Earp's first venture into law enforcement, takes care that we know who is wearing the badge.

Early in the afternoon of August 18, 1873, Wyatt had the sun-scorched plaza almost to himself as he lounged beneath the wooden awning which shaded Beebe's General Store and Brennan's Saloon, next door. At intervals someone passed on the walk, cowboys left one saloon for another, or a sweating horseman rode in from the prairie, hitched his cayuse and sought relief from the blazing heat at a favorite bar. For the most part, the dusty cowtown square was devoid of life, except the drooping horses tethered to the rails and their attendant swarms of flies. Sweltering wild and woolly Ellsworth was as peaceful as a cool green-and-white New England village.

In a saloon beyond Brennan's, Wyatt knew, an "open" poker game was in progress, with stakes of unusual size. Play was so high that the Thompsons had left their faro bank to sit in. When informed of a table rule against guns, Ben and Bill had still been sufficiently intrigued by the size of the pots to send their weapons back to the Grand Central and draw cards. Wyatt had heard that the Thompsons were forcing the play, that Bill was drinking steadily and getting mean. Whereupon he was well satisfied to be out of the game. Wyatt had small fancy for the Thompsons in any case, less for Bill at a poker table with high stakes and drunk.

From the saloon in which the Thompsons were gambling, a violent uproar was followed by the appearance of the brothers on the plaza. They came out of the door on the run, Bill cursing loudly and shouting threats over his shoulder as the pair made for the Grand Central. A moment later, they reappeared from the hotel and headed back toward the saloon, Ben carrying a double-barreled shotgun and Bill, a rifle. At the rail in front of the saloon stood a pair of horses hitched to a hay-wagon and behind this rack the Thompsons took their stand, Bill shouting threats and imprecations and Ben adding profanely insulting invitations to those inside the saloon to "Come out and make your fight."

Wyatt stepped into Beebe's doorway, for cover from stray lead, as the racket of the belligerent brothers drew several hundred persons from the various establishments bordering the plaza as hopeful spectators. Sheriff Whitney hurried from his store, stopping at Beebe's doorway to ask Wyatt if he knew what had started the row. The question was answered by a bystander at the poker game who had sensed that its immediate vicinity was not the safest place in Ellsworth. He had run from the saloon by a rear door and around to the plaza to view forthcoming festivities.

"John Sterling slapped Bill Thompson's face," this onlooker volunteered. "Bill got nasty and John gave him the flat of his hand across the mouth. When Bill invited John to get a gun and meet him outside, John hit him again and knocked him out of his seat. Then Bill and Ben ran after their guns."

Sheriff Whitney was in his shirt-sleeves and palpably unarmed, yet without further hesitation he walked over to the hay-wagon where the Thompsons stood with cocked weapons waiting for someone to come out of the saloon.

"You keep out of this, Sheriff," Ben warned him. "We don't want to hurt you."

"Don't be foolish, Ben," Whitney replied.

Thompson's rejoinder was a torrent of profanity directed at Sterling and his friends, whereupon the sheriff went into the saloon. He returned to the walk with word that Sterling had been forcibly prevented from coming out to fight and had been taken by friends to his camp outside the town by way of the back door.

Whitney feared that Sterling might be shot on sight by one of the Thompsons when he again came into Ellsworth, and to smooth over the quarrel, invited the Thompsons into Brennan's saloon for a drink and a talk. Cow-punchers and merchants went indoors, and as Wyatt moved back to his lounging-place between Brennan's doorway and Beebe's entrance, he again had the plaza to himself. Fifteen minutes later, Whitney came out of the saloon, alone, and stopped to talk.

"They've calmed down a bit," the sheriff reported. "They're inside with a bunch of Texas men."

"Did you take their guns away from them?" Wyatt asked.

"No," Whitney replied, "they wouldn't stand for that."

Before Wyatt had time to comment on this matter, Bill Thompson appeared in Brennan's doorway with Ben's shotgun.

"I'll get a sheriff if I don't get anybody else," he declared.

Wyatt and Whitney turned to face him; Bill fired both barrels of the gun—eighteen buckshot—point-blank into the sheriff's breast, and ran back into the saloon.

Wyatt caught Whitney in his arms.

"I'm done," the sheriff gasped. "Get me home."

At the roar of gunfire, saloon, hotels, and stores spouted five hundred men into the Ellsworth plaza, nine tenths of them Texas gun-toters, an unarmed minority, local citizens. Ben and Bill Thompson walked deliberately out of Brennan's to a string of saddled cowponies at a near-by rail, Ben covering one flank with the rifle, Bill, the other with the shotgun. In front of the Grand Central, Thompson followers collected under George Peshaur, Cad Pierce, Neil Kane, and John Good, to forestall attack, and the brothers swung their gun-muzzles back and forth to menace the store fronts as they argued over ensuing procedure.

Friends of Sheriff Whitney volunteered to take the dying man home and Wyatt Earp turned his attention to the Thompsons. He stepped again into Beebe's entrance, and peered around the door-casing into the plaza for sight of the Ellsworth peace officers. None was in view. Beebe's door opened, and there at Wyatt's shoulder was Happy Jack Morco, Indian fighter and six-gun expert, two belts of ammunition around his waist and a forty-five-Colt's at either hip. Wyatt gave way to let Morco reconnoiter.

"For God's sake, get out of town," Ben Thompson urged Bill. "You shot Sheriff Whitney."

"I know it," Bill replied. "I'd have shot him if he'd been Jesus Christ."

Happy Jack peeped cautiously around the door-casing. Ben took a potshot without sighting his rifle. The bullet struck half an inch above the deputy marshal's head and he ducked for cover.

"Too high," Ben informed Bill with an oath of regret. "Get on that horse and get out of here before Whitney's friends get organized. Take this rifle and give me my shotgun. I'll cover your getaway."

Wyatt realized that the brothers were appropriating a cowpony and exchanging weapons, as the rifle would be preferable for Bill on a lone ride down the trail. Here was Happy Jack's opportunity.

"Jump out and get 'em," Wyatt suggested. "Hurry, while they're switching guns."

"Not me," Happy Jack replied. "Those fellows across the street might get me."

"You'd get both Thompsons first," Wyatt urged, but Morco refused to budge.

Wyatt restrained an impulse to boot the deputy marshal onto the open walk, and peered around the casing again. Bill was in the saddle with the Winchester in front of him; Ben, with the shotgun, backed into the road. To quote the *Ellsworth Reporter:*

He [*Bill*] *then rode slowly out of town, cursing and inviting a fight.*

No one accepted the invitation.

As Bill Thompson rode out of shooting range, Ben, still covering the assembled citizens with his shotgun, backed over to the Grand Central. A Texas man brought out his six-guns. With these favorites buckled in place and the shotgun in the crook of his arm, Ben paraded in front of the hotel shouting taunts and threats at the town of Ellsworth in general and at her peace officers in profane particular. At his back were a hundred Texas men, half of them man-killers of record, the rest more than willing to be. Peshaur, Pierce, Good, and Kane were slightly in advance of the crowd. In groups, around the plaza, three or four hundred more Texans were distributed. Every man-jack had six-guns at his hips and a gunhand itching for play. As Ben Thompson halted his tirade momentarily, Cad Pierce sought the limelight.

"I'll give one thousand dollars to anybody who'll knock off another marshal!" he shouted.

As the cowboys yelled appreciation of this offer, Deputy Marshal Brown appeared at the far end of a railroad building. A hundred forty-five-slugs screeched across the plaza, and Brown took cover. To quote *The Reporter* again:

Ben Thompson retained his arms for a full hour after this and no attempt was made to disarm him. Mayor Miller was at his residence. . . . During this long hour, where were the police? No arrest had been made and the street was full of armed men ready to defend Thompson. The police were arming themselves, and, as they claim, just ready to rally out and take alive or dead the violators of the law. They were loading their muskets [*sic*] *just as the mayor, impatient at the delay in making arrests, came along and discharged the whole force. It would have been better to have increased the force and discharged or retained the old police after quiet had been restored. The mayor acted promptly and according to his judgment, but we certainly think it was a bad move. A poor police is better than none, and if, as they claim, they were just ready for work, they should have had a chance to redeem themselves and the honor of the city. Thus the city was left without a police, with no one but Deputy Sheriff Hogue to make arrests.*

Hogue, it chanced, was absent in the country. For some reason unexplained, beyond a statement that it was "not at liberty to do so," the newspaper failed to publish later testimony before Coroner Duck and Police Judge Osborne which furnished a detailed account of events precipitated by the belated appearance of Mayor Jim Miller on the side of the plaza farthest from Ben Thompson.

Wyatt and Happy Jack were still in Beebe's doorway, and Ben Thompson was still strutting up and down before the hotel, when Mayor Miller edged around the corner to the store entrance. Brocky Jack Norton, the marshal, came through Beebe's from the rear; he, too, wore a pair of forty-five-caliber Colt's. Deputy Marshal Brown, armed with a rifle and revolvers, was somewhere behind the railroad shacks. Deputy Marshal Crawford had not made the gesture of plaza appearance. The mayor wasted ten minutes of time and breath in orders to his marshals for Ben Thompson's capture. Neither Brocky Jack nor Happy Jack relished obedience and said so.

Mayor Miller tried another tack. He shouted across the plaza to Thompson, ordering the gunman to lay down his arms and submit to arrest. Ben answered in raucous profanity, at which his followers whooped gleefully. Ellsworth was treed at the tip of the topmost limb.

After urging Happy Jack to jump out and kill the Thompsons, Wyatt had kept silent. But the mayor's pleas to the marshals and contempt for their discretion, abetted by reaction of the cold-blooded fashion in which Sheriff Whitney had been shot down, moved him to comment.

"Nice police force you've got," Wyatt said to Miller.

"Who are you?" the mayor demanded.

"Just a looker-on," Wyatt replied.

"Well, don't talk so much," Miller snapped. "You haven't even got a gun."

As Wyatt was in shirt-sleeves, it was evident that he was unarmed. He seldom carried weapons in the settlements and those he owned were in his hotel room.

"It's none of my business," Wyatt admitted, "but if it was, I'd get me a gun and arrest Ben Thompson or kill him."

Brocky Jack erred.

"Don't pay any attention to that kid, Jim," he interrupted.

But Miller was desperate.

"You're fired, Norton," he said. "You, too, Morco."

The mayor snatched the marshal's badge from Brocky Jack's shirt-front.

"As soon as I can find Brown and Crawford, I'll fire them."

He turned to Wyatt Earp.

"I'll make this your business. You're marshal of Ellsworth. Here's your badge. Go into Beebe's and get some guns. I order you to arrest Ben Thompson."

To the best of Wyatt Earp's recollection, he voiced no formal acceptance of his impromptu appointment as an Ellsworth peace officer. He turned and walked to Beebe's firearms counter and asked for a pair of second-hand forty-fives, with holsters and cartridge belts.

"New guns and holsters," he explained in after years, "might have slowed me down."

Selecting two six-shooters with trigger-dogs that some former gunwise owner had filed to split-second smoothness and a pair of well-worn holsters, Wyatt tested the weapons thoroughly, loaded five cylinders in each, spun them, filled the cartridge-loops, settled the guns on his hips, and walked out to the plaza. He said nothing to Mayor Miller or the two Jacks. Not one of the three offered company or suggestion. Beebe's clerk always asserted that the trio remained huddled in the doorway while the youthful marshal, *pro tem,* walked out to face the deadliest gunman then alive.

Wyatt Earp's short journey across the Ellsworth plaza under the muzzle of Ben Thompson's shotgun established for all time his preëminence among gun-fighters of the West, but the episode has been ignored in written tales. That the camp never shared popular recognition with Wichita and Dodge as a topnotch cowtown, that its glory was but a season long, may have been responsible for the oversight; in any event, narrators of Earp history seem unaware that Wyatt was marshal of Ellsworth for one portentous hour. His appointment was not entered in the records and he was never paid for the service; yet, the amazing single exploit of his brief incumbency was a word-of-mouth sensation in '73, from the Platte to the Rio Grande. From a number of onlookers, who, all uncomprehendingly, were witnesses at the dawning of a new era in the Kansas cowtowns and who later recounted what they saw, has come an authentic picture of the high moment in Ellsworth's lurid heyday, and of Wyatt Earp as he appeared.

As the young man stepped from the shelter of Beebe's door, he pulled at the brim of his black sombrero to set it firmly in place and started diagonally across the plaza toward the Grand Central. Ben Thompson squared around, shifting his shotgun to hold the weapon across his stomach, the fore-end in his left hand, his right on grip and triggers. From that position a single motion would bring it into play.

Ben Thompson was a squarely built, stocky fellow, about five feet eight inches in height. A bloated face, bushy brows above his wide blue eyes, and a sweeping mustache gave him an appearance of greater maturity than his thirty years would justify; and this, as well as his bulkiness, was accentuated as he squatted slightly for effective handling of his gun.

Old-timers have said that Wyatt Earp looked like a boy as he crossed the plaza. Six feet tall, weighing not more than one hundred and fifty-five pounds, he, too, was the owner of good blue eyes; but, in contrast to Thompson's red and puffy countenance, Wyatt's lean and muscular features were smooth-shaven and tanned brown, his slimness further set off by white shirt, black trousers, wide-brimmed black hat, and high-heeled horseman's boots. As he walked, his hands swung easily, conveniently close to his holsters, but making no overt moves.

As Wyatt reached a point possibly fifty yards from Thompson, Cad Pierce said something to which Ben snarled over his shoulder in reply. Pierce subsided, and with the other Texas men waited for Ben to call the turn.

Wyatt Earp had a definite course of action in mind as he advanced toward the hundred or more half-drunken cowboys, any and all of whom were keyed to cutting lose at him with twice that many guns for the mere satisfaction of seeing him die. He knew that to half the men in the crowd he was an utter stranger; the rest might know him by sight or name; he had no fear-inspiring record as a killer, and, so far as anyone in Ellsworth might know, had never used guns against a human adversary in all his life. He realized, too, that he was a target few men in the hundred could miss at fifty yards. That he was heeled with a pair of guns was evident to all; one false or hesitant gesture with either hand and he was fair game for the first to draw.

"I knew what I would do before the mayor pinned Brocky Jack's badge on my shirt," Wyatt said in recalling the affair. "I based my action on my knowledge of Ben Thompson's vanity and of the Texas men in his crowd.

"In the first place, I knew better than to walk out of Beebe's with a gun in my hand. If I had, I would have been filled with lead before I reached the road. But I also knew that, as long as I did not draw, the Texas men would leave it to Ben to make the play; he would have turned and shot down anyone who dared to cut loose before he opened the ball. Whatever happened must first be between him and me.

"So, all I had to do was keep my eye on Ben's shotgun; not on the muzzle, but on his right hand at the grip and trigger-guard. That held my eye on the target I had picked, his stomach just back of his hand. I figured he'd wait for me to get within thirty or forty yards to make his weapon most effective and that he could not get the shotgun into action without 'telegraphing the move,' as a boxer would say, through his wrist. When I saw his wrist move to put his arm muscles into play, I'd go for my guns and I had enough confidence in myself to be certain that I could put at least one slug into his belly before he could pull a trigger.

"I realized that after I'd plugged Ben, some of his crowd might get me, and I had some idea, I suppose, of taking as many with me as I could. Beyond figuring to get Cad Pierce after I got Ben, if that was possible, I don't recall thinking much about that. All I really cared about was heading Thompson into his hole. I intended to arrest him if I could. But it was a moral certainty that he'd try to shoot. If he did, I'd kill him. I could hit a target the size of his stomach ten times out of ten shots with a forty-five at any range up to one hundred yards, and I had perfect confidence in my speed."

When Wyatt Earp was about forty yards distant, Ben Thompson called to him.

"What do you want, Wyatt?" he shouted.

"I want you, Ben," Wyatt replied, walking steadily forward.

Neither Ben Thompson nor any onlooker, and least of all Wyatt Earp, has offered a completely satisfactory explanation for what followed. Thompson made no move with his gun, and did not speak again until Wyatt was less than thirty yards away.

"I'd rather talk than fight," the killer called.

"I'll get you either way, Ben," Wyatt assured him, without halting in his stride.

"Wait a minute," said Thompson. "What do you want me to do?"

"Throw your shotgun into the road, put up your hands, and tell your friends to stay out of this play," Wyatt answered. Less than fifteen yards now separated the men.

"Will you stop and let me talk to you?" Ben asked.

Wyatt halted. He now knew positively that he could take Thompson, alive or dead, whichever way the gunman chose to turn events. He had Ben talking, which is the gravest error possible to a gun-thrower who has serious business at hand.

"What are you going to do with me?" Thompson asked.

"Kill you or take you to jail," Wyatt informed him.

"Brown's over there by the depot with a rifle," Ben objected. "The minute I give up my guns he'll cut loose at me."

"If he does," Wyatt promised, "I'll give you back your guns and we'll shoot it out with him. As long as you're my prisoner, the man that gets you will have to get me."

Thompson hesitated.

"Come on," Wyatt ordered: "throw down your gun or make your fight."

Ben Thompson grinned.

"You win," he said, tossed his shotgun into the road, and shoved both hands above his head.

Wyatt Earp's guns were still in their holsters. Now, for the first time, his hand went to his right hip.

"You fellows get back!" he ordered the Texas men. "Move!"

As they obeyed, Wyatt stepped up to Thompson and unbuckled his prisoner's gunbelts.

"Come on, Ben," he said. "We'll go over to the calaboose."

With the famous Thompson six-guns dangling from their belts in his left hand, Wyatt marched his prisoner across the plaza to Judge V. B. Osborne's court. Until he reached the entrance, no onlookers spoke to him, or moved to follow. Once Wyatt and Ben were inside, the mayor and his erstwhile officers hurried after them. A moment later, five hundred milling men stormed at the narrow doorway, Thompson's friends leading the mob.

Deputy Sheriff Hogue, who had just ridden into town, forced a way through the crowd as a messenger from the Whitney home arrived with the shouted news that the sheriff was dead. The announcement was premature —Whitney actually lived for several hours after the Thompson hearing— but to the mob it was final.

There was talk of lynching, but Wyatt anticipated no serious trouble on that score; real danger would come with any attempt of the Texas men to rescue Ben from the law. The Thompson element dictated his next move. Peshaur, Pierce, Kane, and Good shouldered into the front rank, each with his forty-fives belted to his waist and Pierce carrying the shotgun with which Whitney had been assassinated and which Ben had thrown into the road. Wyatt spoke to Hogue in an undertone, then turned on the gunmen.

"Get out of here!" he ordered. "Pierce, take your crowd outside and keep 'em there. There'll be no lynching and no rescue."

Pierce looked at Thompson.

"Better go, Cad," Ben suggested. "He means what he says."

With the courtroom cleared, Thompson's arraignment proceeded.

"What's the charge?" asked Judge Osborne.

As no one else volunteered a reply, Wyatt suggested that Ben was probably an accessory to murder. The judge turned to Mayor Miller as the proper person to indicate the enormity of Thompson's offense. The mayor hesitated, possibly in embarrassment under the keen blue eye of his hastily selected peace officer, considered the economic importance of the Texas men to the community, then offered as an amendment his opinion that maybe Ben had disturbed the peace.

"Guilty," said the judge. "Twenty-five dollars fine."

Thompson grinned as he peeled the assessment from a roll of greenbacks.

"Do I get my guns?" he inquired.

"Certainly," said the judge. "You have paid your fine and the marshal will restore any property he may have taken from you."

As Thompson reached for his gunbelts, Wyatt issued his last order as an Ellsworth peace officer.

"Ben," he said, "court or no court, don't you put those on here. You carry them straight to the Grand Central, and don't so much as hesitate on the way. I'll be watching you. Keep moving until you're out of my sight. After that, what you do will be none of my business."

Wyatt stood in the courtroom door with his eye on Thompson until the gunman reached his hotel, then turned to Mayor Miller.

"Here," he said, "is your badge, and here are the guns I got at Beebe's. I don't need 'em any longer."

"Don't you want to be marshal of Ellsworth?" Miller asked.

"I do not," Wyatt replied.

"We'll pay you one hundred and twenty-five dollars a month," the mayor offered.

"Ellsworth," Wyatt answered sententiously, "figures sheriffs at twenty-five dollars a head. I don't figure the town's my size."

3. The Enduring Frontier

According to United States census, the American frontier came to an end in 1880. The American frontier, however, was a cultural-historical event as well as a physical fact; and the mores of the frontier continued long after the line of the frontier on the map had disappeared. There are many writers, such as Mabel Elliott, who see the influence of the frontier extending into our own time and shaping our ideas about the nature of crime. A tradition of lawlessness, she argues, echoes in our minds.

All sociologists and criminologists accept the idea that culture in its wider ramifications and that culture conflict in particular provide the matrix out of which much of the modern crime problem emerges. Thus, *e.g.,* we recognize that race, class, national origins and the varying cultural patterns of social behavior provide important sources of cultural conflict and resultant anti-social behavior.

We sometimes forget, however, that the mainsprings of anti-social conduct are as much rooted in the past as they are a function of the present and that in America in particular, crime bears a significant relationship to the folkways and mores of the frontier. As a matter of fact there are numerous evidences that crime itself is written large in these same folkways and mores.

We have all heard the old story of how in Germany all which is allowable is forbidden, whereas in France all that is forbidden is "allowed." In our country we might go even further in asserting that lawlessness has been a part of the devices of social control, and that crimes have been committed which have not only been tacitly allowed, but have had the acceptance and approval of the group. Herein we have an explanation of the confounding confusion presented by the white collar criminal, the corrupt politician, and the ethics of the "robber Barons."

. . .

Out of the West have come some of the finest types of American men and women. But the restive spirit of the pioneer has created much of the pattern of freedom and liberty which has been so characteristic a part of our American way of life. Herein we have the origins of the American rejection of the restraining influences of group life in the cities, a rejection made possible by the existence of the vast open spaces where a man could

From Mabel A. Elliott, "Crime and the Frontier Mores," **American Sociological Review,** Vol. IX (April 1944).

exist without tribute to tax collectors, or law makers, and if he moved fast enough he did not need to defer even to his neighbor's opinion.

. . .

The historical importance of the frontier has found its best expression in the classic work of Frederick J. Turner. None has excelled his description of the Westerward course of civilization in our vast commonwealth. For with the ever-receding frontier any man with sufficient energy might clear a spot in the wilderness and secure for himself a goodly competence through the effective assistance of our homestead laws.

In this conquering of the wilderness we may trace the roots of our particular brand of democracy. Here has developed the exaggerated individualism of the plains and mountain country and our much vaunted American standard of living.

Life on the Western frontier presented many variations. Opening up the fertile prairies was a relatively calm and peaceful business. There was, however, sufficient inland banditry and enough piracy in the steamboat trade to lend color and vitality to the tranquillity of the Ohio and Mississippi valleys. The opening up of the great agricultural states of the North Central area was, in the main, dependent upon orderly men willing to assume the necessary routine tasks. Men engaged in wresting a living from the soil have little occasion for sharp disputes or violent combat. Hence the great agricultural middle west, Ohio, Indiana, Illinois, Iowa, Minnesota and Wisconsin, took on the general orderliness of life characteristic of New England. In these regions the strong motif of Puritanism developed. At the same time the folkways, mores and laws of New England were transplanted to the Western scene. Thus Iowa and Eastern Kansas became more New English than New England.

Those who were seeking a fortune in the Far West and especially those who invaded the mining sections of the Rocky Mountains were pioneers of different character. It is true that many sturdy and courageous men of honor were tempted by considerations of the economic opportunities and advantageous climate to participate in the development of Colorado, Montana, Wyoming, California and the Oregon Country. But here also came the flotsam, outlaws from Eastern states, ex-convicts made bitter by real or fancied injustice, desperadoes. The Western frontier became in fact the haven of refuge for the horse and cattle thief of Nebraska and Kansas, for the escaped burglar from an Eastern penitentiary, for the counterfeiter who might have new opportunity to ply his illicit vocation. Paroled convicts came from Australia, while Mexican outlaws swelled the numbers.

In fact the background of many of our pioneers was so disreputable that a special code of etiquette arose for conversing with strangers. As one Westerner put it:

"Never ask a stranger where he came from or he may draw a trigger. He may very well have come from jail."

Indeed too much inquisitiveness, as Everett Dick expresses it, was "an invitation to gunplay."

In California the signs of the times were well expressed in a song of the day:

Oh what was your name in the States?
Was it Thompson or Johnson or Bates?
Did you murder your wife
And fly for your life?
Say, what was your name in the States?

Legal, religious and educational institutions and controls were virtually non-existent in the mining camps and mountain frontiers. Here, too, there were few women. This meant there was little of the conserving influence of good women or the stabilizing values of family life. The distorted sex ratio in the almost exclusively male population was undoubtedly a factor in the frontier crime rates. This distorted sex ratio brought the inevitable influx of scarlet women who became the hostesses of the gambling dens and night clubs and the dancing partners at the "Hurdy-gurdy" houses which offered the combined facilities of a bar, gambling house and dance hall.

Shooting scrapes and jealous quarrels over the attentions of these willing ladies were a frequent accompaniment of strong liquor, frustrated impulses and the code of the times. According to the latter, no red-blooded man was expected to take silently the curses and insults of his rivals. Personal insults, however much deserved, demanded immediate action. If a mountaineer was denounced as a liar, a thief, or by less mentionable epithets he did not hesitate to annihilate his slanderer. The mountaineer was quick on the trigger, aimed well, and without remorse. Thus we may account for the emotional origins of many a mountaineer murder. Life was cheap, but honor was long on the Western frontier.

. . .

Obviously it is far from this author's belief that the frontier mores explain all or most of our crime rate. Nevertheless, the frontier culture constitutes an important part of our social heritage and explains much of the American's rejection of and disrespect for formal legislative controls. Unlike our European cousins we have had our most serious frontier problems within our own borders. Perhaps, one might add facetiously, herein is one explanation why crime is writ large in the American mores—just as the mores are written in the lack of social consciousness of our forebears. In Europe, on the other hand, there has been much respect for laws within national boundaries, whereas cultural conflicts have led to war. As Turner has pointed out, ours is a democracy born of free land and such a democracy "strong in selfishness and individualism, intolerant of administrative experience and education and pressing individual liberty beyond its proper bounds, has its dangers as well as its benefits."

4. The Fascination of Crime

It is possible, of course, that the ambivalence about the wrongfulness of wrongdoing transcends national boundaries and a particular cultural tradition. No Orchids for Miss Blandish *was a popular crime novel in England in the 1940s and George Orwell was driven to ask why. The impersonality of modern society, the passivity of the average citizen that makes fantasy more real than reality, the brutalizing conditions that breed a taste for brutality—all may alter our concept of crime no matter what the public declarations may be.*

The book [*No Orchids for Miss Blandish*] contains eight full-dress murders, an unassessable number of casual killings and woundings, an exhumation (with a careful reminder of the stench), the flogging of Miss Blandish, the torture of another woman with red-hot cigarette-ends, a strip-tease act, a third-degree scene of unheard-of cruelty and much else of the same kind. It assumes great sexual sophistication in its readers (there is a scene, for instance, in which a gangster, presumably of masochistic tendency, has an orgasm in the moment of being knifed), and it takes for granted the most complete corruption and self-seeking as the norm of human behaviour. The detective, for instance, is almost as great a rogue as the gangsters, and actuated by nearly the same motives. Like them, he is in pursuit of "five hundred grand." It is necessary to the machinery of the story that Mr. Blandish should be anxious to get his daughter back, but apart from this, such things as affection, friendship, good nature or even ordinary politeness simply do not enter. Nor, to any great extent, does normal sexuality. Ultimately only one motive is at work throughout the whole story: the pursuit of power.

It should be noticed that the book is not in the ordinary sense pornography. Unlike most books that deal in sexual sadism, it lays the emphasis on the cruelty and not on the pleasure. Slim, the ravisher of Miss Blandish, has "wet, slobbering lips": this is disgusting, and it is meant to be disgusting. But the scenes describing cruelty to women are comparatively perfunctory. The real high-spots of the book are cruelties committed by men upon other men: above all, the third-degreeing of the gangster, Eddie Schultz, who is lashed into a chair and flogged on the windpipe with truncheons, his arms broken by fresh blows as he breaks loose. In another of Mr. Chase's books, *He Won't Need It Now,* the hero, who is intended to be a sympathetic and perhaps even noble character, is described as stamping on somebody's face, and then, having crushed the man's mouth in, grinding his heel round and round in it. Even when physical incidents of this kind are not occurring, the mental atmosphere of these books is always the same. Their whole theme is the struggle for power and the triumph of the strong over the weak. The big gangsters wipe out the little ones as mercilessly as a pike gobbling up the little fish in a pond; the police kill off the criminals as cruelly as the angler kills the pike. If ultimately one sides with the police against the gangsters, it is merely because they are better organized and more powerful, because, in fact, the law is a bigger racket than crime. Might is right: *voe victis.*

As I have mentioned already, *No Orchids* enjoyed its greatest vogue in 1940, though it was successfully running as a play till some time later. It was, in fact, one of the things that helped to console people for the boredom of being bombed. Early in the war the *New Yorker* had a picture of a little man approaching a news-stall littered with papers with such headlines as "Great Tank Battles in Northern France," "Big Naval Battle in the North Sea," "Huge Air Battles over the Channel," etc. etc. The little man is saying, *"Action Stories,* please." That little man stood for all the drugged millions to whom the world of the gangsters and the prize-ring is more "real," more "tough," than such things as wars, revolutions, earthquakes, famines and pestilences. From the point of view of a reader of *Action Stories,* a description of the London blitz, or of the struggles of the European underground parties, would be "sissy stuff." On the other hand, some puny gun-battle in Chicago, resulting in perhaps half a dozen deaths, would seem genuinely "tough." This habit of mind is now extremely widespread. A soldier sprawls in a muddy trench, with the machine-gun bullets crackling a foot or two overhead, and whiles away his intolerable boredom by reading an American gangster story. And what is it that makes that story so exciting? Precisely the fact that people are shooting at each other with machine-guns! Neither the soldier nor anyone else sees anything curious in this. It is taken for granted that an imaginary bullet is more thrilling than a real one.

The obvious explanation is that in real life one is usually a passive victim, whereas in the adventure story one can think of oneself as being at the centre of events. But there is more to it than that. Here it is necessary to refer again to the curious fact of *No Orchids* being written—with technical errors, perhaps, but certainly with considerable skill—in the American language.

There exists in America an enormous literature of more or less the same stamp as *No Orchids.* Quite apart from books, there is the huge array of "pulp magazines," graded so as to cater to different kinds of fantasy, but nearly all having much the same mental atmosphere. A few of them go in for straight pornography, but the great majority are quite plainly aimed at sadists and masochists. Sold at threepence a copy under the title of *Yank Mags,* these things used to enjoy considerable popularity in England, but when the supply dried up owing to the war, no satisfactory substitute was forthcoming. English imitations of the "pulp magazine" do now exist, but they are poor things compared with the original. English crook films, again, never approach the American crook film in brutality. And yet the career of Mr. Chase shows how deep the American influence has already gone. Not only is he himself living a continuous fantasy-life in the Chicago underworld, but he can count on hundreds of thousands of readers who know what is meant by a "clipshop" or the "hotsquat," do not have to do mental arithmetic when confronted by "fifty grand," and understand at sight a sentence like "Johnnie was a rummy and only two jumps ahead of the nut-factory." Evidently there are great numbers of English people who are partly Americanised in language and, one ought to add, in moral outlook. For there was no popular protest against *No Orchids.* In the end it was withdrawn, but only retrospectively, when a later work, *Miss Callaghan Comes to Grief,* brought Mr. Chase's books to the attention of the authorities. Judging by casual conversations at the time, ordinary readers got a mild thrill out of the obscenities of *No Orchids,* but saw nothing undesirable in the book as a whole. Many people, incidentally, were under the impression that it was an American book reissued in England.

The thing that the ordinary reader *ought* to have objected to—almost certainly would have objected to, a few decades earlier—was the equivocal attitude towards crime. It is implied throughout *No Orchids* that being a criminal is only reprehensible in the sense that it does not pay. Being a policeman pays better, but there is no moral difference, since the police use essentially criminal methods. In a book like *He Won't Need It Now* the distinction between crime and crime-prevention practically disappears. This is a new departure for English sensational fiction, in which till recently there has always been a sharp distinction between right and wrong and a general agreement that virtue must triumph in the last chapter. English books glorifying crime (modern crime, that is—pirates and highwaymen are different) are very rare. Even a book like *Raffles,* as I have pointed out, is governed by powerful taboos, and it is clearly understood that Raffles's crimes must be expiated sooner or later. In America, both in life and fiction, the tendency to tolerate crime, even to admire the criminal so long as he is successful, is very much more marked. It is, indeed, ultimately this attitude that has made it possible for crime to flourish upon so huge a scale. Books have been written about Al Capone that are hardly different in tone from the books written about Henry Ford, Stalin, Lord Northcliffe and all the rest of the "log cabin to White House" brigade. And switching back eighty years, one finds Mark Twain adopting much the same attitude towards the disgusting bandit Slade, hero of twenty-eight murders, and towards the Western desperadoes generally. They were successful, they "made good," therefore he admired them.

3 LIFE IN THE CITY

Whatever may have been the ideas about crime in earlier portions of American experience, rapid growth of industrialization and urbanization radically transformed the meaning of crime in the United States, in both its context and its consequences. Crime became largely an urban matter, often flourishing in the growing slums of makeshift cities.

The same pattern had been seen before in other societies with masses of the poor in an urban setting. In the United States, however, the problem was intensified as members of minority groups were caught up in the painful process of assimilation. It is within this framework that we must try to understand the meaning of crime—not as an isolated act of an individual floating in a vacuum but as part of a life pattern of a person in a particular social and physical environment.

1. A London Slum

We would prefer to forget our slums, for they are a constant reminder of an unfilled social promise. Fortunately, we have a long heritage of writers who refuse to let us forget: Mayhew, Dickens, Marx and Engels, Riis, Harrington . . .

In the following selection by Arthur Morrison describing the Jago, an infamous London slum in the early nineteenth century, we can see a social setting in which crime and delinquency are as natural as breathing.

It was past the mid of a summer night in the Old Jago. The narrow street was all the blacker for the lurid sky; for there was a fire in a farther part of Shoreditch, and the welkin was an infernal coppery glare. Below, the hot, heavy air lay, a rank oppression, on the contorted forms of those who made for sleep on the pavement: and in it, and through it all, there rose from the foul earth and the grimed walls a close, mingled stink—the odour of the Jago.

From where, off Shoreditch High Street, a narrow passage, set across with posts, gave menacing entrance on one end of Old Jago Street, to where the other end lost itself in the black beyond Jago Row; from where Jago Row began south at Meakin Street, to where it ended north at Honey Lane—there the Jago, for one hundred years the blackest pit in London, lay and festered; and half-way along Old Jago Street a narrow archway gave upon Jago Court, the blackest hole in all that pit.

A square of two hundred and fifty yards or less—that was all there was of the Jago. But in that square the human population swarmed in thousands. Old Jago Street, New Jago Street, Half Jago Street lay parallel, east and west: Jago Row at one end and Edge Lane at the other lay parallel also, stretching north and south: foul ways all. What was too vile for Kate Street, Seven Dials, and Ratcliff Highway in its worst day, what was too useless, incapable and corrupt—all that teemed in the Old Jago.

. . .

Cosh-carrying was near to being the major industry of the Jago. The cosh was a foot length of iron rod, with a knob at one end, and a hook (or a ring) at the other. The craftsman, carrying it in his coat sleeves, waited

From Arthur Morrison, **A Child of the Jago** (London, 1896; Baltimore: Penguin Books, 1946). Reprinted by permission of The Westminster Hospital and The National Society for the Prevention of Cruelty to Children.

about dark staircase corners till his wife (married or not) brought in a well drunken stranger: when, with a sudden blow behind the head, the stranger was happily coshed, and whatever was found on him as he lay insensible was the profit of the transaction. In the hands of capable practitioners this industry yielded a comfortable subsistence for no great exertion. Most, of course, depended on the woman: whose duty it was to keep the other artist going in subjects. There were legends of surprising ingatherings achieved by wives of especial diligence: one of a woman who had brought to the cosh some six-and-twenty on a night of public rejoicing. This was, however, a story years old, and many have been no more than an exemplary fiction, designed, like a Sunday School book, to convey a counsel of perfection to the dutiful matrons of the Old Jago.

The man and woman vanished in a doorway near the Jago Row end, where, for some reason, dossers were fewer than about the portal of Jago Court. There conversation flagged, and a broken snore was heard. It was a quiet night, as quietness was counted in the Jago; for it was too hot for most to fight in that stifling air—too hot to do more than turn on the stones and swear. Still the last hoarse yelps of a combat of women came intermittently from Half Jago Street in the farther confines.

In a little while something large and dark was pushed forth from the door-opening near Jago Row which Billy Leary's spouse had entered. The thing rolled over, and lay tumbled on the pavement, for a time unnoted. It might have been yet another would-be sleeper, but for its stillness. Just such a thing it seemed, belike, to two that lifted their heads and peered a few yards off, till they rose on hands and knees and crept to where it lay: Jago rats both. A man it was; with a thick smear across his face, and about his head the source of the dark trickle that sought the gutter deviously over the broken flags. The drab stuff of his pockets peeped out here and there in a crumpled bunch, and his waistcoat gaped where the watch-guard had been. Clearly, here was an uncommonly remunerative cosh—a cosh so good that the boots had been neglected, and remained on the man's feet. These the kneeling two unlaced deftly, and, rising, prize in hand, vanished in the deeper shadow of Jago Row.

A small boy, whom they met full tilt at the corner, staggered out to the gutter and flung a veteran curse after them. He was a slight child, by whose size you might have judged his age at five. But his face was of serious and troubled age. One who knew the children of the Jago, and could tell, might have held him eight, or from that to nine.

He replaced his hands in his trousers' pockets, and trudged up the street. As he brushed by the coshed man he glanced again toward Jago Row, and, jerking his thumb that way, "Done 'im for 'is boots," he piped. But nobody marked him till he reached Jago Court, when old Beveridge, pushing back his hat once more, called sweetly and silkily, "Dicky Perrott!" and beckoned with his finger.

The boy approached, and as he did so the man's skeleton hand suddenly shot out and gripped him by the collar. "It—never—does—to—see—too—much!" Beveridge said, in a series of shouts close to the boy's ear. "Now go home," he added in a more ordinary tone, with a push to make his meaning plain: and straightway relapsed against the wall.

The boy scowled and backed off the pavement. His ragged jacket was coarsely made from one much larger, and he hitched the collar over his shoulder as he shrank toward a doorway some few yards on. Front doors were used merely as firewood in the Old Jago, and most had been burnt there many years ago. If perchance one could have been found still on its hinges, it stood ever open and probably would not shut. Thus at night the Jago doorways were a row of black holes, foul and forbidding.

Dicky Perrott entered his hole with caution, for anywhere, in the passage and on the stairs, somebody might be lying drunk, against whom it would be unsafe to stumble. He found nobody, however, and climbed and reckoned his way up the first stair-flight with the necessary regard for the treads that one might step through and the rails that had gone from the side. Then he pushed open the door of the first-floor back and was at home.

A little heap of guttering grease, not long ago a candle end, stood and spread on the mantelpiece, and gave irregular light from its drooping wick. A thin-railed iron bedstead, bent and staggering, stood against a wall, and on its murky coverings a half-dressed woman sat and neglected a baby that lay by her, grieving and wheezing. The woman had a long dolorous face, empty of expression and weak of mouth.

"Where 'a' you bin, Dicky?" she asked, rather complaining than asking. "It's sich low hours for a boy."

Dicky glanced about the room. "Got anythink to eat?" he asked.

"I dunno," she answered listlessly. "P'raps there's a bit o' bread in the cupboard. I don't want nothin', it's so 'ot. An' father ain't bin 'ome since tea-time."

The boy rummaged and found a crust. Gnawing at this, he crossed to where the baby lay. " 'Ullo, Looey," he said, bending and patting the muddy cheek. " 'Ullo!"

The baby turned feebly on its back, and set up a thin wail. Its eyes were large and bright, its tiny face was piteously flea-bitten and strangely old. "Wy, she's 'ungry, mother," said Dicky Perrott, and took the little thing up.

He sat on a small box, and rocked the baby on his knees, feeding it with morsels of chewed bread. The mother, dolefully inert, looked on and said: "She's that backward I'm quite wore out; more 'n ten months old, an' don't even crawl yut. It's a never-endin' trouble, is children."

She sighed, and presently stretched herself on the bed. The boy rose, and carrying his little sister with care, for she was dozing, essayed to look through the grimy window. The dull flush still spread overhead, but Jago Court lay darkling below, with scarce a sign of the ruinous back yards that edged it on this and the opposite sides, and nothing but blackness between.

The boy returned to his box, and sat. Then he said: "I don't s'pose father's 'avin' a sleep outside, eh?"

The woman sat up with some show of energy. "Wot?" she said sharply. "Sleep out in the street like them low Ranns an' Learys? I should 'ope not. It's bad enough livin' 'ere at all, an' me being used to different things once, an' all. You ain't seen 'im outside, 'ave ye?"

"No, I ain't seen 'im: I jist looked in the court." Then, after a pause: "I 'ope 'e's done a click," the boy said.

His mother winced. "I dunno wot you mean, Dicky," she said, but falteringly. "You—you're gittin' that low an'—"

"Wy, copped somethink, o' course. Nicked somethink. You know."

"If you say sich things as that I'll tell 'im wot you say, 'an 'e'll pay you. We ain't that sort o' people, Dicky, you ought to know. I was alwis kep' respectable an' straight all my life, I'm sure, an'—"

"I know. You said so before, to father—I 'eard: w'en 'e brought 'ome that there yuller prop—the necktie pin. Wy, where did 'e git that? 'E ain't 'ad a job for munse and munse: where's the yannups come from wot's bin for to pay the rent, an' git the toke, an' milk for Looey? Think I dunno? I ain't a kid. I know."

"Dicky, Dicky! you musn't say sich things!" was all the mother could find to say, with tears in her slack eyes. "It's wicked an'—an' low. An' you must alwis be respectable an' straight, Dicky, an' you'll—you'll git on then."

"Straight people's fools, *I* reckon. Kiddo Cook says that, an' 'e's as wide as Broad Street. W'en I grow up I'm goin' to git toffs' clo'es an' be in the 'igh mob. They does big clicks."

"They git put in a dark prison for years an' years, Dicky—an'—an' if you're sich a wicked low boy, father'll give you the strap—'ard," the mother returned, with what earnestness she might. "Gimme the baby, an' you go to bed, go on; 'fore father comes."

Dicky handed over the baby, whose wizen face was now relaxed in sleep, and slowly disencumbered himself of the ungainly jacket, staring at the wall in a brown study. "It's the mugs wot git took," he said, absently. "An quoddin' ain't so bad." Then, after a pause, he turned and added suddenly: "S'pose father'll be smugged some day, eh, mother?"

His mother made no reply, but bent languidly over the baby, with an indefinite pretence of settling it in a place on the bed. Soon Dicky himself, in the short and ragged skirt he had worn under the jacket, burrowed head first among the dingy coverings at the foot, and protruding his head at the farther side, took his accustomed place crosswise at the extreme end.

The filthy ceiling lit and darkened by fits as the candlewick fell and guttered to its end. He heard his mother rise and find another fragment of candle to light by its expiring flame, but he lay still wakeful. After a time he asked: "Mother, why don't you come to bed?"

"Waitin' for father. Go to sleep."

He was silent for a little. But brain and eyes were wide awake, and soon he spoke again. "Them noo 'uns in the front room," he said. "Ain't the man give 'is wife a 'idin' yut?"

"No."

"Nor yut the boy—'umpty-backed 'un?"

"No."

"Seems they're mighty pertickler. Fancy theirselves too good for their neighbours; I 'eard Pigeony Poll say that; on'y Poll said—"

"You mustn't never listen to Pigeony Poll, Dicky. Ain't you 'eard me say so? Go to sleep. 'Ere comes father." There was, indeed, a step on the stairs, but it passed the landing, and went on to the top floor. Dicky lay awake, but silent, gazing upward and back through the dirty window just over his head. It was very hot, and he fidgeted uncomfortably, fearing to turn or toss lest the baby should wake and cry. There came a change in the hue of the sky, and he watched the patch within his view, until the red seemed to gather in spots, and fade a spot at a time. Then at last there was a tread on the stairs, that stayed at the door; and father had come home. Dicky lay still, and listened.

2. The Pattern Repeats Itself

In the United States, more than one hundred years after Jago, it has become apparent that our urban, industrial society has managed to create a persisting culture of poverty locked into urban ghettos. It is far from true that slums are the only areas in which crime and delinquency are to be found, but in such areas there is an amalgamation of environmental forces that greatly increases the likelihood of illegal behavior. The important thing, for the moment, is to see breaking the law as part of a life history rather than as a single gesture or an entry in a row of figures. Jean Evans' account of Johnny Rocco makes clear the need to look at crime and delinquency in context.

Walk through the slum section of any American city some evening. Pause at the poolrooms, the gyms, the dingy bars, the candy stores, and certain street corners where boys and young men gather. Any one of them might be a Johnny Rocco.

Johnny is a short, chunky fellow of twenty. He looks older than his years. His hair, which is dark with a slightly reddish cast, is receding at the temples, thinning on top. His dark, heavy eyebrows, meeting over a slightly aquiline nose, give him an angry, somber look. His eyes are narrow, the skin underneath them tending to be baggy. There is a small narrow scar on his left cheek. His hands are stubby, the fingers square, the nails bitten short. Blue and red tattoos, their edges blurred, decorate both his forearms to just below the wrists. He carries his shoulders stiffly, walking with a cocky rolling gait.

At first contact Johnny seems tough—very tough. "I used to have a heart. I was chicken-hearted," he says contemptuously. "Now I don't give a damn for anyone. Everybody's out for himself. . . ."

"Cops? They're no good. Two-bit phonies and racketeers. I'm old now and I know the rackets they run. They beat the law themselves, and then they go out and arrest some poor kid. The guys outside the law, they'll gyp you, too. You got to watch your step. You can't trust anybody. Your own gang will insult you. Your own family, they'll call you a jerk. I don't team up with anybody. I'm what you call—here today and gone tomorrow."

But as you get to know him, the brassy quality of what he has to say gives way to something else, and the real Johnny begins to emerge.

"All my life—as far as I remember. If I wanted to have something, to be something—No! Never! Not a goddamned lousy thing! Anything I wanted, I never could work it. I never could accomplish—"

Johnny was born in a large Midwestern industrial city. His parents, Italian immigrants, had settled there at the turn of the century. When Johnny was born, there were nine other Rocco children, each about two years younger than the preceding one. Regina, who was twenty when Johnny came along, was the oldest. Then came Francesco, Aldo, Sebastian, Georgio, Paul, Antonio, Carla, and Richard. Two more children came after Johnny was born: David, a year and a half younger than Johnny, and Mike. Mike died in infancy.

The neighborhood where the Roccos lived was known as one of the worst slums in the city. It was known, too, for its high rate of crime and juvenile delinquency. It was a neighborhood of factories, abandoned tumble-down shacks, junk yards, poolrooms, cheap liquor joints, and broken houses with sagging steps and paint peeling from their sides.

Johnny's father worked irregularly—as a bartender, teamster, or day laborer. Two things he did regularly: he drank and he gambled. In his drunken rages he often attacked the children and their mother. The little ones learned to scuttle across the floor like beetles and find shelter under tables or beds, where his kicking feet couldn't reach them.

Johnny's short, dark, excitable mother was always sick and complaining. She suffered from heart disease. The children fought. They were noisy and destructive. There was seldom enough food in the house. The rent was never paid, and Mrs. Rocco lived in constant terror of landlords and evictions. The Roccos moved frequently. They moved every nine or ten months, but never to a better house or neighborhood. They moved through a succession of drafty, sparsely furnished four- and five-room apartments, which were heated by coal or kerosene, the geography of their lives circumscribed by dirt, squalor, and factory and slaughterhouse smells and noises.

Johnny's memories of his early childhood are sporadic. He remembers that when he was a little boy, the family had a dog, Teddy. Teddy got sick and lay beside the kerosene stove, quiet and shivering. Johnny recalls that Teddy was still alive when one of his older brothers put Teddy into a sack half-full of trash, carried him to the garbage dump, and left him there to die.

Johnny remembers visiting another of his brothers at a reform school. That was a little later, and that memory has the quality of a holiday; the reform school, Johnny says, was in a "country-like" place.

Johnny remembers hiding in a snowbank once, when his mother was very angry. He remembers fights between his brothers when his mother stood in the middle of the room screaming, and blood ran from his brothers' noses. And Johnny remembers how his father died. A heavy, regular thumping awoke Johnny one night. He got up and, still dazed with sleep, wandered into the kitchen, where the family usually gathered. His father was lying on the floor.

"Some men my father was out with had dragged him up the stairs and put him there. There was blood on his face. Blood was coming out of his ears. He was holding the leg of the kitchen table with one hand, an' he was moanin', and he kept pounding his foot on the floor. One of my brothers called an ambulance, but he died."

Johnny was then five. One of the city's many social-work agencies through whose hands the Roccos passed has a notation in its records on the death of Johnny's father: "Killed in a drunken brawl by his best friend."

The rest of Johnny's memories, many of them more in the nature of a quality of feeling than of actual remembrance, flow backward and forward in time, a merging of history and experience.

Time out of mind there was trouble in the Rocco family. Johnny knows by a certain "lousy feeling" he's always had; by certain conditions that seem to him to have had no beginning or end; by monotonously repetitious happenings. There were sickness and violence. There was trouble with social-work agencies. The Roccos were known to twenty-five welfare agencies in thirty years. There was trouble with landlords, with the schools where the Rocco children went, with the police.

By the time Johnny's father died, four of the older Rocco children had married and moved away. (Johnny's oldest sister married a drunkard. Four of his brothers contracted "forced marriages" while still in their teens. Two of them have been divorced and remarried; one of them once, the other twice, though the family is Roman Catholic.) What was left of the Rocco family continued in its dismal course, the children getting into one difficulty after another and Mrs. Rocco, sick and confused, and inept, trudging from school to police station to court, listening to complaints about them, and from hospital to welfare agency, asking for help and still more help.

If the Rocco boys ever had any tender feeling for one another, that was lost somewhere in the maelstrom of accumulated want, frustration, and jealousy that was the lot of each of them. As much as possible, the members of the household moved in separate orbits, their paths converging under the family roof only when they paused to sleep or to eat their pasta. Of the seven remaining children only one boy, Georgio, assumed any responsibility toward the others, and that was thrust upon him. He was sixteen, the oldest son in the household, when his father died. If Georgio worked, he contributed part of his earnings to the family. When the rest of the children got so out of hand that Mrs. Rocco implored him to do something, he applied the only discipline he knew: he beat them brutally.

"My brothers—I don't despise them," Johnny says, "but the past I don't forget. They used to push me around. I wasn't afraid of them. I used to tell them: 'Go ahead. Hit me. Hit me. What do I care?' Except Georgio! The fear I had for my brother Georgio, if he threatened me—if he only looked at me—I'm scared of him, that's all."

Johnny slept in a bed with Richard and David. Richard, a dark, scowling boy who was born with a twisted foot, was two years older than Johnny. David, who was a year and a half younger, had congenital syphilis, and suffered from anemia. Johnny always felt that, because his mother was ill and Richard and David were sickly, the three of them were drawn into an alliance from which he was excluded.

"I was the strongest, so I had to sleep across the foot of the bed. Even if I wanted to swap places with them, it was no dice. They wouldn't. And, anyway, my mother wouldn't make them. Those brass beds! You know, they got bars at the end. Jesus! In the winter, those bars are cold. I used to lay there and they'd ball me up against the cold bars. They'd kick my face and my back and pull the covers off. I'd be—half of me out of the covers, freezing, or laying on those bars.

"Sunday mornings, hell, you wanted to sleep. It was cold. Then the fighting would start. They'd be crowding an' pushing an' I'd yell or kick them. It used to make me mad. Then my big brother, Georgio, he'd be laying in his bed in the other room, an' he'd yell: 'Johnny! Come here!'

"Whenever my brother Georgio said: 'Johnny! Come here!' Christ! I'd be scared. Walkin' to the sink or the table, wherever he was—to me, that was walkin' into a death house. I'd get out of the bed an' go up to the bed where he was an' bam! He'd let me have it. He used to give me charley-horses so's I couldn't move my arm. He broke my nose once. My head hit the door an' I went out cold."

The only person in that household Johnny loved was his mother. "Sometimes she was wrong," Johnny says, "but she tried to be good to us. She would just as soon take a meal out of her own mouth and give it to us. But she never favored me. She favored Richie and Davie. Davie—he's dead now—he was her favorite. I was trouble to her. I was always on the outside," Johnny says heavily. "When Davie died she said she wished it was me instead."

Johnny was especially bitter toward David, who was the baby of the family. "I used to lick him. I used to fight and break things. I was always trouble. Even before he was sick, Davie was petted. He got everything, even a bike. I didn't get anything.

"I never went any place. If I went any place, I had to go on my own. My people never took me out to a show or any place with them. On Sundays when all the kids on the corner had money, I didn't. I'd go and clip it. I never had a birthday party. I never had a birthday present outside of what Mr. O'Brien, a friend I had when I was bigger, gave me. . . . Christmases, and I was always in the wrong. Maybe I cracked Davie, or I was yelling, or somebody complained. It was always something. My mother would get my brother Richie something and my brother Davie something.

She'd tell me in advance I wasn't going to get anything. Yeah, it made me mad."

Johnny didn't want to be "always trouble" to his mother. He wanted to show her how much he loved her, but he could never quite reach her. He wanted to make her love and pet him, too, as she did David, but he didn't know how. He had a secret way of paying her tribute: "Money I stole, I would never give to my mother." He earned a little, periodically, selling *True Confession* magazines. He gave her that. Then she, in turn, would give him a dime.

Once, Johnny says, he borrowed a shoe-shine box, "hook-jacked" school, and worked from morning till night. "I made two bucks and a half. Boy! I was hungry, but I wouldn't even buy a roll. I wouldn't even spend something for carfare home. I wanted to give my mother all of it."

But even when Johnny was determined to make his mother love him, he was annoying, he was so insistent. He would rush home after school and make a great show of sweeping the floors or polishing the stove. He would urge and urge his mother to send him on an errand. Tense and watchful for the extravagant praise he craved, he'd even make overtures to David. But something always happened to burst the bubble; a quarrel with David, a rebuff from his mother—and Johnny, overcome with rage, frustration, and self-pity, would swing back to thieving, baiting David, and screaming savagely at his mother.

One of the subterfuges Johnny's fumbling mother resorted to in her efforts to pacify landlords, who were always hounding her, was to keep her screaming, battling children out of the house as much as possible. As soon as each child was old enough to shift for himself, she would turn him out on the streets. One after another the Rocco boys became known to the police. Their father himself had a long court record for assault, disorderliness, drunkenness; five of Johnny's brothers, who started in childhood, ran up police records covering charges of disturbing the peace, breaking and entering, larceny, perjury, assault and battery, bastardy, and malicious injury.

"I was in the police station, too. Plenty!" Johnny says. "Saturdays, they had Kid's Day. We'd be in this long corridor. There'd be all little kids sitting down, niggers and kids with their shoe-shine boxes who'd have to go out shining shoes afterwards. They'd bring us in an' those jerks, the cops, they'd be sitting there. They'd ask us—" Johnny's sentence broke off; then he continued on a new tack.

"Christ! I remember a lot of times I got picked up for something—or maybe staying out late, or suspicion. They'd round us up an' bring us in, an' this cop here, he was always insulting me. 'You little fresh—you little bastard!' He'd belt me or anything he felt like doing. I was just——to him. . . ."

Johnny hadn't been running the streets long when the knowledge was borne in on him that being a Rocco made him "something special"; the reputation of the notorious Roccos, known to neighbors, schools, police, and welfare agencies as "chiselers, thieves, and trouble-makers," preceded him. The cop on the beat, Johnny says, always had some cynical smart-crack to make. Certain homes were barred to him. Certain children were not permitted to play with him. Wherever he went—on the streets, in the neighborhood settlement house, at the welfare agency's penny milk station, at school, where other Roccos had been before him—he recognized himself by a gesture, an oblique remark, a wrong laugh.

. . .

At one point, after he had been at the [Catholic] school for quite a while, he succeeded in gathering a gang of admiring little boys around him. He reacted extravagantly. He swaggered, swore, defied school discipline. He encouraged them to break school rules, too, and incited them to trip or grab and hug girls. The sisters, O'Brien noted, would have liked to see Johnny make friends, but Johnny was far from a wholesome influence and they had begun to get complaints from parents of some of the other children that Johnny was teaching boys to steal and say bad words. Johnny's gang was finally broken up.

"In that school," Johnny says, "they didn't have no playground. They used to block off the street. Once I went up in a tree with some kids. I guess I was showing off. It was the kind of a tree where you strip the leaves off one of the thin branches and make—you know, like a switch. All of us kids were doing it, hanging in the tree, swinging the switches around. The sister caught us. She didn't do anything to the other kids. She said I was the biggest and I was getting the other kids in trouble. She took all the switches away and she took me in all the rooms, in front of all the classes, and she whipped me with those switches. To make an example of me—a jerk, you know—in front of all the kids. I let them know right there that I didn't care what they done to me. I hated them all. I didn't care. I didn't."

One day Johnny folded his arms and, with face ugly and sullen, refused to do any work. The only thing he would say to the sister was that he wanted to return to public school. When Mr. O'Brien came to discuss this with him, Johnny, sitting stiff and upright in his chair, would neither speak to him nor look at him. Lips tightly pursed, his face set in a hard belligerent expression, he stared straight ahead.

Mr. O'Brien talked kindly to Johnny, but Johnny wouldn't answer. He tried talking sternly, but Johnny merely tightened his lips and shrugged his shoulders. O'Brien knew Johnny was unhappy because he was a big boy in a class with little kids. He pointed out that in public school the boys Johnny's size and age were in the upper grades and that there, too, Johnny would be among small children. Johnny indicated that he knew this, but still wanted to go back to the public school. Then Mr. O'Brien reminded him of some of the things the public-school teachers had said to Johnny—that he would never learn to get along anywhere. "I don't agree with them," O'Brien said to Johnny, "but maybe I'll have to admit that I'm wrong and they are right."

Finally Mr. O'Brien rose as if to leave. "All right. I'm sorry about all this," he said. "I'm not mad at you, but I'm a little disappointed. I want to help you if I can, but no one can help you if you don't want to help yourself. All the same, I know you've tried hard. I think you're a good kid."

As he patted Johnny's shoulder in a departing gesture, Johnny grabbed his arm and, burying his face in it, burst into sobs. Mr. O'Brien said Johnny clung to his arm and cried until the material of his coat was crinkled and the tears soaked through. Then he went back to his classroom.

Afterwards O'Brien learned that Johnny had been particularly difficult at home during that period, too, and that he was reporting regularly to the police because he had broken some windows. When Mr. O'Brien asked about that, Johnny burst out: "What am I gonna do? If I play with the big kids, they get me in trouble. If I play with the little kids, I get them in trouble. What am I gonna do?"

Mr. O'Brien, who had a thorough appreciation of Johnny's dilemma, reflected: there is more than one Johnny. There is the winsome, puppy-like boy, grinning, garrulous, grateful for attention, and full of high resolve. There is the "bad" Johnny, cruel, self-centered, his chunky body rigid, "his face set in a hard expression of pure hatred like a little god of evil." Somewhere between the two was the unhappy and perplexed Johnny, impelled by conflicting drives within himself, besieged by conflicting influences from the outside.

There were the gang kids, cocky, street-wise, and seemingly invulnerable, whom Johnny could not help admiring. Though he wanted the prestige of being one of them, he didn't "fit in." There were the "good kids" at school, whom Johnny despised because he was barred from their society, but by whom he wanted to be accepted. There was the paradox of his mother, who, Johnny said, "lived like a saint," yet found lying, cheating, and chiseling from the relief bureau a necessary part of the war for survival. There were the cops, the men who stood for law and order, but who Johnny knew had their little rackets, too. Finally, there was Mr. O'Brien, Johnny's friend and the "big man" whom Johnny wanted to impress and emulate.

Mr. O'Brien realized that in giving Johnny his friendship and help he had also brought Johnny new challenges and conflicts. He realized, too, that in trying to win Johnny from the influences and effects of his environment, he was working against formidable odds.

"The more I learn about this boy and his background, the more convinced I am that it is going to be extremely difficult to achieve any betterment in him in his present environment and home situation," he wrote in his records. "It is going to be a constant fight to keep Johnny from following the pattern so well grooved by each of his brothers."

3. Again

Violence, disorganized families, lack of eduation, unemployment, a desperate search for short-range gratifications—these are as important components of the culture of poverty as is poverty itself. And members of minority groups, particularly Negroes, must add the bitter facts of discrimination that are likely to further increase the sense of alienation and hopelessness for those at the bottom of the social heap. Claude Brown tells what it is like to be a Negro child in New York.

I want to talk about the first Northern urban generation of Negroes. I want to talk about the experiences of a misplaced generation, of a misplaced people in an extremely complex, confused society. This is a story of their searching, their dreams, their sorrows, their small and futile rebellions, and their endless battle to establish their own place in America's greatest metropolis—and in America itself.

The characters are sons and daughters of former Southern sharecroppers. These were the poorest people of the South, who poured into New York City during the decade following the Great Depression. These migrants were told that unlimited opportunities for prosperity existed in New York and that there was no "color problem" there. They were told that Negroes lived in houses with bathrooms, electricity, running water, and indoor toilets. To them, this was the "promised land" that Mammy had been singing about in the cotton fields for many years.

Going to New York was good-bye to the cotton fields, good-bye to "Massa Charlie," good-bye to the chain gang, and, most of all, good-bye to those sunup-to-sundown working hours. One no longer had to wait to get to heaven to lay his burden down; burdens could be laid down in New York.

So, they came, from all parts of the South, like all the black chillun o' God following the sound of Gabriel's horn on that long-overdue Judgment Day. The Georgians came as soon as they were able to pick train fare off the peach trees. They came from South Carolina where the cotton stalks were bare. The North Carolinians came with tobacco tar beneath their fingernails.

They felt as the Pilgrims must have felt when they were coming to

America. But these descendants of Ham must have been twice as happy as the Pilgrims, because they had been catching twice the hell. Even while planning the trip, they sang spirituals as "Jesus Take My Hand" and "I'm On My Way" and chanted, "Hallelujah, I'm on my way to the promised land!"

It seems that Cousin Willie, in his lying haste, had neglected to tell the folks down home about one of the most important aspects of the promised land: it was a slum ghetto. There was a tremendous difference in the way life was lived up North. There were too many people full of hate and bitterness crowded into a dirty, stinky, uncared-for closet-size section of a great city.

Before the soreness of the cotton fields had left Mama's back, her knees were getting sore from scrubbing "Goldberg's" floor. Nevertheless, she was better off; she had gone from the fire into the frying pan.

The children of these disillusioned colored pioneers inherited the total lot of their parents—the disappointments, the anger. To add to their misery, they had little hope of deliverance. For where does one run to when he's already in the promised land?

. . .

One day a few months after I got back from the South, I didn't feel like staying in school, so I went looking for somebody to play hookey with. Bulldog and Toto were in the same class; and as always, Bulldog was sleeping. Toto came out and went back to get Bulldog. This took some time, because their teacher knew they were hookey partners and wouldn't let them out of the class together. So Bulldog had to get the pass, since he couldn't run so fast. We waited for Toto in the backyard across the street from the school. When he came, we all went downtown looking for something to steal. We didn't steal too much that day, so we kept on looking after it got dark. Late that night, we found a good store to break into. It was at Broadway and 147th Street. There were a lot of radios and clocks and electric irons and stuff like that. And the store had a transom that didn't seem to have a burglar alarm on it.

Since Bulldog was slow at running and doing most things, he stayed outside and we passed the stuff out to him. When I had started filling up the third shopping bag, Toto called me to the window. He was still passing the stuff out to Bulldog. Bulldog had fallen asleep, but he was still taking the stuff that Toto was passing to him. He was taking it and passing it to two big white cops behind him.

I thought the cops would take us to the Children's Center on 104th Street. Instead, they took us to a place I had heard about but had never been to before, a place called the Youth House way down on East Twelfth Street.

I remember the day I went to the Youth House because it was four days before Carole's birthday party. Carole was going to be thirteen years old the next Sunday. Everybody was going to be at Carole's party. Well, almost everybody, because I wasn't going to be there now, unless we had a real softhearted judge. Bulldog wouldn't be there either, and he would miss it; he really liked to eat, especially cake and ice cream and stuff like that. Toto couldn't come anyway. We had been in trouble a lot of times before, and Mama wouldn't let him come to our house. She said he was too roguish. Mama said that of all the little rogues I hung out with, Toto was the most roguish-looking one. One time Mama was telling Dad about Toto, and Dad said, "All them little rogues he hangs out wit look like they'll steal anything that ain't nailed down." And Mama said, "Well, Toto is the one who looks like he'll steal the nails and all." But that was all right, because Toto's mother didn't let him hang out with me either, and she probably said the same thing about me.

When we went to court the next day, we didn't get a softhearted judge; we got a mean old colored lady named Judge Bolin. I had seen her picture on a magazine cover one time, that colored magazine that Jackie Robinson, Joe Louis, and Pigmeat use to have their pictures in sometimes. That lady judge looked meaner than she did on the magazine cover. She had a hard-to-hear voice, but you could hear it—everybody in the courtroom was real quiet when she said something. She had a face on her that looked like the hardest thing in the world to do with it would have been to smile. I wondered what would happen if somebody in the courtroom said something funny and she tried to smile at it. I thought that her face would probably crack up from the strain. But that wasn't going to happen anyway, because everybody in the place seemed to be scared of her. It almost made me scared of her. I started to get scared of her too until I saw what was going on. This lady judge was just like the mean old queens I had seen in swordfighting pictures at the Odeon. She was bullying everybody in that courtroom with a low voice, even the men, who seemed like a bunch of turkeys, scared of a woman.

Whenever she wanted to show the people there how bad she was, instead of hitting somebody or yelling at them she just looked at them or talked even softer. When she started talking softer, she was bullying everybody in the queen's courtroom. I thought, It's like she's sayin', "Goddamit, you peasants better shut up and listen to me, 'cause I'm gonna ask you what I said, and everybody who don't know is gonna git his head chopped off!" So the softer she talked, the quieter everybody was and the harder they listened, because their heads depended on it. When she looked at somebody, his head went on the hatchet man's list, and there was nothing he could do but wait for the man with the black hood over his face to come and get him.

I wondered what would happen if I yelled out, "Ain't nobody scared-a you, you ole bitch!" I had never called a lady a bitch, but I called a big girl a bitch one time and ran real fast. I thought that if I didn't act scared, the mean queen would get real mad and would probably send me to that place called Sing Sing. So I did the best thing—stayed real quiet and acted as if I were scared of her too. I thought, This lady judge couldn't have a husband like Dad and be as mean as she is, 'cause Dad would beat her ass. Or would he? Maybe this lady is too mean for anybody to beat, even Dad.

From the minute I laid eyes on the mean queen, I knew she wasn't going to send me home, and she didn't. She gave me another day to come back to court and sent me back to the Youth House. Toto was sent there too, but Bulldog had to go to the Children's Center.

Before we left the court, Mama said, "That judge said you don't come back to court before January 5. Boy, do you know that's next year? You wasn' home for last Christmas, and you won't be home for this one either. And you won't be home for Carole's birthday party next Sunday. It's just November 14, and you only been back in New York three months and four days. Boy, sometimes I git the feelin' you ain't gon never stay home no more."

I told Mama that I didn't care so much about not being home and that if Bulldog had stayed awake, I would have brought Carole the biggest and best birthday present she'd ever had. All Mama did was look at me with tears in her eyes, and I knew she was thinking, Lord, what's the matter with my child?

When the bus was all loaded and ready to take us back to the Youth House, one of the boys in the seat behind me tapped me on the shoulder and said, "Hey, shorty, ain't that your mother standin' on the court stoop?"

"Yeah."

He said, "Man, she's cryin'."

I said, "So what?" as if I didn't care. But I cared; I had to care: that was the first time I had seen Mama crying like that. She was just standing there by herself, not moving, not making a sound, as if she didn't even know it was cold out there. The sun was shining, but it was cold and there was ice on the ground. The tears just kept rolling down Mama's face as the bus started to pull away from the curb. I had to care. Those tears shining on Mama's face were falling for me. When the bus started down the street, I wanted to run back and say something to Mama. I didn't know what. I thought, maybe I woulda said, "Mama, I didn' mean what I said, 'cause I really do care." No, I wouldn'a said that. I woulda said, "Mama, button up your coat. It's cold out here." Yeah, that's what I forgot to say to Mama.

4. The Gangster as Tragic Hero

Mass culture is both effect and cause in our society, expressing and shaping our beliefs. Just as George Orwell found in No Orchids for Miss Blandish *a symbol for what was happening in wartime England, Robert Warshow found in the gangster movie the dark side of American life, the No to the great American Yes. Gangsterism and the search for success in the competitive life of the city, said Warshow, were tragically intertwined. When we inquire into the nature of crime, we must examine the nature of conformity.*

America, as a social and political organization, is committed to a cheerful view of life. It could not be otherwise. The sense of tragedy is a luxury of aristocratic societies, where the fate of the individual is not conceived of as having a direct and legitimate political importance, being determined by a fixed and supra-political—that is, non-controversial—moral order or fate. Modern equalitarian societies, however, whether democratic or authoritarian in their political forms, always base themselves on the claim that they are making life happier; the avowed function of the modern state, at least in its ultimate terms, is not only to regulate social relations, but also to determine the quality and the possibilities of human life in general. Happiness thus becomes the chief political issue—in a sense, the only political issue—and for that reason it can never be treated as an issue at all. If an American or a Russian is unhappy, it implies a certain reprobation of his society, and therefore, by a logic of which we can all recognize the necessity, it becomes an obligation of citizenship to be cheerful; if the authorities find it necessary, the citizen may even be compelled to make a public display of his cheerfulness on important occasions, just as he may be conscripted into the army in time of war.

Naturally, this civic responsibility rests most strongly upon the organs of mass culture. The individual citizen may still be permitted his private unhappiness so long as it does not take on political significance, the extent of this tolerance being determined by how large an area of private life the society can accommodate. But every production of mass culture is a public act and must conform with accepted notions of the public good. Nobody seriously questions the principle that it is the function of mass culture to maintain public morale, and certainly nobody in the mass audience objects to having his morale maintained. At a time when the normal condition of the citizen is a state of anxiety, euphoria spreads over our culture like the broad smile of an idiot. In terms of attitudes towards life, there is very little difference between a "happy" movie like *Good News,* which ignores death and suffering, and a "sad" movie like *A Tree Grows in Brooklyn,* which uses death and suffering as incidents in the service of a higher optimism.

But, whatever its effectiveness as a source of consolation and a means of pressure for maintaining "positive" social attitudes, this optimism is fundamentally satisfying to no one, not even to those who would be most disoriented without its support. Even within the area of mass culture, there always exists a current of opposition, seeking to express by whatever means are available to it that sense of desperation and inevitable failure which optimism itself helps to create. Most often, this opposition is confined to rudimentary or semiliterate forms: in mob politics and journalism, for example, or in certain kinds of religious enthusiasm. When it does enter the field of art, it is likely to be disguised or attenuated: in an unspecific form of expression like jazz, in the basically harmless nihilism of the Marx Brothers, in the continually reasserted strain of hopelessness that often seems to be the real meaning of the soap opera. The gangster film is remarkable in that it fills the need for disguise (though not sufficiently to avoid arousing uneasiness) without requiring any serious distortion. From its beginnings, it has been a consistent and astonishingly complete presentation of the modern sense of tragedy.

In its initial character, the gangster film is simply one example of the movies' constant tendency to create fixed dramatic patterns that can be repeated indefinitely with a reasonable expectation of profit. One gangster film follows another as one musical or one Western follows another. But this rigidity is not necessarily opposed to the requirements of art. There have been very successful types of art in the past which developed such specific and detailed conventions as almost to make individual examples of the type interchangeable. This is true, for example, of Elizabethan revenge tragedy and Restoration comedy.

For such a type to be successful means that its conventions have imposed themselves upon the general consciousness and become the accepted vehicles of a particular set of attitudes and a particular aesthetic effect. One goes to any individual example of the type with very definite expectations, and originality is to be welcomed only in the degree that it intensifies the expected experience without fundamentally altering it. Moreover, the relationship between the conventions which go to make up such a type and the real experience of its audience or the real facts of whatever situation it pretends to describe is of only secondary importance and does not determine its aesthetic force. It is only in an ultimate sense that the type appeals to its audience's experience of reality; much more immediately, it appeals to previous experience of the type itself: it creates its own field of reference.

Thus the importance of the gangster film, and the nature and intensity of its emotional and aesthetic impact, cannot be measured in terms of the place of the gangster himself or the importance of the problem of crime in American life. Those European movie-goers who think there is a gangster on every corner in New York are certainly deceived, but defenders of the "positive" side of American culture are equally deceived if they think it relevant to point out that most Americans have never seen a gangster. What matters is that the experience of the gangster *as an experience of art* is universal to Americans. There is almost nothing we understand better or react to more readily or with quicker intelligence. The Western film, though it seems never to diminish in popularity, is for most of us no more than the folklore of the past, familiar and understandable only because it has been repeated so often. The gangster film comes much closer. In ways that we do not easily or willingly define, the gangster speaks for us, expressing that part of the American psyche which rejects the qualities and the demands of modern life, which rejects "Americanism" itself.

The gangster is the man of the city, with the city's language and knowledge, with its queer and dishonest skills and its terrible daring, carrying his life in his hands like a placard, like a club. For everyone else, there is at least the theoretical possibility of another world—in that happier American culture which the gangster denies, the city does not really exist; it is only a more crowded and more brightly lit country—but for the gangster there is only the city; he must inhabit it in order to personify it: not the real city, but that dangerous and sad city of the imagination which is so much more important, which is the modern world. And the gangster—though there are real gangsters—is also, and primarily, a creature of the imagination. The real city, one might say, produces only criminals; the imaginary city produces the gangster: he is what we want to be and what we are afraid we may become.

Thrown into the crowd without background or advantages, with only those ambiguous skills which the rest of us—the real people of the real city—can only pretend to have, the gangster is required to make his way, to make his life and impose it on others. Usually, when we come upon him, he has already made his choice or the choice has already been made for him, it doesn't matter which: we are not permitted to ask whether at some point he could have chosen to be something else than what he is.

The gangster's activity is actually a form of rational enterprise, involving fairly definite goals and various techniques for achieving them. But this rationality is usually no more than a vague background; we know, perhaps, that the gangster sells liquor or that he operates a numbers racket; often we are not given even that much information. So his activity becomes a kind of pure criminality: he hurts people. Certainly our response to the gangster film is most consistently and most universally a response to sadism; we gain the double satisfaction of participating vicariously in the gangster's sadism and then seeing it turned against the gangster himself.

But on another level the quality of irrational brutality and the quality of rational enterprise become one. Since we do not see the rational and routine aspects of the gangster's behavior, the practice of brutality—the quality of unmixed criminality—becomes the totality of his career. At the same time, we are always conscious that the whole meaning of this career is a drive for success: the typical gangster film presents a steady upward progress followed by a very precipitate fall. Thus brutality itself becomes at once the means to success and the content of success—a success that is defined in its most general terms, not as accomplishment or specific gain, but simply as the unlimited possibility of aggression. (In the same way, film presentations of businessmen tend to make it appear that they achieve their success by talking on the telephone and holding conferences and that success *is* talking on the telephone and holding conferences.)

From this point of view, the initial contact between the film and its audience is an agreed conception of human life: that man is a being with the possibilities of success or failure. This principle, too, belongs to the city; one must emerge from the crowd or else one is nothing. On that basis the necessity of the action is established, and it progresses by inalterable paths to the point where the gangster lies dead and the principle has been modified: there is really only one possibility—failure. The final meaning of the city is anonymity and death.

In the opening scene of *Scarface,* we are shown a successful man; we know he is successful because he has just given a party of opulent proportions and because he is called Big Louie. Through some monstrous lack of caution, he permits himself to be alone for a few moments. We understand from this immediately that he is about to be killed. No convention of the gangster film is more strongly established than this: it is dangerous to be alone. And yet the very conditions of success make it impossible not to be alone, for success is always the establishment of an *individual* preeminence that must be imposed on others, in whom it automatically arouses hatred; the successful man is an outlaw. The gangster's whole life is an effort to assert himself as an individual, to draw himself out of the crowd, and he always dies *because* he is an individual; the final bullet thrusts him back, makes him, after all, a failure. "Mother of God," says the dying Little Caesar, "is this the end of Rico?"—speaking of himself thus in the third person because what has been brought low is not the undifferentiated *man,* but the individual with a name, the gangster, the success; even to himself he is a creature of the imagination. (T. S. Eliot has pointed out that a number of Shakespeare's tragic heroes have this trick of looking at themselves dramatically; their true identity, the thing that is destroyed when they die, is something outside themselves—not a man, but a style of life, a kind of meaning.)

At bottom, the gangster is doomed because he is under the obligation to succeed, not because the means he employs are unlawful. In the deeper layers of the modern consciousness, *all* means are unlawful, every attempt to succeed is an act of aggression, leaving one alone and guilty and defenseless among enemies: one is *punished* for success. This is our intolerable dilemma: that failure is a kind of death and success is evil and dangerous, is—ultimately—impossible. The effect of the gangster film is to embody this dilemma in the person of the gangster and resolve it by his death. The dilemma is resolved because it is *his* death, not ours. We are safe; for the moment, we can acquiesce in our failure, we can choose to fail.

5. Beyond 1984

The emergence of a permanent criminal class—mindlessly violent, totally estranged—is an idea that has occurred to a number of writers. Anthony Burgess, in A Clockwork Orange, *portrays a savage society of the future where delinquent gangs terrorize the streets. Much of the slang is taken from Russian, with "droog" for friend, "mesto" for place, "skorry" for quick or quickly, "veschch" for thing, "horrorshow" (anglicized from "khorosho") for good or well, "peet" for drink, "ptitsa" for "chick," and so on. He adds gypsy cant ("O my brothers"), cockney rhyming slang, American usages, and his own inventions to build the adolescent language of a fictional, mechanical world possibly somewhere ahead of us.*

"What's it going to be then, eh?"

There was me, that is Alex, and my three droogs, that is Pete, Georgie, and Dim, Dim being really dim, and we sat in the Korova Milkbar making up our rassoodocks what to do with the evening, a flip dark chill winter bastard though dry. The Korova Milkbar was a milk-plus mesto, and you may, O my brothers, have forgotten what these mestos were like, things changing so skorry these days and everybody very quick to forget, newspapers not being read much neither. Well, what they sold there was milk plus something else. They had no licence for selling liquor, but there was no law yet against prodding some of the new veshches which they used to put into the old moloko, so you could peet it with vellocet or synthemesc or drencrom or one or two other veshches which would give you a nice quiet horrorshow fifteen minutes admiring Bog And All His Holy Angels and Saints in your left shoe with lights bursting all over your mozg. Or you could peet milk with knives in it, as we used to say, and this would sharpen you up and make you ready for a bit of dirty twenty-to-one, and that was what we were peeting this evening I'm starting off the story with.

Our pockets were full of deng, so there was no real need from the point of view of crasting any more pretty polly to tolchock some old veck in an alley and viddy him swim in his blood while we counted the takings and divided by four, nor to do the ultra-violent on some shivering starry grey-haired ptitsa in a shop and go smecking off with the till's guts. But, as they say, money isn't everything.

The four of us were dressed in the heighth of fashion, which in those days was a pair of black very tight tights with the old jelly mould, as we called it, fitting on the crotch underneath the tights, this being to protect and also a sort of a design you could viddy clear enough in a certain light, so that I had one in the shape of a spider, Pete had a rooker (a hand, that is), Georgie had a very fancy one of a flower, and poor old Dim had a very hound-and-horny one of a clown's litso (face, that is), Dim not ever having much of an idea of things and being, beyond all shadow of a doubting thomas, the dimmest of we four. Then we wore waisty jackets without lapels but with these very big built-up shoulders ("pletchoes" we called them) which were a kind of a mockery of having real shoulders like that. Then, my brothers, we had these off-white cravats which looked like whipped-up kartoffel or spud with a sort of a design made on it with a fork. We wore our hair not too long and we had flip horrorshow boots for kicking.

"What's it going to be then, eh?"

There were three devotchkas sitting at the counter all together, but there were four of us malchicks and it was usually like one for all and all for one. These sharps were dressed in the heighth of fashion too, with purple and green and orange wigs on their gullivers, each one not costing less than three or four weeks of those sharps' wages, I should reckon, and make-up to match (rainbows round the glazzies, that is, and the rot painted very wide). Then they had long black very straight dresses, and on the groody part of them they had little badges of like silver with different malchicks' names on them—Joe and Mike and suchlike. These were supposed to be the names of the different malchicks they'd spatted with before they were fourteen. They kept looking our way and I nearly felt like saying the three of us (out of the corner of my rot, that is) should go off for a bit of pol and leave poor old Dim behind, because it would be just a matter of kupetting Dim a demi-litre of white but this time with a dollop of synthemesc in it, but that wouldn't really have been playing like the game. Dim was very very ugly and like his name, but he was a horrorshow filthy fighter and very handy with the boot.

"What's it going to be then, eh?"

The chelloveck sitting next to me, there being this long big plushy seat that ran round three walls, was well away with his glazzies glazed and sort of burbling slovos like "Aristotle wishy washy works outing cyclamen get forficulate smartish." He was in the land all right, well away, in orbit, and I knew what it was like, having tried it like everybody else had done, but at this time I'd got to thinking it was a cowardly sort of a veshch, O my brothers. You'd lay there after you'd drunk the old moloko and then you got the messel that everything all round you was sort of in the past. You could viddy it all right, all of it, very clear—tables, the stereo, the lights, the sharps and the malchicks—but it was like some veshch that used to be there but was not there not no more. And you were sort of hypnotized by your boot or shoe or a fingernail as it might be, and at the same time you were sort of picked up by the old scruff and shook like you might be a cat. You got shook and shook till there was nothing left. You lost your name and your body and your self and you just didn't care, and you waited till your boot or your finger-nail got yellow, then yellower and yellower all the time. Then the lights started cracking like atomics and the boot or finger-nail or, as it might be, a bit of dirt on your trouser-bottom turned into a big big big mesto, bigger than the whole world, and you were just going to get introduced to old Bog or God when it was all over. You came back to here and now whimpering sort of, with your rot all squaring up for a boohoo-hoo. Now, that's very nice but very cowardly. You were not put on this earth just to get in touch with God. That sort of thing could sap all the strength and the goodness out of a chelloveck.

"What's it going to be then, eh?"

The stereo was on and you got the idea that the singer's goloss was moving from one part of the bar to another, flying up to the ceiling and then swooping down again and whizzing from wall to wall. It was Berti Laski rasping a real starry oldie called "You Blister My Paint." One of the three ptitsas at the counter, the one with the green wig, kept pushing her belly out and pulling it in in time to what they called the music. I could feel the knives in the old moloko starting to prick, and now I was ready for a bit of twenty-to-one. So I yelped: "Out out out out!" like a doggie, and then I cracked this veck who was sitting next to me and well away and burbling a horrorshow crack on the ooko or earhole, but he didn't feel it and went on with his "Telephonic hardware and when the farfarculule gets rubadubdub." He'd feel it all right when he came to, out of the land.

"Where out?" said Georgie.

"Oh, just to keep walking," I said, "and viddy what turns up, O my little brothers."

So we scatted out into the big winter nochy and walked down Marghanita Boulevard and then turned into Boothby Avenue, and there we found what we were pretty well looking for, a malenky jest to start off the evening with. There was a doddery starry schoolmaster type veck, glasses on and his rot open to the cold nochy air. He had books under his arm and a crappy umbrella and was coming round the corner from the Public Biblio, which not many lewdies used those days. You never really saw many of the older bourgeois type out after nightfall those days, what with the shortage of police and we fine young malchickiwicks about, and this prof type chelloveck was the only one walking in the whole of the street. So we goolied up to him, very polite, and I said: "Pardon me, brother."

He looked a malenky bit poogly when he viddied the four of us like that, coming up so quiet and polite and smiling, but he said: "Yes? What is it?" in a very loud teacher-type goloss, as if he was trying to show us he wasn't poogly. I said:

"I see you have books under your arm, brother. It is indeed a rare pleasure these days to come across somebody that still reads, brother."

"Oh," he said, all shaky. "Is it? Oh, I see." And he kept looking from one to the other of we four, finding himself now like in the middle of a very smiling and polite square.

"Yes," I said. "It would interest me greatly, brother, if you would kindly allow me to see what books those are that you have under your arm. I like nothing better in this world than a good clean book, brother."

"Clean," he said. "Clean, eh?" And then Pete skvatted these three books from him and handed them round real skorry. Being three, we all had one each to viddy at except for Dim. The one I had was called *Elementary Crystallography,* so I opened it up and said: "Excellent, really first-class," keeping turning the pages. Then I said in a very shocked type goloss: "But what is this here? What is this filthy slovo? I blush to look at this word. You disappoint me, brother, you do really."

"But," he tried, "but, but."

"Now," said Georgie, "here is what I should call real dirt. There's one slovo beginning with an f and another with a c." He had a book called *The Miracle of the Snowflake*.

"Oh," said poor old Dim, smotting over Pete's shoulder and going too far, like he always did, "it says here what he done to her, and there's a picture and all. Why," he said, "you're nothing but a filthy-minded old skitebird."

"An old man of your age, brother," I said, and I started to rip up the book I'd got, and the others did the same with the ones they had, Dim and Pete doing a tug-of-war with *The Rhombohedral System*. The starry prof type began to creech: "But those are not mine, those are the property of the municipality, this is sheer wantonness and vandal work," or some such slovos. And he tried to sort of wrest the books back off of us, which was like pathetic. "You deserve to be taught a lesson, brother," I said, "that you do." This crystal book I had was very tough-bound and hard to razrez to bits, being real starry and made in days when things were made to last like, but I managed to rip the pages up and chuck them in handfuls of like snowflakes, though big, all over this creeching old veck, and then the others did the same with theirs, old Dim just dancing about like the clown he was. "There you are," said Pete. "There's the mackerel of the cornflake for you, you dirty reader of filth and nastiness."

"You naughty old veck, you," I said, and then we began to filly about with him. Pete held his rookers and Georgie sort of hooked his rot wide open for him and Dim yanked out his false zoobies, upper and lower. He threw these down on the pavement and then I treated them to the old boot-crush, though they were hard bastards like, being made of some new horrorshow plastic stuff. The old veck began to make sort of chumbling shooms—"wuf waf wof"—so Georgie let go of holding his goobers apart and just let him have one in the toothless rot with his ringy fist, and that made the old veck start moaning a lot then, then out comes the blood, my brothers, real beautiful. So all we did then was to pull his outer platties off, stripping him down to his vest and long underpants (very starry; Dim smecked his head off near), and then Pete kicks him lovely in his pot, and we let him go. He went sort of staggering off, it not having been too hard of a tolchock really, going "Oh oh oh," not knowing where or what was what really, and we had a snigger at him and then rifled through his pockets, Dim dancing round with his crappy umbrella meanwhile, but there wasn't much in them. There were a few starry letters, some of them dating right back to 1960 with "My dearest dearest" in them and all that chepooka, and a keyring and a starry leaky pen. Old Dim gave up his umbrella dance and of course had to start reading one of the letters out loud, like to show the empty street he could read. "My darling one," he recited, in this very high type goloss, "I shall be thinking of you while you are away and hope you will remember to wrap up warm when you go out at night." Then he let out a very shoomny smeck—"Ho ho ho"—pretending to start wiping his yahma with it. "All right," I said. "Let it go, O my brothers." In the trousers of this starry veck there was only a malenky bit of cutter (money, that is)—not more than three gollies—so we gave all his messy little coin the scatter treatment, it being hen-korm to the amount of pretty polly we had on us already. Then we smashed the umbrella and razrezzed his platties and gave them to the blowing winds, my brothers, and then we'd finished with the starry teacher type veck. We hadn't done much, I know, but that was only like the start of the evening and I make no appy polly loggies to thee or thine for that. The knives in the milk-plus were stabbing away nice and horrorshow now.

THE LAWYER'S VIEW

In that long, involved social experiment we call the administration of justice, the law has attempted to be as precise as possible in defining what it means by a crime. If the law is too vague, if its definitions are too loose or too unclear, then the state is in a position to declare anything it dislikes a crime, and the door is opened for oppression.

It is not easy to be precise, however, because the conflicts arising in the course of human interaction are complex and filled with the qualifications of particular circumstances. The commandment "Thou shalt not kill," for example, might seem definite enough, but, in fact, our society has come to believe that there are certain exceptions to the rule and that in the name of justice we must recognize that killing is sometimes justifiable or excusable. It is the task of the law to translate general proscriptions into exact and detailed rules.

One of the most crucial elements that the law must take into account is criminal intent. In our legal system it has long been held that if a particular act is to be labeled a crime, the act must be a voluntary effort to inflict harm. This might seem like a simple matter, at first glance, but there are few issues more troublesome as the law tries to draw the line between criminal and noncriminal behavior.

1. Criminal Intent

The willful, malicious intention to inflict harm is sometimes referred to as mens rea *or the "guilty mind"; and, in general, it is claimed that the existence of criminal intent is an indispensable element of a crime. An injury inflicted through accident, under duress, or because of an honest mistake of fact may not be a crime at all. In recent years, however, there has been a growing tendency to define certain acts as crimes regardless of intent, particularly in the area of statutory regulations. In the following decision of the Supreme Court of the United States, the trend receives a setback.*

On a large tract of uninhabited and untilled land in a wooded and sparsely populated area of Michigan, the Government established a practice bombing range over which the Air Force dropped simulated bombs at ground targets. These bombs consisted of a metal cylinder about forty inches long and eight inches across, filled with sand and enough black powder to cause a smoke puff by which the strike could be located. At various places about the range signs read "Danger—Keep Out—Bombing Range." Nevertheless, the range was known as good deer country and was extensively hunted.

Spent bomb casings were cleared from the targets and thrown into piles "so that they will be out of the way." They were not stacked or piled in any order but were dumped in heaps, some of which had been accumulating for four years or upwards, were exposed to the weather and rusting away.

Morissette, in December of 1948, went hunting in this area but did not get a deer. He thought to meet expenses of the trip by salvaging some of these casings. He loaded three tons of them on his truck and took them to a nearby farm, where they were flattened by driving a tractor over them. After expending this labor and trucking them to market in Flint, he realized $84.

Morissette, by occupation, is a fruit stand operator in summer and a trucker and scrap iron collector in winter. An honorably discharged veteran of World War II, he enjoys a good name among his neighbors and has had no blemish on his record more disreputable than a conviction for reckless driving.

The loading, crushing and transporting of these casings were all in broad daylight, in full view of passers-by, without the slightest effort at conceal-

From Morissette v. United States, 342 U.S. 246 (1952), 11.

ment. When an investigation was started, Morissette voluntarily, promptly and candidly told the whole story to the authorities, saying that he had no intention of stealing but thought the property was abandoned, unwanted and considered of no value to the Government. He was indicted, however, on the charge that he "did unlawfully, wilfully and knowingly steal and convert" property of the United States of the value of $84, in violation of 18 U. S. C. § 641, which provides that "whoever embezzles, steals, purloins, or knowingly converts" government property is punishable by fine and imprisonment. Morissette was convicted and sentenced to imprisonment for two months or to pay a fine of $200. The Court of Appeals affirmed, one judge dissenting.

At his trial, Morissette, as he had at all times told investigating officers, testified that from appearances he believed the casings were cast-off and abandoned, that he did not intend to steal the property, and took it with no wrongful or criminal intent. The trial court, however, was unimpressed, and ruled: "[H]e took it because he thought it was abandoned and he knew he was on government property. . . . That is no defense. . . . I don't think anybody can have the defense they thought the property was abandoned on another man's piece of property." The court stated: "I will not permit you to show this man thought it was abandoned. . . . I hold in this case that there is no question of abandoned property." The court refused to submit or to allow counsel to argue to the jury whether Morissette acted with innocent intention. It charged: "And I instruct you that if you believe the testimony of the government in this case, he intended to take it. . . . He had no right to take this property. . . . [A]nd it is no defense to claim that it was abandoned, because it was on private property. . . . And I instruct you to this effect: That if this young man took this property (and he says he did), without any permission (he says he did), that was on the property of the United States Government (he says it was), that it was of the value of one cent or more (and evidently it was), that he is guilty of the offense charged here. If you believe the government, he is guilty. . . . The question on intent is whether or not he intended to take the property. He says he did. Therefore, if you believe either side, he is guilty." Petitioner's counsel contended, "But the taking must have been with a felonious intent." The court ruled, however: "That is presumed by his own act."

The Court of Appeals suggested that "greater restraint in expression should have been exercised," but affirmed the conviction because, "As we have interpreted the statute, appellant was guilty of its violation beyond a shadow of doubt, as evidenced even by his own admissions." Its construction of the statute is that it creates several separate and distinct offenses, one being knowing conversion of government property. The court ruled that this particular offense requires no element of criminal intent. This conclusion was thought to be required by the failure of Congress to express such a requisite and this Court's decisions in *United States* v. *Behrman,* 258 U.S. 280, and *United States* v. *Balint,* 258 U.S. 250.

. . .

The contention that an injury can amount to a crime only when inflicted by intention is no provincial or transient notion. It is as universal and persistent in mature systems of law as belief in freedom of the human will and a consequent ability and duty of the normal individual to choose between good and evil. A relation between some mental element and punishment for a harmful act is almost as instinctive as the child's familiar exculpatory "But I didn't mean to," and has afforded the rational basis for a tardy and unfinished substitution of deterrence and reformation in place of retaliation and vengeance as the motivation for public prosecution. Unqualified acceptance of this doctrine by English common law in the Eighteenth Century was indicated by Blackstone's sweeping statement that to constitute any crime there must first be a "vicious will." Common-law commentators of the Nineteenth Century early pronounced the same principle, although a few exceptions not relevant to our present problem came to be recognized.

Crime, as a compound concept, generally constituted only from concurrence of an evil-meaning mind with an evil-doing hand, was congenial to an intense individualism and took deep and early root in American soil. As the states codified the common law of crimes, even if their enactments were silent on the subject, their courts assumed that the omission did not signify disapproval of the principle but merely recognized that intent was so inherent in the idea of the offense that it required no statutory affirmation. Courts, with little hesitation or division, found an implication of the requirement as to offenses that were taken over from the common law. The unanimity with which they have adhered to the central thought that wrongdoing must be conscious to be criminal is emphasized by the variety, disparity and confusion of their definitions of the requisite but elusive mental element. However, courts of various jurisdictions, and for the purposes of different offenses, have devised working formulae, if not scientific ones, for the instruction of juries around such terms as "felonious intent," "criminal intent," "malice aforethought," "guilty knowledge," "fraudulent intent," "willfulness," *"scienter,"* to denote guilty knowledge, or *"mens rea,"* to signify an evil purpose or mental culpability. By use or combination of these various tokens, they have sought to protect those who were not blameworthy in mind from conviction of infamous common-law crimes.

However, the *Balint* and *Behrman* offenses belong to a category of another character, with very different antecedents and origins. The crimes there involved depend on no mental element but consist only of forbidden acts or omissions. This, while not expressed by the Court, is made clear from examination of a century-old but accelerating tendency, discernible both here and in England, to call into existence new duties and crimes which disregard any ingredient of intent. The industrial revolution multiplied the number of workmen exposed to injury from increasingly powerful and complex mechanisms, driven by freshly discovered sources of energy, requiring higher precautions by employers. Traffic of velocities, volumes and varieties unheard of came to subject the wayfarer to intolerable casualty risks if owners and drivers were not to observe new cares and uniformities of conduct. Congestion of cities and crowding of quarters called for health and welfare regulations undreamed of in simpler times. Wide distribution of goods became an instrument of wide distribution of harm when those who dispersed food, drink, drugs, and even securities, did not comply with reasonable standards of quality, integrity, disclosure and care. Such dangers have engendered increasingly numerous and detailed regulations which heighten the duties of those in control of particular industries, trades, properties or activities that affect public health, safety or welfare.

While many of these duties are sanctioned by a more strict civil liability, lawmakers, whether wisely or not, have sought to make such regulations more effective by invoking criminal sanctions to be applied by the familiar technique of criminal prosecutions and convictions. This has confronted the courts with a multitude of prosecutions, based on statutes or administrative regulations, for what have been aptly called "public" welfare offenses." These cases do not fit neatly into any of such accepted classifications of common-law offenses, such as those against the state, the person, property, or public morals. Many of these offenses are not in the nature of positive aggressions or invasions, with which the common law so often dealt, but are in the nature of neglect where the law requires care, or inaction where it imposes a duty. Many violations of such regulations result in no direct or immediate injury to person or property but merely create the danger or probability of it which the law seeks to minimize. While such offenses do not threaten the security of the state in the manner of treason, they may be regarded as offenses against its authority, for their occurrence impairs the efficiency of controls deemed essential to the social order as presently constituted. In this respect, whatever the intent of the violator, the injury is the same, and the consequences are injurious or not according to fortuity. Hence, legislation applicable to such offenses, as a matter of policy, does not specify intent as a necessary element. The accused, if he does not will the violation, usually is in a position to prevent it with no more care than society might reasonably expect and no more exertion than it might reasonably exact from one who assumed his responsibilities. Also, penalties commonly are relatively small, and conviction does no grave damage to an offender's reputation. Under such considerations, courts have turned to construing statutes and regulations which make no mention of intent as dispensing with it and holding that the guilty act alone makes out the crime. This has not, however, been without expressions of misgiving.

. . .

Neither this Court nor, so far as we are aware, any other has undertaken to delineate a precise line or set forth comprehensive criteria for distinguishing between crimes that require a mental element and crimes that do not. We attempt no closed definition, for the law on the subject is neither settled nor static. The conclusion reached in the *Balint* and *Behrman* cases has our approval and adherence for the circumstances to which it was there applied. A quite different question here is whether we will expand the doctrine of crimes without intent to include those charged here.

Stealing, larceny, and its variants and equivalents, were among the earliest offenses known to the law that existed before legislation; they are invasions of rights of property which stir a sense of insecurity in the whole community and arouse public demand for retribution, the penalty is high and, when a sufficient amount is involved, the infamy is that of a felony, which, says Maitland, is ". . . as bad a word as you can give to man or thing." State courts of last resort, on whom fall the heaviest burden of interpreting criminal law in this country, have consistently retained the requirement of intent in larceny-type offenses. If any state has deviated, the exception has neither been called to our attention nor disclosed by our research.

Congress, therefore, omitted any express prescription of criminal intent from the enactment before us in the light of an unbroken course of judicial decision in all constituent states of the Union holding intent inherent in this class of offense, even when not expressed in a statute. Congressional silence as to mental elements in an Act merely adopting into federal statutory law a concept of crime already so well defined in common law and statutory interpretation by the states may warrant quite contrary inferences than the same silence in creating an offense new to general law, for whose definition the courts have no guidance except the Act. Because the offenses before this Court in the *Balint* and *Behrman* cases were of this latter class, we cannot accept them as authority for eliminating intent from offenses incorporated from the common law. Nor do exhaustive studies of state court cases disclose any well-considered decisions applying the doctrine of crime without intent to such enacted common-law offenses, although a few deviations are notable as illustrative of the danger inherent in the Government's contentions here.

The Government asks us by a feat of construction radically to change the weights and balances in the scales of justice. The purpose and obvious effect of doing away with the requirement of a guilty intent is to ease the prosecution's path to conviction, to strip the defendant of such benefit as he derived at common law from innocence of evil purpose, and to circumscribe the freedom heretofore allowed juries. Such a manifest impairment of the immunities of the individual should not be extended to common-law crimes on judicial initiative.

The spirit of the doctrine which denies to the federal judiciary power to create crimes forthrightly admonishes that we should not enlarge the reach of enacted crimes by constituting them from anything less than the incriminating components contemplated by the words used in the statute. And where Congress borrows terms of art in which are accumulated the legal tradition and meaning of centuries of practice, it presumably knows and adopts the cluster of ideas that were attached to each borrowed word in the body of learning from which it was taken and the meaning its use will convey to the judicial mind unless otherwise instructed. In such case, absence of contrary direction may be taken as satisfaction with widely accepted definitions, not as a departure for them.

We hold that mere omission from § 641 of any mention of intent will not be construed as eliminating that element from the crimes denounced.

. . .

As we read the record, this case was tried on the theory that even if criminal intent were essential its presence (a) should be decided by the court (b) as a presumption of law, apparently conclusive, (c) predicated upon the isolated act of taking rather than upon all of the circumstances. In each of these respects we believe the trial court was in error.

Where intent of the accused is an ingredient of the crime charged, its existence is a question of fact which must be submitted to the jury. State court authorities cited to the effect that intent is relevant in larcenous crimes are equally emphatic and uniform that it is a jury issue. The settled practice and its reason are well stated by Judge Andrews in *People* v. *Flack,* 125 N. Y. 324, 334, 26 N. E. 267, 270:

> *It is alike the general rule of law and the dictate of natural justice that to constitute guilt there must be not only a wrongful act, but a criminal intention. Under our system (unless in exceptional cases), both must be found by the jury to justify a conviction for crime. However clear the proof may be, or however incontrovertible may seem to the judge to be the inference of a criminal intention, the question of intent can never be ruled as a question of law, but must always be submitted to the jury. Jurors may be perverse; the ends of justice may be defeated by unrighteous verdicts, but so long as the functions of the judge and jury are distinct, the one responding to the law, the other to the facts, neither can invade the province of the other without destroying the significance of trial by court and jury. . . .*

It follows that the trial court may not withdraw or prejudge the issue by instruction that the law raises a presumption of intent from an act. It often is tempting to cast in terms of a "presumption" a conclusion which a court thinks probable from given facts. The Supreme Court of Florida, for example, in a larceny case, from selected circumstances which are present in this case, has declared a presumption of exactly opposite effect from the one announced by the trial court here:

> . . . *But where the taking is open and there is no subsequent attempt to conceal the property, and no denial, but an avowal, of the taking a strong presumption arises that there was no felonious intent, which must be repelled by clear and convincing evidence before a conviction is authorized. . . .* Kemp v. State, *146 Fla. 101, 104, 200 So. 368, 369.*

We think presumptive intent has no place in this case. A conclusive presumption which testimony could not overthrow would effectively eliminate intent as an ingredient of the offense. A presumption which would permit but not require the jury to assume intent from an isolated fact would prejudge a conclusion which the jury should reach of its own volition. A presumption which would permit the jury to make an assumption which all the evidence considered together does not logically establish would give to a proven fact an artificial and fictional effect. In either case, this presumption would conflict with the overriding presumption of innocence with which the law endows the accused and which extends to every element of the crime. Such incriminating presumptions are not to be improvised by the judiciary. Even congressional power to facilitate convictions by substituting presumptions for proof is not without limit. *Tot* v. *United States,* 319 U. S. 463.

Moreover, the conclusion supplied by presumption in this instance was one of intent to steal the casings, and it was based on the mere fact that defendant took them. The court thought the only question was, "Did he intend to take the property?" That the removal of them was a conscious and intentional act was admitted. But that isolated fact is not an adequate basis on which the jury should find the criminal intent to steal or knowingly convert, that is, *wrongfully* to deprive another of possession of property. Whether that intent existed, the jury must determine, not only from the act of taking, but from that together with defendant's testimony and all of the surrounding circumstances.

Of course, the jury, considering Morissette's awareness that these casings were on government property, his failure to seek any permission for their removal and his self-interest as a witness, might have disbelieved his profession of innocent intent and concluded that his assertion of a belief that the casings were abandoned was an afterthought. Had the jury convicted on proper instructions it would be the end of the matter. But juries are not bound by what seems inescapable logic to judges. They might have concluded that the heaps of spent casings left in the hinterland to rust away presented an appearance of unwanted and abandoned junk, and that lack of any conscious deprivation of property or intentional injury was indicated by Morissette's good character, the openness of the taking, crushing and transporting of the casings, and the candor with which it was all admitted. They might have refused to brand Morissette as a thief. Had they done so, that too would have been the end of the matter.

2. The Changing Law

The aim of criminal law today, according to most writers, is deterrence or reformation rather than retribution. But if an act is involuntary, if there is no criminal intent, there is nothing to be deterred or reformed, and punishment is the infliction of pain without purpose.

To what extent, then, is criminal behavior involuntary? Our answer to the question has changed as our understanding of human behavior has changed, and so too has criminal law. Alcoholism, for example, once defined as a crime, is now coming to be defined as a disease and outside the scope of penal sanctions.

In the following selection, Joe B. Driver claims that his alcoholism is not a crime and his imprisonment is cruel and unusual punishment. The court agrees.

The question is whether a chronic alcoholic, as appellant Joe B. Driver has been proved and confesses to be, can Constitutionally be criminally convicted and sentenced, as he was, for public drunkenness.

Admitting the truth of the charge under the North Carolina statute, he grounded his defense on the Eighth Amendment, applied to the States under the due process clause of the Fourteenth, barring the infliction of "cruel and unusual" punishment. His argument may be condensed in this syllogism: Driver's chronic alcoholism is a disease which has destroyed the power of his will to resist the constant, excessive consumption of alcohol; his appearance in public in that condition is not his volition, but a compulsion symptomatic of the disease; and to stigmatize him as a criminal for this act is cruel and unusual punishment.

This plea failed in the State courts. State v. Driver, 262 N.C. 92, 136 S.E.2d 208 (1964). Thereupon he unsuccessfully petitioned the Federal district court for habeas corpus to procure release from imprisonment ordered on his sentence. Driver v. Hinnant, 243 F.Supp. 95 (E.D. N.C.-1965). From this denial he appeals.

We find merit in his petition. Accordingly we must vacate the judgment on review and remand for the further proceedings later outlined.

The State statute is N.C. Gen. Stat. § 14–335 reading as follows:

From Driver v. Hinnant, **Federal Reporter** (2nd series), Vol. 356 (St. Paul, Minn.: West Publishing Company, 1966), pp. 763–765.

If any person shall be found drunk or intoxicated on the public highway, or at any public place or meeting, in any county . . . herein named, he shall be guilty of a misdemeanor, and upon conviction shall be punished as is provided in this section:

12. In . . . Durham [*County*] *. . . by a fine, for the first offense, of not more than fifty dollars ($50.00), or imprisonment for not more than thirty days; for the second offense within a period of twelve months, by a fine of not more than one hundred dollars ($100.00), or imprisonment for not more than sixty days; and for the third offense within any twelve months' period such offense is declared a misdemeanor, punishable as a misdemeanor within the discretion of the court.*

As more than a three-time repeater in Durham County, Driver was sentenced to imprisonment for two years for each of two offenses occurring on December 18 and 19, 1963, respectively, the terms running concurrently. While he pleaded guilty, the evidence taken as a guide to an appropriate sentence conclusively proved him a chronic alcoholic, his inebriation in public view an involuntary exhibition of the infirmity. The District Judge had no doubts about it. Actually, it is a concessum in the case.

Driver was 59 years old. His first conviction for public intoxication occurred at 24. Since then he has been convicted of this offense more than 200 times. For nearly two-thirds of his life he has been incarcerated for these infractions. Indeed, while enlarged on bail pending determination of this appeal, he has been twice convicted for like violations.

Thus the question here is beyond the difficult determination of whether an accused is a chronic alcoholic. Our discussion and decision, it must be recalled throughout, presuppose an indisputable finding that the offender is a "chronic alcoholic." As defined by the National Council on Alcholism, he is a "person who is powerless to stop drinking and whose drinking seriously alters his normal living pattern." The American Medical Association defines "alcoholics" as "those excessive drinkers whose dependence on alcohol has attained such a degree that it shows a noticeable disturbance or interference with their bodily or mental health, their interpersonal relations, and their satisfactory social and economic functioning." The World Health Organization recognizes alcoholism "as a chronic illness that manifests itself as a *disorder of behavior*." (Accent added.) It is known that alcohol can be addicting, and it is the addict—the involuntary drinker—on whom our decision is now made. Hence we exclude the merely excessive—steady or spree—voluntary drinker.

This addiction—chronic alcoholism—is now almost universally accepted medically as a disease. The symptoms, as already noted, may appear as "disorder of behavior." Obviously, this includes appearances in public, as here, unwilled and ungovernable by the victim. When that is the conduct for which he is criminally accused, there can be no judgment of criminal conviction passed upon him. To do so would affront the Eighth

Amendment, as cruel and unusual punishment in branding him a criminal, irrespective of consequent detention or fine.

Although his misdoing objectively comprises the physical elements of a crime, nevertheless no crime has been perpetrated because the conduct was neither actuated by an evil intent nor accompanied with a consciousness of wrongdoing, indispensable ingredients of a crime. Morissette v. United States, 342 U.S. 246, 250–252, 72 S.Ct. 240, 96 L.Ed. 288 (1952). Nor can his misbehavior be penalized as a transgression of a police regulation—malum prohibitum—necessitating no intent to do what it punishes. The alcoholic's presence in public is not his act, for he did not will it. It may be likened to the movements of an imbecile or a person in a delirium of a fever. None of them by attendance in the forbidden place defy the forbiddance.

This conclusion does not contravene the familiar thesis that voluntary drunkenness is no excuse for crime. The chronic alcoholic has not drunk voluntarily, although undoubtedly he did so originally. His excess now derives from disease. However, our excusal of the chronic alcoholic from criminal prosecution is confined exclusively to those acts on his part which are compulsive as symptomatic of the disease. With respect to other behavior—not characteristic of confirmed chronic alcoholism—he would be judged as would any person not so afflicted.

Of course, the alcohol-diseased may by law be kept out of public sight. Equally true, the North Carolina statute does not punish them solely for drunkenness, but rather for its public demonstration. But many of the diseased have no homes or friends, family or means to keep them indoors. Driver examples this pitiable predicament, for he is apparently without money or restraining care.

Robinson v. State of California, supra, 370 U.S. 660, 82 S.Ct. 1417 (1962), sustains, if not commands, the view we take. While occupied only with a State statute declaring drug addiction a misdemeanor, the Court in the concurrences and dissents, as well as in the majority opinion, enunciated a doctrine encompassing the present case. The California statute criminally punished a "status"—drug addiction—involuntarily assumed: the North Carolina Act criminally punishes an involuntary symptom of a status—public intoxication. In declaring the former violative of the Eighth Amendment, we think pari ratione, the *Robinson* decision condemns the North Carolina law when applied to one in the circumstances of appellant Driver. All of the opinions recognize the inefficacy of such a statute when it is enforced to make involuntary deportment a crime.

The Constitutional premise of *Robinson,* and so apt here, is found in the opinion, 370 U.S. at 666, 82 S.Ct. at 1420:

It is unlikely that any State at this moment in history would attempt to make it a criminal offense for a person to be mentally ill, or a leper, or to be afflicted with a venereal disease. A State might determine that the general health and welfare require that the victims of these and other human afflictions be dealt with by compulsory treatment, involving quarantine, confinement, or sequestration. But, in the light of contemporary human knowledge, a law which made a criminal offense of such a disease would doubtless be universally thought to be an infliction of cruel and unusual punishment in violation of the Eighth and Fourteenth Amendments.

The Director of the Prison Department of North Carolina, has patly and pithily termed the prosecution of the chronic alcoholic. Driver, he said, is one of the "unfortunates whose only offense is succumbing publicly to the disease of alcoholism."

We do not annul the North Carolina statute. It is well within the State's power and right to deter and punish public drunkenness, especially to secure others against its annoyances and intrusions. Robinson v. State of California, supra, 370 U.S. 660, 664, 82 S.Ct. 1417. To this end any intoxicated person found in the street or other public areas may be taken into custody for inquiry or prosecution. But the Constitution intercedes when on arraignment the accused's helplessness comes to light. Then it is that no *criminal* conviction may follow.

The upshot of our decision is that the State cannot stamp an unpretending chronic alcoholic as a criminal if his drunken public display is involuntary as the result of disease. However, nothing we have said precludes appropriate detention of him for treatment and rehabilitation so long as he is not marked a criminal.

3. The Light of Reason

The question "What Is a Crime?" is actually two questions in one. At one level we can ask if a particular type of behavior is criminal as defined by law; at another level we can ask why the law arrives at a particular set of definitions. Morris Cohen disentangles the two with the trained hand of a legal philosopher.

In passing moral judgments as we all sooner or later inevitably do in regard to legal and other human arrangements, we generally oscillate between the appeal to self-evident principles and the appeal to the obvious demands of the specific situation before us. This seems a highly unsatisfactory procedure to those who feel that certainty must be found in one or the other terminus, else all our moral judgments fail for lack of an assured support. This essay is based on the view that such oscillation is under certain logical precautions and scientific systematization the only proper procedure,—that to trust rigid principles regardless of specific consequences makes for inhuman absolutism, while to rely on nothing but the feeling of the moment leads to brutal anarchy. Consider the ethical atomists who think that life breaks itself up into a number of separate autonomous situations, each immediately revealing its own good or proper solution to our conscience, intuition, or intuitive reason, intelligence or common sense. When these moralists are confronted by a challenge to any of their particular judgments, they generally adduce some reason or at least cite an analogous case, thus involving explicitly or implicitly an appeal to some determining principle more abstract and wider than the specific case before them. On the other hand, those who rely on principles to decide specific cases do, and have to, defend these principles by showing that they lead to the proper consequences. By a consideration of some of the ethical problems of the criminal law, I wish to illustrate the truth that the procedure from principles to facts and from facts to principles, without assuming either to be absolute or unquestionable, does not at all lead to complete moral nihilism, but rather clarifies the process of building a systematic view of what the law should do, even though it tolerates a certain amount of probabilism and pluralism in taking into account the wide variations of social conditions and sentiments.

In the law school's curriculum and in the text-books, the criminal law

From Morris R. Cohen, "Moral Aspects of the Criminal Law," **Reason and Law** (New York: Collier Books, 1961). Reprinted by permission of The Yale Law Journal Company and Fred B. Rothman & Company from **The Yale Law Journal,** Vol. 49, pp. 987 ff.

appears as a distinct and strictly delimited province; and practitioners generally leave it to a separate branch of their profession, by no means the highest in income and prestige. But if you ask the man in the street what he understands by *law* he will generally mention the prohibition against theft, murder or some other punishable offense. As in other cases the layman, while devoid of well-defined and properly elaborated ideas, still touches the root of the matter. The criminal law may properly be viewed not only as a branch but also as a basic phase of the whole legal system.

. . .

It is sometimes asserted that the civil law protects the private interests of individuals while the criminal law protects the interests of the state or community. But this contrast is of little value. I do not wish to dispute the fact that the interest in preventing sacrilege or other grave public danger was one of the origins of criminal procedure, and that offenses against the king or government have been and still are generally the most severely punished. But it is hardly necessary to call attention to the vital interests of the state not only in protecting but in promoting private industry and commerce from which it derives its support. Surely no interest of the state is so dear to it as the collection of taxes. Yet the non-payment of a real estate tax is not always a crime. An absolute differentiation between the substance of the criminal and of the civil law is indeed clearly impossible so long as the same act may be the basis of either a civil suit or a criminal prosecution. The difference here clearly resolves itself into one of procedure.

In the United States today, it seems very easy to distinguish between criminal and civil procedure on the ground that in the former some state official is in duty bound to prosecute, whereas a civil action is brought by a private individual acting at his pleasure. We must add however that state officials are also bound to bring certain civil suits, and in England the attorney general may intervene in tort cases between private parties. This is not to deny that there are today some differences between civil and criminal procedure, *i.e.,* the one in regard to the burden of proof. But it is well to remember that these differences are far from prevailing in all legal systems and are apt to appear more important in theory than in the actual practice of our jury trials. In any case, up to the second decade of the nineteenth century the common law allowed a private action or "appeal" for murder and other injuries.

These considerations are not intended to deny that legislatures and courts can, do, and should call certain acts criminal and provide some distinctive procedures for dealing with them. The general desire for security demands that everyone know, with a fair degree of certainty, what is and what is not criminal. The fear that some innocent act may be branded as criminal is as horrible as the older paralyzing fear of unconscious unintentional sin. What I wish to insist on is that the criminal law is an integral part of the legal system and is subject to the same considerations which do and should influence the whole. More specifically, the criminal law cannot be distinguished from the rest by any difference of moral principle. Some crimes, to be sure, are shocking; but there are many crimes that are felt to be much less reprehensible than many outrageous forms of injustice, cruelty or fraud, which the law does not punish at all, or else makes their perpetrator liable to money damages in a civil suit. It is well to remember that Moses murdered an Egyptian and fled the country, that Socrates was, by a majority of his fellow citizens that voted, found guilty of a crime, and that George Washington and others would have been treated as criminals if the American Revolution had been as unsuccessful as was the Scotch rebellion under Sir William Wallace. Those who, like Kant, regard obedience to the law as an absolute duty, must logically deny the moral right of any revolution. But this cannot be carried out consistently, since most, if not all, established governments, even the Constitution of the United States, have arisen out of revolutions and military conquest. Some dim, uncomfortable perception of this may be responsible for Kant's remarkable prohibition of any inquiry as to how the existing government acquired its authority.

An adequate discussion of justice in the criminal law must, therefore, deal with all the ethical issues of the law generally, such as the principle of equality, the adjustment of conflicting interests, or the relation between respect for personality and the demands of social responsibility and solidarity. But this study will be limited to a few questions that are in the forefront of current discussion as to the criminal law.

With this question "What Is a Crime?", we are at once plunged into an ancient and persistent controversy. On one hand, we have the legalists who urge that any act or omission is a crime when, and only when, it is declared to be such by the legislative power or by those who speak with the authority of the law; an act may be sinful, immoral or contrary to the public good, but it is not a crime unless it is legally so declared. On the other hand, we have those who claim this view to be superficial, and who insist that no legislature can or should treat anything as a crime unless it is so in fact or in the nature of things. This issue dates back to the old Greek controversy of the fifth century B.C. between those who saw everything determined by nature and those who pressed the claims of convention or human legislation. To Aristotle may be traced the classical compromise of distinguishing between those acts which are crimes by nature (*mala per se*) and are prohibited among all peoples, and those others (*mala prohibita*) which are prohibited only in certain places by special legislation. This view has been largely influential in molding the classical doctrine of natural rights in the criminal as well as in other branches of the law. In point of fact, however, no one has ever made a critical catalogue of the acts which have actually been prohibited by all peoples at all times. Almost all those who insist that there are *mala per se* put into that class those acts which in an undefined way seem to them to be shocking. But they do not give any clear criterion by which to judge what acts should thus be included and what acts should be excluded from the category of crime.

The oldest traditions view crime as a violation of some eternal law set by the gods, nature or reason. These find expression in two forms, the theologic and the rationalist (more properly intuitive). Both have the advantage over the positivist that they do not have to use empirical evidence to establish absolute distinctions between what is and what is not properly a crime.

1. *The theologic point of view.* This is the older and still the most widespread. It regards the criminal law, and indeed all law, as divinely ordained for all time by Manu or by Zeus, given by Jahweh to Moses or to Mohammed by Allah. Without entering into any theologic controversy, it may be granted as an historic fact that communities as a rule do not allow any one who pleases to decide what acts the divine will has ordained as criminal. That is a function left in fact to some recognized authorities, *e.g.,* priests, religiously trained judges, scribes who interpret certain texts, or the like. When the judgment of these authorities can in any way be questioned, there is some attempt to justify it on the basis of reason and human history. Thus great moralists of the Catholic church, such as St. Thomas, are not willing to rest the distinction between what are and what are not crimes on mere authority. The divine Will is not despotically arbitrary, but is viewed as essentially rational and just. Hence in practice, theologic moralists appeal also to a rationalist view of human nature and experience.

Of course, there are theologians who insist that the essence of crime is the violation of the divine will, and that our frail human reason cannot determine what is just or unjust for the Perfect Whole. Mankind is quite accustomed to double standards of morality, different for men and women, for the state and individual, and for divine and human persons. Thus it is not wrong for Jahweh to harden Pharaoh's heart or to send a lying spirit to Ahab in order to punish him. It is not even wrong to put an evil design into David's heart in order to punish innocent children of Israel by either killing them by the plague or else depriving them of their parents. But the persistent efforts to explain such incidents and to justify the ways of God show a general disinclination to view God's law or will as entirely devoid of what seems to us rational or just.

Moreover, not all sins or violations of God's law are treated by theologians as crimes. Many evil acts are left to the direct punishment of the divine power here or hereafter, *e.g.,* covetousness, sex relations that are prohibited by the divine but not by human law, uncharitable attitudes to others, or failure to honor our parents. The Catholic church, claiming divine authority, does not today urge that the state make it a penal offense to disbelieve the dogma of trans-substantiation or of the immaculate conception of the Virgin Mary, or to hold those views as to the relation of the Holy Ghost to the Father and Son which make heretics of all the Greek orthodox. If blasphemy is still a crime in some of our states, it is defended on the alleged ground of protecting the public peace. Suicide is very often viewed as a direct violation of divine law. But few care to see criminal punishment meted out to one who has been unsuccessful in his attempt at it; and we may suspect that when suicide was treated as a felony, the fact that this deprived the heirs of the felon of his property and gave it to the king or church was an important motive or factor in the case.

2. *The point of view of moral intuition.* Of those who have attempted to give us an absolute moral basis for a penal code, Kant is the foremost. He rejects the claims of all authority, secular or sacred, as inconsistent with the autonomy of the free will in ethical relations. The universal principle of all moral conduct, the categorical imperative to live so that the maxim of our action can become a principle of universal legislation, is not the source but rather a formula for what conscience, moral faith or "practical reason" immediately dictates as our duty in any specific case. In the end Kant falls back on the assumption that just as our moral conscience tells us that "Thou shalt not kill," is an absolute duty for the individual, so is "You shall kill the murderer" an equally absolute duty for the community. If a society is to be absolved, the last murderer must be executed, else the blood of the victim will be on the heads of those who fail to do so.

While the Kantian theory is fairly close to the popular conscience, which often regards the prevailing *mores* as eternal laws of nature and reason, it fails as a guide in the determination of what specific acts are or ought to be treated as criminal.

Not all violations of moral laws are crimes (*e.g.,* lying). But why is not truth-telling as important for the preservation of the moral order as the protection of property? We all agree that murder should be a crime. But such agreement is purely verbal unless we are agreed as to what is murder. Surely, not all instances of killing can be regarded as criminal, even on Kantian grounds. What distinction does he offer between excusable or even commendable homicide, and murder? No one today regards it as criminal to kill a man in self-defense. But the line between justifiable and unjustifiable fear of attack varies and is somewhat arbitrarily fixed by law. In international relations, it is hopeless to fix a sharp line between an offensive and defensive war, even though in extreme cases the distinction is clear even to those not involved in the combat.

None of us think of the official executioner as a murderer. Though he is obviously not of the highest dignity, and we may not agree with De Maistre that the whole state rests on him, he is still a public servant. Nihilists who condemned and executed some of the brutal underlings of the czar were branded as murderers by his advisers who ordered, one Sunday morning, the shooting of a number of people that came to present a petition. Shall we say that the moral conscience of mankind is clear as to who in these instances was guilty of murder? The soldiers who kill in war are brave heroes, and on both sides they are said to be defending their country. But may not their obedience to their officers make wars of unjust aggression possible?

I am not arguing that there is no such thing as morally revolting criminal murder, simply because in the nature of things there is not any sharp line to define it. That would be like arguing that there is no difference between day and night because there is no sharp line but rather a twilight zone between them. But I am calling attention to the inadequacy of the intuitionists' account which supposes that the common conscience has a clear and universally acknowledged answer as to when an act is or is not criminal.

Similar considerations hold in regard to theft. Apart from existing law, it is hard to say what does and what does not morally belong to another. Especially is this true in modern society when no man can point to anything and say, "This is exclusively the product of my own work in which I received no help from others." For, in fact, the author of a book, or the farmer who raises crops, has been supported by others during his work, and the relative value of his services is largely determined by the conditions created by the legal system. The notion of theft is relatively clear if it denotes taking something in a way that the law prohibits. But on purely moral grounds, apart from the law, it is by no means clear. Is it immoral for a manufacturer to copy the brilliant ideas that his rival has developed? If the design of a dress should be made property by law on the analogy of copyright, then imitating it will become theft. Among many primitive peoples there is no sense of private property in food. But it is a grave theft for one man to sing the personal song of another. Before the copyright laws, there was no conception of property in the literary composition itself. But when the legal rules in regard to property change, our moral duties in respect to it change.

Even if there were an absolute duty to obey the law always (which is dubious), legislation in a modern state would still have to go beyond traditional morality precisely because the latter does not offer sufficiently definite rules to regulate the life of people that in fact have conflicting notions of right and wrong. We see this in the conflicting claims of different classes of society, *e.g.,* employer and employee. The truth is that our specific moral rules are not, as is often assumed, fixed for all time, but vary with changing conditions; and to maintain the order necessary for the good life, we must have the power to terminate controversies definitively. This involves rules that generally are not free from all elements of arbitrariness. Moral duties thus become more definite and clear after the law is enacted. A consideration of the law of marriage and divorce will make this clear. Bigamy is repugnant to the general conscience of today. But was it adulterous for the Old Testament patriarchs to marry more than one wife, even two sisters? Is it adulterous today to marry two sisters successively, if death or divorce comes between the two marriages? Many who regard free love as horrible, see no objection to free divorce. Arbitrary legislation does in fact change our judgments as to what is moral and immoral in given situations, and the law makes crimes of acts that were not so before the legislation took place.

The positivists who wish to develop a science of criminology, and who believe that a science can deal only with facts of existence, find it difficult to admit that what is a crime is determined by legislation. They are thus forced to maintain that certain acts are criminal by nature, whether committed by men, beasts or even plants. Unfortunately, however, they do not tell us what traits distinguish a criminal from any other act. What for instance makes it criminal for the sensitive plant to feed on insects? Are not birds similarly guilty, and do not fish live by devouring other fish? It seems that the positivists are here following the old doctrine of the Stoic moralists that nature decrees certain acts as impermissible even to animals, so that those who violate this decree are guilty of crimes against nature. But unless we believe in supernatural ordinances or in a devil who interferes with our nature, we must apply the term natural to everything that actually takes place, in the field of legislation as well as in the field of "unnatural" or "abnormal" animal behavior.

The most thoroughgoing attempt to define natural crime is that of Garofalo who identifies it with those harmful actions which shock the moral sense of pity and probity of all civilized people. This moral sense, he holds, is not only unaffected by legislation which makes acts criminal that were not so before, but it is independent also of the circumstances and exigencies of any given epoch. But how can positivists who identify science with determinism hold that social changes can occur without having any effect on what is deemed criminal? Garofalo admits the obvious and well authenticated fact that laws as to what constitutes crime do vary, but he thinks that the sentiments of pity and probity are the same among all civilized peoples. But who are civilized people? The naive answer is: those whose views are like our own, from which it follows that our ancestors were not, and that other people with different conceptions of the requisities of pity and probity are not, civilized. This use of the term *civilized* seems amazingly naive, but it is supported by the fashionable assumption that there is a cosmic law according to which all people must, regardless of diverse circumstances in their environment, evolve along the same uniform line of which we today represent the highest point. There is, however, no scientific evidence, logic or empirical, for any such law. As a matter of historic fact, not only do different "civilized" peoples vary in their moral sense or sentiment as to what pity and probity require, but within any community there is a large variation in this respect. And which view, or way of feeling, will prevail depends on temporal changes that do not follow any one line but are dependent on so many circumstances or factors that the future is unpredictable.

It is hardly necessary to show that hatred, pugnacity and brutality have not only been human traits at all times, but have been glorified in religion and literature. Consider the command in Deuteronomy to exterminate all the inhabitants of a conquered city, or the ferocious ending of the touching psalm "By the Rivers of Babylon," not to mention the obvious delight in wholesale slaughter in the Book of Esther, or the record of pious, God-fearing Puritans in their treatment of Indians, or their participation in the Negro slave traffic. Moreover, when we reflect on the tortures imposed by the Inquisition, the brutalities of civil war (and even of the economic struggle), or how certain contemporary rulers have risen to power not only by the practice but by the very glorification of brutality, it does not seem that the latter trait is found only among those in prison.

Civilized Italians and Germans at the time that Garofalo wrote might have been shocked at the suggestion that their people would ever be capable of perpetrating the cruelties which Fascists and Nazis have exercised on their opponents or even on innocent children who happened to live in Ethiopian villages or to be of Jewish ancestry. Yet those responsible for these acts have become national heroes and their cruelty has become the virtue of fortitude and patriotic devotion to the national state.

Within American society today, there is a violent difference of feeling or sentiment in regard to birth control. There are those who consider it an abominable crime against nature, so that spreading information about it or abetting it should remain a penal offense. On the other hand, there are those who feel strongly that the best interests of society demand that such information be more widely diffused. The question as to which party will prevail cannot be answered by any law of evolution such as Spencer's. It depends upon such factors among others as legislation for improved and more ample housing.

In the end Garofalo admits that besides natural crime there are many offenses which even civilized peoples do and should punish. The latter category will be found to include most of the offenses of our criminal law. Garofalo himself mentions not only political crimes, such as meetings to conspire against the government, seditious utterances, prohibited political demonstrations, refusal to perform required military or other services to the state, irregularities in the conduct of elections, etc., but also clandestine prostitution, smuggling, helping prisoners to escape, and the like. Now if all these are not natural crimes, our prisons contain very many who have not committed any natural crime, while many who practice gross cruelty and improbity in business or elsewhere are not in prison at all. There is therefore no ground for the basic assumption of the "anthropologic" school of criminology, that the physical or mental traits common to prisoners are distinctive of natural criminals.

Positivistic sociologists and jurists as well as moralists often identify crime with acts which are contrary to the social interests or endanger social existence. But the most obvious reflection shows that this begs the question. Acts are criminal not because they *are* harmful, but because they are *deemed* harmful by those who make or interpret the law. The most serious crimes are sometimes those acts that in the judgment of enlightened and heroically unselfish people will best promote the common good, for example, criticism of the errors of established governments or churches. The history of the martyrs of religion and science amply indicates that acts deemed criminal at a given time in a given community often turn out to be of the greatest value for human life.

In the past the most heinous crimes (judging by the severity of the punishment) have been sacrilege or ceremonial defilement, witchcraft and heresy. Doubtless these were regarded with terror because they were supposed to endanger society by bringing down the wrath of gods that are not careful to discriminate between the guilty and innocent when they send down their lightning or plagues. But what any community regards as most dangerous is not eternally fixed in the nature of things, but varies from time to time and from locality to locality in ways which we cannot always explain. Moreover, it is not always the feeling of danger that makes us regard certain acts as punishable. The causes of social irritation and active resentment are wider. Children in New York have stoned men for wearing straw hats after September 15th, and Mexican peasants have burnt new orange groves planted by foreigners for no other reason than the dislike of any novelty in their vicinity.

5 MATTERS OF DEBATE

A basic assumption in our thinking of criminal law is that legal rules should be based on legitimate authority. That is to say, those who formulate the rules must be recognized as having the right to do so, and the rules are to be obeyed not simply from fear but from a sense of obligation or moral duty.

In many areas of the law, however, we may find the legitimacy of legal rules being called into question. The law may be challenged as a matter of principle, as in the case of Henry David Thoreau or Martin Luther King. The demands of the law may become doubtful under the press of disaster, as in the case of the sinking lifeboat described by Edmond Cahn. Or the rightfulness of the law may become uncertain, as Howard Becker points out, when people feel that the rules are being forced upon them by outsiders.

The important point is that when we try to understand the nature of crime, we must be aware that we are dealing with rules that are not always regarded as legitimate by all people under all circumstances. And, as we shall see shortly, this variation is one of the vital elements in explaining why the rules are or are not obeyed.

1. A Majority of One

Unjust laws exist, said Henry David Thoreau. Shall we be content to obey them? In protest against the society of his time, he refused to pay his poll tax and went to jail. But who is to draw the line between enlightened resistance to bad law and meaningless anarchy? Thoreau placed his faith in the individual conscience—and, in fact, he would have wondered where else the decision could be made.

Unjust laws exist: shall we be content to obey them, or shall we endeavor to amend them, and obey them until we have succeeded, or shall we transgress them at once? Men generally, under such a government as this, think that they ought to wait until they have persuaded the majority to alter them. They think that, if they should resist, the remedy would be worse than the evil. But it is the fault of the government itself that the remedy *is* worse than the evil. *It* makes it worse. Why is it not more apt to anticipate and provide for reform? Why does it not cherish its wise minority? Why does it cry and resist before it is hurt? Why does it not encourage its citizens to be on the alert to point out its faults and *do* better than it would have them? Why does it always crucify Christ, and excommunicate Copernicus and Luther, and pronounce Washington and Franklin rebels?

One would think, that a deliberate and practical denial of its authority was the only offense never contemplated by government; else, why has it not assigned its definite, its suitable and proportionate penalty? If a man who has no property refuses but once to earn nine shillings for the state, he is put in prison for a period unlimited by any law that I know, and determined only by the discretion of those who placed him there; but if he should steal ninety times nine shillings from the state, he is soon permitted to go at large again.

If the injustice is part of the necessary friction of the machine of government, let it go, let it go: perchance it will wear smooth,—certainly the machine will wear out. If the injustice has a spring, or a pulley, or a rope, or a crank, exclusively for itself, then perhaps you may consider whether the remedy will not be worse than the evil; but if it is of such a nature that it requires you to be the agent of injustice to another, then, I say, break the law. Let your life be a counter friction to stop the machine. What I have to

From Henry David Thoreau, **Walden and Civil Disobedience**, edited by N. H. Pearson (New York: Holt, Rinehart and Winston, Inc., 1955). Reprinted by permission.

do is to see, at any rate, that I do not lend myself to the wrong which I condemn.

As for adopting the ways which the state has provided for remedying the evil, I know not of such ways. They take too much time, and a man's life will be gone. I have other affairs to attend to. I came into this world, not chiefly to make this a good place to live in, but to live in it, be it good or bad. A man has not everything to do, but something; and because he cannot do *everything,* it is not necessary that he should do *something* wrong. It is not my business to be petitioning the Governor or the Legislature any more than it is theirs to petition me; and if they should not hear my petition, what should I do then? But in this case the state has provided no way: its very Constitution is the evil. This may seem to be harsh and stubborn and unconciliatory; but it is to treat with the utmost kindness and consideration the only spirit that can appreciate or deserves it. So is all change for the better, like birth and death, which convulse the body.

I do not hesitate to say, that those who call themselves Abolitionists should at once effectually withdraw their support, both in person and property, from the government of Massachusetts and not wait till they constitute a majority of one, before they suffer the right to prevail through them. I think that it is enough if they have God on their side, without waiting for that other one. Moreover, any man more right than his neighbors constitutes a majority of one already.

2. To Form a More Perfect Union

The battle for civil rights is one of the most significant social movements of our time. In this struggle, Martin Luther King had never ceased to call for nonviolent resistance, and this position often meant a willingness to go to jail. If breaking the law can be interpreted by some individuals as a moral act, then crime has more than one meaning; and a thoughtless acceptance of all laws may be no easy path to virtue.

The nonviolent resisters can summarize their message in the following simple terms: We will take direct action against injustice without waiting for other agencies to act. We will not obey unjust laws or submit to unjust practices. We will do this peacefully, openly, cheerfully because our aim is to persuade. We adopt the means of nonviolence because our end is a community at peace with itself. We will try to persuade with our words, but if our words fail, we will try to persuade with our acts. We will always be willing to talk and seek fair compromise, but we are ready to suffer when necessary and even risk our lives to become witnesses to the truth as we see it.

The way of nonviolence means a willingness to suffer and sacrifice. It may mean going to jail. If such is the case the resister must be willing to fill the jail houses of the South. It may even mean physical death. But if physical death is the price that a man must pay to free his children and his white brethren from a permanent death of the spirit, then nothing could be more redemptive.

What is the Negro's best defense against acts of violence inflicted upon him? As Dr. Kenneth Clark has said so eloquently, "His only defense is to meet every act of barbarity, illegality, cruelty and injustice toward an individual Negro with the fact that 100 more Negroes will present themselves in his place as potential victims." Every time one Negro school teacher is fired for believing in integration, a thousand others should be ready to take the same stand. If the oppressors bomb the home of one Negro for his protest, they must be made to realize that to press back the rising tide of the Negro's courage they will have to bomb hundreds more, and even then they will fail.

Faced with this dynamic unity, this amazing self-respect, this willingness to suffer, and this refusal to hit back, the oppressor will find, as oppressors have always found, that he is glutted with his own barbarity. Forced to stand before the world and his God splattered with the blood of his brother, he will call an end to his self-defeating massacre.

American Negroes must come to the point where they can say to their white brothers, paraphrasing the words of Gandhi: "We will match your capacity to inflict suffering with our capacity to endure suffering. We will meet your physical force with soul force. We will not hate you, but we cannot in all good conscience obey your unjust laws. Do to us what you will and we will still love you. Bomb our homes and threaten our children; send your hooded perpetrators of violence into our communities and drag us out on some wayside road, beating us and leaving us half dead, and we will still love you. But we will soon wear you down by our capacity to suffer. And in winning our freedom we will so appeal to your heart and conscience that we will win you in the process."

Realism impels me to admit that many Negroes will find it difficult to follow the path of nonviolence. Some will consider it senseless; some will argue that they have neither the strength nor the courage to join in such a mass demonstration of nonviolent action. As E. Franklin Frazier points out in *Black Bourgeoisie,* many Negroes are occupied in a middle-class struggle for status and prestige. They are more concerned about "conspicuous consumption" than about the cause of justice, and are probably not prepared for the ordeals and sacrifices involved in nonviolent action. Fortunately, however, the success of this method is not dependent on its unanimous acceptance. A few Negroes in every community, unswervingly committed to the nonviolent way, can persuade hundreds of others at least to use nonviolence as a technique and serve as the moral force to awaken the slumbering national conscience. Thoreau was thinking of such a creative minority when he said: "I know this well, that if one thousand, if one hundred, if ten men whom I could name—if ten honest men only—aye, if one honest man, in the state of Massachusetts, ceasing to hold slaves, were actually to withdraw from the copartnership, and be locked up in the county jail therefore, it would be the abolition of slavery in America. For it matters not how small the beginning may seem to be, what is once well done is done forever."

3. Life in a Lifeboat

Are we ever justified in taking the life of another to save our own? This is the issue confronted by Edmond Cahn in his account of nine crew members and thirty-two passengers adrift in a sinking lifeboat.

At the very end of the piece, Cahn suggests that perhaps the earth is like the lifeboat of the William Brown *and that the problem of duty is one of our common moral dilemmas. We can begin to see how one's sense of obligation to the law can be broken by the force of circumstances.*

Holmes was a seaman on the William Brown, *which set sail from Liverpool for Philadelphia in 1841. The ship struck an iceberg some 250 miles from Newfoundland and soon began to sink. Two boats were lowered. The captain, various members of the crew, and a passenger got into one of them and, after six days on the open sea, were picked up and brought to land. The other boat was called the "long-boat"; it was leaky and might easily be swamped. Into it Holmes jumped along with the first mate, seven other seaman, and thirty-two passengers—about twice as many as the boat could hold under the most favorable conditions of wind and weather. Just as the long-boat was about to pull away from the wreck, Holmes, hearing the agonized cries of a mother for her little daughter who had been left behind in the panic, dashed back at the risk of instant death, found the girl and carried her under his arm into the long-boat. The sailors rowed and the passengers bailed, but the over-weighted long-boat, drifting between blocks of floating ice, sank lower and lower as a steady rain fell on the sea. The wind began to freshen, the sea grew heavy, and waves splashed over the bow. Then, after the first mate had twice given the order, Holmes and the rest of the crew began to throw the male passengers overboard. Two married men and a little boy were spared, but the fourteen remaining male passengers were cast over, and two women—devoted sisters of one of the victims—voluntarily leaped to join their brother in his death. The long-boat stayed afloat. The next morning Holmes spied a sail in the distance, exerted himself heroically to attract notice of the passing vessel, and eventually brought about the rescue of everyone left in the boat.*

When the survivors arrived in Philadelphia, the mate and most of the seamen, hearing talk of prosecution, disappeared. Holmes was put on trial for manslaughter.

In his charge to the jury as to the law, the judge stated that passengers must be saved in preference to all seamen except those who are indispensable to

From Edmond Cahn, **The Moral Decision: Right and Wrong in the Light of the Amercian Law** (Bloomington: Indiana University Press, 1955). Reprinted by permission.

operating the boat. If no seaman can possibly be dispensed with, then the victims must be chosen from among the passengers by casting lots, provided—as in this case—there is time enough to do so.

The jury found Holmes guilty but recommended mercy. He was sentenced to six months' imprisonment at hard labor, in addition to the nine months he had already spent in jail awaiting his trial.

No human being has ever asked to be born and no hour passes without its toll of perfectly sane suicides. The two sisters in the Holmes case are not to be looked upon as sacrificing themselves for the benefit of their fellow-passengers or as acting in irrational panic. They no longer possessed anything of worth to yield up as a sacrifice, for without their brother whom they loved, they simply did not care to remain in this life. And so they took their departure from it quite calmly, one of them pausing only long enough to ask for a dress to put around her. If the value of being alive is to be taken for granted as self-evident, how can it be denied so often and with such irrevocable sincerity?

This question could never be resolved if our appraisal of human life were a strictly *subjective process.* From the subjective point of view, the value of being alive varies not only from man to man according to the individual's relative status and destiny; more than that, it varies within the estimation of each selfsame individual from hour to hour according to his mood, the way the sun feels on the pores of his skin, and the chemicals bubbling in his viscera.

Suddenly, life may seem precious because a member of the opposite sex has smiled and extended a compliment, or because an unexpected copper coin has been found in the pocket of an old coat. Another time it may taste like filthy grit in the mouth because a certain letter has not arrived, because a cripple has come into view, or because some cluster of strangers have burst into an unexplained fit of laughter, the proverbial "laughter of fools—like the crackling of thorns under a pot." A moment later, the incident has slipped into the past and the mood becomes neutral again. All these states may be very real to the one who experiences them, but they fluctuate too irrationally and violently to furnish any standard for moral judgment.

When we turn to *objective* examinations of the value of being alive, it would be wiser not to expect a very optimistic appraisal. Considering the sum-total of human woe, disease, and bafflement, we may wonder that a net result of positive value—however small—is ever arrived at. An objective appraisal entitled to great consideration has been preserved for us in the Babylonian Talmud, which recounts how one famous school of rabbis disputed with another famous school for two and a half years. One school held it would have been better if man had not been created, and the other school contended it was better that man had been created than if he had not been created. At the end of that period, they finally took a vote, and it was found that the majority held it would have been much better had man not been created, but that since he had been created, it is his duty to examine his past actions, or according to others, to be careful of his future actions.

This estimate brings us to some very important distinctions that must be kept in view at all points in our study. They are distinctions between an *answer,* a *rule for conduct,* and a *decision.* These rabbis were giving an answer to a general question, an answer that embodied certain attitudes, empirical observations, and value judgments. They were not making either a rule for conduct or a decision, that is, either a standard for judging and punishing or a disposition of some specific human predicament to which the attitudes and evaluations developed in the *answer* might become applicable in one way or another. To answer that it would have been better if man had not been created is not the same as to legislate that a man in general has the right to save his life by ending the life of someone else, or to decide that Seaman Holmes in particular was justified under all the circumstances of his own unique crisis. On the contrary, the Talmud itself rejects the plea of necessity as an excuse for taking life. Thus it is that judgments change their tenor when they are meant to be acted on in the incidents of daily living.

The objective view does not hold that under every conceivable human set of circumstances each human life has an indestructible value. As everyone knows, the law has its published list of justifiable homicides (killing in self-defense) and excusable homicides (killing by mere accident); it drafts men into the armed forces to risk death in defense of their country, and if they commit certain types of crime, it deliberately puts them to death by hanging, asphyxiation, or electrocution. To hold that my life is not worth enough objectively to justify saving it by destroying yours is not necessarily to assign a very high value to either life. When cases arise in the civil courts involving suits for money-compensation, it is notorious that more money will be awarded for an injury that, with at least the appearance of permanency, takes away one's economic earning-power than for an injury that, with indisputable permanency, takes away one's life; and in most cases where the person killed is too young an infant to have demonstrated his capacity to earn money, very little will be granted to his family by way of damages.

Interestingly enough, the United States Supreme Court and the British House of Lords, though confronting the question in connection with quite different types of litigation, both decided unanimously that to be alive is in the eyes of the law preferable to not being alive. The American opinion, written by Justice Holmes, affords an example of strictly objective appraisal. A man by the name of Perovich had been convicted of murder in the first degree and was sentenced to be hanged. President Taft commuted his sentence to life-imprisonment. Perovich claimed the President had no power to do this without obtaining his consent, because the Constitution gave the President only a right to "pardon" an offense completely, to shorten the period of imprisonment, or reduce the amount of a fine, but not the right to change one form of punishment (death) to another (life-imprisonment). This contention Holmes rejected, saying: "By common understanding imprisonment for life is a less penalty than death." Just to continue in the land of the living—though with expectations as wretched as Perovich's—was held to be somewhat better than death. The appraisal was objective: Perovich the murderer could not have been jettisoned with impunity if Seaman Holmes had found him in the long-boat.

Once we grant that every human life has some value, the American courts give us very little additional information by which to ascertain the elements of that value. This vagueness—justifiable perhaps for other considerations but disappointing to our inquiry—is due to the fact that, when a person sues because he has been injured or his estate sues because he has been killed, American courts do not *separately* evaluate the loss he sustained in having his expectancy of life shortened or terminated, nor do they award separate damages for the abbreviation of this life expectancy. They usually consider the loss of expectancy as part of the general claim for damages. The English do segregate this item and, doing so, have found it necessary to state officially what elements should go into evaluating the loss of an expected portion of one's life. Suppose a child is killed—deprived of his expectancy of life—at the age of two and one-half: is the judge warranted in telling the jury that, when they come to assess the damages, they may presume "that human life is, on the whole, good"? If the judge sits without a jury, may he presume so?

No—in the unanimous judgment of the House of Lords, Britain's highest court—he may not. He may not make this optimistic assumption, then consult the statistical tables of mortality and life expectancy, and go on in a crude fashion to allow so many pounds sterling for each year that the child has lost. "It would be fallacious to assume, for this purpose, that all human life is continuously an enjoyable thing, so that the shortening of it calls for compensation, to be paid to the deceased's estate, on a quantitative basis. The ups and downs of life, its pains and sorrows, as well as its joys and pleasures—all that makes up 'life's fitful fever'—have to be allowed for in the estimate."

What, then, should the trier of the facts take into consideration in such a case? What view should guide him in evaluating the child's lost prospect of happiness? His view should be directed to the circumstances of the specific individual life that has been destroyed; it should be *projective*. "If the character or habits of the individual were calculated to lead him to a future of unhappiness or despondency, that would be a circumstance justifying a smaller award. It is significant that, at any rate in one case of which we were informed, the jury refused to award any damages under this [loss of expectancy of life] head at all." Nor should the test be whether the deceased person *subjectively* had the ability to appreciate that staying alive would bring him a measure of happiness: what, for instance, could an infant know on that score? It is necessary rather to estimate "what kind of future on earth the victim might have enjoyed, whether he had justly estimated that future or not." Here in this case of an extremely young victim, the high court saw so many uncertainties as to the child's future prospects, so many unsettled possibilities and lurking risks, that the award must be smaller than for some mature individual, whose prospects would have become more definite and susceptible of calculation as the years flowed by.

Prospects—what are "prospects" when we come to estimate the chances of happiness in life? Are they the "great expectations," perhaps, that former generations conceived of in terms of comfortable inheritances, well-kept lawns, and the solemn descent of social rank? Quite a few commoners filled with dreams and envies might be inclined to think so; but not the House of Lords. They knew better, and nobly said:

"I would add that, in the case of a child, as in the case of an adult, I see no reason why the proper sum to be awarded should be greater because the social position or prospects of worldly possessions are greater in one case than another. Lawyers and judges may here join hands with moralists and philosophers and declare that the degree of happiness to be attained by a human being does not depend on wealth or status." (On hearing which, the moralist, not accustomed to or altogether comfortable in such august company, may murmur: Wisdom consists in recognizing the worthlessness of the baubles *before* one holds them in his hands.)

Having announced these principles, the House of Lords then proceeded to reduce by five-sixths the sum the trial judge had awarded on the mistaken assumption "that human life is, on the whole, good." Two hundred pounds would be quite enough, and would have been excessive "if it were not that the circumstances of the infant were most favourable." The amount seems small for a whole life's expectancy, and cynics may remark that any of the high judges would willingly have paid his doctor much more to prolong his own existence for just a few months. But pounds for a life that still breathes are incommensurable with pounds for a life that can never breathe again, incommensurable in practical terms because we cannot know what horrors the dead infant was spared by its death, incommensurable in moral terms because the doctor's fee is a purchase only of his services, not of that which cannot morally be bought, or sold, or trafficked in. The House of Lords was evaluating what had been lost and was irrecoverable; the life of a living unharmed child is not in the same realm as the pound sterling.

But if a living person is incommensurable with money, is he commensurable with something else—that is, with other living humans? The United States Court in the Holmes case must have thought he was, for it announced that, if passengers or sailors, as the case may be, must be thrown into the sea in order to save the other members of the group, the terrible choice should be made by casting lots. Shall we assent to this?

The sailor, says the Court, must sacrifice himself first, unless he cannot be dispensed with. Why? Is not his life worth as much or as little as the passenger's? Of course it is, but he has burdened it with a very specific duty, and, though the circumstances of the long-boat might appear so desperate as to cancel all other social conventions and civil obligations, this one they could not cancel because it was expressly conceived and designed to yoke him in just such a plight, to bind him in conscience and in law, and to drive him open-eyed and willing to whatever course might be necessitated, including his own extinction. The power to preserve one's life is not a right where it has been put in pledge not for money or merchandise but for the lives of others, and where war, disaster at sea, or some other stroke of maleficent chance forecloses the pledge. Holmes needed no judge's summons when he scurried back to the sinking *William Brown* to rescue the little girl who had been left aboard. For—whatever the value of being alive may be—we all know perfectly well that there are many things more valuable; and while we hope both openly and secretly that we shall not be called upon to demonstrate our scheme of values at the cost of our lives, we must hold on to believing in our capacity to make ourselves do so, even if the occasion should prove so cruel as to allow time for reflection.

In the long-boat, there was such time, time—if passengers must be thrown into the sea—to select by casting lots. The judge said that would have been the only acceptable procedure, analogous in its outcome to a choice made not by man but by "destiny." Since some must be killed or all must die, let "destiny" choose among them. Some must be killed, it seemed, for the male passengers did not volunteer to lighten the boat by leaving it; on the contrary, before being thrust into the sea, they had tried by offers of bribes and by main force to stay aboard. "Women and children first" may or may not have been the maxim that governed their conduct in the initial moments of panic; they could not agree that it remained applicable after many long hours had passed and the men could take thought in their desperation.

It is rather presumptuous of us—sitting dry in our safety—to pass judgment of any kind on those poor wretches in the long-boat. May we be spared ever coming to a pass like theirs, spared the bleakness of such a choice! May we likewise be spared the duty of serving on a jury in any comparable case, or of charging a jury with the law as to what men are required to do in an ultimate crisis! If we feel free now to offer comments on the setting in which Holmes was compelled to do what he did, let us at least cling to the grace of humility and of self-doubt. Let us rather judge Holmes' judge than Holmes. It was the judge who pointed to casting lots as the single permissible solution.

In the literature of our subject, at least three different opinions have been voiced concerning the resort to lots. One is that lots must be used because no one has suggested a better alternative method of selection. The second view is that matters of this kind should be left to the judgment of the jury as individual cases may arise and that it is unwise to erect any rigid legal rule to control the actions of people in such dire necessity. The third view is that we should reject lots because while life remains there may be ground for hope and no one can be quite certain that a rescuing sail will not come into sight. (This third view seems to deny that we can ever reach enough certainty as to our factual beliefs to be morally justified in the action we take, but Judge Cardozo, the author of this view, would probably have been among the first to repudiate such a position. Only the actual disappearance of the long-boat under the water would afford a mathematical certainty that time had run out.)

It seems to me that we are dealing here with what may be called "morals of the last days"; that is to say, such morals as men may be summoned to display when all the usual differences between man and man become irrelevant because the differences have to do with a life that continues—if not for one, then for another. The crisis in the long-boat was apocalyptic in character, the kind of crisis in which, as Jesus saw, family ties, earthly possessions, and distinctions of every conceivable kind become null and void. In a strait of this extremity, all men are reduced—or raised, as one may choose to denominate it—to members of the genus, mere congeners and nothing else. Truly and literally, all were "in the same boat," and thus none could be saved separately from the others.

I am driven to conclude that otherwise—that is, if none sacrifice themselves of free will to spare the others—they must all wait and die together. For where all have become congeners, pure and simple, no one can save himself by killing another. In such a setting and at such a price, he has no moral individuality left to save. Under the terms of the moral constitution, it will be *wholly* his self that he kills in his vain effort to preserve himself. The "morals of the last days" leave him a generic creature only; in such a setting, so remote from the differentiations of normal existence, every person in the boat embodies the entire genus. Whoever saves one, saves the whole human race; whoever kills one, kills mankind.

So, in all humility, I would put aside the talk of casting lots, not only because the crisis involves stakes too high for gambling and responsibilities too deep for destiny, but also because no one can win in such a lottery, no one can survive intact by means of the killing.

Finally, would it be permissible to suggest that this planet we live on is not entirely unlike the long-boat of the *William Brown?* By all means, provided one bears in mind that at most the metaphor can provide only a moral attitude or an answer, not a moral decision.

4. Who Makes the Rules?

If the law is not to be mere coercion, people must consent to the rules that guide their lives. It is doubtful, however, if such consent can ever be achieved if people do not have a hand in formulating what the rules will be. Howard Becker argues that for some people there are social rules, including legal rules, that are viewed as no more than an arbitrary imposition. Our theories about the causes of behavior that deviates from the rules cannot afford to ignore the sense of alienation of those who feel they have played no part in the making of the law.

I have been using the term "outsiders" to refer to those people who are judged by others to be deviant and thus to stand outside the circle of "normal" members of the group. But the term contains a second meaning, whose analysis leads to another important set of sociological problems: "outsiders," from the point of view of the person who is labeled deviant, may be the people who make the rules he had been found guilty of breaking.

Social rules are the creation of specific social groups. Modern societies are not simple organizations in which everyone agrees on what the rules are and how they are to be applied in specific situations. They are, instead, highly diffentiated along social class lines, ethnic lines, occupational lines, and cultural lines. These groups need not and, in fact, often do not share the same rules. The problems they face in dealing with their environment, the history and traditions they carry with them, all lead to the evolution of different sets of rules. Insofar as the rules of various groups conflict and contradict one another, there will be disagreement about the kind of behavior that is proper in any given situation.

Italian immigrants who went on making wine for themselves and their friends during Prohibition were acting properly by Italian immigrant standards, but were breaking the law of their new country (as, of course, were many of their Old American neighbors). Medical patients who shop around for a doctor may, from the perspective of their own group, be doing what is necessary to protect their health by making sure they get what seems to them the best possible doctor; but, from the perspective of the physician, what they do is wrong because it breaks down the trust the patient ought to put in his physician. The lower-class delinquent who fights for his "turf" is only doing what he considers necessary and right, but teachers, social workers, and police see it differently.

While it may be argued that many or most rules are generally agreed to by all members of a society, empirical research on a given rule generally reveals variation in people's attitudes. Formal rules, enforced by some specially constituted group, may differ from those actually thought appropriate by most people. Factions in a group may disagree on what I have called actual operating rules. Most important for the study of behavior ordinarily labeled deviant, the perspectives of the people who engage in the behavior are likely to be quite different from those of the people who condemn it. In this latter situation, a person may feel that he is being judged according to rules he has had no hand in making and does not accept, rules forced on him by outsiders.

To what extent and under what circumstances do people attempt to force their rules on others who do not subscribe to them? Let us distinguish two cases. In the first, only those who are actually members of the group have any interest in making and enforcing certain rules. If an orthodox Jew disobeys the laws of kashruth only other orthodox Jews will regard this as a transgression; Christians or nonorthodox Jews will not consider this deviance and would have no interest in interfering. In the second case, members of a group consider it important to their welfare that members of certain other groups obey certain rules. Thus, people consider it extremely important that those who practice the healing arts abide by certain rules; this is the reason the state licenses physicians, nurses, and others, and forbids anyone who is not licensed to engage in healing activities.

To the extent that a group tries to impose its rules on other groups in the society, we are presented with a second question: Who can, in fact, force others to accept their rules and what are the causes of their success? This is, of course, a question of political and economic power. Later we will consider the political and economic process through which rules are created and enforced. Here it is enough to note that people are in fact always *forcing* their rules on others, applying them more or less against the will and without the consent of those others. By and large, for example, rules are made for young people by their elders. Though the youth of this country exert a powerful influence culturally—the mass media of communication are tailored to their interests, for instance—many important kinds of rules are made for our youth by adults. Rules regarding school attendance and sex behavior are not drawn up with regard to the problems of adolescence. Rather, adolescents find themselves surrounded by rules about these matters which have been made by older and more settled people. It is considered legitimate to do this, for youngsters are considered neither wise enough nor responsible enough to make proper rules for themselves.

In the same way, it is true in many respects that men make the rules for women in our society (though in America this is changing rapidly).

Negroes find themselves subject to rules made for them by whites. The foreign-born and those otherwise ethnically peculiar often have their rules made for them by the Protestant Anglo-Saxon minority. The middle class makes rules the lower class must obey—in the schools, the courts, and elsewhere.

Differences in the ability to make rules and apply them to other people are essentially power differentials (either legal or extralegal). Those groups whose social position gives them weapons and power are best able to enforce their rules. Distinctions of age, sex, ethnicity, and class are all related to differences in power, which accounts for differences in the degree to which groups so distinguished can make rules for others.

In addition to recognizing that deviance is created by the responses of people to particular kinds of behavior, by the labeling of that behavior as deviant, we must also keep in mind that the rules created and maintained by such labeling are not universally agreed to. Instead, they are the object of conflict and disagreement, part of the political process of society.

PART II

WHAT CAUSES CRIME ?

INTRODUCTION[1]

James F. Short, Jr.

The "Why?" of crime and delinquency is of interest to a variety of people—to policemen and parents, judges and juries, social workers and social scientists, and to the public at large, which puzzles over the apparent paradox of widespread criminal and delinquent behavior in an age of such technological accomplishment and affluence as the world has never known.

Our ideas about crime causation similarly are shaped by a variety of influences—by theological and moral premises, by mass media, and by the arguments of persons who have participated in crime as well as those who have systematically studied crime. In this essay, however, our interest is not so much in "Who done it?" in the popular sense as it is in the state of scientific knowledge concerning crime causation. We will adopt the perspective of scholarly inquiry, because we are interested in objective, systematic, and generalized knowledge of the nature of crime and criminals rather than insight or knowledge about why a particular crime was committed by a particular individual. This does not mean, however, that all other perspectives will be ignored, for scientists and scholars can profit from the experience and observations of others. But it does mean that we will rest our conclusions on appraisal of evidence that has been collected within the framework of science. For example, several of the selections in Part I of this anthology consist of accounts from fiction, from highly personal experience, or from those who are vitally involved in the fight for civil liberties or the control of crime. They are interesting and informative. But now we must look at the accumulated body of systematic knowledge about crime causation.

The bulk of the systematic research and literature on crime causation represents the efforts of partisans of psychological and sociological perspectives. Both groups attempt to make sense out of facts (or assumed facts) about crime and delinquency, criminals and delinquents. They do so often from fundamentally different points of view, and these differences give rise to many arguments between them. These controversies turn out to be rather pointless, however, when it is recognized that all behavior results from combinations of *actors* and *situations* in which action occurs. Psychologists and social psychologists approach the study of any phenomenon chiefly from the perspective of the individual—his attitudes, values, temperament, and so on, all of which are likely to be grouped under the term "personality." They are concerned with the process of learning and personality development and with the reaction of different personalities to common situations. Sociologists, on the other hand, mainly focus on the nature of social systems and on how behavior is distributed within these systems. They observe that behavior—including crime and delinquency—is not randomly distributed in any population, but systematically varies among different categories of persons. Their major interest is how these categories of persons "fit in" with various social systems, on status and role variations in these systems, and on the cultural and institutional arrangements within the systems. Both of these perspectives—the individual and the nature of social systems—are legitimate and important if crime and delinquency are to be understood and controlled with any effectiveness.

Despite centuries of human concern with "deviant" behavior, such as crime and delinquency, and decades of scientific attention, we possess little certain knowledge of causation. We know a great deal about the *correlates* of crime and delinquency—how they vary in relation to other phenomena. But this does not mean that we possess equal knowledge of causation. There are many explanations that help to make sense out of many of the facts concerning crime and delinquency. But no explanation makes sense out of all that is known. This essay and the selections that follow are concerned with both the facts of crime and delinquency and their interpretation in the form of theories that purport to be, or strive toward, a general explanation of these phenomena. Posing the problem in this manner means that we will not be interested specifically in what motivated Joe X to commit murder, burglary, or vandalism, but, instead, in what is known about general patterns of motivation and the general process of learning and its development in persons, young and old, male and female, and so on. We will be interested in specific factors associated with particular crimes only to the extent that they help us to understand general patterns and contribute to general explanations.

Without attempting to cover the history of theories concerning crime and delinquency or the precise nature of all theories now held by one "school" or another, we will sketch major variations in the behavior to be explained and the state of current theoretical formulations. It is appropriate to begin the search for explanation with biological theories of crime. Man is, after all, a biological creature—subject to the law of heredity like other animals, the result of an extremely long process of evolution. Life begins as a process of biological creation, and biological factors are important to human behavior throughout life. Another reason to begin at this point, however, is that the first type of scientific study of criminals involved examination of biological features of criminals, as shown briefly in the selection from Cesare Lombroso that follows this essay. In Europe, L. A. J. Quetelet and others who were pioneers in the study of human ecology had earlier begun investigation of the social distribution of criminal acts, but it was Lombroso and his followers who first focused systematically on the *criminal* in an attempt to study him by objective means.

The notion that criminals represent a distinct biological type has been effectively disposed of by subsequent investigations with better samples, but the search continues, as noted by the editors of this volume. Studies of siblings, including twins, and of other biological phenomena, such as glandular functioning and body type, suggest that biological factors and processes always interact with social phenomena to bring about such correlations as exist between them and crime and delinquency. These biological phenomena include intelligence, which is now recognized as extremely varied in nature and the product of complex interactions of biological heritage and social experience. Much remains to be discovered concerning these matters, and the growing area of common interest of biological and social science—sometimes called sociobiology—promises to yield new insights and knowledge concerning the etiology of crime and delinquency.

The conclusion that biological phenomena *interact* with social experiences in the production of crime is hardly surprising. Crime, after all, is a matter of legal definition, and, as noted in Part I, definitions of what constitutes crime vary enormously from time to time and from place to place. Quite aside from contrary evidence concerning strict biological determinism of crime, it is well to note that many biological factors alleged to "cause" crime are *constants*—that is, they remain the same over time and place where definitions of crime vary greatly. They are constant, also, among individuals who exhibit very different behavior patterns, including criminal and noncriminal behavior. A constant factor cannot produce change except in combination with a changing factor. Thus, when we wish to understand why crime is more prevalent among males than among females, we do not seek an explanation in the biological facts of sex, because the difference between male and female crime rates varies greatly under different (changing) circumstances. These differences have been much greater in earlier periods of our history than they are today. They are also smaller among some social groups than among others and for some offenses than for others. This explanation does not mean that sex is thereby dismissed as a possible motivating factor in some types of criminal behavior or that being male or female is unimportant to understanding behavior. But the biological fact of being male or female cannot itself explain the variation expressed in different rates of crime.

The question we must answer, therefore, is what is the nature of the circumstances that produce these variations? The same question applies to all empirical regularities of crime, whether the effort be to explain why particular individuals have become criminal (or why they have not) or why the ratio of criminals to noncriminals is higher in one group than another.

A complete catalog of empirical regularities of crime and delinquency is beyond the scope of this essay, but a few examples will serve to introduce our further consideration of explanatory theories.

1. Crime rates are higher for males than for females, with much variation as noted above.
2. Crime rates vary by age. In the total population, crime is especially characteristic of young persons. The "age of maximum criminality" varies greatly by offense and by sex, but "for all crimes, and for each specific crime, the rate decreases steadily from the age of maximum criminality to the end of life."[2]
3. Crime rates vary among different racial and ethnic groups. Within

each group, however, crime rates also vary greatly, in response to social conditions. Thus, as immigrant groups came to this country, rates of delinquency among their children characteristically were very high. As these groups entered into the "mainstream" of American life, and as they were accepted into this mainstream, rates of delinquency correspondingly decreased. Present high-rate groups include Negroes, Puerto Ricans, and Mexicans—all of whom have experienced great difficulty in achieving acceptance in the United States. American Orientals—an apparent exception to this overall pattern because of their low delinquency rates—have retained their cultural identity, for a variety of reasons, to a much greater degree than have other incoming groups.

4. As measured by crimes known to the police, arrests, court appearances, and convictions, crime and delinquency are heavily concentrated in the slum sections of larger cities. They are directly related, also, to the degree of urbanization, although in recent years rural and suburban rates have tended to rise more rapidly than urban rates. Within cities, delinquency rates are highest in blighted, inner-city areas characterized by physical deterioration, the encroachment of industry, and the concentration of other social problems such as poverty, suicide, and mental illness. The geographical concentration of delinquency over the years for both boys and girls (whether measured by arrests, truancy rates, first court appearances, or recidivism) has led social scientists to refer to these areas of concentration as "delinquency areas." Rates for other areas vary inversely with their distance from delinquency areas.
5. On the basis of ecological findings that show a close association between delinquency rates and poverty, social class has come to be considered an important variable in the etiology of delinquency. In large cities, data gathered by means of field observation and self-reports confirm official records suggesting the greater likelihood of involvement in delinquency by lower-class children. However, studies conducted in several small cities and towns fail to demonstrate greater delinquency involvement by lower-class youngsters. A few studies of middle- and upper-class delinquency exist but much additional research is needed. The existence of white collar crime, that is, crime committed by a person of respectability and high social status in the course of his occupation, reminds us that neither social class nor poverty and its associated problems can account for all crime although these factors may be quite relevant to explanations of particular types of crime.
6. Although the research literature fails to demonstrate the existence of a criminal or delinquent personality as such, there is little doubt that persons characterized by various personality disturbances are more vulnerable to the stresses of life; and they are more likely to choose delinquent "solutions" to their problems than are those whose personalities are less disturbed. There is strong presumptive evidence that delinquents are characterized by a general lack of social abilities —for whatever reason—than are nondelinquents.

Although a part of all these variations may be due to differences in official discovery (and, hence, reporting) of offenses and offenders and in handling cases once discovery is made, their persistence in study after study, by investigators of considerable sophistication, suggests that they are not simply statistical artifacts and, thus, cannot be "explained away." On a very broad theoretical level, these variations suggest a conclusion of the greatest importance, namely, that *crime and delinquency are types of social behavior and they are closely related to other forms of social behavior.*

Given certain facts that a theory (or theories) must "fit," one way to approach the problem of causation is to ask what high-rate groups have in common—or, more specifically, what types of social experiences occur with greater frequency among these groups than among low-rate groups. Again, we note that this question may be phrased in the terms of a variety of perspectives. What types of personalities become delinquent or criminal in these groups? What types of experiences produce such personalities? Or, focusing more specifically on criminal or delinquent behavior, to what extent and how are crime and delinquency learned? How do the social systems in which different categories of persons participate contribute to differential experiences relative to crime?

A great many ideas have been offered in an attempt to answer such questions. No single theory has proved adequate to the task, although some theories are able to make sense out of more of the data than are others. It may be that crime refers to such varied phenomena that a general explanatory theory is impossible. Donald R. Cressey reminds us, however, that

> *General theories about criminal behavior as a whole should guide the research and theory directed at explaining particular kinds of criminal behavior and studies of particular kinds of criminal behavior should lead to either strengthening or modifying the general theories. If no one general theory can explain all criminal behavior, then it is desirable to define precisely the areas to which it does apply, so that several congruous theories will, when taken together, explain all crime.*[3]

The remainder of this essay will examine a few of the more promising leads suggested by recent theories and empirical investigations. The search for explanation, both psychological and sociological, typically takes one of two forms. Investigators either study all offenders in a particular population, for example, a court, a prison, or a clinic; or they make some prior selection of a particular *type* of offender from such a population, for example, an auto thief, a sex offender, or an embezzler. Typically, also, the investigator focuses on factors or processes of particular interest to his own theoretical persuasion, rather than on the totality of the offender's experience or background. As a result of these differences, it is often not clear just how the findings from one study or set of studies contribute to a general theory of criminal behavior or to particular kinds of such behavior. This situation, it must be admitted, makes it difficult to summarize what is known about crime and delinquency causation.

The complexity of the psychology of crime, from both legal and behavioral points of view, will be clear from the selections included under this topic in this volume. The classic psychoanalytic position—delineating as basic components of personality the id, ego, and superego—is well represented by the Franz Alexander and Hugo Staub selection. Here, all behavior is seen to result in part from the balance achieved between "drive energy," which is fundamentally biological in nature, and the sense of reality and conscience that develop through socialization experiences. In the process of "growing up," innate forces or energy sources (conceptualized as sexual in nature in the classic statement of the position, but broadened somewhat by later formulations) must be both gratified and controlled by the individual. One learns through experience to cope both with the restrictions of the external environment and with internalized values (including his conscience). Psychoanalysts stress the importance to basic personality structure of very early socialization experiences, particularly in the family.

Psychoanalysts and psychiatrists thus remind us that any person is a potential criminal and that "Every man has within him the capacity to commit the most objectionable antisocial acts, no matter how civilized or sophisticated his social training has made him."[4] Although "Any weakness of the control system is believed to be conducive to criminality,"[5] not all criminal or delinquent acts are seen as resulting from defects in this system, and crime in some situations may be quite rational and psychologically "healthy." This point of view sees crime as "an adaptation to life stress."[6] It recognizes the relevance for such adaptation of many aspects of the human condition, noting that crime "is best understood in terms of the manner in which the individual experiences the biological, psychological, and socially determined situations of his existence."[7]

In their attempt to understand more fully the variety and complexity of the phenomena so loosely labeled as crime and delinquency, scholars of both psychological and sociological persuasion have proposed a variety of classifications of such behavior. Seymour L. Halleck notes:

All psychiatric classifications separate delinquency which appears to be socially learned behavior from delinquency which is believed to be related to individual psychopathology. Psychiatrists concede that a child who has a stable home life and a relatively well-integrated personality can become a delinquent if he is exposed to a social environment which condones antisociality.[8]

Halleck also notes that psychiatric classifications of delinquency "seem to rely upon judgments of the degree of unreasonableness of the delinquent's behavior."[9]

Socialized or environmentally determined delinquents are described as behaving in a more reasonable manner than unsocialized delinquents. . . . Even the most sociologically determined delinquent act is often motivated by wishes which are not ordinarily examined closely enough to determine the extent of their actual "normality." At the same time the emotionally disturbed delinquent will not violate the law unless confronted with certain social conditions.[10]

For their part, sociologists apparently (to the investigator) have focused on consistent and homogeneous behavior patterns and have sought to understand them by reference to the social conditions with which they are associated and to nonpathological learning processes. Sociologists are quick to point out that the existence of fundamental drives in every individual cannot explain why some persons "choose" a delinquent or criminal way of behaving as a solution to problems of stress, whereas others behave in a conventional manner frequently despite great personal and environmental stress. Psychiatrists, too, are much concerned with these problems and admit that the theory of crime as adaptation to life stress "is primarily useful in understanding maladaptive or unreasonable criminal behavior."[11] There is, in fact, increasing evidence of interest in the data and theories of their counterparts in related disciplines by both psychological and sociological protagonists.

Among sociologists the most widely held general theory of crime and delinquency considers that persons learn these behaviors in the same way that they learn conventional behaviors, that is, in interaction with persons in a process of communication. The most influential learning environments consist of intimate, personal groups, and these are regarded as primary in the acquisition of motives, values, and rationalizations conducive to crime and of the techniques of crime. Edwin Sutherland referred to this theory as "differential association," by which he meant that through association with other persons one becomes exposed to both criminal and noncriminal patterns of behavior. A person becomes delinquent (or criminal) "because of an excess of definitions favorable to violations of law."[12] The research problem then becomes one of specifying the nature of one's associations; specifically, Sutherland suggested the importance of the frequency, priority, duration, and intensity of associations conducive to criminal and conventional behavior, respectively. Sociologists have found answers to these questions in studies of juvenile groupings, such as those by Frederic M. Thrasher,[13] and Clifford R. Shaw and Henry D. McKay,[14] and in the articles by James F. Short, Jr., and Fred L. Strodtbeck, and by Harold Finestone, as reported in this volume, as well as in studies of the adult organization of crime. These "reference groups" are found to be important in establishing and maintaining one's self-image and the standards by which personal conduct is judged acceptable or unacceptable. When they have looked at the family life of delinquent youngsters to see what may have accounted for their exposure to patterns of delinquency, sociologists have tended to emphasize structural or cultural characteristics rather than psychic stress or the unconscious processes and mechanisms, which are the hallmark of psychiatric theories and investigations. There is, however, much overlapping between the two viewpoints and general agreement that experiences that expose the child to criminal values and opportunities are conducive to criminality. The amount of exposure necessary to produce particular types of delinquents or criminals is not easily resolved by the data. The precise mechanisms by which a delinquent act is produced are not clearly understood, and psychiatrists are more likely to emphasize the importance of stress produced by disturbed interpersonal relationships, whereas sociologists tend to emphasize available cultural opportunities and strains in the social structure that produce them.

Thus, sociologists have pointed to the fact that in blighted inner-city areas where crime, delinquency, and other social ills are concentrated, the traditional institutions of social control do not function effectively—large proportions of families are broken by separation, divorce, or death; political ignorance, apathy, or cynicism leads to manipulation from outside interests and ineffective representation; economic conditions of poverty and expressive religious movements without power to influence social conditions abound; control over behavior is relegated in many instances to inherently unstable institutional forms, such as gangs and semipublic gatherings on the street, in taverns, in poolrooms, and in private residences, all of which are turned to economic advantage as the location for "partying" behavior. The more traditional of these institutional forms tend to be dominated by interests outside the community rather than by indigenous leadership and participation. This picture has remained the same over successive generations of immigrants who have settled in these communities, complicated by the great cultural variation characteristic of immigrant groups. The "melting-pot" tradition in the United States was not produced without cost to those who were uprooted from traditional cultures and placed, many times at great disadvantage, in new cultural settings. Conflict between old and new cultures frequently created misunderstandings and great stress, particularly among the young who could not—or would not, because they were oriented toward the new life—retreat into the cultural islands established in the areas of first settlement by their parents.

Immigrant adjustment, disorganizing though it may have been, was temporary and self-healing. Most groups became assimilated into the mainstream of life in the United States and culture conflict disappeared, to be remembered—even celebrated—only on special occasions, such as the ethnic holiday St. Patrick's Day. Negro communities also possess these same self-healing tendencies, as recent research dramatically suggests.[15] Other traditions were also brought to this country by immigrant groups, including crime in various stages and types of organization. These, too, found fertile ground, as Daniel Bell's analysis demonstrates so brilliantly. Clearly, culture conflict is not a function simply of differing ethnic traditions but is firmly imbedded in the very fabric of "respectable" society as well.

This fabric is the focus of still another major sociological approach to the study of crime and delinquency. Robert K. Merton and others have pointed to stresses within American society that arise as a result of an open-class ideology, combined with emphasis upon material success and restricted opportunity for the achievement of success.[16] High aspirations are created for all to achieve the "good life," but different racial, ethnic, and class groupings are unequal in available opportunities for realization of these aspirations. "In this setting," Merton enjoins, "a cardinal American virtue, 'ambition,' promotes a cardinal American vice, 'deviant behavior.' "[17] Modifications and elaborations of this theory have sought to explain the emergence of a variety of delinquent and criminal subcultures, whereby certain patterns become "traditional," with common values, norms of conduct, and social arrangements among those who participate in these subcultures. Examples include conflict, criminal, and retreatist (largely use of drugs) delinquent subcultures, and various types of white collar, professional, and organized crime among adults. Juvenile and adult subcultures of these types are related in important and complex ways, just as are legitimate, or conventional, subcultures among youth and adults. The presence in a community of either or both legitimate and illegitimate opportunities and learning environments, and their relations with one another, are important factors in determination of the amount and type of criminal activity in the community.[18]

There is disagreement among sociologists, as there is among psychiatrists, concerning the precise mechanisms responsible for criminal and delinquent behavior and the degree of influence that should be attributed to various factors and processes. There is great need, and great opportunity, for articulation of theories at both of these levels. Both have been more successful in isolating important classes of variables, and in limited studies of their impact, than in accumulating and integrating knowledge gained within and between levels. Although much has been learned, no type of crime or delinquency has been studied thoroughly from both of these perspectives.

Conclusion

Crime and delinquency cannot be understood apart from the social and cultural contexts in which they occur. This is as true of types of crime that seem most often associated with psychological stress as it is of those where no such stress is present, or at least apparent. Cultural values define to an important degree what will be considered stressful and provide the framework within which interpersonal relations, including those within the family, occur. This conclusion is of great importance because interpersonal relations are the major source of stress related to personality disturbance.

It is not necessary to invoke pathologies of personality to explain many types of crime, for example, white collar crime, organized and professional crime, and much crime and delinquency that are specifically condoned within local cultural milieux. Particular individuals who participate in these patterns of behavior may, indeed, be characterized by psychological pathology, but many who participate apparently are not so characterized, and the existence of the pattern of crime or delinquency cannot be explained as the result of personal pathology.

Privately held values of individuals are less important to understanding why and in what form crime and delinquency occur than are the values of social systems in which these individuals participate and their status(es) and interaction with others in these systems. As an example, the behavior of Junior Johnson in the bootleg trade described in the selection from Tom Wolfe is unintelligible in terms of personal values, except as these reflect the cultural values of the system in which this action occurred. Similarly, white collar criminals are participants in social systems that prescribe types of behavior, some of which are in violation of laws. Their behavior is understandable (and predictable) only in terms of these prescriptions—rather than their personal values, which, after all, are quite respectable and certainly noncriminal in a conventional sense. The most important values in understanding the behavior of professional criminals and participants in organized crime are, as Sutherland and Bell argue so cogently, the values of the social systems in which these people are involved—including, particularly in the latter case, the values of success and admiration of the successful and the "extraordinary talent for compromise in politics and extremism in morality" that characterize the "American way of life." The behavior of Finestone's "cats" and Short and Strodtbeck's gang boys is unintelligible except in terms of the subcultures and the specific groups in which they participate. Particularly in the latter case, the status of a boy in his gang is seen to be important in defining situations that require action and in determining the appropriateness of a given action. Apropos the major point of this paragraph, values of the gang boys studied by Short and Strodtbeck and their associates were examined and compared with those of nongang boys from the same neighborhoods as the gang boys and of nongang boys from middle-class neighborhoods. The gang boys were found to espouse both the moral validity and the legitimacy of conventional middle-class values. In this respect they did not differ from either lower- or middle-class nongang boys. Within the group setting, however, the gang boys did not support these values and, in fact, actively discouraged their expression. Group values were not directed toward violation of the law, *as such,* but carrying them into action often involved the boys in law violation, as in such behavior as drinking, "making out" sexually, smoking marijuana, or interacting with members of rival gangs.

In all these types of behavior, it is clear that more is involved in causation than either "definitions favorable to violation of law," in the language of the most widely held sociological theory of criminal learning and motivation, or reaction to stress or the release of fundamental (and universal) drives deep within the human personality. In addition to the cultural and systemic considerations discussed above, we note that the fact that behavior is criminal often is irrelevant to the specific motivation of individual participants in such behavior. Although motivation is an extremely complex matter, it is clear that the motivation to engage in criminal and other types of deviant behavior often is provided by such conventionally applauded values as status among one's peers and loyalty to them, superior performance in one's job, and the achievement of political power and monetary reward. Still, the bulk (in terms of numbers of offenses) of "crime," consisting of small property offenses committed repeatedly by a vast army of "ordinary" criminals, is not readily understood—by social scientists or by anyone else.

We note, finally, that the control of crime and delinquency involves processes that are important to causation of these phenomena. Crime and delinquency are "social roles" as well as legally proscribed behaviors. The individual who is arrested and brought before a court and charged with an offense thereby acquires a new social definition, to be remarked upon in social discourse and remembered when important decisions are made, for example, when he seeks a job, credit, or a loan. The "labeling" phenomenon associated with the law and processes of law enforcement is an important aspect of crime causation that has been recently emphasized by social scientists.[19]

It will be clear to the reader of this anthology that not all the facts are in concerning crime and delinquency—their definition, etiology, and control. It should be clear that all the facts will *never* be in concerning these matters, given the complex and rapidly changing nature of our society. Crime and delinquency are integral to this society—they are brought into existence by legal definition, and they change with the law; the behaviors so designated are social in nature, responsive to social as well as psychological stress and/or development. The best we can do—but it is a great deal—is to continue the systematic and objective study of man in all his complexity, individually and collectively, in groups and in institutional arrangements, and to insist that efforts at the control of these phenomena be based on knowledge so generated. This does not mean that considerations of value to society should be neglected. Quite the contrary, for these considerations are paramount to the study of man—which, after all, is the proper study of mankind.

Notes

1. Material for this essay is based especially on the following sources: Albert K. Cohen and James F. Short, Jr., "Juvenile Delinquency," in Robert K. Merton and Robert A. Nisbet (eds.), *Contemporary Social Problems* (New York: Harcourt, Brace & World, 1966), Chap. 2; Donald R. Cressey, "Crime," in *ibid.,* Chap. 3; Robert A. Gordon, "Social Level, Social Disability, and Gang Interaction," *American Journal of Sociology,* 73 (July 1967), 42–62; Seymour L. Halleck, *Psychiatry and the Dilemmas of Crime* (New York: Harper & Row, 1967); James F. Short, Jr., "Juvenile Delinquency: The Sociocultural Context," in Lois W. Hoffman and Martin L. Hoffman (eds.), *Review of Child Development Research* (New York: Russell Sage Foundation, 1966), Vol. II; the President's Commission on Law Enforcement and Administration of Justice, *Task Force Report: Crime and Its Impact—An Assessment* (Washington, D.C.: U.S. Government Printing Office, 1967); the President's Commission on Law Enforcement and Administration of Justice, *Task Force Report: Juvenile Delinquency and Youth Crime* (Washington, D.C.: U.S. Government Printing Office, 1967).
2. Cressey, *op. cit.,* p. 147.
3. *Ibid.,* p. 182.
4. Halleck, *op. cit.,* p. 60.
5. *Ibid.,* p. 61.
6. *Ibid.,* p. 63.
7. *Ibid.*
8. *Ibid.,* p. 134.
9. *Ibid.,* p. 135.
10. *Ibid.*
11. *Ibid.,* p. 196.
12. Edwin H. Sutherland and Donald R. Cressey, *Principles of Criminology,* 6th ed. (Philadelphia: Lippincott, 1960).
13. Frederic M. Thrasher, *The Gang* (Chicago: University of Chicago Press, 1927; abridged, 1963).
14. Clifford R. Shaw and Henry D. McKay, *Juvenile Delinquency and Urban Areas* (Chicago: University of Chicago Press, 1942).
15. Henry D. McKay, "A Note on the Trends in Rates of Delinquency in Certain Areas of Chicago," in *Task Force Report: Juvenile Delinquency and Youth Crime, op. cit.,* pp. 114–118.
16. Robert K. Merton, *Social Theory and Social Structure,* rev. ed. (New York: Free Press, 1957).
17. *Ibid.,* p. 146.
18. For a review of these theories and data related to them, see James F. Short, Jr. (ed.), *Gang Delinquency and Delinquent Subcultures* (New York: Harper & Row, 1968).
19. See, for example, Howard S. Becker (ed.), *The Other Side: Perspectives on Deviance* (New York: Free Press, 1964).

Suggestions for Further Reading

Becker, Howard S. (ed.). *The Other Side: Perspectives on Deviance.* New York: Free Press, 1964.

Brown, Claude. *Manchild in the Promised Land.* New York: Macmillan, 1965.

Clinard, Marshall B., and Richard Quinney. *Criminal Behavior Systems: A Typology.* New York: Holt, Rinehart and Winston, 1967.

Cloward, Richard A., and Lloyd Ohlin. *Delinquency and Opportunity: A Theory of Delinquent Gangs.* New York: Free Press, 1960.

Cohen, Albert K. *Delinquent Boys.* New York: Free Press, 1955.

Giallombardo, Rose (ed.). *Juvenile Delinquency.* New York: Wiley, 1960.

Halleck, Seymour. *Psychiatry and the Dilemmas of Crime.* New York: Harper & Row, 1967.

Matza, David. *Delinquency and Drift.* New York: Wiley, 1964.

Maurer, David W. *The Big Con.* New York: Pocket Books, 1949.

Merton, Robert K. *Social Theory and Social Structure.* Rev. ed. New York: Free Press, 1957.

———, and Robert A. Nisbet (eds.). *Contemporary Social Problems.* New York: Harcourt, Brace & World, 1966.

President's Commission on Law Enforcement and Administration of Justice. *Task Force Report: Crime and Its Impact—An Assessment.* Washington, D.C.: U.S. Government Printing Office, 1967.

———. *Task Force Report: Organized Crime.* Washington, D.C.: U.S. Government Printing Office, 1967.

Shaw, Clifford R. *The Jack-Roller: A Delinquent Boy's Own Story.* Chicago: University of Chicago Press, 1966.

———, and Henry D. McKay. *Juvenile Delinquency and Urban Areas.* Rev. ed. Chicago: University of Chicago Press, 1968.

Short, James F., Jr. (ed.). *Gang Delinquency and Delinquent Subcultures.* New York: Harper & Row, 1968.

———, and Fred L. Strodtbeck, *Group Process and Gang Delinquency.* Chicago: University of Chicago Press, 1965.

Sutherland, Edwin H. *The Professional Thief.* Chicago: University of Chicago Press, 1937.

———, and Donald R. Cressey. *Principles of Criminology.* 6th ed. Philadelphia: Lippincott, 1960.

Thrasher, Frederic M. *The Gang: A Study of 1,313 Gangs in Chicago.* Abridged ed. Chicago: University of Chicago Press, 1963.

Wolfgang, Marvin E., Leonard Savitz, and Norman Johnston (eds.). *The Sociology of Crime and Delinquency.* New York: Wiley, 1962.

1 THE BIOLOGY OF CRIME

There is a beguiling neatness and simplicity in theories that argue that crime is caused by biological factors. The mysteries of human learning, values, motives, and the influence of participation in social groups are all avoided, and we somehow find it fitting to think that bad or defective behavior has its source in the bad or defective physical make-up of the individual.

Unfortunately, such theories have not weathered well, and their claims are generally believed to have little scientific merit. Cesare Lombroso, in the latter part of the nineteenth century was among the first to develop ideas about the "born criminal," and, indeed, he is sometimes referred to as the father of modern criminology. But the evidence has not been kind to his ideas or to those of his latter-day followers such as Earnest Albert Hooton. The correlation between characteristics of the soma *and the* psyche *seems at best to be a weak one.*

The battle over nature versus nurture is not finished, however. In recent years, a group of scientists including such men as Konrad Lorenz has begun to reexamine the influence of man's biological nature on his behavior with a good deal of sophistication and close, empirical observation. Most of their work has been confined to studies of animal behavior, but at least they have managed to make us consider again the possible biological basis of man's aggressiveness.

1. The Criminal Type

Cesare Lombroso's belief that criminals were marked by atavistic characteristics or throwbacks to more primitive forms is clearly little more than a mistaken speculation. Marvin Wolfgang, in reviewing the work of Lombroso, has contended that modern criminologists have been too quick to criticize his findings when they no longer take the time to read his books. This countercriticism undoubtedly contains a good deal of truth, but the fact remains that there are few reputable scholars who can accept Lombroso's notions about the criminal's dullness to the sense of touch, retreating forehead, and so on—although the notions linger on in popular thought.

The born criminal shows in a proportion reaching 33% numerous specific characteristics that are almost always atavistic. Those who have followed us thus far have seen that many of the characteristics presented by savage races are very often found among born criminals. Such, for example, are: the slight development of the pilar system; low cranial capacity; retreating forehead; highly developed frontal sinuses; great frequency of Wormian bones; early closing of the cranial sutures; the simplicity of the sutures; the thickness of the bones of the skull; enormous development of the maxillaries and the zygomata; prognathism; obliquity of the orbits; greater pigmentation of the skin; tufted and crispy hair; and large ears. To these we may add the lemurine appendix; anomalies of the ear; dental diastemata; great agility; relative insensibility to pain; dullness of the sense of touch; great visual acuteness; ability to recover quickly from wounds; blunted affections; precocity as to sensual pleasures; greater resemblance between the sexes; greater incorrigibility of the woman (Spencer); laziness; absence of remorse; impulsiveness; physiopsychic excitability; and especially improvidence, which sometimes appears as courage and again as recklessness changing to cowardice. Besides these there is great vanity; a passion for gambling and alcoholic drinks; violent but fleeting passions; superstition; extraordinary sensitiveness with regard to one's own personality; and a special conception of God and morality.

. . .

From Cesare Lombroso, **Crime: Its Causes and Remedies** (Boston: Little, Brown and Company, 1918). Reprinted by permission.

We may add that the atavism of the criminal, when he lacks absolutely every trace of shame and pity, may go back far beyond the savage, even to the brutes themselves. Pathological anatomy helps prove our position by showing in the case of the criminal a greater development of the cerebellum, a rarer union of the calcarine fissure with the parieto-occipital, the absence of folds in the passage of Gratiolet, the gutterlike shape of the nasal incisure, the frequency of the olecranial foramen, extra ribs and vertebræ, and especially the histological anomalies discovered by Roncoroni in the cortex of the cerebrum of criminals, that is to say, the frequent absence of granular layers, and the presence of nerve cells in the white matter, and immense pyramidal cells. In seeking for analogies beyond our own race we come upon the explanation of the union of the atlas with the occipital bone, the prominence of the canine teeth, the flattening of the palate, and the median occipital fossa, occurring among criminals as with the lemurs and rodents; as also the prehensile foot, the simplicity of the lines of the palm, motor and sensory left-handedness. We recall also the tendency to cannibalism even without desire for vengeance, and still more that form of sanguinary ferocity, mingled with lubricity, of which examples are furnished us by Gille, Verzeni, Legier, Bertrand, Artusio, the Marquis of Sade, and others, with whom atavism was accompanied by epilepsy, idiocy, or general paralysis, but who always recall the pairing of animals, preceded by ferocious and sanguinary contests to overcome the reticence of the female or to conquor rivals.

These facts prove clearly that the most horrible crimes have their origin in those animal instincts of which childhood gives us a pale reflection. Repressed in civilized man by education, environment, and the fear of punishment, they suddenly break out in the born criminal without apparent cause, or under the influence of certain circumstances, such as sickness, atmospheric influences, sexual excitement, or mob influence. We know that certain morbid conditions, such as injuries to the head, meningitis, and chronic intoxication, or certain physiological conditions like pregnancy and senility, produce derangements in the nutrition of the nervous centers, and in consequence atavistic retrogressions. We can see, then, how they may facilitate the tendency to crime, and when we take into account the short distance that separates the criminal from the savage, we come to understand why convicts so easily adopt savage customs, including cannibalism, as was observed in Australia and Guiana. When we note, further, how children, until they are educated, are ignorant of the difference between vice and virtue, and steal, strike, and lie without the least compunction, we easily understand the great precocity in crime, and see why it is that the majority of abandoned children and orphans end by becoming criminals.

2. Nature Versus Nurture

The argument as to whether man's patterns of behavior are innate or acquired through learning reached its greatest intensity in the first several decades of this century. Some portion of the argument, at least, had been due to the extreme statements made by those on opposite sides of the theoretical fence in which all human behavior (including deviant behavior) became either a product of the genes or an exact reflection of social norms. It is a virtue of the following piece, by Dunn and Dobzhansky, that man is seen as a physical and social being growing up in a physical and social environment.

Several investigators in different countries (United States, Holland, Germany) combed prisons for members of twin pairs among the inmates. When a twin was found efforts were made to locate his co-twin brother and to determine whether the latter did or did not have a criminal record. A total of 111 pairs of identical twins were investigated, and in 80 cases both co-twins were found to have had criminal records of various kinds. Among the same number (111 pairs) of two-egg twins, only 38 pairs consisted of co-twins both of whom had criminal records, while in the remaining 73 pairs one of the twins was convicted for some crime while his co-twin was not known to have broken any law. Clearly, then, one-egg twins are more often similar in having criminal records than are two-egg twins.

What, however, do these facts mean? One of the investigators described his findings in a book entitled *Crime as Destiny*. To him and to some others, the "coincidences in the lives of identical twins mean that heredity has the inevitability of fate." Some shocked proponents of the importance of the environment declared that there must be something wrong with the data, since everybody knows that crime is a social phenomenon, and, as a consequence, it just cannot be due to heredity.

It may nevertheless be useful to restrain one's excitement and to look at the data once more dispassionately. Indeed, there is nothing in the observations to show that the individuals who committed crimes, and were caught at it, would have done so had they been brought up differently. Perhaps some of them would have become pillars of society, or judges and lawyers, instead of defendants and convicts. Even in the environments in which they actually lived, some identical twin brothers of the criminals appeared to be

From L. C. Dunn and Th. Dobzhansky, **Heredity, Race, and Society** (New York: New American Library, 1946). Reprinted by permission.

law-abiding citizens. Therefore their heredities did not necessarily predestine them to careers of crime. Nor is there anything to show that some of those who are reputed to be virtuous and respectable would not have gone astray had they lived in environments conducive to crime. All the data do show is, then, that people with similar heredities tend to react more similarly than do people with different heredities.

The dependence of mental traits on both heredity and environment can also be demonstrated by studies on foster children. When children are distributed to foster homes, it is unavoidable that some of them will be placed in more and others in less favorable environments. One can, then, compare the intelligence and other traits in children who grow up in different environments. Such comparisons are especially interesting if, as often happens, the families which take foster children also have children of their own. Suppose, for the sake of argument, that the intelligence of a growing child is determined solely by his environment. The intelligence of foster children should then be proportional to that of "own" children of the adopting families. If, on the contrary, intelligence were due to heredity alone, there would be no consistent relationship between the intelligence test scores of foster and of own children. The actual situation is intermediate between these extremes. Foster children show higher I.Q.'s in homes in which own children have higher I.Q.'s, and vice versa. This attests to the importance of the environment. But this is not the whole story. In the most favorable foster homes foster children average lower in performance than do own children; in the less favored families foster children show, on the contrary, an average performance superior to own children. This shows the presence of a hereditary component in the development of the qualities which the I.Q. tests measure.

Perhaps it will help to summarize the current views about the Nature-Nurture problem to employ an allegory, which however must not be pushed too far or taken too literally. In the formation of each human trait there is a kind of lock-and-key arrangement between the inborn Nature and the surrounding Nurture. Nature provides a great variety of locks, and Nurture many different keys. Each trait has its own class of locks and will respond to a limited number of keys. Some locks do not at present respond to any keys provided by the existing variety of environments. Thus, some mental defectives do not benefit by any kind of advanced education; but only a few years ago diabetics also did not respond to any of the treatments which had been tried. It took a newly invented key, insulin, to fit that peculiar lock. The lock by which "criminal behavior" is regulated is in some persons so set that it does not easily yield to the ordinary keys presented by poverty, defective education, and other bad surroundings. But in other persons the "criminal behavior" locks open with any one of these keys. Knowing that heredity determines only responses to environments but not the presence or absence of a given trait as such, we do not despair when we discover that a child has inherited a tendency to asthma or hay fever. Instead, we try to find out to which particular substance in the environment he is sensitive and then to create an environment in which that substance is rare or absent.

It is true that for many heredities no environments have been found as yet which will change the response appreciably. The heredity which determines our eye color, blood group type, or fingerprint type seems to produce the same traits in all known environments. The skin color, stature and weight are quite certainly hereditary, but they are also sensitive to environment. Psychic characters, such as criminality, are so sensitive to environment that the very fact that heredity has anything at all to do with them was long in dispute. In which class a given trait belongs depends, however, on how much we know about the trait in question, as the example of diabetes and insulin shows.

On the whole, modern biology has strengthened the hands of those who try to improve the minds and bodies of men by improving the conditions in which they live. The normal mental and emotional "Natures" are very responsive to "Nurtures" of education and social influences. The "personality" is influenced by education, training, opportunities, cultural contacts and similar factors. It is acquired by us through our experience.

3. The Critics Respond

The idea that behavior which is labeled criminal by society must have its roots in biological pathology keeps reappearing and keeps getting knocked down. The most serious attempt in recent decades to resurrect a theory of biological defects as the source of crime has been that of Earnest Albert Hooton, an eminent physical anthropologist. As indicated in the following review by Robert K. Merton and M. F. Ashley Montagu of Crime and the Man *and* The American Criminal *(Cambridge, Mass.: Harvard University Press, 1939), Hooton's efforts have suffered the same fate as those of his predecessors.*

Professor Hooton in two works recently published in the combined fields of physical anthropology and criminology has propounded some highly unorthodox theories and stated some startling conclusions. Already the popular press is heralding the more lurid of these conclusions and it may no doubt be expected that additional publicity of this sort will follow upon the appearance of the two succeeding volumes of *The American Criminal*. In this massive report, Hooton has presented the results of twelve years of research representing the most extensive investigation of the physical characters of a criminal series of populations as compared with civilian populations that has yet appeared. It may at once be stated that this work will occupy as conspicuous a place in the history of criminology as the works of his predecessors in the field, Lombroso and Goring. It is the mantle of Lombroso, patched with some pieces from that of Max Nordau, rather than that of Goring—which Hooton spurns—that has descended upon the shoulders of Hooton. He wears it most gracefully. We are convinced that this vigorously tendentious study of the American criminal will have a most stimulating effect upon that largely neglected branch of human biology which is concerned to discover the relations between body, mind, and society; or shall we say heredity, conduct, and culture? It is a work which simply bristles with controversial points.

Since Hooton's work seems destined to exert an appreciable effect upon the thought of all those who make themselves acquainted with it, as well as upon the thought of many who do not, it is desirable that the significance

From Robert K. Merton and M. F. Ashley Montagu, "Crime and the Anthropologist." Reproduced by permission of the American Anthropological Association from the **American Anthropologist**, Vol. 42, pp. 384–408 (July–September, 1940).

of his results be critically examined from as many aspects as possible, for its implications are of the greatest importance. The study is of such magnitude that even the present forerunners of what promises to be a monumental report cannot be adequately discussed in a paper of this length. At most all that we can venture to do here is to consider some features of the framework of the research, some of its more general conclusions, and certain methodological assumptions which have been adopted. We shall hereafter refer to *The American Criminal* (the first of "three ponderous volumes, each positively bristling with statistical documentation") as *AC*, and to *Crime and the Man* (the summary volume of Lowell Institute Lectures) as *CM*.

As a consequence of his researches Hooton has been forced into the un-American position of espousing the cause of the angels. It may seem from what we say here that we have been forced into the opposite extreme of embracing the cause of the criminals. That is only apparently so. Actually, what we wish to do here is to suggest that the differences between the angels and the criminals are only skin deep; that the criminals may not have sprouted wings as the angels have done, not because it was not in them to do so, but because their wings were clipped before they were ready to try them.

Both of Hooton's works are introduced with ingenious attacks upon anticipated criticism and a series of *ad hominem* rejoinders-in-advance to any who may venture to voice their disagreement with the author's conclusions. "The categorical denials of hereditary influences in crime which are commonly emitted by sociologists" (*AC*, 4) and other "humanitarian practitioners" who "have poured out so much blood and treasure upon the investigation of the causes of crime" have not led us any nearer to a solution of the causative elements in criminal behavior. Hence, it is implied, the author's categorical affirmations that "criminals are organically inferior" and that "the primary cause of crime is biological inferiority" are more likely to do so. The statement of the case in terms of these mutually exclusive alternatives adds considerably to the dialectical flavor of the argument if not to our knowledge of the causation of crime. As we shall have occasion to see, this posing of false dilemmas is one of the more frequent polemical devices which Hooton utilizes in the analysis of his data.

Hooton defines a criminal as "a person who is under sentence in a penal institution, having been convicted for an antisocial act punishable by commitment to such an institution." (*AC*, 7.) He points out that "Crimes are obviously infractions of more or less arbitrary social rules, and whether an act is or is not accounted a crime, depends not only upon the nature of that act, but also upon the attitude of society toward it, which may differ radically from time to time and in diversely constituted political, social, and ethnic groups." (*AC*, 7.) "The criminal is a person distinguished by the commission of an overt act against society and he exemplifies for us an extreme of human conduct, thus making himself an excellent subject for the investigation of the relation of physique to behavior." (*AC,* 8.)

It is because the criminal exemplifies an "extreme" of human conduct that he was selected by Hooton for the investigation of the possible relation of physique to conduct. The object of the investigation is stated at the conclusion of the second chapter (*CM,* 33), which is significantly entitled *The Organic Basis of Crime,* as being "Specifically [the examination of] the physical characteristics of a large series of anti-social individuals in order to find out whether their varied types of delinquency are associated with their anthropological characters, and whether they are physically distinguished from those of us who are, perhaps temporarily, at large, and at least, putatively, law-abiding."

An indication of Hooton's dispassionate approach—in contrast, presumably, to Goring's "emotional preconception" which Hooton decries—is afforded by his initial comment "upon one stupid objection . . . to the effect that it is useless to study incarcerated criminals because they represent only the failures of those habitually and purposefully engaged in anti-social pursuits." (*AC,* 10.) In such an extreme form, this objection, whether "stupid" or not, would rule out most studies of criminals, since only those who are incarcerated are usually available for study. But it is still possible, and for some purposes relevant, that incarcerated criminals are not a representative sample (with respect to intelligence, economic status, race, nationality and rural-urban composition) of those who commit crimes. Selective arrests, and more importantly, selective commitments in terms of economic status and race are attested by many conversant with the facts; the differential in the case of Negroes seems to be especially marked. Hooton himself finds it convenient to adduce possible differentials in "rates of apprehension and conviction" between rural and urban criminals when he writes that "in rural life sparsity of population and restricted criminal opportunity lead . . . to easy detection and apprehension of persons responsible for crimes" in relative contrast to urban offenders. (*AC,* 288. Criminologists have indicated additional selective elements in this connexion.) It is at least possible, then, that some of the apparent sociological and physical differentials between criminals and civilians would be eliminated, were allowances made for the selective elements in commitment. Hooton is of course at liberty to define the "criminal" as he wishes, but he is not free to assume as an unchallengeable axiom that prisoners are in all relevant respects representative of the total population of those who have committed one or more illegal acts. To insinuate an axiom is not to demonstrate a fact. This consideration is mentioned here, not so much for its intrinsic importance—the fact remains that unconfined criminals and the anthropometrist's calipers have little chance to meet—but simply to bring out the author's tendency to demolish exaggerated propositions and hence to obscure the essential issue.

The study of the *Old American Criminal* reports on 4212 native white prisoners of native white parentage from nine states and a civilian (non-criminal) check sample of 313 (146 Nashville firemen and 167 residents of Massachusetts). Observations included at least 33 anthropometric measurements and indices, ten sociological categories and 33 morphological categories for each person. It should be noted that almost one-half of the civilian check group are firemen; in an occupation for which, Hooton observes, "the physical qualifications are rather stringent." He also notes that "the principal objection to them is that they are inclined to be fat," but feels compelled to add that they have the further liabilities of being of uniform social and economic status, in contrast to the criminal sample, and that their urban residence contrasts with the dominantly rural residence of the criminals when not incarcerated. In other words, as far as half the crucial check sample is concerned, the civilians are in many respects distinctly selected. However, it is comforting to learn that the Nashville civilians and the Tennessee villains are at least ethnically comparable.

Another part of the check group consists of Massachusetts militiamen and "in as much as enlistment in the militia is contingent upon the passing of a physical examination, it may be assumed that its members are, on the whole, of superior physique to the criminals" who, presumably, do not need to pass a formal physical examination. (*AC,* 34.) One may readily sympathize with Hooton's difficulty in obtaining a suitable check sample, but the fact still remains that a research of this magnitude proceeded with a clearly loaded check group. That the Tennessee civilian sample, with its various physical and social idiosyncrasies, proves disturbing to Hooton may be inferred from the frequency of such remarks as: "the Tennessee firemen show an unduly high mean," "the Tennessee firemen are perhaps broader in the face than an unselected (*sic*) civilian group would be," "the plump and sedentary fire-fighters," "the big-jowled firemen," "the excess weight of the Tennessee firemen," *etc.* (*AC,* 208 *ff.*) Despite all this, we are told that the Tennessee series probably "affords the more reliable results," "for the Massachusetts criminal series includes a brachycephalic French element almost absent from the civilian series." (*AC,* 216.) Another liability of the Massachusetts civilian series is the intrusion of the personal equation of "Observer C" with respect to some morphological items. Thus, the Tennessee civilian sample is the more reliable, and if this be so, then rough indeed is this "roughly comparable sample of civilians." To what extent are observed "biological" differences attributable to the bias of the sample? In view of some of the inferences which Hooton later feels justified in drawing, this bias becomes a grievous inadequacy, to say the least. It should be noticed, however, that Hooton has zealously ascertained and emphasized some of these sources of bias, both slight and pronounced, in his data.

. . .

Hooton finds that "on the whole, the biological superiority of the civilian to the delinquent is quite as certain as his sociological superiority." (*CM,*

376.) "The evidence," he writes, "that the criminals are derived from the baser biological stuff of their various ethnic stocks seems to me to be conclusive, although" he adds, "it might be argued that they came from families which are the anthropological victims of environmental depression." (*CM,* 379.)

Hooton finds that the "First generation criminals seem to adhere more closely than first generation civilians to the squat, broad-faced types which are often characteristic of the foreign born emigrant from Europe," and he goes on to make the astonishing suggestion that "It seems possible that such biological inadaptability, such phylogenetic conservatism, is responsible for the association of primitive features with retarded culture in modern savages." (*CM,* 379.)

It need hardly be said that for this suggestion there exists not the slightest factual support, but unexceptionally the evidence completely and unequivocally proves the contrary; that modern "savages" are biologically at least as perfectly adapted to the environments in which they live as the white man is to his. With respect to culture, it apparently requires to be pointed out that the culture of "savages," with rare exceptions, is anything but "retarded." It is a misunderstanding of the nature of culture, and of the history of our own, to speak of the culture of simpler peoples as retarded. Primitive cultures are no less complex and developed in their own ways than our own; unless, of course, we set out with the assumption that the standards of thought and material organization which Western culture has attained, as a consequence of the countless fertilizing cross currents and eddies of other cultures to which Western man has for the past few thousand years been exposed, are the measures of all cultures. Is it necessary to point out that not more than two thousand years ago, many peoples now esteemed "retarded" by us, might have judged the ancestors of all the potential and actual readers of this article as irremediably physically and culturally retarded, with quite as much justice as is implicit in Hooton's suggestion? It would seem that Hooton might profitably include an historical dimension in his biologistic judgments.

What, furthermore, it would be interesting to know, are the "primitive features" which are thought to be associated with the "retarded culture" of "modern savages"? As far as the physical structure of "modern savages" is concerned, there is no ground whatever for the belief that it is characterized by quantitatively or qualitatively more "primitive features" than is the physical structure of Western man. It is in such pronouncements as these that Hooton reveals his strong bias in favor of the belief that certain kinds of physical characters are probably associated with certain kinds of mental and social functioning.

Two distinct interpretative tendencies run throughout the work: one, a cautious and admirably restrained effort to assay the significance of biological factors in the determination of the incidence of criminal behavior; the other, a pugnacious and flamboyant insistence on the biological determination of crime. These two views do not rest comfortably in the same book but, conveniently enough, they are usually segregated. Thus, we have such careful disclaimers of extreme biological determinism as these:

This is very far from an insistence upon the direct causal relationship between the physical minutiae of an animal and his psychological processes—much less his behavior. All of these are varied expressions of the organism bound up together in their common heredity and modified in their several directions by the common environment. (AC, *6.*)

Similarly, it may be worth while to examine the physical characteristics of large groups of criminals to discover whether they are in any sense physically homogeneous, and if so whether they are distinguishable from non-criminals. Here again there is no necessary implication of causality—at least in the sense of a direct relationship between the physical characteristics of criminals and their antisocial conduct. (AC, *8.*)

The lawless habits of a racial or ethnic group may be persistently linked with its hereditary physique, although in a mainly non-casual relationship. (AC, *296.*)

These straightforward formulations of problems in criminal anthropology seem to us to be unexceptionable. But these moderate statements are soon forgotten in the fervor of formulating conclusions. In spite of all these laudable protestations that a statistical association is not to be confused with a causal relationship, Hooton insists that "the variation in physique and body build is *certainly causally* related to nature of offense." (*AC,* 296; italics inserted.) And this, despite the absence of adequate evidence to demonstrate the causal connexion which he holds to be incontestable. In an equally forthright fashion, Hooton tells his Lowell Institute audience: "You may say that this is tantamount to a declaration that the *primary cause* of crime is biological inferiority—and this is exactly what I mean." (*CM,* 130; italics inserted.) In fact, as he warms to his subject, he evidently means much more than that. Hooton believes that he now has sufficient evidence for the following dictum:

I deem human [*biological*] *deterioration to be ultimately responsible not only for crime, but for the evils of war, the oppression of the populace by totalitarian states, and for all of the social catacylsms which are rocking the world and under which civilization is tottering.* (CM, *393.*)

He does not tell us whether the recent "bear market" on the Stock Exchange is likewise attributable to this same biological degeneration. The sibylline abandon with which one of our most eminent physical anthropologists bestows these *obiter dicta* upon a Lowell Institute audience augurs ill for the more exact correlation between fact, inference and conclusion which we have assumed to characterize the scientific method. Extrapolations such as these pique the imagination and bedevil the intellect. One of Hooton's more interesting implications is that we either accept and act upon these views or slink back into our self-constituted caverns of democratic ignorance and despair to await the impending collapse of civilization. (See his concluding remarks in *CM.*) If we are to escape the day of Biological Judgment we must act—before too long. Only the "ruthless elimination of inferior types" can save us. The concluding words of Hooton's monograph are these:

Criminals are organically inferior. Crime is the resultant of the impact of environment upon low grade human organisms. It follows that the elimination of crime can be effected only by the extirpation of the physically, mentally and morally unfit, or by their complete segregation in a socially aseptic environment. (AC, *309.*)

In his call to arms, Hooton is especially prone to such horrendous catchwords as "biological inferiority," "organic degeneration," "biological deterioration." Thus, we are told that "criminals present a united front of biological inferiority," (*AC,* 300) and that "criminals as a group represent an aggregate of sociologically inferior and biologically inferior individuals." (*AC,* 304.) Without holding any particular brief for criminals, one may nevertheless inquire: what does Hooton concretely mean by inferiority in these connexions? As we shall see, his "answers" are either contradictory, equivocal or darkly implicit. In comparing his criminal and civilian samples—the latter, be it remembered, consist of exactly 313 persons (146 Nashville firemen and 167 Massachusetts militiamen and Boston out-patients)—he finds seven metrical and indicial items in which there are unquestionably significant *differences* (which persist when civilian and criminal aggregates are compared as a whole and when intra-state comparisons of civilians and criminals are made). What are these *differences* which, we must infer, unquestionably signify *inferiority?* The first is age. The criminals are 3.80 years younger than the civilians. Youth, presumably, is to be included in this homespun category of biological inferiority. "The hoary head is a crown of glory." (*Proverbs,* xvi, 31.) It hardly comes as an unheralded discovery that the age-group of maximum criminality is in the young-adult period and that this age-group varies with the type of offense. The study of crime statistics had long ago led to this finding.

The second term involving statistically significant differences between the civilians and criminals is weight: the criminals are 11.70 pounds lighter, on the average, and this difference is 10.83 p.e. Presumably, deficiency of weight as compared with the "roly-poly" firemen, *et al.,* is a mark of biological inferiority. In view of the frequently observed association between body weight and socio-economic status, might it not be advisable to equate the status of the criminal and check samples, before treating differences of weight as "biological" differences? Or are we to make the further assumption that socio-economic status is also biologically determined?

The five other indubitable differences involve the criminals' deficiencies in chest breadth, head circumference, upper face height, nose height and ear length. One awaits with some impatience the demonstration that these deficiences represent biological inferiority, as one awaits the proof that these "significant differences" mean anything more than a difference between two statistics computed from separate samples of such a magnitude that the probability that the samples were drawn from the same universe is inappreciable. We already know that Hooton's samples were drawn from different universes, and what we would be interested to know is why Hooton fastened upon a difference of a biological nature, rather than upon the many other characters of difference which are socio-economically known to exist between the civilians and criminals, as the causative factor in criminality. Statistically significant differences tell us no more than that the statistics involved are of different values; they do not tell us *why* or how they came to be so. The extrapolation of the "biological" factor, to the exclusion of all others, may satisfy Hooton's critical sense, but it does not satisfy ours.

. . .

Since Hooton himself does not indicate any systematically applied criteria of inferiority, these may tentatively be supplied. We may take Hooton's detailed records of anthropometric and indicial differentiation by offense groups, and classify each of the characters in the ten offense groups, by which the criminals differ significantly from the compared civilians, as characters which may be regarded as primitive, advanced or progressive, and indifferent; assuming those characters to be primitive which are more anthropoid-like than the Apollo-like characters which we tend to regard as advanced, and taking indifferent characters to be those, such as weight or stature, which can hardly be judged as either primitive or advanced. In short, in order to lean over backwards and give Hooton the benefit of every possible and every doubtful argument, we here classify his 39 anthropometric and indicial characters—including some which speciously support his case but which he has himself rejected as inadequate—by the very arbitrary standard of the structure of the existing anthropoid apes, the chimpanzee and the gorilla. A character is by us taken to be "advanced" when it exhibits features which are furthest removed from the conditions characterizing the apes. A "primitive" character is taken to be one that is "less" removed than the advanced character from the condition characteristic of the apes. Thus, for example, in the apes the antero-posterior diameter of the chest is relatively very great, whereas in man the chest is relatively comparatively flat; hence, when criminals exhibit a greater chest breadth than the civilian sample we have classified that as a "primitive" character for the criminals, even though in this respect the criminals obviously resemble the civilians considerably more closely than they do the apes.

. . .

Hooton set himself a task of unusual magnitude. His data appear to be inadequate for answering some of the questions with which he was fundamentally concerned. The substantial result of his research is an unparalleled array of metrical, indicial and morphological data, the significance of which still remains largely to be established. Should these researches be extended, it is to be hoped that a sociological perspective will not be so conspicuously absent in the interpretation of the data and that a systematic effort will be made to equate some of the social, economic and cultural attributes of the civilian and criminal samples, before the facile conclusion is reached that one is dealing with exclusively "biological" data. Moreover, it would seem expedient to abandon the extreme biologistic preconception which is manifest in various sections of the present interpretation and to consider in more detail the interrelations of the biological and socio-cultural factors in the determination of criminal behavior. (See the beginnings of such an effort, *AC,* 274 *ff.*) The practice of setting up false dilemmas, the frequent implication that sociological and biological interpretations are mutually exclusive, serves to mislead not only the reader of this work but possibly the author as well. It may well be that many of these exaggerations arose from a polemical context; in that event, it would seem more sagacious to take the facts and let the polemics go. Above all, it would appear expedient for an impartial investigator to disentangle himself from the illusion that scientific toughmindedness requires the assumption of biological determinism or that socio-cultural facts are born simply of the observer's sentiments and self-induced phantasies. This general biologism thwarts an adequate interpretation of an impressive mound of statistical data.

4. The Search Continues

In the past few years, a new brand of biology has gained widespread attention. It has centered on the study of animal behavior and has explored such matters as the sense of territory, membership in animal groups, forms of play, and so on. Konrad Lorenz contends that much of this work has profound implications for human society, although many scientists in other disciplines object to such generalizations. In any event, Lorenz sees man's aggressive behavior not as a product of biological defect but as an inevitable result of his "normal" physical endowment. The search for biological causes of criminal behavior may have been transformed, but has not yet been completely abandoned.

Anthropologists concerned with the habits of Australopithecus have repeatedly stressed that these hunting progenitors of man have left humanity with the dangerous heritage of what they term "carnivorous mentality." This statement confuses the concepts of the carnivore and the cannibal, which are, to a large extent, mutually exclusive. One can only deplore the fact that man has definitely not got a carnivorous mentality! All his trouble arises from his being a basically harmless, omnivorous creature, lacking in natural weapons with which to kill big prey, and, therefore, also devoid of the built-in safety devices which prevent "professional" carnivores from abusing their killing power to destroy fellow members of their own species. A lion or a wolf may, on extremely rare occasions, kill another by one angry stroke, but, as I have already explained in the chapter on behavior mechanisms functionally analogous to morality, all heavily armed carnivores possess sufficiently reliable inhibitions which prevent the self-destruction of the species.

In human evolution, no inhibitory mechanisms preventing sudden manslaughter were necessary, because quick killing was impossible anyhow; the potential victim had plenty of opportunity to elicit the pity of the aggressor by submissive gestures and appeasing attitudes. No selection pressure arose in the prehistory of mankind to breed inhibitory mechanisms preventing the killing of conspecifics until, all of a sudden, the invention of artificial weapons upset the equilibrium of killing potential and social inhibitions.

When it did, man's position was very nearly that of a dove which, by some unnatural trick of nature, has suddenly acquired the beak of a raven. One shudders at the thought of a creature as irascible as all prehuman primates are, swinging a well-sharpened hand-ax. Humanity would indeed have destroyed itself by its first inventions, were it not for the very wonderful fact that inventions and responsibility are both the achievements of the same specifically human faculty of asking questions.

Not that our prehuman ancestor, even at a stage as yet devoid of moral responsibility, was a fiend incarnate; he was by no means poorer in social instincts and inhibitions than a chimpanzee, which, after all, is—his irascibility not withstanding—a social and friendly creature. But whatever his innate norms of social behavior may have been, they were bound to be thrown out of gear by the invention of weapons. If humanity survived, as, after all, it did, it never achieved security from the danger of self-destruction. If moral responsibility and unwillingness to kill have indubitably increased, the ease and emotional impunity of killing have increased at the same rate. The distance at which all shooting weapons take effect screens the killer against the stimulus situation which would otherwise activate his killing inhibitions. The deep, emotional layers of our personality simply do not register the fact that the crooking of the forefinger to release a shot tears the entrails of another man. No sane man would even go rabbit hunting for pleasure if the necessity of killing his prey with his natural weapons brought home to him the full, emotional realization of what he is actually doing.

The same principle applies, to an even greater degree, to the use of modern remote-control weapons. The man who presses the releasing button is so completely screened against seeing, hearing, or otherwise emotionally realizing the consequences of his action, that he can commit it with impunity—even if he is burdened with the power of imagination. Only thus can it be explained that perfectly good-natured men, who would not even smack a naughty child, proved to be perfectly able to release rockets or to lay carpets of incendiary bombs on sleeping cities, thereby committing hundreds and thousands of children to a horrible death in the flames. The fact that it is good, normal men who did this, is as eerie as any fiendish atrocity of war!

. . .

In 1955 I wrote a paper, "On the Killing of Members of the Same Species": "I believe—and human psychologists, particularly psychoanalysts, should test this—that present-day civilized man suffers from insufficient discharge of his aggressive drive. It is more than probable that the evil effects of the human aggressive drives, explained by Sigmund Freud as the results of a special death wish, simply derive from the fact that in prehistoric times intra-specific selection bred into man a measure of aggression drive for which in the social order of today he finds no adequate outlet." If these words contain an element of reproach against psychoanalysis, I must here withdraw them. At the time of writing, there were already some psychoanalysts who did not believe in the death wish and rightly explained the self-destroying effects of aggression as misfunctions of an instinct that was essentially life-preserving. Later, I came to know one psychiatrist and psychoanalyst who, even at that time, was examining the problem of the hypertrophy of aggression owing to intra-specific selection.

Sydney Margolin, in Denver, Colorado, made very exact psychoanalytical and psycho-sociological studies on Prairie Indians, particularly the Utes, and showed that these people suffer greatly from an excess of aggression drive which, under the ordered conditions of present-day North American Indian reservations, they are unable to discharge. It is Margolin's opinion that during the comparatively few centuries when Prairie Indians led a wild life consisting almost entirely of war and raids, there must have been an extreme selection pressure at work, breeding extreme aggressiveness. That this produced changes in the hereditary pattern in such a short time is quite possible. Domestic animals can be changed just as quickly by purposeful selection. Margolin's assumption is supported by the fact that Ute Indians now growing up under completely different educational influences suffer in exactly the same way as the older members of their tribe who grew up under the educational system of their own culture; moreover, the pathological symptoms under discussion are seen only in those Prairie Indians whose tribes were subjected to the selection process described.

Ute Indians suffer more frequently from neurosis than any other human group, and again and again Margolin found that the cause of the trouble was undischarged aggression. Many of these Indians feel and describe themselves as ill, and when asked what is the matter with them they can only say, "I am a Ute!" Violence toward people not of their tribe, and even manslaughter, belong to the order of the day, but attacks on members of the tribe are extremely rare, for they are prevented by a taboo the severity of which it is easy to understand, considering the early history of the Utes: a tribe constantly at war with neighboring Indians and, later on, with the white man, must avoid at all costs fights between its own members. Anyone killing a member of the tribe is compelled by strict tradition to commit suicide. This commandment was obeyed even by a Ute policeman who had shot a member of his tribe in self-defense while trying to arrest him. The offender, while under the influence of drink, had stabbed his father in the femoral artery, causing him to bleed to death. When the policeman was ordered by his sergeant to arrest the man for manslaughter—it was obviously not murder—he protested, saying that the man would want to die since he was bound by tradition to commit suicide and would do so by resisting arrest and forcing the policeman to shoot him. He, the policeman, would then have to commit suicide himself. The more than short-sighted sergeant stuck to his order, and the tragedy took place exactly as predicted.

This and other of Margolin's records read like Greek tragedies: an inexorable fate forces crime upon people and then compels them to expiate voluntarily their involuntarily acquired guilt.

It is objectively convincing, indeed it is proof of the correctness of Margolin's interpretation of the behavior of Ute Indians, that these people are particularly susceptible to accidents. It has been proved that accident-proneness may result from repressed aggression, and in these Utes the rate of motor accidents exceeds that of any other car-driving human group. Anybody who has ever driven a fast car when really angry knows—in so far as he is capable of self-observation in this condition—what strong inclination there is to self-destructive behavior in a situation like this. Here even the expression "death wish" seems apt.

. . .

Aggressive behavior and killing inhibitions represent only one special case among many in which phylogenetically adapted behavior mechanisms are thrown out of balance by the rapid change wrought in human ecology and sociology by cultural development. In order to explain the function of responsible morality in re-establishing a tolerable equilibrium between man's instincts and the requirements of a culturally evolved social order, a few words must first be said about social instincts in general. It is a widely held opinion, shared by some contemporary philosophers, that all human behavior patterns which serve the welfare of the community, as opposed to that of the individual, are dictated by specifically human rational thought. Not only is this opinion erroneous, but the very opposite is true. If it were not for a rich endowment of social instincts, man could never have risen above the animal world. All specifically human faculties, the power of speech, cultural tradition, moral responsibility, could have evolved only in a being which, before the very dawn of conceptual thinking, lived in well-organized communities. Our prehuman ancestor was indubitably as true a friend to his friend as a chimpanzee or even a dog, as tender and solicitous to the young of his community and as self-sacrificing in its defense, aeons before he developed conceptual thought and became aware of the consequences of his actions.

2 THE PSYCHOLOGY OF CRIME

If the effort to find the causes of crime in biological factors has yet to be successful, there are still those students of criminal behavior who are convinced that the causes must lie somewhere within the individual. They look, however, not for defects of the body but for defects in the mind. Mental deficiency, psychosis, or some other form of psychological pathology is claimed as the major force lying behind most violations of criminal law.

In the so-called M'Naghten Rules, the law has long recognized a limited type of mental illness—a defect of reason—as a possible cause of criminal behavior; and it has held that the imposition of punishment would be cruel and barbaric for persons suffering from this version of insanity. With the Durham decision in the 1950s, however, the types of mental illness recognized by the law were greatly expanded and it seemed possible that our system of punishment might need to be heavily revised—if, indeed, most crimes were rooted in psychological abnormality.

Actually, it has never been shown that most criminals suffer from mental illness or that the incidence of mental illness among criminals is markedly different from that of the general population. Psychopathy, for example, has been claimed by some writers to be a significant cause of crime, but they have never been able to marshal satisfactory evidence to support the contention. Franz Alexander and Hugo Staub, in spelling out the classical psychoanalytic position, are somewhat more modest in their argument; and Thomas Szasz urges still greater caution in examining theories about psychological abnormality.

1. The M'Naghten Rules

Few concepts of the law have been more sharply criticized than the concept of insanity as set forth in the M'Naghten Rules—or more warmly defended. On the one hand there are those who see the law's view of mental illness as hopelessly outdated and restricted. On the other hand there are those who argue that if we modify the M'Naghten Rules we will open the door to every possible excuse for crime. The M'Naghten case is now more than a hundred years old, but in the following account by John Biggs we can see the main issues that still dominate much of the discussion today.

In 1843 Daniel M'Naghten, a Scotsman, standing in a London garden adjacent to Prime Minister Robert Peel's residence, shot Edward Drummond, Peel's principal secretary, believing him to be Peel. In the quaint words of the indictment, Drummond "languished, and languishing, did die." M'Naghten was charged with first-degree murder. That M'Naghten was "insane" at the time he committed the crime no man can doubt today. He was subject to delusions of persecution as well as hallucinations, and his conduct in London, as proved by the sworn evidence of the witnesses, was mad indeed. His trial for murder took place on March 3 and 4, 1843, in the Central Criminal Court of London, popularly known as the "Old Bailey."

. . .

The jury rendered a verdict of "Not guilty, on the ground of insanity." M'Naghten was removed to the Bethlehem Hospital, to await the Crown's pleasure. He was transferred to Broadmoor in March of 1864, and died there on May 3, 1865, probably of *diabetes mellitus*. His hospital record states as to his chief delusion: "[He] imagines the Tories are his enemies."

The result of the trial immediately came under hot attack. Contemporaneous editorials prove this. Similar editorials are written today and spring from identical motivation. Editorials from the *Illustrated London News* prove my point. One, that of March 11, 1843, shows that it was the writer's opinion that M'Naghten was only simulating insanity and that soft-headed judges and doctors had let him escape the stern hand of justice. It was suggested that Bedlam, the "Eden of St. George's Fields," was a soft and pleasant place and that a more distant place of confinement should be

From John Biggs, Jr., **The Guilty Mind: Psychiatry and the Law of Homicide** (New York: Harcourt, Brace & World, Inc., 1955). Reprinted by permission of the author.

set up immediately on Norfolk Island. A second editorial, one week later, reiterated the same concepts, and stated that Bedlam was a "retreat of idleness" and that perhaps M'Naghten and other criminals were "profitably insane." Immediate curative legislation was suggested. There was heated debate in both the House of Lords and the House of Commons as to the propriety of M'Naghten's fate.

Queen Victoria herself wrote a letter to Sir Robert Peel. Her dissatisfaction with the administration of justice was manifest. Her letter reads:

*Buckingham Palace, 12*th March, *1843.*

The Queen returns the paper of the Lord Chancellor's to Sir Robert Peel with her best thanks.

The law may be perfect, but how is it that whenever a case for its application arises, it proves to be of no avail? We have seen the trials of Oxford and MacNaghten conducted by the ablest lawyers of the day—Lord Denman, Chief Justice Tindal, and Sir Wm. Follett,—and they allow *and* advise *the Jury to pronounce the verdict of* Not Guilty *on account of* Insanity,—*whilst* everybody *is morally* convinced *that both malefactors were perfectly conscious and aware of what they did! It appears from this, that the force of the law is entirely put into the judge's hands, and that it depends merely upon his charge whether the law is to be applied or not. Could not the Legislature lay down that rule which the Lord Chancellor does in his paper, and which Chief Justice Mansfield did in the case of Bellingham; and why could not the judges be* bound *to interpret the law in* this *and* no other *sense in their charges to the Juries?*

The House of Lords decided "to take the opinion of the Judges on the law governing such cases." The judges of the common law courts could be called upon by the House of Lords for information on questions of law. Accordingly all fifteen judges attended the House of Lords the following June and five questions of law were propounded by the Lords to them.

Lord Chief Justice Tindal answered for all the fifteen common law judges save Mr. Justice Maule, who gave a separate set of answers. Tindal said: "The first question proposed by your Lordship is this: 'What is the law respecting alleged crimes committed by persons afflicted with insane delusion in respect of one or more particular subjects or persons; as, for instance, where at the time of the commission of the alleged crime the accused knew he was acting contrary to law, but did the act complained of with a view, under the influence of insane delusion, of redressing or revenging some supposed grievance or injury, or of producing some supposed public benefit?'

"In answer to which question, assuming that your Lordships' inquiries are confined to those persons who labour under such partial *delusions* only, and are not in other respects insane, we are of the opinion that, notwithstanding the party accused did the act complained of with a view, under the influence of insane delusion, of redressing or revenging some supposed grievance or injury, or of producing some public benefit, he is nevertheless punishable according to the nature of the crime committed, *if he knew at the time of committing such crime that he was acting contrary to law;* by which expression we understand your Lordships to mean *the law of the land.*

"Your Lordships are pleased to inquire of us, secondly, 'What are the proper questions to be submitted to the jury, where a person alleged to be afflicted with insane delusion respecting one or more particular subjects or persons, is charged with the commission of a crime (murder, for example), and insanity is set up as a defence?' And, thirdly, 'In what terms ought the question to be left to the jury as to the prisoner's state of mind at the time when the act was committed?' And as these two questions appear to us to be more conveniently answered together, we have to submit our opinion to be, that the jurors ought to be told in all cases that every man *is to be presumed to be sane,* and to possess a sufficient degree of reason to be responsible for his crimes, *until the contrary be proved* to their satisfaction; and that to establish a defence on the ground of insanity, it must be clearly proved that, at the time of the committing of the act, the party accused was labouring *under such a defect of reason, from disease of the mind, as not to know the nature and quality* of the act he was doing; or if he did know it, that *he did not know that he was doing what was wrong.* The mode of putting the latter part of the question to the jury on these occasions has generally been, whether the accused at the time of doing the act knew *the differences between right and wrong:* which mode, though rarely, if ever, leading to any mistake with the jury, is not, as we conceive, so accurate when put generally and in the abstract, as when put with reference to the party's knowledge of right and wrong in respect to the very act with which he is charged. *If the question were to be put as to the knowledge of the accused solely and exclusively with reference to the law of the land, it might tend to confound the jury, by* inducing them to believe that *an actual knowledge of the law of the land was essential in order to lead to a conviction;* whereas the law is administered upon the principle that every one must be taken conclusively to know it, without proof that he does know it. *If the accused was conscious that the act was one which he ought not to do, and if that act was at the same time contrary to the law of the land, he is punishable;* and the usual course therefore has been to leave the question to the jury, whether the party accused had a sufficient degree of reason to know that he was doing an act that was wrong: and this course we think is correct, accompanied with such observations and explanations as the circumstances of each particular case may require.

"The fourth question which your Lordships have proposed to us is this:—'If a person under an insane delusion as to existing facts, commits an offense in consequence thereof, is he thereby excused?' *To which question the answer must of course depend on the nature of the delusion:* but, making the same assumption as we did before, namely, that he labours under such partial delusion only, and is not in other respects insane, we think he must be considered in the same situation as to responsibility as if the facts with respect to which the delusion exists were real. For example, if under the influence of his delusion he supposes another man to be in the act of attempting to take away his life, and he kills that man, as he supposes, in self-defence, he would be exempt from punishment. If his delusion was that the deceased had inflicted injury to his character and fortune, and he killed him in revenge for such supposed injury, he would be liable to punishment.

"The question lastly proposed by your Lordships is:—'Can a medical man conversant with the disease of insanity, who never saw the prisoner previously to the trial, but who was present during the whole trial and the examination of all the witnesses, be asked his opinion as to the state of the prisoner's mind at the time of the commission of the alleged crime, or his opinion whether the prisoner was conscious at the time of doing the act that he was acting contrary to law, or whether he was labouring under any and what delusion at the time?' In answer thereto, we state to your Lordships, that we think the medical man, under the circumstances supposed, cannot in strictness be asked his opinion in the terms above stated, because each of those questions involves the determination of the truth of the facts deposed to, which it is for the jury to decide, and the questions are not mere questions upon a matter of science, in which case such evidence is admissible. But where the facts are admitted or not disputed, and the question becomes substantially one of science only, it may be convenient to allow the question to be put in that general form, though the same cannot be insisted on as a matter of right." (Emphasis added)

The origin and very nature of the answers detract from their weight. Sir James Stephen has stated: "I cannot help feeling however, and I know that some of the most distinguished judges on the Bench have been of the same opinion, that the authority of the answers is questionable, and it appears to me that when carefully considered they leave untouched the most difficult questions connected with the subject, and lay down propositions liable to be misunderstood, though they might, and I think ought to be, construed in a way which would dispose satisfactorily of all cases whatever."

2. A Modern View

The decision of Judge David L. Bazelon in the Durham case marked a possible turning point in the law's attitude toward the relationship between crime and mental disorder. A "defect of reason" was no longer taken as the only form of mental illness that would be recognized, and the way had been opened for a profound reconsideration of the precise link between criminal behavior and psychological disorder. It is too soon, however, to tell if the Durham decision is the first of many similar decisions or merely an insignificant dent in the M'Naghten Rules, which are still in effect in most jurisdictions.

Monte Durham was convicted of housebreaking, by the District Court sitting without a jury. The only defense asserted at the trial was that Durham was of unsound mind at the time of the offense. We are now urged to reverse the conviction (1) because the trial court did not correctly apply existing rules governing the burden of proof on the defense of insanity, and (2) because existing tests of criminal responsibility are obsolete and should be superseded.

Durham has a long history of imprisonment and hospitalization. In 1945, at the age of 17, he was discharged from the Navy after a psychiatric examination had shown that he suffered "from a profound personality disorder which renders him unfit for Naval service." In 1947 he pleaded guilty to violating the National Motor Theft Act and was placed on probation for one to three years. He attempted suicide, was taken to Gallinger Hospital for observation, and was transferred to St. Elizabeths Hospital, from which he was discharged after two months. In January of 1948, as a result of a conviction in the District of Columbia Municipal Court for passing bad checks, the District Court revoked his probation and he commenced service of his Motor Theft sentence. His conduct within the first few days in jail led to a lunacy inquiry in the Municipal Court where a jury found him to be of unsound mind. Upon commitment to St. Elizabeths, he was diagnosed as suffering from "psychosis with psychopathic personality." After 15 months of treatment, he was discharged in July 1949 as "recovered" and was returned to jail to serve the balance of his

From Durham v. United States, **Federal Reporter** (2nd series), Vol. 214 (St. Paul, Minn.: West Publishing Company), pp. 864–876.

sentence. In June 1950 he was conditionally released. He violated the conditions by leaving the District. When he learned of a warrant for his arrest as a parole violator, he fled to the "South and Midwest obtaining money by passing a number of bad checks." After he was found and returned to the District, the Parole Board referred him to the District Court for a lunacy inquisition, wherein a jury again found him to be of unsound mind. He was readmitted to St. Elizabeths in February 1951. This time the diagnosis was "without mental disorder, psychopathic personality." He was discharged for the third time in May 1951. The housebreaking which is the subject of the present appeal took place two months later, on July 13, 1951.

According to his mother and the psychiatrist who examined him in September 1951, he suffered from hallucinations immediately after his May 1951 discharge from St. Elizabeths. Following the present indictment, in October 1951, he was adjudged of unsound mind in proceedings under § 4244 of Title 18 U.S.C., upon the affidavits of two psychiatrists that he suffered from "psychosis with psychopathic personality." He was committed to St. Elizabeths for the fourth time and given subshock insulin therapy. This commitment lasted 16 months—until February 1953—when he was released to the custody of the District Jail on the certificate of Dr. Silk, Acting Superintendent of St. Elizabeths, that he was "mentally competent to stand trial and . . . able to consult with counsel to properly assist in his own defense."

He was thereupon brought before the court on the charge involved here. The prosecutor told the court:

So I take this attitude, in view of the fact that he has been over here [St. Elizabeths] a couple of times and these cases that were charged against him were dropped, I don't think I should take the responsibility of dropping these cases against him; then Saint Elizabeths would let him out on the street, and if that man committed a murder next week then it is my responsibility. So we decided to go to trial on one case, that is the case where we found him right in the house, and let him bring in the defense, if he wants to, of unsound mind at the time the crime was committed, and then Your Honor will find him on that, and in your decision send him back to Saint Elizabeths Hospital, and then if they let him out on the street it is their responsibility.

Shortly thereafter, when the question arose whether Durham could be considered competent to stand trial merely on the basis of Dr. Silk's ex parte statement, the court said to defense counsel:

I am going to ask you this, Mr. Ahern: I have taken the position that if once a person has been found of unsound mind after a lunacy hearing, an ex parte certificate of the superintendent of Saint Elizabeths is not sufficient to set aside that finding and I have held another lunacy hearing. That has been my custom. However, if you want to waive that you may do it, if you admit that he is now of sound mind.

The court accepted counsel's waiver on behalf of Durham, although it had been informed by the prosecutor that a letter from Durham claimed need of further hospitalization and by defense counsel that ". . . the defendant does say that even today he thinks he does need hospitalization; he told me that this morning." Upon being so informed, the court said, "Of course, if I hold he is not mentally competent to stand trial I send him back to Saint Elizabeths Hospital and they will send him back again in two or three months." In this atmosphere Durham's trial commenced.

His conviction followed the trial court's rejection of the defense of insanity in these words:

I don't think it has been established that the defendant was of unsound mind as of July 13, 1951, in the sense that he didn't know the difference between right and wrong or that even if he did, he was subject to an irresistible impulse by reason of the derangement of mind.

While, of course, the burden of proof on the issue of mental capacity to commit a crime is upon the Government, just as it is on every other issue, nevertheless, the Court finds that there is not sufficient to contradict the usual presumption of [sic] *the usual inference of sanity.*

There is no testimony concerning the mental state of the defendant as of July 13, 1951, and therefore the usual presumption of sanity governs.

While if there was some testimony as to his mental state as of that date to the effect that he was incompetent on that date, the burden of proof would be on the Government to overcome it. There has been no such testimony, and the usual presumption of sanity prevails.

. . .

Mr. Ahern, I think you have done very well by your client and defended him very ably, but I think under the circumstances there is nothing that anybody could have done. [Emphasis supplied.]

We think this reflects error requiring reversal.

In Tatum v. United States we said, "When lack of mental capacity is raised as a defense to a charge of crime, the law accepts the general experience of mankind and presumes that all people, including those accused of crime, are sane." So long as this presumption prevails, the prosecution is not required to prove the defendant's sanity. But "as soon as 'some evidence of mental disorder is introduced, . . . sanity, like any other fact, must be proved as part of the prosecution's case beyond a reasonable doubt.' " Here it appears that the trial judge recognized this rule but failed to find "some evidence." We hold that the court erred and that the requirement of "some evidence" was satisfied.

In Tatum we held that requirement satisfied by considerably less than is present here. Tatum claimed lack of memory concerning the critical events and three lay witnesses testified that he appeared to be in "more or less of a trance," or "abnormal," but two psychiatrists testified that he was of "sound mind" both at the time of examination and at the time of the crime. Here, the psychiatric testimony was unequivocal that Durham was of unsound mind at the time of the crime. Dr. Gilbert, the only expert witness heard, so stated at least four times . . . Intensive questioning by the court failed to produce any retraction of Dr. Gilbert's testimony that the "period of insanity would have embraced the date July 13, 1951." And though the prosecution sought unsuccessfully in its cross- and recross-examination of Dr. Gilbert to establish that Durham was a malingerer who feigned insanity whenever he was trapped for his misdeeds, it failed to present any expert testimony to support this theory. In addition to Dr. Gilbert's testimony, there was testimony by Durham's mother to the effect that in the interval between his discharge from St. Elizabeths in May 1951, and the crime "he seemed afraid of people" and had urged her to put steel bars on his bedroom windows.

Apparently the trial judge regarded this psychiatric testimony as "no testimony" on two grounds: (1) it did not adequately cover Durham's condition on July 13, 1951, the date of the offense; and (2) it was not directed to Durham's capacity to distinguish between right and wrong. We are unable to agree that for either of these reasons the psychiatric testimony could properly be considered "no testimony."

Following Dr. Gilbert's testimony that the condition in which he found Durham on September 3, 1951 was progressive and did not "arrive overnight," Dr. Gilbert responded to a series of questions by the court:

> *Q.* [*Court*]. *Then is it reasonable to assume that it is not possible to determine* how far *this state of unsound mind had progressed by July 13th? Isn't that so? A.* [*Dr. Gilbert*]. *As to the seriousness of the symptoms as compared with them and the time I observed him, that's true, except that his travels were based, according to his statement to me, on certain of the symptoms and his leaving Washington, his giving up his job and work and leaving the work that he had tried to do.*
>
> *Q. But you can't tell, can you,* how far *those symptoms had progressed and become worse by the 13th of July? A. No, not* how far *they were, that is correct."* [*Emphasis supplied.*]

Thereafter, when the prosecutor on recross asked Dr. Gilbert whether he would change his opinion concerning Durham's mental condition on July 13, 1951, if he knew that Durham had been released from St. Elizabeths just two months before as being of sound mind, the court interrupted to say: "Just a minute. The Doctor testified in answer to my question that he doesn't know and he can't express a definite opinion as to his mental condition on the 13th of July." This, we think, overlooks the witness' unequivocal testimony on direct and cross-examination, and misconceives what he had said in response to questioning by the court, namely, that certain symptoms of mental disorder antedated the crime, although it was impossible to say how far they had progressed.

Moreover, any conclusion that there was "no testimony" regarding Durham's mental condition at the time of the crime disregards the testimony of his mother. Her account of his behavior after his discharge from

St. Elizabeths in May 1951 was directly pertinent to the issue of his sanity at the time of the crime.

On re-direct examination, Dr. Gilbert was asked whether he would say that Durham "knew the difference between right and wrong on July 13, 1951; that is, his ability to distinguish between what was right and what was wrong." He replied: "As I have stated before, if the question of the right and wrong were propounded to him he could give you the right answer." Then the court interrupted to ask:

The Court. No, I don't think that is the question, Doctor—not whether he could give a right answer to a question, but whether he, himself, knew the difference between right and wrong in connection with governing his own actions. . . . If you are unable to answer, why, you can say so; I mean, if you are unable to form an opinion.

The Witness. I can only answer this way: That I can't tell how much the abnormal thinking and the abnormal experiences in the form of hallucinations and delusions—delusions of persecution—had to do with his anti-social behavior.

I don't know how anyone can answer that question categorically, except as one's experience leads him to know that most mental cases can give you a categorical answer of right and wrong, but what influence these symptoms have on abnormal behavior or anti-social behavior—

The Court. Well, your answer is that you are unable to form an opinion, is that it?

The Witness. I would say that that is essentially true, for the reasons that I have given.

Later, when defense counsel sought elaboration from Dr. Gilbert on his answers relating to the "right and wrong" test, the court cut off the questioning with the admonition that "you have answered the question, Doctor."

The inability of the expert to give categorical assurance that Durham was unable to distinguish between right and wrong did not destroy the effect of his previous testimony that the period of Durham's "insanity" embraced July 13, 1951. It is plain from our decision in Tatum that this previous testimony was adequate to prevent the presumption of sanity from becoming conclusive and to place the burden of proving sanity upon the Government. None of the testimony before the court in Tatum was couched in terms of "right and wrong."

Finally, even assuming *arguendo* that the court, contrary to the plain meaning of its words, recognized that the prosecution had the burden of proving Durham's sanity, there would still be a fatal error. For once the issue of insanity is raised by the introduction of "some evidence," so that the presumption of sanity is no longer absolute, it is incumbent upon the trier of fact to weigh and consider "the whole evidence, including that supplied by the presumption of sanity . . ." on the issue of "the capacity in law of the accused to commit" the crime. Here, manifestly, the court as the trier of fact did not and could not weigh "the whole evidence," for it found there was "no testimony concerning the mental state" of Durham.

For the foregoing reasons, the judgment is reversed and the case is remanded for a new trial.

It has been ably argued by counsel for Durham that the existing tests in the District of Columbia for determining criminal responsibility, *i.e.,* the so-called right-wrong test supplemented by the irresistible impulse test, are not satisfactory criteria for determining criminal responsibility. We are urged to adopt a different test to be applied on the retrial of this case. This contention has behind it nearly a century of agitation for reform.

A. The right-wrong test, approved in this jurisdiction in 1882, was the exclusive test of criminal responsibility in the District of Columbia until 1929 when we approved the irresistible impulse test as a supplementary test in Smith v. United States. The right-wrong test has its roots in England. There, by the first quarter of the eighteenth century, an accused escaped punishment if he could not distinguish "good and evil," *i.e.,* if he "doth not know what he is doing, no more than . . . a wild beast." Later in the same century, the "wild beast" test was abandoned and "right and wrong" was substituted for "good and evil." And toward the middle of the nineteenth century, the House of Lords in the famous M'Naghten case restated what had become the accepted "right-wrong" test in a form which has since followed, not only in England but in most American jurisdictions as an exclusive test of criminal responsibility:

. . . the jurors ought to be told in all cases that every man is to be presumed to be sane, and to possess a sufficient degree of reason to be responsible for his crimes, until the contrary be proved to their satisfaction; and that, to establish a defence on the ground of insanity, it must be clearly proved that, at the time of the committing of the act, the party accused was labouring under such a defect of reason, from disease of the mind, as not to know the nature and quality of the act he was doing, or, if he did know it, that he did not know he was doing what was wrong.

As early as 1938, Isaac Ray, one of the founders of the American Psychiatric Association, in his now classic Medical Jurisprudence of Insanity, called knowledge of right and wrong a "fallacious" test of criminal responsibility. This view has long since been substantiated by enormous developments in knowledge of mental life. In 1928 Mr. Justice Cardozo said to the New York Academy of Medicine: "Everyone concedes that the present [legal] definition of insanity has little relation to the truths of mental life."

Medico-legal writers in large number, The Report of the Royal Commission on Capital Punishment 1949–1953, and The Preliminary Report by the Committee on Forensic Psychiatry of the Group for the Advancement of Psychiatry present convincing evidence that the right-and-wrong test is "based on an entirely obsolete and misleading conception of the nature of insanity." The science of psychiatry now recognizes that a man is an integrated personality and that reason, which is only one element in that personality, is not the sole determinant of his conduct. The right-wrong test, which considers knowledge or reason alone, is therefore an inadequate guide to mental responsibility for criminal behavior. As Professor Sheldon Glueck of the Harvard Law School points out in discussing the right-wrong tests, which he calls the knowledge tests:

It is evident that the knowledge tests unscientifically abstract out of the mental make-up but one phase or element of mental life, the cognitive, which, in this era of dynamic psychology, is beginning to be regarded as not the most important factor in conduct and its disorders. In brief, these tests proceed upon the following questionable assumptions of an outworn era in psychiatry: (1) that lack of knowledge of the "nature or quality" of an act (assuming the meaning of such terms to be clear), or incapacity to know right from wrong, is the sole or even the most important symptom of mental disorder; (2) that such knowledge is the sole instigator and guide of conduct, or at least the most important element therein, and consequently should be the sole criterion of responsibility when insanity is involved; and (3) that the capacity of knowing right from wrong can be completely intact and functioning perfectly even though a defendant is otherwise demonstrably of disordered mind.

Nine years ago we said:

The modern science of psychology . . . does not conceive that there is a separate little man in the top of one's head called reason whose function is to guide another unruly little man called instinct, emotion, or impulse in the way he should go.

By its misleading emphasis on the cognitive, the right-wrong test requires court and jury to rely upon what is, scientifically speaking, inadequate, and most often, invalid and irrelevant testimony in determining criminal responsibility.

The fundamental objection to the right-wrong test, however, is not that criminal irresponsibility is made to rest upon an inadequate, invalid or indeterminable symptom or manifestation, but that it is made to rest upon *any* particular symptom. In attempting to define insanity in terms of a symptom, the courts have assumed an impossible role, not merely one for which they have no special competence. As the Royal Commission emphasizes, it is dangerous "to abstract particular mental faculties, and to lay it down that unless these particular faculties are destroyed or gravely impaired, an accused person, whatever the nature of his mental disease, must be held to be criminally responsible . . ." In this field of law as in others, the fact finder should be free to consider all information advanced by relevant scientific disciplines.

Despite demands in the name of scientific advances, this court refused to alter the right-wrong test at the turn of the century. But in 1929, we reconsidered in response to "the cry of scientific experts" and added the irresistible impulse test as a supplementary test for determining criminal responsibility. Without "hesitation" we declared, in Smith v. United States, "it to be the law of this District that, in cases where insanity is interposed as a defense, and the facts are sufficient to call for the application of the rule of irresistible impulse, the jury should be so charged." We said:

. . . The modern doctrine is that the degree of insanity which will relieve the accused of the consequences of a criminal act must be such as to create in his mind an uncontrollable impulse to commit the offense charged. This impulse must be such as to override the reason and judgment and obliterate the sense of right and wrong to the extent that the accused is deprived of the power to choose between right and wrong. The mere ability to distinguish right from wrong is no longer the correct test either in civil or criminal cases, where the defense of insanity is interposed. The accepted rule in this day and age, with the great advancement in medical science as an enlightening influence on this subject, is that the accused must be capable, not only of distinguishing between right and wrong, but that he was not impelled to do the act by an irresistible impulse, which means before it will justify a verdict of acquittal that his reasoning powers were so far dethroned by his diseased mental condition as to deprive him of the will power to resist the insane impulse to perpetrate the deed, though knowing it to be wrong.

As we have already indicated, this has since been the test in the District.

Although the Smith case did not abandon the right-wrong test, it did liberate the fact finder from exclusive reliance upon that discredited criterion by allowing the jury to inquire also whether the accused suffered from an undefined "diseased mental condition [which] deprive[d] him of the will power to resist the insane impulse . . ." The term "irresistible impulse," however, carries the misleading implication that "diseased mental condition[s]" produce only sudden, momentary or spontaneous inclinations to commit unlawful acts.

As the Royal Commission found:

. . . In many cases . . . this is not true at all. The sufferer from [melancholia, for example] experiences a change of mood which alters the whole of his existence. He may believe, for instance, that a future of such degradation and misery awaits both him and his family that death for all is a less dreadful alternative. Even the thought that the acts he contemplates are murder and suicide pales into insignificance in contrast with what he otherwise expects. The criminal act, in such circumstances, may be the reverse of impulsive. It may be coolly and carefully prepared; yet it is still the act of a madman. This is merely an illustration; similar states of mind are likely to lie behind the criminal act when murders are committed by persons suffering from schizophrenia or paranoid psychoses due to disease of the brain.

We find that as an exclusive criterion the right-wrong test is inadequate in that (a) it does not take sufficient account of psychic realities and scientific knowledge, and (b) it is based upon one symptom and so cannot validly be applied in all circumstances. We find that the "irresistible impulse" test is also inadequate in that it gives no recognition to mental illness characterized by brooding and reflection and so relegates acts caused by such illness to the application of the inadequate right-wrong test. We conclude that a broader test should be adopted.

. . .

The rule we now hold must be applied on the retrial of this case and in future cases is not unlike that followed by the New Hampshire court since 1870. It is simply that an accused is not criminally responsible if his unlawful act was the product of mental disease or mental defect.

We use "disease" in the sense of a condition which is considered capable of either improving or deteriorating. We use "defect" in the sense of a condition which is not considered capable of either improving or deteriorating and which may be either congenital, or the result of injury, or the residual effect of a physical or mental disease.

Whenever there is "some evidence" that the accused suffered from a diseased or defective mental condition at the time the unlawful act was committed, the trial court must provide the jury with guides for determining whether the accused can be held criminally responsible. We do not, and indeed could not, formulate an instruction which would be either appropriate or binding in all cases. But under the rule now announced, any instruction should in some way convey to the jury the sense and substance of the following: If you the jury believe beyond a reasonable doubt that the accused was not suffering from a diseased or defective mental condition at the time he committed the criminal act charged, you may find him guilty. If you believe he was suffering from a diseased or defective mental condition when he committed the act, but believe beyond a reasonable doubt that the act was not the product of such mental abnormality, you may find him guilty. Unless you believe beyond a reasonable doubt either that he was not suffering from a diseased or defective mental condition, or that the act was not the product of such abnormality, you must find the accused not guilty by reason of insanity. Thus your task would not be completed upon finding, if you did find, that the accused suffered from a mental disease or defect. He would still be responsible for his unlawful act if there was no causal connection between such mental abnormality and the act. These questions must be determined by you from the facts which you find to be fairly deducible from the testimony and the evidence in this case.

The questions of fact under the test we now lay down are as capable of determination by the jury as, for example, the questions juries must determine upon a claim of total disability under a policy of insurance where the state of medical knowledge concerning the disease involved, and its effects, is obscure or in conflict. In such cases, the jury is not required to depend on arbitrarily selected "symptoms, phases or manifestations" of the disease as criteria for determining the ultimate questions of fact upon which the claim depends. Similarly, upon a claim of criminal irresponsibility, the jury will not be required to rely on such symptoms as criteria for determining the ultimate question of fact upon which such claim depends. Testimony as to such "symptoms, phases or manifestations," along with other relevant evidence, will go to the jury upon the ultimate questions of fact which it alone can finally determine. Whatever the state of psychiatry, the psychiatrist will be permitted to carry out his principal court function which, as we noted in Holloway v. U. S., "is to inform the jury of the character of [the accused's] mental disease [or defect]." The jury's range of inquiry will not be limited to, but may include, for example, whether an accused, who suffered from a mental disease or defect did not know the difference between right and wrong, acted under the compulsion of an irresistible impulse, or had "been deprived of or lost the power of his will . . ."

Finally, in leaving the determination of the ultimate question of fact to the jury, we permit it to perform its traditional function which, as we said in Holloway, is to apply "our inherited ideas of moral responsibility to individuals prosecuted for crime . . ." Juries will continue to make moral judgments, still operating under the fundamental precept that "Our collective conscience does not allow punishment where it cannot impose blame." But in making such judgments, they will be guided by wider horizons of knowledge concerning mental life. The question will be simply whether the accused acted because of a mental disorder, and not whether he displayed particular symptoms which medical science has long recognized do not necessarily, or even typically, accompany even the most serious mental disorder.

The legal and moral traditions of the western world require that those who, of their own free will and with evil intent (sometimes called *mens rea*), commit acts which violate the law, shall be criminally responsible for those acts. Our traditions also require that where such acts stem from and are the product of a mental disease or defect as those terms are used herein, moral blame shall not attach, and hence there will not be criminal responsibility. The rule we state in this opinion is designed to meet these requirements.

3. Does Psychopathy Exist?

As a popular explanation for criminal behavior, few categories of psychological abnormality seem to have greater appeal than psychopathy. It seems so inevitable, so self-evident, that crimes would be committed by the "asocial, aggressive, highly impulsive person," as the psychopath is described in the following selection, by William and Joan McCord. Unfortunately, many psychiatrists are doubtful that psychopathy exists as a meaningful diagnostic entity; and there is some question that our understanding is much increased by saying asocial, aggressive, or impulsive acts are committed because people are asocial, aggressive, or impulsive.

A sweaty crowd jammed the courtroom and gaped at a slender, passive young man sitting in the dock. He seemed detached from the melee, bored by the complicated legal process. If the papers had not splashed his picture across the front pages, few people would have known that this was the defendant, William Cook—"Billy the Kid"—brutal slayer of five human beings.

In his few years of life, Cook had been a terrible scourge to society. His youth had been spent in fights, homosexual orgies, and robberies. His adult life, short as it was, had culminated in the killing of a fellow robber, in the murder of an innocent man and wife, and—most shockingly—in the shooting of their two children.

This was the day the crowd awaited. Today Billy Cook would "get what was coming to him." What could he possibly deserve but death? The crowd had little patience with the legal process that led to this moment. They despised the hairsplitting psychiatrists who had maintained that Cook was "mentally ill, although not insane." Few of the spectators understood the esoteric arguments among the expert witnesses. Three defense psychiatrists had asserted that Cook was "psychopathic." The prosecution agreed but added, to the joy of the crowd, "So what?"

As the judge read the sentence, a dissatisfied rustle swept through the crowd. Not death, but "300 years in Alcatraz" was Billy Cook's fate. Few heard or cared to hear what the judge so solemnly added: "Billy Cook is a symbol of society's failure."

To save itself from other Billy Cooks, society must come to understand the psychopathic personality. Psychopathy, possibly more than other mental disorders, threatens the safety, the serenity, and the security of American life. From the ranks of the psychopaths come political demagogues, the most violent criminals, the riot leaders, sexual misfits, and drug addicts. Psychologist Robert Lindner has observed: "Hydra-headed and slippery to the touch though it is, psychopathy represents the most expensive and most destructive of all known forms of aberrant behavior." Not only does the psychopath cost society dearly, but he represents such a unique, fascinating example of the human species that the understanding of his disorder can contribute greatly to our general knowledge of human nature. For, as later chapters will show, he rests at one extreme of the continuum of human variety: he is the unsocialized man, the "lone wolf," the stranger to social intercourse.

Just what is psychopathy? For 150 years, science has known of the psychopath's existence; for at least 140 years, scientists have quarreled over the definition of his disorder.

A minority has maintained that the psychopathic personality, as a distinct clinical syndrome, does not exist. One of these dissenters, psychiatrist Olof Kinberg, commented a few years ago: "[The concept] should be abrogated as theoretically unsatisfactory, practically misleading and destructive to scientific thinking." And Dr. Leo Kanner has commented, "A psychopath is somebody you don't like." Few of those who have dealt with criminals, worked in mental hospitals, or participated in social casework would agree with Kinberg or Kanner. Indeed, most investigators believe that the concept not only has meaning, but that it is indispensable. Even Kinberg surreptitiously recognized that certain individuals require a special classification. "In the good old times," he admitted, "one exported such cases to the U.S.A. where most of them went to the dogs or were sent back by their consulates."

Although most social scientists admit the existence of the psychopath, they have extraordinary difficulty in defining his disease. As a psychiatrist with long experience recently exclaimed: "I know an elephant when I see one, but damned if I can define one!"

Much of the difficulty with definition has, however, been superficial and overly stressed. Hervey Cleckly, an American psychiatrist with vast experience with psychopaths, has observed, "At a meeting of the American Psychiatric Association, or a staff conference at a state hospital, if a physician expresses an opinion to one of his colleagues about a psychopath, it is clearly, and at once, understood that he is not speaking of a cyclothymic or schizoid personality or of ordinary homosexuality but of the grave character and behavior disorder so familiar to most psychiatrists as a distinct and easily recognizable entity." Below their surface argument, most social scientists postulate a common core of psychopathy with which many would agree: *The psychopath is an asocial, aggressive, highly impulsive person, who feels little or no guilt and is unable to form lasting bonds of affection with other human beings.*

4. Id, Ego, and Superego

Freudian theory has radically altered our ideas about the human psyche, and although psychoanalysis is now undergoing critical review by many scientists, it has provided an invaluable key to a number of problems in criminal behavior, as indicated in the following piece by Franz Alexander and Hugh Staub. The authors carefully avoid a gross stereotype of the criminal and try to develop a classification that takes into account the variety of men who break the law. It is an essential step, if we are to separate the causes that underlie the bewildering array of behavior classified as crime.

We inferred already that any attempt to establish definite criminal types, biologically discernible from the normal personality, fails to take into consideration the great number of the more or less asocial individuals. The relatively very small number of individuals who, as a result of degeneracy, i.e., heredity or prenatal defects of development, are incapable of social adjustment, do not represent characteristically the class of criminal individuals.

The majority of criminals are not different physically and grossly psychologically from the normal individual; the deviation from the normal is a matter of development, which depends more on the life history of the person than upon heredity; in other words, the greatest number of criminals could under different circumstances have developed into normal individuals. The attempt of Lombroso and his school to draw a sharp line between the normal and the criminal comes from the narcissistic wish of the scientist to separate himself and his normal fellow men from the criminal, as if the latter belonged to a different race of beings, different biologically and recognizable through definite, easily discernible physical signs. Any attempt to cross out this artificial line of demarcation is met with the same affective opposition as was the Darwinian theory of evolution, which injured the human pride by making man evolve from a line of animals.

The psychoanalytic study of unconscious psychic life leads to the conviction that every part of the human personality, which is socially adjusted, represents a later and comparatively labile product of a special evolution.

However, within the innermost nucleus of the personality, which is both quantitatively and dynamically much more powerful, it is impossible to differentiate normal from criminal impulses. The human being enters the world as a criminal, i.e., socially not adjusted. During the first years of his life, the human individual preserves his criminality to the fullest degree. His actual social adjustment begins only at the time after the Œdipus complex is overcome. This happens during the so-called latency period which was described by Freud. This period begins between the ages of four and six, and ends at puberty. It is at this period that the development of the criminal begins to differentiate itself from that of the normal. The future normal individual succeeds (mostly in the latency period) in partly repressing his genuine criminal instinctive drives, and thus cuts them out of motor expression, and partly in transforming them into socially acceptable striving; the future criminal more or less fails in carrying out this adjustment.

The criminal carries out in his actions his natural unbridled instinctual drives; he acts as the child would act if it only could. The repressed, and therefore unconscious criminality of the normal man finds a few socially harmless outlets, like the dream and phantasy life, neurotic symptoms and also some transitional forms of behavior which are less harmless, like duelling, boxing, bull fights and, occasionally, the free expression of one's criminality in war.

No better proof for the general criminality of mankind could be found than the proof which would be brought about by the daring experiment of depriving, say, the Spanish nation of its bull fights, the Americans of their boxing and football games, old Europe of its soldier game and the world of its penal codes. The universal criminality of man of today demands violent, purely physical outlets; without them it would become transformed into a battle of all against all.

The only difference between the criminal and the normal individual is that the normal man partially controls his criminal drives and finds outlets for them in socially harmless activities. This power of controlling, and of the domestication of the primitive, unsocial tendencies is acquired by the individual as a result of education. In other words, criminality, generally speaking, is not a congenital defect but a defect in the bringing up; this statement does not cover certain borderline cases which should be considered separately. Our contention will become clearer if we could imagine that all the children of the world between the ages of two to six should suddenly become physically superior to the adult and were thus able to dominate the adult to the same degree as the adult dominates the child. These children, let us imagine further, would then set themselves to act out all their phantasies. These Gulliverian giant children dominating a world of dwarf-like adults would present a hundred-per-cent criminality in action.

The first drive in relation to the outside world which the newly born individual experiences is the drive to grasp, to dominate. This drive in its earliest expression appears in the form of the cannibalistic possession of the breast of the mother, a sort of a partial eating up of the mother. The psychic content of this drive on this level is known in the psychoanalytic theory of instinctual drives as the *oral-sadistic* phase of development of the individual. The pregenital sexuality of the suckling finds its satisfaction in the mouth activity while sucking the mother's breast, the nipple or the bottle or the thumb. In this phase one is naturally unable to find any trace of the future social attitude, i.e., the tendency to consider the interests of others.

Disturbances in the normal functioning during this instinctual phase, particularly any educational mistake in the process of weaning, might influence the educability of the individual along the lines of social relationships. Individuals who at every frustration of a wish show a tendency to violent action, who react to any postponement of a pleasure with uncontrollable impatience, prove frequently to have been orally spoiled children; these individuals serve as a proof of how exceptionally long indulgence during the period of sucking reappears with a vengeance in an adult. But weaning must inevitably come some day, and such spoiled babies respond to it with spiteful resistance; they do not want to give up a rightfully acquired habit. Abraham and Alexander consider that the deepest roots of kleptomania are to be found in the history of this period.

The child finds itself compelled for the first time to submit to the wishes of the adult when it begins to be taught habits of cleanliness. At first the child experiences a definite pleasure in relation to its excretory functions; this pleasure consists either of holding back or expressing the excreta; this pleasure, as well as the coprophilic tendencies of the child, is considerably interfered with when the adult begins to present demands for orderliness, cleanliness, and propriety.

Interference with its primitive instinctual drives brings the child to the realization that its sovereignty is badly encroached upon; it becomes impossible for the child to utilize the excretory processes whenever and in whatever manner it wishes, and thus to derive pleasure from them whenever it wishes, in whatever manner and degree it wishes. One of the chief characteristics of this anal erotism is that it gives one a sense of power, a feeling that one's pleasures do not depend upon others; for, in contrast to breast or bottle, which can and are always taken away and therefore are connected with a feeling of insecurity, the excrements are products created by the child itself, and take the place of the breast or bottle as a source of pleasure. In other words, the source of oral pleasure is always in the hands of the adult, while the fecal masses, hidden within the body, are outside the reach of grown-ups who want to dominate.

The psychoanalytic literature has not yet considered with sufficient detail this strong drive for independence, the spite with which it is connected, and the high self-esteem of the anal phase of development. It was first recognized by Freud as stubbornness of the anal erotic; it is a sort of overcompensation for the sad experiences met with in the oral phase in which the child depended for pleasure on the whim of the mother.

However, sooner or later, the child learns to control and regulate its sphincter activity, because it is afraid of being censured and punished by the adults. The first crime which all humans, without exception, sooner or later commit is the violation of the prescription for cleanliness. Under the rule of this penal code of the nursery, man for the first time becomes acquainted with the punishment which the world metes out to the individual transgressors. Ferenczi, therefore, is right when he speaks of the "sphincter morality" as the beginning and foundation of adult human morality. As a prototype of certain refractory criminals who persist in their spiteful rejection of social demands, one can imagine a baby sitting on its little chamber pot persistently rejecting any demands coming from the outside; it sits in this sovereign position and feels superior to the grown-ups.

At the moment when the child begins to impose inhibitions on the demands of its own sphincter, it makes the first decisive step toward the adjustment to the outside world; at that moment it creates an inhibitory agency within its own personality, and this agency from now on demands from within what the outside world demanded heretofore. In other words, a definite part of the child's personality identifies itself with the demands of the person who is bringing it up. We thus deal here with an identification with a *demand,* i.e., a partial identification with a person; at a later phase the child will identify itself with an adult *person* as a whole instead of with a demand only.

This education to cleanliness becomes a prototype for the future restrictions of instinctual life; a disturbance during this phase of development may naturally serve as a cause of a future disturbance in one's social adjustment.

The anal character traits which were described by Freud, Jones, and Abraham, in their exaggerated form present a number of anti-social and criminal characteristics.

The exaggerated, unsocial, stubborn bluntness of some violators of the law corresponds to the unyielding persistence of infantile anal spite. The characteristic self-centered stubbornness of the anal character acquires in the majority of criminals the form of proud, inaccessible spite, which is directed against all humanity.

In the course of the development of every child we find that its interests gradually broaden, and in addition to its relationship to its own physiological processes it tries to establish a relationship with the outer world. The instinctual drives in the phases of oral and anal development which were just mentioned were psychologically concerned with intake of food and its elimination; instinctual pleasure was derived from these two processes. However, in view of the fact that they begin to be directed toward objects of the outer world, they approach for the first time a psychological level of the adult individual. As is to be expected, the first objects of the outside world toward which the child's interest is directed are the immediate members of the family. Thus, the relationship of the child to father, mother, brothers and sisters, becomes the central problem of the future adult individual. The psychological management of these relationships on the part of the growing human being becomes definitely the decisive factor in the whole development and functioning of the adult person. After thirty years of therapeutic work and psychoanalytical research this point may be considered definitely proved. The way in which the child overcomes the conflicts arising from this situation determines whether it will develop into a healthy or sick individual, or whether his general behavior will be that of a socially adjusted person or that of a criminal. We should like to emphasize now, and we shall be able to prove later in these pages, that psychoneurosis and criminality are defects in one's social adjustment; they hardly differ from one another in their respective psychological contents; the differences are those of psychological dynamics. Both the neurotic and the criminal fell victims to their incapacity of finding a socially acceptable solution of the conflicts which the relationships to the various members of the family engendered. The neurotic expresses symbolically by means of his symptoms, which are socially innocuous, the same things which the criminal does by means of real actions. This important fact opens to us a promising method of study; we can understand the psychological content of a criminal act through the psychoanalysis of the neuroses.

We thus come to the fundamental problem as to which are the circumstances responsible for the fact that, in some individuals, the unconscious criminal phantasy finds it sufficient to come to expression in the substitution form of a neurotic symptom, while in other individuals it demands the motor expression in the form of criminal acts. This problem requires the consideration of the economic and structural characteristics of the psychic apparatus; it is a problem dealing with the relative strength of inhibitory psychic agencies as compared with the pressure coming from the undomesticated remnants of our instinctual drives. We shall be able to throw light on the problem if we consider the data acquired by psychoanalysis with regard to the structural and dynamic development of the human personality.

It is self-evident that, in order to gain an understanding of criminality, we shall have to investigate the process by means of which a socially adjusted Ego develops out of a great homogeneous reservoir of instincts which originally were unsocial; this reservoir of instinctual drives is called the Id.

The two pregenital phases of adjustment which were described above, oral and anal, are but preparatory to the first great necessity, which demands that the object relationship to parents and siblings be transformed into relationships of a social nature.

The problem which the child has to solve is this: it must bring his original sexual attitude toward the parent of the opposite sex into some sort of harmony with its attitude toward the parent of the same sex. The little son, for instance, who had dropped the objectless pleasure-seeking of oral and anal nature, lives under the pressure of a sexual wish for his mother; although this wish does not always appear in consciousness, it is always and definitely present in the unconscious. Under the pressure of this wish the little son is thrown into sexual rivalry with his father, who becomes his sexual competitor, as it were.

The fear of the father, who is stronger, comes to expression as castration anxiety; this anxiety inhibits the active masculine drive; the passive feminine tendencies which are always present in man as a result of his natural biological bisexuality and of oral fixations may, under the pressure of castration anxiety, come to the foreground; hence, a passive feminine attitude toward the more powerful father may set in. One and the same person may thus be simultaneously loved in a passive feminine way and hated because of competition. The little boy finds himself in a state of conflict due to ambivalence of feeling. This situation which is charged with such conflicting emotions presses the boy to find a way out. He then attempts to look upon his father as the prototype of what he himself wants to be; he wants to become like father, i.e., to identify himself with him. This identification is originally presented by a phantasy in which the child hopes to replace the father in the latter's sexual role; however, this identification carries with it also the following consequences: the role of the father as a person who rules and forbids is taken over by the personality of the child; the prototype father is thus introjected and as a result a new partial personality is erected within the personality of the son; this partial personality acts as a representative of the father, as it were, and functions as an organ inhibiting the primitive instinctual impulses of the boy.

The child, at the time, is not yet physiologically mature and is as yet unable to function sexually as the father does; the full expression of this function must therefore wait; the *inhibitory* functions, however, become effective *at once*. Thus the first real social adjustment appears to be a result of compromise between a drive toward a lustful pleasure and the prohibition of this drive. In other words, the individual succeeds in restricting the expression of instinctual impulses in the hope that in the future real gratification will be secured. This compromise is not satisfactory to the psychic life of the child, which for the time being is guided only by the pleasure principle; it must be accepted, however, under the pressure of fear of pain, which unavoidably arises at the very moment when an attempt is made to obtain the gratification of forbidden instinctual demands. Hence a complete identification with father becomes impossible; for physiological incapacity and castration anxiety prevent it; this identification does not go beyond the function of inhibition and a few sublimatory reactions.

The child has to console himself with the hope that a complete identification will be achieved at some future date ("When I grow up, I will . . .

etc."); for the present, he finds consolation for his renunciation in that he is loved (by father).

The wish for being loved, according to Freud, plays a greater role in the life of the girl than in that of the boy; the boy's wish is stimulated mainly by the fear of the punishing father.

Our investigations are substantially limited to those of men, because men continue to play a dominant role, not only in criminality, but in the general structure of society. Our conclusions, however, are valid for both sexes.

The fear of the father, the wish to be loved by him, and the tendency to take him as a model, thus represent the main springs in the process of identification as far as its inhibitory effect is concerned—an effect actually wished by the son. This identification produces an inner psychic agency which represents simultaneously an inhibitory function and an ideal to be achieved. This part of the personality, i.e., the social part of it, we call the Superego; it is differentiated from the rest of the Ego.

In summing up, we may say that the differentiation of the Superego from the rest of the personality could be described as a process which is dominated by the pleasure principle. Fear of punishment and of loss of love; in other words, the avoidance of real pain, and the craving to obtain positive pleasure by means of being loved, the hope that the future will provide many possibilities for gratification through complete identification with the educator, present the instinctual springs for the formation of the Superego.

As a result of this new formation within the Ego, a part of this Ego accepts and incorporates within itself the social demands of the environment, of the parents and of all other persons who have to do with the education of the child; this part of the Ego functions as a Superego and inhibits the forbidden instinctual impulses. The relationship between the Superego and the rest of the personality is thus a sort of a replica of the relationship which originally existed between the child and the adult who brought him up. Thus the original conflict between parent and the child becomes transformed into an inner psychic conflict between two parts of the same personality, the Superego and the Ego. The fear of real punishment (castration anxiety) becomes transformed into fear of one's own conscience, i.e., the fear becomes internalized; the Ego feels it facing its Superego. In the same way, the wish to be loved by one's parents becomes internalized as a striving to remain in harmony with one's own conscience.

It is characteristic of all psychoneuroses and of the majority of criminals that the formation and proper organization of a Superego within their respective personalities remains imperfect. The organization of the Ego and the Superego into a harmonious unit fails, the Superego remains a sort of a foreign body within their personalities; there is a constant persisting tension between the Ego and the Superego; the Ego strives to regain its original independence and to follow as it once did the primitive, unsocial impulses of the Id. This striving for independence, however, is always thwarted by the threatening presence of both reality and the demands of the Superego.

This existence of the Superego as a foreign body within the personality can be best observed in a child during the early period of Superego development. One can observe a definite period, during which the Superego is still greatly dependent upon real persons, who serve as prototypes for its development. The brilliant observations of Anna Freud proved that during this transitional stage the child behaves according to a sort of double standard; in the presence of the parents it behaves in accordance with their demands for good behavior and thus follows the pressure coming from its own Superego; yet when alone it returns at once to its primitive unsocial nature. We had the opportunity to observe this phenomenon in a three-year-old child. As it was getting off its chamber pot it looked on its own feces with unconcealed delight and exclaimed. "It smells so nice"; at that moment it noticed its mother and added with a guilty conscience, "No, whee!" During this period, when the Superego just begins to become an integral part of the personality, but is not yet entirely incorporated into it as a solid unit, one may best observe how the Ego tries to rid itself of this burdensome inhibitory agency. Only gradually and under the constant educative pressure from the adults is a successful introjection accomplished.

It must be borne in mind, however, that in the majority of adults, and throughout their lives, there always remains a certain dependence of the superego on its prototypes. As soon as confidence in authority is lost, the inner power of the Superego becomes shattered. It would undoubtedly be difficult to find a man who would persist in remaining righteous if the whole world about him were violating all social restrictions.

Let us return to and clarify our considerations of the role of the sense of justice, which we reviewed above. We pointed out that, when the sense of justice is sufficiently injured, the inner restrictions of our instincts weaken and a number of repressed impulses break through; we stated that injustice was perceived by the Ego as a breaking of a silent social contract; the powerful restricting agencies of social life not having made good their promises, the Ego feels that it need not continue the policy of renunciation. The details of this social process become clearer now; it is under the pressure of the Superego that the Ego agreed to accept all the most important and fundamental restrictions on the instinctual impulses. The Superego is the inner representative of reality which demands renunciation; its inhibitory power, as we have seen, is more or less dependent upon the relationship which exists between the Ego and authority; when the Ego loses its confidence in those representing authority, the Superego, as the latter's psychic representative, loses to the same extent the power which it holds over the instinctual life of man.

We may then describe the regressive phenomenon which takes place in case of injury to the sense of justice as a process in which the Superego loses its inhibitory power over the Ego; the Ego then unopposed follows the tendencies of the Id. The remarkable thing in this, like in any other regressive phenomena, is the tendency to expand. The injustice may be related to a very insignificant matter, but the reactive breaking-through of repressed impulses not infrequently upsets the oldest and the most fundamental cultural restrictions. Michael Kohlass, who unjustly lost two horses, derives from this minor injury the right to kill. Such manner of thinking is reminiscent of that of the youngster who says: "When the parents are unjust, I have a right to do everything." We now can see clearly that our psychic apparatus took over the restrictions imposed by civilization reluctantly and, in fact, unwillingly.

Those instinctual restrictions which are developmentally the oldest, and which are most fundamental in the process of social formations, come entirely from the inhibitory power of the Superego and not from any prohibitions imposed from the outside. We may say incidentally that these fundamental social trends of man are derived chiefly from the tendencies which come from the Œdipus complex. We shall consider later the details of this interesting phenomenon.

On the whole, however, the civilized man of today still continues to follow the pattern of his childhood, and most of his self-renunciations are due to the fear of punishment. This inhibitory fear is covered by a thin layer of moral, but not yet quite organized inner inhibitions, which come from the youngest fringes of the Superego. The reason why the breaking-through of the repressed instinctual impulses has the tendency to expand is that, in case of even a relatively minor injustice on the part of the constituted authorities, the deepest, the apparently solidly organized inhibitions become threatened and loosened. Thus, for instance, we observed the following phenomenon: A political criminal in prison, who naturally considered his punishment unjust, had during his prison term vivid incestuous dreams accompanied by nocturnal emissions. Even the inhibition of incestuous wishes was thus lifted while the man suffered at the hands of what he thought the unjust law; it was as if the prisoner had said to himself: "If my father (the State) treats me in this fashion, then I don't need to respect his privileges and may take mother." Children use this mode of thinking quite readily, in order to weaken the moral authority of their parents; neurotics and neurotic criminals utilize the same method in order to weaken their own conscience, and thus to grant the Ego a free hand in the matter of gratifying its anti-social tendencies. As one of the writers expressed it elsewhere, they bribe or disarm their conscience by means of a voluntary acceptance of some suffering. All forms of psychoneuroses are based on this "bribery" mechanism; they represent a compromise made by the Ego in order to obtain simultaneous gratification of both the prohibited Id drives and the demands of the Superego.

In other words, in a neurosis the unadjusted Id tendencies succeed in gaining a substitutive gratification, despite the presence of a strict social agency within the personality. The same mechanisms which are at work in the production of a neurosis are operative in the behavior of the greatest majority of criminals. The difference between the neurotic and the criminal consists in the following: the neurotic symptom is a gratification which permits of no complete expression in action and is only of subjective significance to the neurotic himself. The neurotic suffering has the meaning of a self-inflicted punishment; the criminal gratification, however, is obtained by means of a real act which is directed against the outside world, and the consequence, the punishment, appears to be inflicted by the outside world. The neurosis thus appears to be a later development in the evolution of man, a sort of intrapsychic replica of the more primitive process—crime and punishment.

A neurosis, like the history of a crime, consists of two phases: in the first, a gratification of a wish which is not acceptable to reality or the Superego takes place; in the second, a punishment, a suffering sets in as a reaction of society or the Superego against the forbidden gratification.

The large group of criminals who show a psychic organization akin to the one of the neurotic patient, i.e., those who show the presence of an inner conflict between the social and anti-social tendencies of their personality, we shall call the group of *Neurotic Criminals*. Under this designation, we shall group those criminals who show unconscious psychic processes that might have led to the development of a neurosis. Modern psychiatry calls such criminals psychopathic personalities, hysterical or epileptic personalities, who, according to Aschaffenburg and other psychiatrists, make up the bulk of all transgressors of the law. The only difference between them and the psychoneurotics is that in the latter the tension between unconscious tendencies and repressing forces is resolved *autoplastically* (symptom), while in the former it is resolved *alloplastically* (criminal acts).

Later on we shall attempt to prove that this type of criminal is neither frightened away, nor inhibited, nor made a better person by the reaction of present-day society, i.e., by punishment, for in such cases of neurotic criminality punishment acts as a temptation to crime, and criminality is thus furthered instead of stopped.

Thus we may definitely recognize the existence of a group of criminals in whom the prototypes of social behavior remain foreign to the Ego.

There are also criminals who betray no tension between their instinctual drives and social demands; from the practical point of view this type is very important. Aichhorn, in his book *Wayward Youth,* describes this variety of criminal, particularly the young one. Aichhorn came to the conclusion that these individuals have not only a criminal Ego, but also a criminal Superego; they are well adjusted to the criminal prototypes of their social conscience and to their criminal environment; hence they live in accordance with the dictates of a special criminal morality; this means that they did carry out the process of identification with the interests of a community, but this community is not that of law-abiding citizens.

We must remember that the normal, non-criminal individual does not share the ideas of the whole community to which he belongs, for, as a rule, he belongs to a certain class, to a sort of a caste that has a special ideology of its own. The psychological content of the ideals and of the Superego of a proletarian differs considerably from those of an aristocrat; those of a pacifist and a militarist are also different; what one considers criminal, the other considers as a postulate of the highest ethical type. The psychological structure of the criminal mentioned above does not differ from that of a normal individual. He merely belongs to a social class that lives by different standards. We shall call this group the group of *Normal Criminals.* It will be again noted that these individuals are well adjusted to a totally different community, and that within the limits of that community they are normal social beings. The internal conflict between Ego and Superego is not present, or, at any rate, not greater than in the case of a normal person. Only the exaggerated conceit of a scientist, who is bound and determined to defend the standards of a definite social organization, will make one seek biological points of differentiation between these individuals and ourselves.

We think, therefore, that these criminals are to be looked upon as normal persons who had the misfortune of adjusting themselves to a weaker part of the community. Many of these, if they were brought up outside the criminal environment, would have grown up to be highly adjusted social individuals in our sense of the word. Nothing shows this point clearer than the romantic literature dealing with the criminal; all its traditions and literary presentations bear witness to bravery, spirit of sacrifice, sympathy with the weaker, chivalry, etc.

Thus we have two groups of criminals, one which is psychically sick and another which is psychically healthy, but socially abnormal; there is a third group which, as compared with these two, includes but a very small minority of criminals; yet forensic medicine has been and still is paying greater attention to this minority. We have in mind those criminals who were either retarded in their development because of defective biological growth or those whose psychological personality was destroyed by some organic processes (idiots, paretics, schizophrenics and epileptics).

The transition from this group to that of the neurotic is not easy to denote. To take schizophrenia as an example—it has not yet been definitely established to what degree constitutional factors and the general history of the individual are respectively responsible for the disease; in some cases, it appears one factor is more responsible than the other; in other cases, the reverse appears to be true. To cite another instance, we may refer to epilepsy, which appears to present a sort of a transitional form between psychoneurosis and organic disease.

At any rate, the criminals belonging to this group are not so much products of the psychological pressure which environment or life circumstances exerted on them, as they are victims of organic processes or heredity; we shall designate them as *criminals who are organically conditioned.*

We thus delimit three large classes of criminals:

I. *The neurotic criminal,* whose hostile activity against society is a result of an intrapsychic conflict between the social and anti-social components of his personality; this conflict, like that of a psychoneurosis, comes from impressions of earliest childhood and from circumstances of later life (psychological etiology).

II. *The normal criminal,* whose psychic organization is similar to that of the normal individual, except that he identified himself with criminal prototypes (sociological etiology).

III. The criminal whose criminality is conditioned by some pathological process of *organic* nature (biological etiology).

These three classes consist of individuals who, as a result of some definite, organic or psychic factors, become criminals; they are *chronic criminals;* there exists in addition a number of normal individuals who, under certain specific conditions become *acute criminals.* The criminal act of the *acute type* is not characteristic of any special group of people; as a matter of fact, every human individual, without exception, under certain conditions and situations is capable of a transgression of the law. The outstanding factor in such crimes is not the peculiarity of the person who committed it, but the singularity of the circumstances which lead to it. While such criminals cannot be fitted into any special typological scheme, and while they are least of all important from the social standpoint, psychologically they are extremely interesting. Moreover, from the standpoint of pronouncing a just verdict, it is of greatest practical importance to make a correct diagnosis of a crime of this type; for in such cases one need not undertake any special treatment, or take any measures in order to avoid the repetition of the crime.

All these classes and forms of criminality which we have just outlined fall between two extreme types of criminality, which occupy the opposite poles of our scheme and which are conceivable only theoretically.

On the one end we find the pure criminal, who had not formed any Superego to represent the demands of society within him; this criminal, when and if he does restrict his anti-social tendencies, does so without any inner urge and unwillingly; he does it merely because he is afraid of the outside authorities. At the other extreme end of our scheme we should find the perfectly adjusted social individual, who without any inner conflict considers the interests of the community before he considers his own; in other words, his Superego and Ego would be fused into one. In reality it is impossible to find these conflict-less individuals; only intermediary types can be found. These intermediary types (every single civilized individual belongs to one of the intermediary types) do not possess a homogeneous psychological organization; they always experience a certain tension between the primitive and socialized parts of the psychic apparatus.

In so far as these pages are devoted to the psychology of the criminal, we shall consider chiefly the *neurotic* and the *acute* criminal. The *normal criminal* and the majority of the professional criminals belonging to this type shall occupy our attention only in so far as we shall attempt to review critically the whole problem of criminality. As to the criminals whose criminality is based on pathological organic conditions, they belong to that chapter of penal jurisprudence and legal medicine which best succeeded in solving the problem of diagnosis and treatment; for such cases a strict scientific psychology may be dispensed with; gross descriptive psychiatry usually suffices.

5. A Psychiatrist Expresses Doubt

As we pointed out, the validity of many psychoanalytic ideas is much debated today. Some of the most critical and informed voices come from the ranks of psychiatrists themselves, and Dr. Thomas Szasz raises some important and disturbing issues. His discussion takes us a little away from the major point we have been considering—the role of psychological factors as a cause of crime—but he makes us confront a problem that illuminates our concern. What do we really mean by mental illness? If we call the criminal sick, what are the consequences?

Psychiatry today is in the curious position of being viewed simultaneously with too much reverence and with undue contempt. Indeed, thoughtful Americans can be roughly divided between those who dismiss all forms of psychiatric practice as worthless or harmful and those who regard it as a panacea for crime, unhappiness, political fanaticism, promiscuity, juvenile delinquency—and virtually every other moral, personal, and social ill of our time.

The adherents of this exaggerated faith are, I believe, the larger and certainly the more influential group in shaping contemporary social policy. It is they who beat the drums for large-scale mental-health programs and who use the prestige and the services of a massive psychiatric establishment as a shield of illusion, concealing some ugly realities we would rather not face. Thus when we read in the paper that the alcoholic, the rapist, or the vandal needs or will be given "psychiatric care," we are reassured that the problem is being solved or, in any event, effectively dealt with, and we dismiss it from our minds.

I contend that we have no right to this easy absolution from responsibility. In saying this I do not, as a practicing psychiatrist, intend to belittle the help which my profession can give to some troubled individuals. We have made significant progress since the pre-Freudian era when psychiatry was a purely medical and custodial enterprise. In contemporary America, much of psychiatric practice consists of psychotherapy, and much of psychiatric theory is psychological and social, rather than biological and medical.

Our refusal to recognize this difference—that is, between deviations from biological norms which we usually call "illness," and deviations from social norms which we call "mental illness" (or crime, delinquency,

From Thomas S. Szasz, "What Psychiatry Can and Cannot Do," **Harper's Magazine**, CCXXIX (February 1964), 50–53. Reprinted by permission of the author.

etc.)—has made it possible to popularize the simplistic clichés of current mental-health propaganda. One of these, for instance, is the deceptive slogan, "Mental illness is like any other illness." This is not true; psychiatric and medical problems are not fundamentally similar. In curing a disease like syphilis or pneumonia, the physician benefits both the patient and society. Can the psychiatrist who "cures" a "neurosis" make the same claim? Often he cannot, for in "mental illness" we find the individual *in conflict* with those about him—his family, his friends, his employer, perhaps his whole society. Do we expect psychiatry to help the individual—or society? If the interests of the two conflict, as they often do, the psychiatrist can help one only by harming the other.

Let us, for example, examine the case of a man I will call Victor Clauson. He is a junior executive with a promising future, a wife who loves him, and two healthy children. Nevertheless he is anxious and unhappy. He is bored with his job which he believes saps his initiative and destroys his integrity; he is also dissatisfied with his wife, and convinced he never loved her. Feeling like a slave to his company, his wife, and his children, Clauson realizes that he has lost control over the conduct of his life.

Is this man "sick"? And if so, what can be done about it? At least half a dozen alternatives are open to him. He could throw himself into his present work or change jobs or have an affair or get a divorce. Or he could develop a psychosomatic symptom such as headaches and consult a doctor. Or, as still another alternative, he could seek out a psychotherapist. Which of these alternatives is the *right* one for him? The answer is not easy.

For in fact, hard work, an affair, a divorce, a new job may all "help" him; and so may psychotherapy. But "treatment" cannot change his external, social situation; only he can do that. What psychoanalysis (and some other therapies) *can* offer him is a better knowledge of himself, which may enable him to make *new choices* in the conduct of his life.

Is Clauson "mentally sick"? If we so label him, what then is he to be cured of? Unhappiness? Indecision? The consequences of earlier unwise decisions?

These are problems in living, not diseases. And by and large it is such problems that are brought to the psychiatrist's office. To ameliorate them he offers not treatment or cure but psychological counseling. To be of any avail this process requires a consenting, cooperative client. There is, indeed, no way to "help" an individual who does not want to be a psychiatric patient. When treatment is *imposed* on a person, inevitably he sees it as serving not his own best interests, but the interests of those who brought him to the psychiatrist (and who often pay him).

Take the case of an elderly widow I will call Mrs. Rachel Abelson. Her husband was a successful businessman who died five years ago, bequeathing part of his estate of $4 million to his children and grandchildren, part to charities, and one-third to his wife. Mrs. Abelson had always been a frugal woman, whose life revolved around her husband. After he died, however, she changed. She began to give her money away—to her widowed sister, to charities, and finally to distant relatives abroad.

After a few years, Mrs. Abelson's children remonstrated, urging her to treat herself better instead of wasting her money on people who had long managed by themselves. But Mrs. Abelson persisted in doing what she felt was "the right thing." Her children were wealthy; she enjoyed helping others.

Finally, the Abelson children consulted the family attorney. He was equally dismayed by the prospect that Mrs. Abelson might spend all the money she controlled in this fashion. Like the children, he reasoned that if Mr. Abelson had wanted to help his third cousin's poverty-stricken daughters in Romania, he could have done so himself; but he never did. Convinced they ought to carry out the essence of their father's intention and keep the money in the family, the Abelson children petitioned to have their mother declared mentally incompetent to manage her affairs. Thereafter Mrs. Abelson became inconsolable. Her bitter accusations and the painful scenes that resulted only convinced her children that she really was mentally abnormal. When she refused to enter a private sanitarium voluntarily, she was committed by court order. She died two years later, and her will—leaving most of her assets to distant relatives—was easily broken on psychiatric grounds.

Like thousands of other involuntary mental patients, Mrs. Abelson was given psychiatric care in the hope of changing behavior offensive to others. Indeed, what was Mrs. Abelson's illness? Spending her money unwisely? Disinheriting her sons? In effect, recourse to psychiatry provided Mrs. Abelson's children with a socially acceptable solution for their dilemma, not hers. To an appalling degree state mental hospitals perform a like function for the less affluent members of our society.

Out of all too many comparable cases, I will cite that of a man we may call Tim Kelleher, who worked steadily as a truck driver for forty years, supporting a wife and nine children. In his early sixties, Kelleher found jobs getting scarcer. Now in his late seventies, he has not worked for over a decade. Since his wife died a few years ago he has lived with one or another of his children.

For two years his daughter Kathleen, mother of four, has been caring for him. Because the old man has grown progressively senile and burdensome, Kathleen's husband wants to shift the responsibility to the other children. But they all feel they've done their share.

Mr. Kelleher's future depends on what his family decides to do with him. One of them may still be willing to take care of him, but if not, he will be committed to a state mental hospital. His case will be diagnosed as a "senile psychosis" or something similar. About a third of the patients now in our mental hospitals are such "geriatric" cases. This is how psychiatry meets a purely socioeconomic need.

If Mr. Kelleher or one of his children were even moderately wealthy, they could hire a companion or nurse to care for him at home or they could place him in a private nursing home. There would be no need to label him a "mental patient" and confine him to a building he will never again leave, and where he will doubtless die within a year.

But for the poor, the public mental hospital is often the only way. Such is the plight of Mrs. Anna Tarranti (this is not her real name). At thirty-two—but looking ten years older—she has just been delivered of her seventh child. Her husband is a construction worker, sporadically employed, and a heavy drinker. After each of the last three babies was born, Mrs. Tarranti was so "depressed" that she had to stay in the hospital an extra week or more. Now she complains of exhaustion, cannot eat or sleep, and does not want to see her baby. At the same time she feels guilty for not being a good mother and says she ought to die.

The fact is that Mrs. Tarranti is overwhelmed. She has more children than she wants, a husband who earns only a marginal living, and religious beliefs that virtually prohibit birth control. What should she do? She knows that if she goes home, she'll soon be pregnant again, a prospect she cannot tolerate. She would like to stay in the hospital, but the obstetrical ward is too busy to keep her long without a bona fide obstetrical illness.

Again, psychiatry comes to the rescue. Mrs. Tarranti's condition is diagnosed as a "post-partum depression" and she is committed to the state hospital. As in the case of Mr. Kelleher, society has found no more decent solution to a human problem than involuntary confinement in a mental hospital.

In effect psychiatry has accepted the job of warehousing society's undesirables. Such, alas, has long been its role. More than a hundred years ago, the great French psychiatrist Philippe Pinel observed that "public asylums for maniacs have been regarded as places of confinement for such of its members as have become dangerous to the peace of society."

Nor have we any right to comfort ourselves with the belief that in our enlightened age confinement in a mental institution is really the same as any other kind of hospitalization. For even though we show more compassion and understanding toward the insane than some of our forebears, the fact is that the person diagnosed as mentally ill is stigmatized—particularly if he has been confined in a public mental hospital. These stigmata cannot be removed by mental-health "education," for the root of the matter is our intolerance of certain kinds of behavior.

Most people who are considered mentally sick (especially those confined involuntarily) are so defined by their relatives, friends, employers, or perhaps the police—*not* by themselves. These people have upset the social order—by disregarding the conventions of polite society or by violating laws—so we label them "mentally ill" and punish them by commitment to a mental institution.

The patient knows that he is deprived of freedom because he has annoyed others, not because he is sick. And in the mental hospital, he learns that until he alters his behavior, he will be segregated from society. But even if he changes and is permitted to leave, his record of confinement goes with him. And the practical consequences are more those of a prison than a hospital record. The psychological and social damage thus incurred often far outweighs the benefits of any psychiatric therapy.

Consider, for example, the case of a young nurse I will call Emily Silverman who works in a general hospital in a small city. Unmarried and lonely, she worries about the future. Will she find a husband? Will she have to go on supporting herself in a job that has become drudgery? She feels depressed, sleeps poorly, loses weight. Finally, she consults an internist at the hospital and is referred to a psychiatrist. He diagnoses her trouble as a case of "depression" and prescribes "antidepressant" drugs. Emily takes the pills and visits the psychiatrist weekly, but she remains depressed and begins to think about suicide. This alarms the psychiatrist, who recommends hospitalization. Since there is no private mental hospital in the city, Emily seeks admission to the state hospital nearby. There, after a few months, she realizes that the "treatment" the hospital offers cannot help her solve her problems. She then "recovers" and is discharged.

From now on, Emily is no longer just a nurse; she is a nurse with a "record" of confinement in a state mental hospital. When she tries to return to her job, she will probably find it filled and that there are no openings. Indeed, as an exmental patient she may find it impossible to obtain any employment in nursing. This is a heavy price to pay for ignorance, yet no one warned her of the hazards involved before she decided to enter the hospital for her "depression."

Because the therapeutic potentialities of psychiatry are consistently exaggerated and its punitive functions minimized or even denied, a distorted relationship between psychiatry and the law has evolved in our time.

Years ago some people accused of serious crimes pleaded "insanity." Today they are often charged with it. Instead of receiving a brief jail sentence, a defendant may be branded "insane" and incarcerated *for life* in a psychiatric institution.

This is what happened, for example, to a filling-station operator I will call Joe Skulski. When he was told to move his business to make way for a new shopping center, he stubbornly resisted eviction. Finally the police were summoned. Joe greeted them with a warning shot in the air. He was taken into custody and denied bail, because the police considered his protest peculiar and thought he must be crazy. The district attorney requested a pretrial psychiatric examination of the accused. Mr. Skulski was examined, pronounced mentally unfit to stand trial, and confined in the state hospital for the criminally insane. Through it all, he pleaded for the right to be tried for his offense. Now in the mental hospital he will spend years of fruitless effort to prove that he is sane enough to stand trial. If convicted, his prison sentence would have been shorter than the term he has already served in the hospital.

Joe, like most patients in public mental hospitals, is a victim of social injustice. A wealthy and important man would have a chance, and the means, to rebut the charge of mental illness—as indeed happened when the government last year tried to handle the incident of General Edwin Walker in this fashion.

All this is not to say that our public mental hospitals serve no socially necessary purpose. They do, in fact, perform two essential—and very different—functions. On the one hand, they help *patients* recover from personal difficulties by providing them with room, board, and a medically approved escape from everyday responsibilities. On the other hand, they help *families* (and society) care for those who annoy or burden them unduly. It is important that we sort out these very different services, for unfortunately their goals are not the same. To relieve people annoyed by the eccentricities, failings, or outright meanness of so-called mentally disturbed persons requires that something be done *to* mental patients, not *for* them. The aim here is to safeguard the sensibilities not of the patient, but of those he upsets. This is a moral and social, not a medical, problem. How, for example, do you weigh the right of Mr. Kelleher to spend his declining years in freedom and dignity rather than as a psychiatric prisoner, against the right of his children to lead a "life of their own" unburdened by a senile father? Or the right of Mrs. Tarranti to repudiate overwhelming responsibilities against her husband's and children's need for the services of a full-time wife and mother? Or the right of Mrs. Abelson to give away her money to poor relatives, against her children's claim on their father's fortune?

Granting that there can often be no happy resolution to such conflicts, there is no reason to feel that we are as yet on the right road. For one thing—we still tolerate appalling inequities between our treatment of the rich and the poor. Though it may be no more than a dimly grasped ideal, both medicine and law strive to treat all people equally. In psychiatry, however, we not only fail to approximate this goal in our practice; we do not even value it as an ideal.

We regard the rich and influential psychiatric patient as a self-governing, responsible client—free to decide whether or not to be a patient. But we look upon the poor and the aged patient as a ward of the state—too ignorant or too "mentally sick" to know what is best for him. The paternalistic psychiatrist, as an agent of the family or the state, assumes "responsibility" for him, defines him as a "patient" against his will, and subjects him to "treatment" deemed best for him, with or without his consent.

Do we really need more of this kind of psychiatry?

6. The Delinquent Personality

With the use of sophisticated research designs, statistics, and measurement techniques, John Conger and Wilbur Miller rigorously investigated the relationships among delinquency, personality, intelligence, and socioeconomic status. The entire enrollment of boys in the tenth grade in Denver, Colorado, public schools in 1956 were selected for study. Within this group of 2,348 students, 271 boys had committed some type of illegal act and been brought to juvenile court. These delinquents were individually matched with nondelinquent boys by age, socioeconomic status, IQ, school environment, and ethnic group to control for any differences that might be due to these variables. Although Conger and Miller strongly emphasize that social and personal factors appear to be highly interrelated, their study clearly suggested that important personality differences existed between the two groups. An analysis of school records, especially teacher ratings of students from which a hypothetical delinquency or D-score was derived, seemed to indicate that these personality differences had existed from the very first years in school.

Even in the early school years, differences in personality characteristics and behavior had begun to emerge between future delinquents and their nondelinquent peers. And such differences continued and, indeed, expanded over the years, despite the fact that delinquent-nondelinquent pair members were of the same age and sex; had grown up in similar neighborhoods (not infrequently the same block); had faced similar socioeconomic problems; had, in the case of minority group members, encountered similar problems of discrimination and sociocultural isolation; were of comparable intelligence (at least as measured by IQ tests); and had attended the same schools.

By the end of the third grade, future delinquents were already seen by their teachers as more poorly adapted than their classmates. They appeared to have less regard for the rights and feelings of their peers; less awareness of the need to accept responsibility for their obligations, both as individuals and as members of a group; and poorer attitudes toward authority, including failure to understand the need for rules and regulations in any well-

From John Janeway Conger and Wilbur C. Miller, **Personality, Social Class, and Delinquency** (New York: John Wiley & Sons, Inc. 1966). Reprinted by permission.

ordered social group and the need for abiding by them. They both resented and rejected authority in the school situation. Their over-all social behavior was simply less acceptable, not simply with teachers, but with peers; they had more difficulty in getting along with peers, both in individual one-to-one contacts and in group situations, and were less willing or able to treat others courteously and tactfully, and less able to be fair in dealing with them. In return, they were less well-liked and accepted by their peers. They were significantly less likely than their nondelinquent matches to be viewed as dependable, friendly, pleasant, considerate, and fair.

In the academic situation itself, they were much more easily distracted, daydreamed more, and, in general, had greater difficulty in maintaining attention and sticking to the task at hand until it was completed. They were less likely to display any special ability or interest.

Not surprisingly, these social and academic problems appeared to reflect underlying emotional problems. In the opinion of their teachers, future delinquents more often came from a disturbed home environment, and were considered overly aggressive.

At the end of the sixth grade, future delinquents continued to appear more poorly adapted than their nondelinquent peers, although some areas of difference had become more conspicuous, whereas others had receded in prominence. Thus future delinquents at this age continued to have less regard for the rights and feelings of others and less awareness of the need to accept responsibility for their obligations—both individual and social. They also continued to behave more aggressively and to be less well-liked and accepted by their peers. In short, their over-all social behavior was still clearly less acceptable. In the classroom, the delinquents still appeared more easily distracted, daydreamed more, and showed less persistence. When challenged, they tended to give up more easily.

Although this general picture persisted from the early school years into the 4–6 grade period, there were some additional differences which emerged, as well as some shifts in emphasis. Thus, in the middle school years, future delinquents were much more likely than their nondelinquent matches to receive comments about inconsistent academic performance. They were more likely to be viewed as underachieving, and less likely to be rated as showing good work habits. Socially, it became increasingly clear that future delinquents possessed less over-all leadership ability and had a narrower range of general interest, although, relatively, they were becoming more and more attention-seeking.

On the other hand, resentment toward, and rejection of authority (in the form of the school as an institution, its teachers and its rules) began to differentiate less clearly between delinquents and nondelinquents at this age, possibly because problems with authority are *generally* more common at this age than among school beginners.

By the end of the ninth grade, when our subjects were entering the period where the greatest incidence of delinquent acts occurs, the delinquents manifested differences from their nondelinquent peers in virtually every area of personality functioning and behavior measured through either personality tests or teacher ratings and comments. As viewed by their teachers, the adolescent delinquents continued to display significantly less respect and consideration for the rights of others—both teachers and peers—than the nondelinquents. They were, not surprisingly, much less cooperative in observing school rules and regulations, and in meeting their responsibilities as members of a social group. Furthermore, at this age the delinquents showed a much greater resentment toward, and rejection of, authority relative to their nondelinquent peers than was true in grades 4–6. It appears that in the years between middle childhood and adolescence the attitudes of the nondelinquents toward authority improved considerably, while among delinquents, they continued to deteriorate.

Relations with peers remained significantly poorer among the delinquents during adolescence, in the opinion of their teachers. They manifested less friendliness toward their classmates, and, in turn, were less well-liked and accepted by them.

In the academic situation, the delinquents continued, as they had throughout their schooling, to have greater difficulty than their nondelinquent matches. Their work habits were still significantly poorer; they were more careless in their work, appeared more often to be working below their capabilities, and needed much more supervision from teachers. Attendance was more often a problem among these youths.

As had been the case ever since kindergarten, the delinquents appeared more distractible in the school situation than their nondelinquent peers. They showed much less capacity for sustained attention, daydreamed more, and when challenged academically, tended to give up more easily.

In adolescence, the delinquents still appeared to their teachers as less well-adjusted than the nondelinquents. Thus they were rated as more lacking in self-confidence and self-respect, less cheerful and happy, less well-adjusted to their own and the opposite sex, and more attention-seeking. Again, home problems reentered the picture, with delinquents much more likely to have "disturbed home environment" mentioned spontaneously by their teachers as a significant problem in the youth's daily life and over-all adjustment.

Of considerable interest is the fact that these impressions of teachers concerning the poorer adjustment of the delinquents seemed to find agreement in the reports of the boys themselves, as judged from the psychological testing at the end of junior high school. Thus in the various group tests the delinquents displayed significantly *fewer* mental health assets and significantly *more* liabilities. In particular, they appeared to feel less capable of establishing close personal relationships with either peers or adults, especially the latter. They described themselves as having many fewer interests in life, and emerged as generally lacking in enthusiasm. Not unexpectedly, they appeared significantly less impressed by the dominant ethical values and goals of American middle-class culture than their nondelinquent matches.

Perhaps somewhat more surprisingly, in the areas of emotional stability, general maturity, and behavior symptomatology, the delinquents also tended to view themselves in much the same way as their teachers had pictured them. Thus the delinquents emerged in the testing as more: egocentric, childishly demanding, inconsiderate, thoughtless, and given to petty expressions of pique (although they might not have cared to use these particular labels for the implicit and explicit attitudes they expressed). They also acknowledged feelings of depression and discouragement, mood swings, daydreaming, and oversensitivity more frequently than their nondelinquent peers. And they admitted more often to a variety of somatic and behavioral expressions of anxiety and hypochondriacal preoccupations. Finally, they also appeared significantly more likely than the nondelinquents to respond to environmental pressures (particularly from parents or other authority-figures) with hostility, rejection, or simply withdrawal from the situation, rather than by acceptance, either for their own sake or that of others.

One cannot help but be impressed by the early emergence of over-all personality and behavioral differences between future delinquents and their nondelinquent matches, nor by the continuity that exists in these differences from one age period to another, despite some shifts in emphasis, and despite the fact that the personality pictures of both delinquents and nondelinquents become more complete and increasingly differentiated in the later school years. Delinquents—who manifested much greater distractibility and poorer attention, less regard for others and less sense of responsibility, poorer peer relationships, and generally poorer over-all adjustment (as indicated by D-scores) in the earliest school years—continued to have similar difficulties throughout their development. Furthermore, it is interesting and rather surprising to note that the increase with age in the number of traits distinguishing delinquent and nondelinquent groups does not appear to have been accompanied by a comparative increase in the ability of individual traits occurring both at adolescence and at earlier age periods to differentiate the groups, although there was some increase. Thus, for example, in the case of D-score (which was available for all age periods) the mean difference between delinquents and nondelinquents was only slightly greater at adolescence than it had been in the period from kindergarten through the third grade. In addition, the percentage of cases in which a delinquent pair-member's score was higher than that of his nondelinquent match increased only slightly between the early school years and adolescence. In brief, the discrimination value of individual traits in the early school years was almost as good as that obtained in the later school years.

3 THE SOCIOLOGY OF CRIME

Unlike the biologist and the psychologist who tend to concentrate on the individual in the study of crime, the sociologist devotes most of his attention to the social environment and the nature of social relationships. Crime, after all, usually involves a criminal and a victim—a pattern of interaction, however brief or violent, between two or more individuals; and thus crime is a social act.

It is a basic assumption of sociology that most social behavior is not innate or instinctive or idiosyncratic. Rather, it is largely learned by a process in which social rules, goals, and values are taken over from others. According to the sociologist, a large part of the rules, goals, and values guiding criminal and delinquent behavior is learned in much the same way as the law-abiding person acquires the sentiments that keep him within the law. From this point of view, then, a good deal of crime is seen as the response of a normal individual to an abnormal environment rather than as the behavior of an abnormal individual "inventing" crime, as it were, on his own.

1. The Correlates of Crime

In trying to uncover the causes of criminal behavior, we must come to grips with the known facts concerning the relationship between crime and a number of other social characteristics, such as age, sex, ethnic background, socioeconomic status, and so on. Over the years we have accumulated a large body of data about these relationships, and any theory that pretends to provide a full explanation of crime must take them into account.

As the following reading by Donald Cressey makes clear, the correlates of crime are not themselves causes in any meaningful sense. They do, however, point the way to social mechanisms, to aspects of social structure, and to socially implanted features of the individual that give rise to violations of criminal law.

Despite all their limitations, statistics on crime give information important to our understanding of crime and to hypotheses and theories about it. Similarities and differences in crime rates for certain categories of persons are so consistent that a gross relationship between the category and crime can reasonably be concluded to exist. In these cases, it is practical to assume that if the part of an observed relationship which is due merely to the methods of collecting statistics were eliminated, a real relationship would still remain. After specifying this assumption, we can go ahead and use the statistics. Even if they are gross, relationships which consistently appear and which cannot be readily "explained away" by citing the inadequacy of crime statistics must be taken into account in any theory of crime and criminality. There are at least six types of such consistent relationships that are of great theoretical significance to students of crime and criminality.

Variation by Age

Many varieties of statistics, in many jurisdictions, in many different years, collected by many types of agencies, uniformly report such a high incidence of crime among young persons, as compared with older persons, that it may reasonably be assumed that there is a statistically significant difference between the rate of crime among young adults and the rate among other age groups. Statistics are likely to exaggerate the crime rate of young adults: old people may have prestige enough to avoid fingerprinting and arrest, and young children might not be arrested as readily as either young adults or old adults, leaving young adults to bear the responsibility for more than their share of all the crimes committed. But there does seem to be a difference, even if it is not as great as the statistics indicate when they are taken at face value. In this sense, there are two general relationships between age and criminality.

A. For all crimes, taken collectively, the age of maximum criminality is in the adolescent period. American statistics on crimes known to the police show the maximum age of general criminality to be between the ages of 18 and 24, but these data probably are more subject to the bias indicated above than are the English statistics, which show that males between the ages of 12 and 13 have the highest crime rates of all male age groups, and that females aged 16 and 17 have higher crime rates than any other female age group.

B. The age of maximum criminality is not the same under all conditions. The extent to which the crime rate among young persons exceeds the crime rate among other age groups varies by offense, sex, place, and time:

1. The age of maximum criminality varies with the type of crime. Automobile theft and burglary, for example, are concentrated in the age group 15–19, while murder, embezzlement, and gambling offenses are committed by persons who are much older.

2. The age of maximum criminality varies by sex. Generally speaking, females commit crimes at later ages than do males. In 1963, for example, 54 percent of the males arrested for larceny were under 18 years of age, but only 40 percent of the females arrested for the same offense were under 18. Yet sex offenses, narcotic drug offenses, crimes against family and children, driving while intoxicated, and homicide and forgery appear earlier in the lives of women than in the lives of men. In 1963, 6 percent of the females and 1 percent of the males arrested for crimes against family and children were under age 18.

3. The age of first delinquency varies from place to place. In areas of high rates of delinquency, the children who become delinquent do so at an earlier age than do the children living in areas with low rates of delinquency.

4. The type of crime most frequently committed by persons of various ages varies from place to place. In some areas of Chicago, delinquent boys between 12 and 13 years old commit burglaries, while in other areas delinquent boys of those ages commit petty larcenies or engage in gang violence. In rural areas, offenders of any specified age are likely to be

convicted of crimes different from those committed by offenders of the same age who live in urban areas.

5. For all crimes, and for each specific crime, the rate decreases steadily from the age of maximum criminality to the end of life. Thus, burglary and automobile theft decrease rather regularly after ages 15–19, as does the crime rate generally; homicide decreases rather regularly after ages 20–29, where it is concentrated. Consistently, the number of first offenders per 1000 persons of any given age decreases regularly after ages 15–19. Some crimes decrease more dramatically with increasing age than do others; for example, the evidence is fairly conclusive that larceny decreases in old age more than do sex offenses.

6. The crime rates among different age groups vary from time to time. The crime rate among old people seems to have declined since the time of World War I, while the crime rate among young adults seems to have been increasing.

7. Both the probability that a crime will be repeated and the length of time between first and second offenses vary with the age at which the first offense is committed. Generally speaking, the younger a person is when he commits his first offense, the higher the probability that he will commit a second offense and the shorter the interval between first offense and second offense.

In sum, the available statistics on crime tell us that young persons have higher crime rates than older persons but that there are variations in the ratio of young persons to old persons in the criminal population. Thus, crime rates vary with age, but in any age group the rates vary with specific social conditions.

Variations by Sex

Sex status is of greater statistical significance in differentiating criminals from noncriminals than any other trait. If an investigator were asked to use a single trait to predict which persons in a town of 10,000 population would become criminals, he would make the fewest mistakes if he simply chose sex status and predicted criminality for the males and noncriminality for the females. He would be wrong in many cases, for most of the males would not become criminals, and a few of the females would become criminals. But he would be wrong in more cases if he used any other single trait, such as age, race, family background, or a personality characteristic. As is the case with age, there are two general relationships to be observed between crime and sex status.

A. The crime rate for men is greatly in excess of the rate for women—in all nations, all communities within a nation, all age groups, all periods of history for which organized statistics are available, and for all types of crime except those peculiar to women, such as infanticide and abortion. In the United States, at present, the rate of arrest of males is about ten times the rate of arrest for females; about 15 times as many males as females are committed to correctional institutions of all kinds; and about 20 times as many males as females are committed to the state and federal prisons and reformatories housing serious offenders. Even if the statistics are grossly biased against males, they can reasonably be interpreted to mean that *some* excess of crime among males is present.

B. The extent to which the crime rate among males exceeds the crime rate among females is not the same under all conditions. There are variations in the sex ratio in crime, just as there are variations in the age ratio in crime:

1. The extent to which the rate for males exceeds the rate for females varies from one nation to another. In Algeria, Tunis, Japan, and Ceylon, male criminals and delinquents are seen to be 3000 or 4000 times as numerous as female criminals. In Australia, Western Europe, the United States, and other nations in which females have great freedom and are viewed as almost equal in social standing to men, the rate for females is closest to the rate for males, although males remain greatly overrepresented in the criminal population.

2. The extent to which the rate for males exceeds the rate for females varies with the social positions of the sexes in different groups within a nation. An analysis of statistics in prewar Poland indicated sex ratios that ranged from 176 to 1163 in 42 groups in categories according to age, province of residence, rural-urban residence, religion, and civil status. (The sex ratio always is expressed as the number of males per 100 females. A ratio over 100, therefore, means that males exceed females, while a ratio less than 100 means that females exceed males.) In the United States, the sex ratio is less extreme among Negroes than it is among whites, and it is probable that Negro males and females more closely resemble each other in social standing than do white males and females. In 1964 the sex ratio among 3000 Negroes placed on probation by the United States District Courts was 576, but the ratio among 9000 whites was 867, and the ratio among 267 American Indians was 927.

3. The extent to which the rate for males exceeds the rate for females varies with the size of community residence. In American cities the crime rate of females is closer to the crime rate of males than is the case in rural areas and small towns. In rural areas reporting arrests to the Federal Bureau of Investigation in 1963, the sex ratio for all crimes was 1209; for cities with over 2500 population it was 755, and for suburban areas it was 834. In the same year, the sex ratio among persons arrested for larceny was 1490 in rural areas, 396 in cities, and 441 in suburban areas. For the crime of burglary, the sex ratios were more nearly the same in the three types of community—2960 in rural areas, 2880 in cities, and 3570 in suburban areas.

4. The extent to which the crime rate among males exceeds the crime

rate among females varies with age. In the United States, the sex ratio among persons committed to penal institutions tends to increase with increasing age. At ages 15–17 the sex ratio is about 1300, while at 60–64 it is about 2500. Similar variations have been found in Sweden and eight other European nations.

5. The extent to which the crime rate among males exceeds the crime rate among females varies with area of residence within a city. Generally, the higher the crime rate of an area the lower the sex ratio in crime. However, it has been shown that some areas with high delinquency rates also have unusually high sex ratios among their delinquents.

6. The extent to which the crime rate among males exceeds the crime rate among females varies with time. There is some evidence that the sex ratio is decreasing. Females were 5 per cent of the persons under age 18 whose arrests were reported to the FBI in 1938, 10 percent in 1947, 12.7 in 1957, and 15.3 in 1963. In time of war, when women take over some of the jobs usually performed by men, and when women in other ways tend to become more nearly equal to men in social standing, the sex ratio in crime declines.

7. Among young criminals, the extent to which the crime rate for males exceeds the crime rate for females varies with the degree of integration in the family. Among delinquents from broken homes the sex ratio is lower than it is among delinquents from unbroken, "integrated" homes. Further, there is some evidence from specialized studies that the sex ratio in delinquency is lower in families in which male children outnumber the females than in families in which the number of each sex is more nearly equal.

To summarize, the available statistics indicate that males have much higher crime rates than females but that the ratio of male criminals to female criminals varies with specific social situations.

Variations by Race

A number of studies have shown that, in the United States, Negroes are more likely to be arrested, indicted, and convicted than are whites who commit the same offenses. Similarly, it has been shown that Negroes have less chance than whites to receive probation, a suspended sentence, parole, commutation of a death sentence, or a pardon. Thus, almost an "index" of the crime rate is likely to exaggerate the rate for Negroes, as compared with the rate among whites. However, it is also true that many crimes committed by Negroes against other Negroes receive no official attention from the police or criminal courts, and this practice of overlooking some crimes offsets to some unknown degree the bias in other arresting, reporting, and recording practices. At least three localized studies have shown that the racial membership of the victim is of great importance in determining the official reactions to crimes committed by Negroes. Like the situation with age and sex, there are two general relationships between crime and race, though here our observations are confined to the United States.

A. The official statistics indicate that the crime rate of Negroes exceeds the rate of whites. The number of arrests of Negroes per 100,000 Negroes is about three times the number of arrests of whites per 100,000 whites. The rate of commitment of Negroes to state and federal prisons is about six times the white rate.

B. The extent to which the crime rate of Negroes exceeds the crime rate of whites varies with social conditions. In some conditions the rate for Negroes is not as far in excess of the rate for whites as it is in other conditions, and in still other conditions the rate for Negroes is lower than the rate for whites:

1. The extent to which the rate for Negroes exceeds the rate for whites varies with regions of the United States. The excess is highest in the western states and lowest in the southern states, with northern states occupying an intermediate position. In Philadelphia in 1954, Negroes made up 20 percent of the population but accounted for 50 percent of the arrests; in Michigan at about the same time, Negroes were 7 percent of the population and about 40 percent of the prison population. The differences in rates are not distributed in the same way for all offenses; for homicide, for example, the difference is greatest in the South and least in New England.

2. The extent to which the crime rate of Negroes exceeds the crime rate of whites varies with sex status. In 1964, 205 white women were placed on federal probation for each 100 Negro women placed on probation, but 313 white men were committed for each 100 Negro men.

3. The extent to which the crime rate of Negroes exceeds the crime rate of whites varies with offense. When based on imprisonment rates, the excess is greatest for assault and homicide and lowest for rape. One study indicated that in Virginia the rates for forgery and for drunken driving actually are lower among Negroes than among whites, but this does not take into account the fact that literacy and automobile ownership are probably less frequent among Negroes. Another study indicated that large cities with a high percentage of Negroes in their populations had higher arrest rates for murder than did large cities with only small percentages of Negroes. It also is known that the excess of crime among Negroes is higher for second offenses than it is for first offenses.

4. The extent to which the crime rate of Negroes exceeds that of whites varies with the area of residence within a city. Studies of Houston and Baltimore show that the Negro delinquency rate is lowest in those areas having the greatest proportion of Negroes in their populations and highest in those areas with relatively low proportions of Negroes to whites. In northern cities, on the other hand, the Negro crime and delinquency rates are higher in segregated than in nonsegregated areas.

5. The extent to which the crime rate of Negroes exceeds the crime rate

of whites varies with time. There is no precise evidence on this point, but it seems probable that the amount of excess has been increasing. An earlier study indicated that in three decades the Negro juvenile delinquency rate in Chicago increased seven times, while the Negro population increased only three times. The comparable rate and population increases for whites is not available.

In short, such statistics as are available indicate that Negroes have higher crime rates than whites but that the ratio of crime rates among Negroes to crime rates among whites varies with specific social situations.

Variations by Nativity

During the years when immigration was at its height, it was generally believed that there was an undue amount of crime among the foreign-born. While assimilation of vast numbers of immigrants is no longer a serious social problem in the United States, analysis of the data on crime among immigrants remains a sociological problem of great theoretical significance. The following two observations about nativity and crime can be made.

A. Such statistics as are available indicate that the crime rate among the foreign-born in the United States is less than that of native whites with the same age, sex, and rural-urban distribution. When computed on the basis of population numbers alone, the crime rate of immigrants is about half that of whites. Similarly, in Australia the crime rate of native Australians is about twice the rate for the immigrants arriving since World War II. When correction is made for the age and sex distributions of the two groups, the crime rates become more nearly equal but still show less crime among immigrants than among native whites.

B. The extent to which the crime rate of native whites exceeds the rate among immigrants is not the same under all social conditions.

1. The extent to which the crime rate among native whites exceeds the crime rate of the foreign-born varies with offense. Certain types of crime are characteristic of one immigrant group, while another type of crime is characteristic of a different immigrant group. Usually, these same types of crime are also characteristic of the home countries. Italy has a high rate of homicide, and Italian immigrants in the United States also have a high homicide rate, as compared to either other immigrant groups or natives. Drunkenness is rare in Italy but frequent in Ireland; Italian immigrant groups have low arrest rates for drunkenness, but Irish immigrants have rather high rates for that offense.

2. The extent to which the crime rate of native whites exceeds the rate among foreign-born persons varies from one immigrant group to another. In 1955, Eastern European immigrants in Australia had crime rates about three times as high as Southern European immigrants and almost twice as high as Northern European immigrants. Similarly, in the United States in

the years when immigration was at its height, persons of Irish nativity had crime rates three to five times as high as German immigrants. The crime rate among Japanese immigrants is exceptionally low.

3. The extent to which the crime rate of native whites exceeds the rate among the foreign-born varies from one native white group to another. The native white sons of immigrants tend to have crime rates higher than those of their fathers but lower than other native whites. In 1933, the rate of commitment of immigrants to state and federal prisons was lower than the commitment rate for the sons of immigrants in all but one of the 28 states for which data were available. Also, sons of immigrants tend to commit crimes characteristic of the receiving country, while, as indicated, the immigrants themselves commit crimes characteristic of the home country.

4. The amount of the excess of crime among the native-born varies with age. Among immigrants who arrive in the United States when they are in early childhood, the crime rate is higher than among immigrants arriving in middle age. Young immigrants take on the relatively high crime rate of native whites to a greater extent than do middle-aged immigrants.

5. The extent to which the crime rate of native whites exceeds that of immigrants varies with the length of time the immigrants have been in the host country. Both immigrants and their sons tend to take on the crime rate of the specific part of the country in which they locate. A study of crime rates in France in the nineteenth century indicated that migrants moving from one province to another changed their crime rates in the direction of the rate of the host province, whether the rate in the host province was higher or lower than the rate in the province from which they migrated. In the first five years of residence in an area of high delinquency in Los Angeles, 5 percent of the children in an immigrant group appeared before the juvenile court; after five more years, 46 percent appeared; and after another ten years 83 percent of the children came before the court. The delinquency rate increased with length of stay in the area, presumably because the immigrant group was assimilating that part of American culture which it experienced, including the delinquency rates. It is safe to assume, on the basis of the study of France, that if the immigrant group had had a high crime rate and had settled in an area of low delinquency rates, their rate would have decreased with increased length of stay.

Variations by Size of Community

Statistics from many countries, and in many periods of time, indicate that urban areas have higher crime rates than rural areas. Again, two general types of relationship between crime and size of community can be observed.

A. Official statistics indicate that the number of serious crimes per 100,000 population increases with the size of the community. In 1963, the rate of robberies known to the police increased from 10.7 in rural areas to 11.1 in towns of less than 10,000 population, to 159.5 in cities of over 250,000, and to 205.8 in cities with over a million inhabitants. Offenses committed by rural criminals might not be reported or recorded as readily as offenses committed in urban areas, but the urban rate generally so far exceeds the rural rate that it is reasonable to conclude that there is in fact a great excess of crime in urban places. Moreover, a large proportion of urban crime also is overlooked, and it is not at all certain that this proportion is any less than the proportion of rural crime that is overlooked.

B. The extent to which the crime rate in urban areas exceeds the crime rate in rural areas is not the same under all conditions. In some rural areas the crime rate, especially for some types of offenses, is higher than the rate in urban areas.

1. The amount of the excess of crime in urban areas varies by offense. In American cities of over 250,000, murder and rape rates are about five times as high as the rates in towns less than 10,000; burglary and larceny rates are about twice as high; automobile theft about four times as high, and robbery about fourteen times as high.

2. The amount of the excess of crime in urban areas varies by area. In an earlier period, frontier towns, river towns, and resort towns were noted for high crime rates, despite the fact that they were not large in size. In contemporary American states containing rural mining and logging towns, the amount of excess is less than in states where rural communities are engaged in agriculture. A study of the Chicago area by Sutherland indicated that burglaries and robberies of banks did not decrease steadily with distance from the city, as was the case for burglary and robbery of chain stores and drug stores; banks in the suburbs had higher rates of robbery and burglary than banks in the center of the city. Similarly, Lottier found that in the Detroit area murder, assault, rape, and robbery were more concentrated in the city than were burglary, automobile theft, and larceny.

3. The amount of excess of crime in urban areas varies in time. There is evidence that as improved communication and transportation have reduced the differences between urban and rural districts, the differences in the crime rates of the two areas have decreased. In the United States, the rural rate has since about 1945 been increasing more rapidly than the urban rate. Similar trends have been noted for European countries.

Variations by Social Class

The reliability of the official statistics on the socioeconomic class backgrounds of criminals has been questioned even more severely than have statistics on variables like age, race, and area of residence. Many persons maintain that the law enforcement processes tend to select working-class persons, just as they tend to select Negroes. Thus it is believed that if a member of the working class and a member of the upper class are equally guilty of some offense, the person on the lower level is more likely to be arrested, convicted, and committed to an institution. Further, some white-collar crimes are not included in sets of official crime statistics. Reckless is confident that if statistical procedures could be corrected, the distribution of crime by social classes in the United States would show a bimodal curve, with high peaks for members of the upper class and the lower class and a low valley for members of the middle class. However, the statistics on ordinary crime so consistently show an overrepresentation of lower-class persons that it is reasonable to assume that there is a real difference between the behavior of the members of this class and the members of other social classes, so far as criminality is concerned. If this assumption is made, the following two general observations are warranted.

A. In the United States, official statistics indicate that the largest proportion of criminal populations come from the working class, and there is also some evidence that the crime rate of working-class persons exceeds the crime rate of other persons. In institutionalized populations, about two-thirds to three-fourths of the men, and about nine-tenths of the women, are members of the working class. A Wisconsin study found that 12 percent of the population of the state was unskilled but that 33 percent of the parents of the state's institutionalized delinquent boys and 53 percent of the parents of its institutionalized delinquent girls were unskilled. In a famous study of social classes in a New England community, it was found that the two lower classes constituted 57 percent of the city's population but accounted for 90 percent of the arrests made during a seven-year period. Many other studies have shown similar overrepresentations of working-class people in criminal populations. One study found that prison inmates rank themselves lower than they rank their fathers on socioeconomic status, perhaps indicating that the prisoners were unable to maintain the family level of status, let alone improve it through upward mobility. Studies of the areas of criminals' residence also indicate high crime rates in areas occupied by persons of low socioeconomic status.

B. The extent of overrepresentation of working-class persons in the criminal population is not the same under all conditions. In some situations, working-class people have crime rates lower than those of other classes:

1. The ratio of working-class persons to other persons in the criminal population varies by social group. In the Japanese colony in Seattle prior to World War II, delinquency and crime rates were very low, despite the fact that the residents were of the working class and were in as great poverty as residents of the area surrounding the colony, who had high rates. Members of the working class who live in rural areas, similarly, have relatively low crime rates. Females living in areas where most residents are of low socioeconomic status have low crime rates. Also, members of some groups in extreme poverty have literally starved to death rather than violate laws.

Finally, it is obvious that most working-class persons do not become criminals and that, therefore, something other than working-class membership is involved. Even in areas of great poverty and high crime rates, large proportions of the residents do not become criminals.

2. The ratio of working-class persons to other persons varies by offense. Most studies showing high ratios of working-class persons have concentrated on crimes against property, such as larceny and burglary. There is some evidence, however, that the ratio is somewhat lower for sex offenses, and in fact the crime rates of the working class may be lower than those of other classes for some sex offenses. Similarly, a study conducted in Detroit indicated that working-class persons are not as overrepresented in the population of automobile thieves as they are in other delinquent and criminal populations. And, of course, working-class persons have lower crime rates than other persons for offenses such as embezzlement, misrepresentation in advertising, violation of antitrust laws, and issuing worthless stocks. The person's position in the occupational structure determines the opportunities for some kinds of crime and also determines whether or not a person will possess the skills necessary to perpetrating some types of offenses.

Conclusion

Although the above are only some of the social conditions with which crime rates vary, the list is sufficiently long to enable us to draw the important conclusion that crime is social behavior that is closely associated with other kinds of social behavior. One set of facts indicates that the crime rate is higher for young adults than for persons in later life, higher for men than for women, higher for Negroes than for whites, higher for native-born than for foreign-born, higher in cities than in rural areas, and higher for the working class than for other social classes. Such differences may be described as ratios—the age ratio in crime, the sex ratio in crime, etc. A second set of facts points up the fact that these ratios are not constant. They vary in definite ways.

These ratios, and variations in ratios, make up some of the facts that a general explanation of crime must fit. They may be called definitive facts, for they define or limit the explanations of crime that can be considered valid. For example, an explanation that attributes crime to poverty helps make good sense out of the overrepresentation of Negroes and working-class persons in the general criminal population, but the theory falls flat when it is recalled that women, who are equal in poverty with men, have very low crime rates; when it is recalled that immigrants, who are probably at least as poor as their sons, sometimes have crime rates lower than their sons; when it is recalled that even poor Negroes and working-class persons do not have high crime rates if they live in rural areas, and so on. Similarly, an explanation of crime in terms of a trait of aggression or other personality characteristic must show that the characteristic is much more frequent among men than among women, among Negro women than white women, among young persons as compared to old persons, etc.; and it also must show that the trait occurs infrequently among immigrant groups, Negroes who live in segregated areas, middle-class persons, etc.

2. Differential Association

In the 1920s and 1930s, explanations of criminal behavior were very likely to place an excessive emphasis on psychiatric disorders or to break down into a hodgepodge of unrelated facts. With the publication of Edwin H. Sutherland's theory of differential association, however, the field gained a large measure of coherence, and the normality of much criminal behavior was brought more sharply into focus.

Today it is clear that the theory of differential association cannot cover all types of criminal behavior, and that its portrayal of the learning process is far too mechanical and crude.

Nonetheless, Sutherland's formulation stands out as a landmark in the history of criminology, and it has guided a generation of sociologists as they have tried to unravel the complexities of crime.

The scientific explanation of a phenomenon may be stated either in terms of the factors which are operating at the moment of the occurrence of a phenomenon or in terms of the processes operating in the earlier history of that phenomenon. In the first case the explanation is mechanistic, in the second historical or genetic; both are desirable. The physical and biological scientists favor the first of these methods and it would probably be superior as an explanation of criminal behavior. Efforts at explanations of the mechanistic type have been notably unsuccessful, perhaps largely because they have been concentrated on the attempt to isolate personal and social pathologies. Work from this point of view has, at least, resulted in the conclusion that the immediate factors in criminal behavior lie in the person-situation complex. Person and situation are not factors exclusive of each other, for the situation which is important is the situation as defined by the person who is involved. The tendencies and inhibitions at the moment of the criminal behavior are, to be sure, largely a product of the earlier history of the person, but the expression of these tendencies and inhibitions is a reaction to the immediate situation as defined by the person. The situation operates in many ways, of which perhaps the least important is the provision of an opportunity for a criminal act. A thief may steal from a fruit stand when the owner is not in sight but refrain when the owner is in sight; a bank burglar may attack a bank which is poorly protected but refrain from attacking a bank protected by watchmen and burglar alarms. A corporation which manufactures automobiles seldom or never violates the Pure Food and Drug Law but a meat-packing corporation violates this law with great frequency.

The second type of explanation of criminal behavior is made in terms of the life experience of a person. This is an historical or genetic explanation of criminal behavior. This, to be sure, assumes a situation to be defined by the person in terms of the inclinations and abilities which the person has acquired up to that date. The following paragraphs state such a genetic theory of criminal behavior on the assumption that a criminal act occurs when a situation appropriate for it, as defined by a person, is present.

Genetic Explanation of Criminal Behavior. The following statement refers to the process by which a particular person comes to engage in criminal behavior.

1. *Criminal behavior is learned.* Negatively, this means that criminal behavior is not inherited, as such; also, the person who is not already trained in crime does not invent criminal behavior, just as a person does not make mechanical inventions unless he has had training in mechanics.

2. *Criminal behavior is learned in interaction with other persons in a process of communication.* This communication is verbal in many respects but includes also "the communication of gestures."

3. *The principal part of the learning of criminal behavior occurs within intimate personal groups.* Negatively, this means that the impersonal agencies of communication, such as picture shows and newspapers, play a relatively unimportant part in the genesis of criminal behavior.

4. *When criminal behavior is learned, the learning includes (a) techniques of committing the crime, which are sometimes very complicated, sometimes very simple; (b) the specific direction of motives, drives, rationalizations, and attitudes.*

5. *The specific direction of motives and drives is learned from definitions of the legal codes as favorable or unfavorable.* In some societies an individual is surrounded by persons who invariably define the legal codes as rules to be observed, while in others he is surrounded by persons whose definitions are favorable to the violation of the legal codes. In our American society these definitions are almost always mixed and consequently we have culture conflict in relation to the legal codes.

6. *A person becomes delinquent because of an excess of definitions favorable to violation of law over definitions unfavorable to violation of law.* This is the principle of differential association. It refers to both criminal and anti-criminal associations and has to do with counteracting forces. When persons become criminal, they do so because of contacts with criminal patterns and also because of isolation from anti-criminal patterns. Any

person inevitably assimilates the surrounding culture unless other patterns are in conflict; a Southerner does not pronounce "r" because other Southerners do not pronounce "r." Negatively, this proposition of differential association means that associations which are neutral so far as crime is concerned have little or no effect on the genesis of criminal behavior. Much of the experience of a person is neutral in this sense, e.g., learning to brush one's teeth. This behavior has no negative or positive effect on criminal behavior except as it may be related to associations which are concerned with the legal codes. This neutral behavior is important especially as an occupier of the time of a child so that he is not in contact with criminal behavior during the time he is so engaged in the neutral behavior.

7. *Differential associations may vary in frequency, duration, priority, and intensity.* This means that associations with criminal behavior and also associations with anti-criminal behavior vary in those respects. "Frequency" and "duration" as modalities of associations are obvious and need no explanation. "Priority" is assumed to be important in the sense that lawful behavior developed in early childhood may persist throughout life, and also that delinquent behavior developed in early childhood may persist throughout life. This tendency, however, has not been adequately demonstrated, and priority seems to be important principally through its selective influence. "Intensity" is not precisely defined but it has to do with such things as the prestige of the source of a criminal or anti-criminal pattern and with emotional reactions related to the associations. In a precise description of the criminal behavior of a person these modalities would be stated in quantitative form and a mathematical ratio be reached. A formula in this sense has not been developed and the development of such a formula would be extremely difficult.

8. *The process of learning criminal behavior by association with criminal and anti-criminal patterns involves all of the mechanisms that are involved in any other learning.* Negatively, this means that the learning of criminal behavior is not restricted to the process of imitation. A person who is seduced, for instance, learns criminal behavior by association but this process would not ordinarily be described as imitation.

9. *While criminal behavior is an expression of general needs and values, it is not explained by those general needs and values since non-criminal behavior is an expression of the same needs and values.* Thieves generally steal in order to secure money, but likewise honest laborers work in order to secure money. The attempts by many scholars to explain criminal behavior by general drives and values, such as the happiness principle, striving for social status, the money motive, or frustration, have been and must continue to be futile since they explain lawful behavior as completely as they explain criminal behavior. They are similar to respiration, which is necessary for any behavior but which does not differentiate criminal from non-criminal behavior.

It is not necessary, at this level of explanation, to explain why a person has the associations which he has; this certainly involves a complex of many things. In an area where the delinquency rate is high a boy who is sociable, gregarious, active, and athletic is very likely to come in contact with the other boys in the neighborhood, learn delinquent behavior from them, and become a gangster; in the same neighborhood the psychopathic boy who is isolated, introvert, and inert may remain at home, not become acquainted with the other boys in the neighborhood, and not become delinquent. In another situation, the sociable, athletic, aggressive boy may become a member of a scout troop and not become involved in delinquent behavior. The person's associations are determined in a general context of social organization. A child is ordinarily reared in a family; the place of residence of the family is determined largely by family income; and the delinquency rate is in many respects related to the rental value of the houses. Many other factors enter into this social organization, including many of the small personal group relationships.

The preceding explanation of criminal behavior was stated from the point of view of the person who engages in criminal behavior. It is possible, also, to state theories of criminal behavior from the point of view of the community, nation, or other group. The problem, when thus stated, is generally concerned with crime rates and involves a comparison of the crime rates of various groups or the crime rates of a particular group at different times. One of the best explanations of crime rates from this point of view is that a high crime rate is due to social disorganization. The term "social disorganization" is not entirely satisfactory and it seems preferable to substitute for it the term "differential social organization." The postulate on which this theory is based, regardless of the name, is that crime is rooted in the social organization and is an expression of that social organization. A group may be organized for criminal behavior or organized against criminal behavior. Most communities are organized both for criminal and anti-criminal behavior and in that sense the crime rate is an expression of the differential group organization. Differential group organization as an explanation of a crime rate must be consistent with the explanation of the criminal behavior of the person, since the crime rate is a summary statement of the number of persons in the group who commit crimes and the frequency with which they commit crimes.

3. Crime and Deviance

It is obvious that not all of the behavior of which society disapproves is illegal; nor is all illegal behavior regarded as a clear and serious deviation from the mores of society. Nonetheless, a great deal of criminal behavior does fall into the category of deviance, and the social scientist has hoped that by examining crime from a more general theoretical viewpoint he can gain a greater understanding of the particular type of behavior that we label a violation of law.

In the following selection by Robert Merton, social behavior is analysed in terms of the individual's goals and the means he has for attaining them. The emphasis is on the socially created disjunction between the two and it is this disjunction that is seen as a major source of the impulse pushing the individual into criminality.

Until recently, and all the more so before then, one could speak of a marked tendency in psychological and sociological theory to attribute the faulty operation of social structures to failures of social control over man's imperious biological drives. The imagery of the relations between man and society implied by this doctrine is as clear as it is questionable. In the beginning, there are man's biological impulses which seek full expression. And then, there is the social order, essentially an apparatus for the management of impulses, for the social processing of tensions, for the "renunciation of instinctual gratifications," in the words of Freud. Nonconformity with the demands of a social structure is thus assumed to be anchored in original nature. It is the biologically rooted impulses which from time to time break through social control. And by implication, conformity is the result of an utilitarian calculus or of unreasoned conditioning.

With the more recent advancement of social science, this set of conceptions has undergone basic modification. For one thing, it no longer appears so obvious that man is set against society in an unceasing war between biological impulse and social restraint. The image of man as an untamed bundle of impulses begins to look more like a caricature than a portrait.

For another, sociological perspectives have increasingly entered into the analysis of behavior deviating from prescribed patterns of conduct. For whatever the role of biological impulses, there still remains the further question of why it is that the frequency of deviant behavior varies within different social structures and how it happens that the deviations have different shapes and patterns in different social structures. Today, as then, we have still much to learn about the processes through which social structures generate the circumstances in which infringement of social codes constitutes a "normal" (that is to say, an expectable) response.

. . .

The framework set out in this essay is designed to provide one systematic approach to the analysis of social and cultural sources of deviant behavior. Our primary aim is to discover how some *social structures exert a definite pressure upon certain persons in the society to engage in nonconforming rather than conforming conduct.* If we can locate groups peculiarly subject to such pressures, we should expect to find fairly high rates of deviant behavior in these groups, not because the human beings comprising them are compounded of distinctive biological tendencies but because they are responding normally to the social situation in which they find themselves. Our perspective is sociological. We look at variations in the *rates* of deviant behavior, not at its incidence. Should our quest be at all successful, some forms of deviant behavior will be found to be as psychologically normal as conformist behavior, and the equation of deviation and psychological abnormality will be put in question.

. . .

No society lacks norms governing conduct. But societies do differ in the degree to which the folkways, mores and institutional controls are effectively integrated with the goals which stand high in the hierarchy of cultural values. The culture may be such as to lead individuals to center their emotional convictions upon the complex of culturally acclaimed ends, with far less emotional support for prescribed methods of reaching out for these ends. With such differential emphases upon goals and institutional procedures, the latter may be so vitiated by the stress on goals as to have the behavior of many individuals limited only by considerations of technical expediency. In this context, the sole significant question becomes: Which of the available procedures is most efficient in netting the culturally approved value? The technically most effective procedure, whether culturally legitimate or not, becomes typically preferred to institutionally prescribed conduct. As this process of attenuation continues, the society becomes unstable and there develops what Durkheim called "anomie" (or normlessness).

The working of this process eventuating in anomie can be easily glimpsed in a series of familiar and instructive, though perhaps trivial, episodes. Thus, in competitive athletics, when the aim of victory is shorn of its institutional trappings and success becomes construed as "winning the game" rather than "winning under the rules of the game," a premium is implicitly set upon the use of illegitimate but technically efficient means. The star of the opposing football team is surreptitiously slugged; the wrestler incapacitates his opponent through ingenious but illicit techniques; university alumni covertly subsidize "students" whose talents are confined to the athletic field. The emphasis on the goal has so attenuated the satisfactions deriving from sheer participation in the competitive activity that only a successful outcome provides gratification. Through the same process, tension generated by the desire to win in a poker game is relieved by successfully dealing one's self four aces or, when the cult of success has truly flowered, by sagaciously shuffling the cards in a game of solitaire. The faint twinge of uneasiness in the last instance and the surreptitious nature of public delicts indicate clearly that the institutional rules of the game are *known* to those who evade them. But cultural (or idiosyncratic) exaggeration of the success-goal leads men to withdraw emotional support from the rules.

. . .

We here consider five types of adaptation, as these are schematically set out in the following table, where (+) signifies "acceptance," (−) signifies "rejection," and (±) signifies "rejection of prevailing values and substitution of new values."

A TYPOLOGY OF MODES OF INDIVIDUAL ADAPTATION

Modes of Adaptation	*Culture Goals*	*Institutionalized Means*
I. Conformity	+	+
II. Innovation	+	−
III. Ritualism	−	+
IV. Retreatism	−	−
V. Rebellion	±	±

Examination of how the social structure operates to exert pressure upon individuals for one or another of these alternative modes of behavior must be prefaced by the observation that people may shift from one alternative to another as they engage in different spheres of social activities. These categories refer to role behavior in specific types of situations, not to personality. They are types of more or less enduring response, not types of personality organization. To consider these types of adaptation in several spheres of conduct would introduce a complexity unmanageable within the confines of this chapter. For this reason, we shall be primarily concerned with economic activity in the broad sense of "the production, exchange, distribution and consumption of goods and services" in our competitive society, where wealth has taken on a highly symbolic cast.

I. Conformity

To the extent that a society is stable, adaptation type I—conformity to both cultural goals and institutionalized means—is the most common and widely diffused. Were this not so, the stability and continuity of the society could not be maintained. The mesh of expectancies constituting every social order is sustained by the modal behavior of its members representing conformity to the established, though perhaps secularly changing, culture patterns. It is, in fact, only because behavior is typically oriented toward the basic values of the society that we may speak of a human aggregate as comprising a society. Unless there is a deposit of values shared by interacting individuals, there exist social relations, if the disorderly interactions may be so called, but no society. It is thus that, at mid-century, one may refer to a Society of Nations primarily as a figure of speech or as an imagined objective, but not as a sociological reality.

Since our primary interest centers on the sources of *deviant* behavior, and since we have briefly examined the mechanisms making for conformity as the modal response in American society, little more need be said regarding this type of adaptation, at this point.

II. Innovation

Great cultural emphasis upon the success-goal invites this mode of adaptation through the use of institutionally proscribed but often effective means of attaining at least the simulacrum of success—wealth and power. This response occurs when the individual has assimilated the cultural emphasis upon the goal without equally internalizing the institutional norms governing ways and means for its attainment.

From the standpoint of psychology, great emotional investment in an objective may be expected to produce a readiness to take risks, and this attitude may be adopted by people in all social strata. From the standpoint of sociology, the question arises, which features of our social structure predispose toward this type of adaptation, thus producing greater frequencies of deviant behavior in one social stratum than in another?

On the top economic levels, the pressure toward innovation not infrequently erases the distinction between business-like strivings this side of the mores and sharp practices beyond the mores. As Veblen observed, "It is not easy in any given case—indeed it is at times impossible until the courts have spoken—to say whether it is an instance of praiseworthy salesmanship or a penitentiary offense." The history of the great American fortunes is threaded with strains toward institutionally dubious innovation as is attested by many tributes to the Robber Barons. The reluctant admiration often expressed privately, and not seldom publicly, of these "shrewd, smart and successful" men is a product of a cultural structure in which the sacrosanct goal virtually consecrates the means. This is no new phenomenon. Without assuming that Charles Dickens was a wholly accurate observer of the American scene and with full knowledge that he was anything but impartial, we cite his perceptive remarks on the American

love of "smart" dealing: which gilds over many a swindle and gross breach of trust; many a defalcation, public and private; and enables many a knave to hold his head up with the best, who well deserves a halter. . . . The merits of a broken speculation, or a bankruptcy, or of a successful scoundrel, are not gauged by its or his observance of the golden rule, "Do as you would be done by," but are considered with reference to their smartness. . . . The following dialogue I have held a hundred times: "Is it not a very disgraceful circumstance that such a man as So-and-so should be acquiring a large property by the most infamous and odious means, and notwithstanding all the crimes of which he has been guilty, should be tolerated and abetted by your Citizens? He is a public nuisance, is he not?" "Yes sir," "A convicted liar?" "Yes, sir." "He has been kicked and cuffed, and caned?" "Yes, sir." "And he is utterly dishonorable, debased, and profligate?" "Yes, sir." "In the name of wonder, then, what is his merit?" "Well, sir, he is a smart man."

In this caricature of conflicting cultural values, Dickens was of course only one of many wits who mercilessly probed the consequences of the heavy emphasis on financial success. Native wits continued where alien wits left off. Artemus Ward satirized the commonplaces of American life until they seemed strangely incongruous. The "crackerbox philosophers," Bill Arp and Petroleum Volcano [later Vesuvius] Nasby, put wit in the service of iconoclasm, breaking the images of public figures with unconcealed pleasure. Josh Billings and his alter ego, Uncle Esek, made plain what many could not freely acknowledge, when he observed that satisfaction is relative since "most of the happiness in this world konsists in possessing what others kant git." All were engaged in exhibiting the social functions of tendentious wit, as this was later to be analyzed by Freud, in his monograph on *Wit and Its Relation to the Unconscious,* using it as "a weapon of attack upon what is great, dignified and mighty, [upon] that which is shielded by internal hindrances or external circumstance against direct disparagement. . . ." But perhaps most in point here was the deployment of wit by Ambrose Bierce in a form which made it evident that *wit* had not cut away from its etymological origins and still meant the power by which one knows, learns, or thinks. In his characteristically ironical and deep-seeing essay on "crime and its correctives," Bierce begins with the observation that "Sociologists have long been debating the theory that the impulse to commit crime is a disease, and the ayes appear to have it—the disease." After this prelude, he describes the ways in which the successful rogue achieves social legitimacy, and proceeds to anatomize the discrepancies between cultural values and social relations.

The good American is, as a rule, pretty hard on roguery, but he atones for his austerity by an amiable toleration of rogues. His only requirement is that he must personally know the rogues. We all "denounce" thieves loudly enough if we have not the honor of their acquaintance. If we have, why, that is different —unless they have the actual odor of the slum or the prison about them. We may know them guilty, but we meet them, shake hands with them, drink with them and, if they happen to be wealthy, or otherwise great, invite them to our houses, and deem it an honor to frequent theirs. We do not "approve their methods"—let that be understood; and thereby they are sufficiently punished. The notion that a knave cares a pin what is thought of his ways by one who is civil and friendly to himself appears to have been invented by a humorist. On the vaudeville stage of Mars it would probably have made his fortune.

[*And again:*] *If social recognition were denied to rogues they would be fewer by many. Some would only the more diligently cover their tracks along the devious paths of unrighteousness, but others would do so much violence to their consciences as to renounce the disadvantages of rascality for those of an honest life. An unworthy person dreads nothing so much as the withholding of an honest hand, the slow, inevitable stroke of an ignoring eye.*

We have rich rogues because we have "respectable" persons who are not ashamed to take them by the hand, to be seen with them, to say that they know them. In such it is treachery to censure them; to cry out when robbed by them is to turn state's evidence.

One may smile upon a rascal (most of us do many times a day) if one does not know him to be a rascal, and has not said he is; but knowing him to be, or having said he is, to smile upon him is to be a hypocrite—just a plain hypocrite or a sycophantic hypocrite, according to the station in life of the rascal smiled upon. There are more plain hypocrites than sycophantic ones, for there are more rascals of no consequence than rich and distinguished ones, though they get fewer smiles each. The American people will be plundered as long as the American character is what it is; as long as it is tolerant of successful knaves; as long as American ingenuity draws an imaginary distinction between a man's public character and his private—his commercial and his personal. In brief, the American people will be plundered as long as they deserve to be plundered. No human law can stop, none ought to stop it, for that would abrogate a higher and more salutary law: "As ye sow, ye shall reap."

Living in the age in which the American robber barons flourished, Bierce could not easily fail to observe what became later known as "white-collar crime." Nevertheless, he was aware that not all of these large and dramatic departures from institutional norms in the top economic strata are known, and possibly fewer deviations among the lesser middle classes come to light. Sutherland has repeatedly documented the prevalence of "white-collar criminality" among businessmen. He notes, further, that many of these crimes were not prosecuted because they were not detected or, if detected, because of "the status of the business man, the trend away from punishment, and the relatively unorganized resentment of the public against white-collar criminals." A study of some 1,700 prevalently middle-class individuals found that "off the record crimes" were common among wholly "respectable" members of society. Ninety-nine per cent of those questioned confessed to having committed one or more of 49 offenses under the penal law of the State of New York, each of these offenses being sufficiently serious to draw a maximum sentence of not less than one year. The mean number of offenses in adult years—this excludes all offenses committed before the age of sixteen—was 18 for men and 11 for women. Fully 64% of the men and 29% of the women acknowledged their guilt on one or more counts of felony which, under the laws of New York is ground for depriving them of all rights of citizenship. One keynote of these findings is expressed by a minister, referring to false statements he made about a commodity he sold, "I tried truth first, but it's not always successful." On the basis of these results, the authors modestly conclude that "the number of acts legally constituting crimes are far in excess of those officially reported. Unlawful behavior, far from being an abnormal social or psychological manifestation, is in truth a very common phenomenon."

But whatever the differential rates of deviant behavior in the several social strata, and we know from many sources that the official crime statistics uniformly showing higher rates in the lower strata are far from complete or reliable, it appears from our analysis that the greatest pressures toward deviation are exerted upon the lower strata. Cases in point permit us to detect the sociological mechanisms involved in producing these pressures. Several researches have shown that specialized areas of vice and crime constitute a "normal" response to a situation where the cultural emphasis upon pecuniary success has been absorbed, but where there is little access to conventional and legitimate means for becoming successful. The occupational opportunities of people in these areas are largely confined to manual labor and the lesser white-collar jobs. Given the American stigmatization of manual labor *which has been found to hold rather uniformly in all social classes,* and the absence of realistic opportunities for advancement beyond this level, the result is a marked tendency toward deviant behavior. The status of unskilled labor and the consequent low income cannot readily compete *in terms of established standards of worth* with the promises of power and high income from organized vice, rackets and crime.

For our purposes, these situations exhibit two salient features. First, incentives for success are provided by the established values of the culture *and* second, the avenues available for moving toward this goal are largely limited by the class structure to those of deviant behavior. It is the *combination* of the cultural emphasis and the social structure which produces intense pressure for deviation. Recourse to legitimate channels for "getting in the money" is limited by a class structure which is not fully open at each level to men of good capacity. Despite our persisting open-class-ideology, advance toward the success-goal is relatively rare and notably difficult for those armed with little formal education and few economic resources. The dominant pressure leads toward the gradual attenuation of legitimate, but by and large ineffectual, strivings and the increasing use of illegitimate, but more or less effective, expedients.

. . .

In societies such as our own, then, the great cultural emphasis on pecuniary success for all and a social structure which unduly limits practical recourse to approved means for many set up a tension toward innovative practices which depart from institutional norms. But this form of adaptation presupposes that individuals have been imperfectly socialized so that they abandon institutional means while retaining the success-aspiration. Among those who have fully internalized the institutional values, however, a comparable situation is more likely to lead to an alternative response in which the goal is abandoned but conformity to the mores persists. This type of response calls for further examination.

III. Ritualism

The ritualistic type of adaptation can be readily identified. It involves the abandoning or scaling down of the lofty cultural goals of great pecuniary success and rapid social mobility to the point where one's aspirations can be satisfied. But though one rejects the cultural obligation to attempt "to get ahead in the world," though one draws in one's horizons, one continues to abide almost compulsively by institutional norms.

It is something of a terminological quibble to ask whether this represents genuinely deviant behavior. Since the adaptation is, in effect, an internal decision and since the overt behavior is institutionally permitted, though not culturally preferred, it is not generally considered to represent a social problem. Intimates of individuals making this adaptation may pass judgment in terms of prevailing cultural emphases and may "feel sorry for them," they may, in the individual case, feel that "old Jonesy is certainly in a rut." Whether this is described as deviant behavior or no, it clearly represents a departure from the cultural model in which men are obliged to strive actively, preferably through institutionalized procedures, to move onward and upward in the social hierarchy.

We should expect this type of adaptation to be fairly frequent in a society which makes one's social status largely dependent upon one's achievements. For, as has so often been observed, this ceaseless competitive struggle produces acute status anxiety. One device for allaying these anxieties is to lower one's level of aspiration—permanently. Fear produces inaction, or more accurately, routinized action.

The syndrome of the social ritualist is both familiar and instructive. His implicit life-philosophy finds expression in a series of cultural clichés: "I'm not sticking *my* neck out," "I'm playing safe," "I'm satisfied with what I've got," "Don't aim high and you won't be disappointed." The theme threaded through these attitudes is that high ambitions invite frustration and danger whereas lower aspirations produce satisfaction and security. It is a response to a situation which appears threatening and excites distrust. It is the attitude implicit among workers who carefully regulate their output to a constant quota in an industrial organization where they have occasion to fear that they will "be noticed" by managerial personnel and "something will happen" if their output rises and falls. It is the perspective of the frightened employee, the zealously conformist bureaucrat in the teller's cage of the private banking enterprise or in the front office of the public works enterprise. It is, in short, the mode of adaptation of individually seeking a *private* escape from the dangers and frustrations which seem to them inherent in the competition for major cultural goals by abandoning these goals and clinging all the more closely to the safe routines and the institutional norms.

If we should expect *lower-class* Americans to exhibit Adaptation II—"innovation"—to the frustrations enjoined by the prevailing emphasis on large cultural goals and the fact of small social opportunities, we should expect *lower-middle class* Americans to be heavily represented among those making Adaptation III, "ritualism." For it is in the lower middle class that parents typically exert continuous pressure upon children to abide by the moral mandates of the society, and where the social climb upward is less likely to meet with success than among the upper middle class. The strong disciplining for conformity with mores reduces the likelihood of Adaptation II and promotes the likelihood of Adaptation III. The severe training leads many to carry a heavy burden of anxiety. The socialization patterns of the lower middle class thus promote the very character structure most predisposed toward ritualism, and it is in this stratum, accordingly, that the adaptive pattern III should most often occur.

But we should note again, as at the outset of this chapter, that we are here examining *modes of adaptation* to contradictions in the cultural and social structure: we are not focusing on character or personality types. Individuals caught up in these contradictions can and do move from one type of adaptation to another. Thus it may be conjectured that some ritualists, conforming meticulously to the institutional rules, are so steeped in the regulations that they become bureaucratic virtuosos, that they over-conform precisely because they are subject to guilt engendered by previous nonconformity with the rules (*i.e.,* Adaptation II). And the occasional passage from ritualistic adaptation to dramatic kinds of illicit adaptation is well-documented in clinical case-histories and often set forth in insightful fiction. Defiant outbreaks not infrequently follow upon prolonged periods of over-compliance. But though the psychodynamic mechanisms of this type of adaptation have been fairly well identified and linked with patterns of discipline and socialization in the family, much sociological research is still required to explain why these patterns are presumably more frequent in certain social strata and groups than in others. Our own discussion has merely set out one analytical framework for sociological research focused on this problem.

IV. Retreatism

Just as Adaptation I (conformity) remains the most frequent, Adaptation IV (the rejection of cultural goals and institutional means) is probably the least common. People who adapt (or maladapt) in this fashion are, strictly speaking, *in* the society but not *of* it. Sociologically, these constitute the true aliens. Not sharing the common frame of values, they can be included as members of the *society* (in distinction from the *population*) only in a fictional sense.

In this category fall some of the adaptive activities of psychotics, autists, pariahs, outcasts, vagrants, vagabonds, tramps, chronic drunkards and drug addicts. They have relinquished culturally prescribed goals and their behavior does not accord with institutional norms. This is not to say that in some cases the source of their mode of adaptation is not the very social structure which they have in effect repudiated nor that their very existence within an area does not constitute a problem for members of the society.

From the standpoint of its sources in the social structure, this mode of adaptation is most likely to occur when *both* the culture goals and the institutional practices have been thoroughly assimilated by the individual and imbued with affect and high value, but accessible institutional avenues are not productive of success. There results a twofold conflict: the interiorized moral obligation for adopting institutional means conflicts with pressures to resort to illicit means (which may attain the goal) and the individual is shut off from means which are both legitimate and effective. The competitive order is maintained but the frustrated and handicapped individual who cannot cope with this order drops out. Defeatism, quietism and resignation are manifested in escape mechanisms which ultimately lead him to "escape" from the requirements of the society. It is thus an expedient which arises from continued failure to near the goal by legitimate measures and from an inability to use the illegitimate route because of internalized prohibitions, *this process occurring while the supreme value of the success-goal has not yet been renounced.* The conflict is resolved by abandoning *both* precipitating elements, the goals and the means. The escape is complete, the conflict is eliminated and the individual is asocialized.

In public and ceremonial life, this type of deviant behavior is most heartily condemned by conventional representatives of the society. In contrast to the conformist, who keeps the wheels of society running, this deviant is a non-productive liability; in contrast to the innovator who is at least "smart" and actively striving, he sees no value in the success-goal which the culture prizes so highly; in contrast to the ritualist who conforms at least to the mores, he pays scant attention to the institutional practices.

Nor does the society lightly accept these repudiations of its values. To do so would be to put these values into question. Those who have abandoned the quest for success are relentlessly pursued to their haunts by a society insistent upon having all its members orient themselves to success-striving. Thus, in the heart of Chicago's Hobohemia are the book stalls filled with wares designed to revitalize dead aspirations.

The Gold Coast Book Store is in the basement of an old residence, built back from the street, and now sandwiched between two business blocks. The space in front is filled with stalls, and striking placards and posters.

These posters advertise such books as will arrest the attention of the down-and-out. One reads: ". . . Men in thousands pass this spot daily, but the majority of them are not financially successful. They are never more than two jumps ahead of the rent men. Instead of that, they should be more bold and daring," "Getting Ahead of the Game," before old age withers them and casts them on the junk heap of human wrecks. If you want to escape this evil fate—the fate of the vast majority of men—come in and get a copy of The Law of Financial Success. *It will put some new ideas in your head, and put you on the highroad to success. 35 cents.*

There are always men loitering before its stalls. But they seldom buy. Success comes high, even at thirty-five cents, to the hobo.

But if this deviant is condemned in real life, he may become a source of gratification in fantasy-life. Thus Kardiner has advanced the speculation that such figures in contemporary folklore and popular culture bolster "morale and self-esteem by the spectacle of man rejecting current ideals and expressing contempt for them." The prototype in the films is of course Charlie Chaplin's bum.

He is Mr. Nobody and is very much aware of his own insignificance. He is always the butt of a crazy and bewildering world in which he has no place and from which he constantly runs away into a contented do-nothingness. He is free from conflict because he has abandoned the quest for security and prestige, and is resigned to the lack of any claim to virtue or distinction. [*A precise characterological portrait of Adaptation IV.*] *He always becomes involved in the world by accident. There he encounters evil and aggression against the weak and helpless which he has no power to combat. Yet always, in spite of himself, he becomes the champion of the wronged and oppressed, not by virtue of his great organizing ability but by virtue of homely and insolent trickiness by which he seeks out the weakness of the wrongdoer. He always remains humble, poor, and lonely, but is contemptuous of the incomprehensible world and its values. He therefore represents the character of our time who is* perplexed by the dilemma either of being crushed in the struggle to achieve the socially approved goals of success and power (*he achieves it only once—in* The Gold Rush) or of succumbing to a hopeless resignation and flight from them. *Charlie's bum is a great comfort in that he gloats in his ability to outwit the pernicious forces aligned against him if he chooses to do so and affords every man the satisfaction of feeling that the ultimate flight from social goals to loneliness is an act of* choice *and not a symptom of his defeat. Mickey Mouse is a continuation of the Chaplin saga.*

This fourth mode of adaptation, then, is that of the socially disinherited who if they have none of the rewards held out by society also have few of the frustrations attendant upon continuing to seek these rewards. It is, moreover, a privatized rather than a collective mode of adaptation. Although people exhibiting this deviant behavior may gravitate toward centers where they come into contact with other deviants and although they may come to share in the subculture of these deviant groups, their adaptations are largely private and isolated rather than unified under the aegis of a new cultural code. The type of collective adaptation remains to be considered.

V. Rebellion

This adaptation leads men outside the environing social structure to envisage and seek to bring into being a new, that is to say, a greatly modified social structure. It presupposes alienation from reigning goals and standards. These come to be regarded as purely arbitrary. And the arbitrary is precisely that which can neither exact allegiance nor possess legitimacy, for it might as well be otherwise. In our society, organized movements for rebellion apparently aim to introduce a social structure in which the cultural standards of success would be sharply modified and provision would be made for a closer correspondence between merit, effort and reward.

But before examining "rebellion" as a mode of adaptation, we must distinguish it from a superficially similar but essentially different type, *ressentiment.* Introduced in a special technical sense, by Nietzsche, the concept of *ressentiment* was taken up and developed sociologically by Max Scheler. This complex sentiment has three interlocking elements. First, diffuse feelings of hate, envy and hostility; second, a sense of being powerless to express these feelings actively against the person or social stratum evoking them; and third, a continual re-experiencing of this impotent hostility. The essential point distinguishing *ressentiment* from rebellion is that the former does not involve a genuine change in values. *Ressentiment* involves a sour-grapes pattern which asserts merely that desired but unattainable objectives do not actually embody the prized values—after all, the fox in the fable does not say that he abandons all taste for sweet grapes; he says only that these particular grapes are not sweet. Rebellion, on the other hand, involves a genuine transvaluation, where the direct or vicarious experience of frustration leads to full denunciation of previously prized values—the rebellious fox simply renounces the prevailing taste for sweet grapes. In *ressentiment,* one condemns what one secretly craves; in rebellion, one condemns the craving itself. But though the two are distinct, organized rebellion may draw upon a vast reservoir of the resentful and discontented as institutional dislocations become acute.

When the institutional system is regarded as the barrier to the satisfaction of legitimized goals, the stage is set for rebellion as an adaptive response. To pass into organized political action, allegiance must not only be withdrawn from the prevailing social structure but must be transferred to new groups possessed of a new myth. The dual function of the myth is to locate the source of large-scale frustrations in the social structure and to portray an alternative structure which would not, presumably, give rise to frustration of the deserving. It is a charter for action. In this context, the functions of the counter-myth of the conservatives—briefly sketched in an earlier section of this chapter—become further clarified: whatever the source of mass frustration, it is not to be found in the basic structure of the society. The conservative myth may thus assert that these frustrations are in the nature of things and would occur in *any* social system: "Periodic mass unemployment and business depressions can't be legislated out of existence; it's just like a person who feels good one day and bad the next." Or, if not the doctrine of inevitability, then the doctrine of gradual and slight adjustment: "A few changes here and there, and we'll have things running as ship-shape as they can possibly be." Or, the doctrine which deflects hostility from the social structure onto the individual who is a "failure" since "every man really gets what's coming to him in this country."

The myths of rebellion and of conservatism both work toward a "monopoly of the imagination" seeking to define the situation in such terms as to move the frustrate toward or away from Adaptation V. It is above all the renegade who, though himself successful, renounces the prevailing values that becomes the target of greatest hostility among those in rebellion. For he not only puts the values in question, as does the out-group, but he signifies that the unity of the group is broken. Yet, as has so often been noted, it is typically members of a rising class rather than the most depressed strata who organize the resentful and the rebellious into a revolutionary group.

4. Up Through the Underworld

Crimes against the person (such as assault) or crimes against property (such as theft) attract a good deal of public attention, but there are other kinds of crime of equal or greater importance. Some writers, for example, have argued that organized crime centering on gambling, narcotics, and prostitution is one of the most serious aspects of the crime problem today. Daniel Bell traces the growth of the rackets in the United States and their links with the legitimate social order.

In the 1890's, the Reverend Dr. Charles Parkhurst, shocked at the open police protection afforded New York's bordellos, demanded a state inquiry. In the Lexow investigation that followed, the young and dashing William Travers Jerome staged a set of public hearings that created sensation after sensation. He badgered "Clubber" Williams, First Inspector of the Police Department, to account for wealth and property far greater than could have been saved on his salary; it was earned, the Clubber explained laconically, through land speculation "in Japan." Heavy-set Captain Schmittberger, the "collector" for the "Tenderloin precincts"—Broadway's fabulous concentration of hotels, theaters, restaurants, gaming houses, and saloons—related in detail how protection money was distributed among the police force. Crooks, policemen, public officials, businessmen, all paraded across the stage, each adding his chapter to a sordid story of corruption and crime. The upshot of these revelations was reform—the election of William L. Strong, a stalwart businessman, as mayor, and the naming of Theodore Roosevelt as police commissioner.

It did not last, of course, just as previous reform victories had not lasted. Yet the ritual drama was re-enacted. Twenty years ago the Seabury investigation in New York uncovered the tin-box brigade and the thirty-three little MacQuades. Jimmy Walker was ousted as Mayor and in came Fiorello La Guardia. Tom Dewey became district attorney, broke the industrial rackets, sent Lucky Luciano to jail and went to the Governor's chair in Albany. Then reform was again swallowed up in the insatiable maw of corruption until Kefauver and the young and dashing Rudolph Halley threw a new beam of light into the seemingly bottomless pit.

How explain this repetitious cycle? Obviously the simple moralistic distinction between "good guys" and "bad guys," so deep at the root of the

From Daniel Bell, "Crime as an American Way of Life," **Antioch Review,** XIII (June 1953), 131–154.

reform impulse, bears little relation to the role of organized crime in American society. What, then, does?

Americans have had an extraordinary talent for compromise in politics and extremism in morality. The most shameless political deals (and "steals") have been rationalized as expedient and realistically necessary. Yet in no other country have there been such spectacular attempts to curb human appetites and brand them as illicit, and nowhere else such glaring failures. From the start America was at one and the same time a frontier community where "everything goes," and the fair country of the Blue Laws. At the turn of the century the cleavage developed between the Big City and the small-town conscience. Crime as a growing business was fed by the revenues from prostitution, liquor and gambling that a wide-open urban society encouraged and which a middle-class Protestant ethos tried to suppress with a ferocity unmatched in any other civilized country. Catholic cultures rarely have imposed such restrictions, and have rarely suffered such excesses. Even in prim and proper Anglican England, prostitution is a commonplace of Piccadilly night life, and gambling one of the largest and most popular industries. In America the enforcement of public morals has been a continuing feature of our history.

Some truth may lie in Svend Ranulf's generalization that moral indignation is a peculiar fact of middle-class psychology and represents a disguised form of repressed envy. The larger truth lies perhaps in the brawling nature of American development and the social character of crime. Crime, in many ways, is a Coney Island mirror, caricaturing the morals and manners of a society. The jungle quality of the American business community, particularly at the turn of the century, was reflected in the mode of "business" practiced by the coarse gangster elements, most of them from new immigrant families, who were "getting ahead," just as Horatio Alger had urged. In the older, Protestant tradition the intense acquisitiveness, such as that of Daniel Drew, was rationalized by a compulsive moral fervor. But the formal obeisance of the ruthless businessman in the workaday world to the church-going pieties of the Sabbath was one that the gangster could not make. Moreover, for the young criminal, hunting in the asphalt jungle of the crowded city, it was not the businessman with his wily manipulation of numbers but the "man with the gun" who was the American hero. "No amount of commercial prosperity," once wrote Teddy Roosevelt, "can supply the lack of the heroic virtues." The American was "the hunter, cowboy, frontiersman, the soldier, the naval hero." And in the crowded slums, the gangster. He was a man with a gun, acquiring by personal merit what was denied to him by complex orderings of a stratified society. And the duel with the law was the morality play *par excellence:* the ganster, with whom rides our own illicit desires, and the prosecutor, representing final judgment and the force of the law.

Yet all this was acted out in a wider context. The desires satisfied in extra-legal fashion were more than a hunger for the "forbidden fruits" of conventional morality. They also involved, in the complex and ever shifting structure of group, class and ethnic stratification, which is the warp and woof of America's "open" society, such "normal" goals as independence through a business of one's own, and such "moral" aspirations as the desire for social advancement and social prestige. For crime, in the language of the sociologists, has a "functional" role in the society, and the urban rackets—the illicit activity organized for continuing profit rather than individual illegal acts—is one of the queer ladders of social mobility in American life. Indeed, it is not too much to say that the whole question of organized crime in America cannot be understood unless one appreciates (1) the distinctive role of organized gambling as a function of a mass consumption economy; (2) the specific role of various immigrant groups as they one after another became involved in marginal business and crime; and (3) the relation of crime to the changing character of the urban political machines.

As a society changes, so does, in lagging fashion, its type of crime. As American society became more "organized," as the American businessman became more "civilized" and less "buccaneering," so did the American racketeer. And just as there were important changes in the structure of business enterprise, so the "institutionalized" criminal enterprise was transformed too.

In the America of the last fifty years the main drift of society has been toward the rationalization of industry, the domestication of the crude self-made captain of industry into the respectable man of manners, and the emergence of a mass-consumption economy. The most significant transformation in the field of "institutionalized" crime was the increasing relative importance of gambling as against other kinds of illegal activity. And, as a multi-billion-dollar business, gambling underwent a transition parallel to the changes in American enterprise as a whole. This parallel was exemplified in many ways: in gambling's industrial organization (e.g., the growth of a complex technology such as the national racing wire service and the minimization of risks by such techniques as lay-off betting); in its respectability, as was evidenced in the opening of smart and popular gambling casinos in resort towns and in "satellite" adjuncts to metropolitan areas; in its functional role in a mass-consumption economy (for sheer volume of money changing hands, nothing has ever surpassed this feverish activity of fifty million American adults); in the social acceptance of the gamblers in the important status world of sport and entertainment, i.e., "café society."

In seeking to "legitimize" itself, gambling had quite often actually become a force against older and more vicious forms of illegal activity. In 1946, for example, when a Chicago mobster, Pat Manno, went down to Dallas, Texas, to take over gambling in the area for the Accardo-Guzik combine, he reassured the sheriff as to his intent as follows: "Something I'm against, that's dope peddlers, pickpockets, hired killers. That's one thing I can't stomach, and that's one thing the fellows up there—the group won't stand for, things like that. They discourage it, they even go to headquarters and ask them why they don't do something about it."

Jimmy Cannon once reported that when the gambling raids started in Chicago, the "combine" protested that, in upsetting existing stable relations, the police were only opening the way for ambitious young punks and hoodlums to start trouble. Nor is there today, as there was twenty or even forty years ago, prostitution of major organized scope in the United States. Aside from the fact that manners and morals have changed, prostitution *as an industry* doesn't pay as well as gambling. Besides, its existence threatened the tacit moral acceptance and quasi-respectability that gamblers and gambling have secured in the American way of life. It was, as any operator in the field might tell you, "bad for business."

The criminal world of the last decade, its tone set by the captains of the gambling industry, is in startling contrast to the state of affairs in the two decades before. If a Kefauver report had been written then, the main "names" would have been Lepke and Gurrah, Dutch Schultz, Jack "Legs" Diamond, Lucky Luciano, and, reaching back a little further, Arnold Rothstein, the czar of the underworld. These men (with the exception of Luciano, who was involved in narcotics and prostitution) were in the main industrial racketeers. Rothstein, it is true, had a larger function: he was, as Frank Costello became later, the financier of the underworld—the pioneer big businessman of crime, who, understanding the logic of co-ordination, sought to *organize* crime as a source of regular income. His main interest in this direction was in industrial racketeering, and his entry was through labor disputes. At one time, employers in the garment trades hired Legs Diamond and his sluggers to break strikes, and the Communists, then in control of the cloakmakers union, hired one Little Orgie to protect the pickets and beat up the scabs; only later did both sides learn that Legs Diamond and Little Orgie were working for the same man, Rothstein.

Rothstein's chief successors, Lepke Buchalter and Gurrah Shapiro, were able, in the early '30's, to dominate sections of the men's and women's clothing industries, of painting, fur dressing, flour trucking, and other fields. In a highly chaotic and cut-throat industry such as clothing, the racketeer, paradoxically, played a stabilizing role by regulating competition and fixing prices. When the NRA came in and assumed this function, the businessman found that what had once been a quasi-economic service was now pure extortion, and he began to demand police action. In other types of racketeering, such as the trucking of perishable foods and water-front loading, where the racketeers entrenched themselves as middlemen—taking up, by default, a service that neither shippers nor truckers wanted to assume—a pattern of accommodation was roughly worked out and the rackets assumed a quasi-legal veneer. On the water-front, old-time racketeers perform the necessary function of loading—but at an exorbitant price, and this monopoly was recognized by both the union and the shippers, and tacitly by government. (See my case study "The Last of the Business Rackets," in the June, 1951 issue of *Fortune*.)

But in the last decade and a half, industrial racketeering has not offered much in the way of opportunity. *Like American capitalism itself, crime shifted its emphasis from production to consumption.* The focus of crime became the direct exploitation of the citizen as consumer, largely through gambling. And while the protection of these huge revenues was inextricably linked to politics, the relation between gambling and "the mobs" became more complicated.

Although it never showed up in the gross national product, gambling in the last decade was one of the largest industries in the United States. The Kefauver Committee estimated it as a twenty-billion-dollar business. This figure has been picked up and widely quoted, but in truth no one knows what the gambling "turnover" and "take" actually is, nor how much is bet legally (pari-mutuel, etc.) and how much illegally. In fact, the figure cited by the committee was arbitrary and arrived at quite sloppily. As one staff member said: "We had no real idea of the money spent. . . . The California crime commission said twelve billion. Virgil Peterson of Chicago estimated thirty billion. We picked twenty billion as a balance between the two."

If comprehensive data are not available, we do know, from specific instances, the magnitude of many of the operations. Some indications can be seen from these items culled at random:

—James Carroll and the M & G syndicate did a 20-million-dollar annual business in St. Louis. This was one of the two large books in the city.

—The S & G syndicate in Miami did a 26-million-dollar volume yearly; the total for all books in the Florida resort reached 40 millions.

—Slot machines were present in 69,786 establishments in 1951 (each paid $100 for a license to the Bureau of Internal Revenue); the usual average is three machines to a license, which would add up to 210,000 slot machines in operation in the United States. In legalized areas, where the betting is higher and more regular, the average gross "take" per machine is $50 a week.

—The largest policy wheel (i.e. "numbers") in Chicago's "Black Belt" reported taxable net profits for the four-year period from 1946 through 1949, after sizable deductions for "overhead," of $3,656,968. One of the large "white" wheels reported in 1947 a gross income of $2,317,000 and a net profit of $205,000. One CIO official estimated that perhaps 15 per cent of his union's lower echelon officials are involved in the numbers racket (a steward, free to roam a plant, is in a perfect situation for organizing bets).

If one considers the amount of betting on sports alone—an estimated six billion on baseball, a billion on football pools, another billion on basketball, six billion on horse racing—then Elmo Roper's judgment that "only the food, steel, auto, chemical, and machine-tool industries have a greater volume of business" does not seem too far-fetched.

While gambling has long flourished in the United States, the influx of the big mobsters into the industry—and its expansion—started in the '30's when repeal of Prohibition forced them to look about for new avenues of enterprise. Gambling, which had begun to flower under the nourishment of rising incomes, was the most lucrative field in sight. To a large extent the shift from bootlegging to gambling was a mere transfer of business operations. In the East, Frank Costello went into slot machines and the operation of a number of ritzy gambling casinos. He also became the "banker" for the Erickson "book," which "laid off" bets for other bookies. Joe Adonis, similarly, opened up a number of casinos, principally in New Jersey. Across the country, many other mobsters went into bookmaking. As other rackets diminished, and gambling, particularly horse-race betting, flourished in the '40's, a struggle erupted over the control of racing information.

Horse-race betting requires a peculiar industrial organization. The essential component is time. A bookie can operate only if he can get information on odds up to the very last minute before the race, so that he can "hedge" or "lay off" bets. With racing going on simultaneously on many tracks throughout the country, this information has to be obtained speedily and accurately. Thus, the racing wire is the nerve ganglion of race betting.

The racing-wire news service got started in the '20's through the genius of the late Moe Annenberg, who had made a fearful reputation for himself as Hearst's circulation manager in the rough-and-tumble Chicago newspaper wars. Annenberg conceived the idea of a telegraphic news service which would gather information from tracks and shoot it immediately to scratch sheets, horse parlors, and bookie joints. In some instances, track owners gave Annenberg the rights to send news from tracks; more often, the news was simply "stolen" by crews operating inside or near the tracks. So efficient did this news distribution system become, that in 1942, when a plane knocked out a vital telegraph circuit which served an Air Force field as well as the gamblers, the Continental Press managed to get its racing wire service for gamblers resumed in fifteen minutes, while it took the Fourth Army, which was responsible for the defense of the entire West Coast, something like three hours.

Annenberg built up a nationwide racing information chain that not only distributed wire news but controlled sub-outlets as well. In 1939, harassed by the Internal Revenue Bureau on income tax, and chivvied by the Justice Department for "monopolistic" control of the wire service, the tired and aging Annenberg simply walked out of the business. He did not sell his interest, or even seek to salvage some profit; he simply gave up. Yet, like any established and thriving institution, the enterprise continued, though on a decentralized basis. James Ragen, Annenberg's operations manager, and likewise a veteran of the old Chicago circulation wars, took over the national wire service through a dummy friend and renamed it the Continental Press Service.

The salient fact is that in the operation of the Annenberg and Ragen wire service, formally illegal as many of its subsidiary operations may have been (i.e. in "stealing" news, supplying information to bookies, etc.) gangsters played no part. It was a business, illicit, true, but primarily a business. The distinction between gamblers and gangsters, as we shall see, is a relevant one.

In 1946, the Chicago mob, whose main interest was in bookmaking rather than gambling casinos, began to move in on the wire monopoly. Following repeal, the Capone lieutenants had turned, like Lepke, to labor racketeering. Murray ("The Camel") Humphries muscled in on the teamsters, the operating engineers, and the cleaning-and-dyeing, laundry, and linen-supply industries. Through a small-time punk, Willie Bioff, and union official George Browne, Capone's chief successors, Frank ("The Enforcer") Nitti and Paul Ricca, came into control of the motion-picture union and proceeded to shake down the movie industry for fabulous sums in order to "avert strikes." In 1943, when the government moved in and smashed the industrial rackets, the remaining big shots, Charley Fischetti, Jake Guzik, and Tony Accardo decided to concentrate on gambling, and in particular began a drive to take over the racing wire.

In Chicago, the Guzik-Accardo gang, controlling a sub-distributor of the racing news service, began tapping Continental's wires. In Los Angeles, the head of the local distribution agency for Continental was beaten up by hoodlums working for Mickey Cohen and Joe Sica. Out of the blue appeared a new and competitive nationwide racing information and distribution service, known as Trans-American Publishing, the money for which was advanced by the Chicago mobs and Bugsy Siegel, who, at the time, held a monopoly of the bookmaking and wire-news service in Las Vegas. Many books pulled out of Continental and bought information from the new outfit, many hedged by buying from both. At the end of a year, however, the Capone mob's wire had lost about $200,000. Ragen felt that violence would erupt and went to the Cook County district attorney and told him that his life had been threatened by his rivals. Ragen knew his competitors. In June 1946 he was killed by a blast from a shotgun.

Thereafter, the Capone mob abandoned Trans-American and got a "piece" of Continental. Through their new control of the national racing-wire monopoly, the Capone mob began to muscle in on the lucrative Miami gambling business run by the so-called S & G syndicate. For a long time S & G's monopoly over bookmaking had been so complete that when New York gambler Frank Erickson bought a three months' bookmaking concession at the expensive Roney Plaza Hotel, for $45,000, the local police, in a highly publicized raid, swooped down on the hotel; the next year the

Roney Plaza was again using local talent. The Capone group, however, was tougher. They demanded an interest in Miami bookmaking, and, when refused, began organizing a syndicate of their own, persuading some bookies at the big hotels to join them. Florida Governor Warren's crime investigator appeared—a friend, it seemed, of old Chicago dog-track operator William Johnston, who had contributed $100,000 to the Governor's campaign fund—and began raiding bookie joints, but only those that were affiliated with S & G. Then S & G, which had been buying its racing news from the local distributor of Continental Press, found its service abruptly shut off. For a few days the syndicate sought to bootleg information from New Orleans, but found itself limping along. After ten days' war of attrition, the five S & G partners found themselves with a sixth partner, who, for a token "investment" of $20,000 entered a Miami business that grossed $26,000,000 in one year.

While Americans made gambling illegal, they did not in their hearts think of it as wicked—even the churches benefited from the bingo and lottery crazes. So they gambled—and gamblers flourished. Against this open canvas, the indignant tones of Senator Wiley and the shocked righteousness of Senator Tobey during the Kefauver investigation rang oddly. Yet it was probably this very tone of surprise that gave the activity of the Kefauver Committee its piquant quality. Here were some Senators who seemingly did not know the facts of life, as most Americans did. Here, in the person of Senator Tobey, was the old New England Puritan conscience poking around in industrial America, in a world it had made but never seen. Here was old-fashioned moral indignation, at a time when cynicism was rampant in public life.

Commendable as such moralistic fervor was, it did not make for intelligent discrimination of fact. Throughout the Kefauver hearings, for example, there ran the presumption that all gamblers were invariably gangsters. This was true of Chicago's Accardo-Guzik combine, which in the past had its fingers in many kinds of rackets. It was not nearly so true of many of the large gamblers in America, most of whom had the feeling that they were satisfying a basic American urge for sport and looked upon their calling with no greater sense of guilt than did many bootleggers. After all, Sherman Billingsley did start out as a speakeasy proprietor, as did the Kriendlers of the "21" Club; and today the Stork Club and the former Jack and Charlie's are the most fashionable night and dining spots in America (one prominent patron of the Stork Club: J. Edgar Hoover).

The S & G syndicate in Miami, for example (led by Harold Salvey, Jules Levitt, Charles Friedman, Sam Cohen, and Edward (Eddie Luckey) Rosenbaum was simply a master pool of some two hundred bookies that arranged for telephone service, handled "protection," acted as bankers for those who needed ready cash on hard-hit books, and, in short, functioned somewhat analogously to the large factoring corporations in the textile field or the credit companies in the auto industry. Yet to Kefauver, these S & G men were "slippery and arrogant characters. . . . Salvey, for instance, was an old-time bookie who told us he had done nothing except engage in bookmaking or finance other bookmakers for twenty years." When, as a result of committee publicity and the newly found purity of the Miami police, the S & G syndicate went out of business, it was, as the combine's lawyer told Kefauver, because the "boys" were weary of being painted "the worst monsters in the world." "It is true," Cohen acknowledged, "that they had been law violators." But they had never done anything worse than gambling, and "to fight the world isn't worth it."

Most intriguing of all were the opinions of James J. Carroll, the St. Louis "betting commissioner," who for years had been widely quoted on the sports pages of the country as setting odds on the Kentucky Derby winter book and the baseball pennant races. Senator Wiley, speaking like the prosecutor in Camus's novel, *The Stranger,* became the voice of official morality:

SENATOR WILEY: Have you any children?
MR. CARROLL: Yes, I have a boy.
SENATOR WILEY: How old is he?
MR. CARROLL: Thirty-three.
SENATOR WILEY: Does he gamble?
MR. CARROLL: No.
SENATOR WILEY: Would you like to see him grow up and become a gambler, either professional or amateur?
MR. CARROLL: No . . .
SENATOR WILEY: All right. Is your son interested in your business?
MR. CARROLL: No, he is a manufacturer.
SENATOR WILEY: Why do you not get him into the business?
MR. CARROLL: Well, psychologically a great many people are unsuited for gambling.

Retreating from this gambit, the Senator sought to pin Carroll down on his contributions to political campaigns:

SENATOR WILEY: Now this morning I asked you whether you contributed any money for political candidates or parties, and you said not more than $200 at any one time. I presume that does not indicate the total of your contributions in any one campaign, does it?
MR. CARROLL: Well, it might, might not, Senator. I have been an "againster" in many instances. I am a reader of *The Nation* for fifty years and they have advertisements calling for contributions for different candidates, different causes. . . . They carried an advertisement for George Norris; I contributed, I think, to that, and to the elder La Follette.

Carroll, who admitted to having been in the betting business since 1899, was the sophisticated—but not immoral!—counterpoint to moralist Wiley. Here was a man without the stigmata of the underworld or underground; he was worldly, cynical of official rhetoric, jaundiced about people's motives, he was—an "againster" who believed that "all gambling legislation originates or stems from some group or some individual seeking special interests for himself or his cause."

Asked why people gamble, Carroll distilled his experiences of fifty years with a remark that deserves a place in American social history: "I really don't know how to answer the question," he said. "I think gambling is a biological necessity for certain types. I think it is the quality that gives substance to their daydreams."

In a sense, the entire Kefauver materials, unintentionally, seem to document that remark. For what the Committee revealed time and time again was a picture of gambling as a basic institution in American life, flourishing openly and accepted widely. In many of the small towns, the gambling joint is as open as a liquor establishment. The town of Havana, in Mason County, Illinois, felt miffed when Governor Adlai Stevenson intervened against local gambling. In 1950, the town had raised $15,000 of its $50,000 budget by making friendly raids on the gambling houses every month and having the owners pay fines. "With the gambling fines cut off," grumbled Mayor Clarence Chester, "the next year is going to be tough."

Apart from the gamblers, there were the mobsters. But what Senator Kefauver and company failed to understand was that the mobsters, like the gamblers, and like the entire gangdom generally, were seeking to become quasi-respectable and establish a place for themselves in American life. For the mobsters, by and large, had immigrant roots, and crime, as the pattern showed, was a route of social ascent and place in American life.

The mobsters were able, where they wished, to "muscle in" on the gambling business because the established gamblers were wholly vulnerable, not being able to call on the law for protection. The Senators, however, refusing to make any distinction between a gambler and a gangster, found it convenient to talk loosely of a nationwide conspiracy of "illegal" elements. Senator Kefauver asserted that a "nationwide crime syndicate does exist in the United States, despite the protestations of a strangely assorted company of criminals, self-serving politicians, plain blind fools, and others who may be honestly misguided, that there is no such combine." The Senate Committee report states the matter more dogmatically: "There is a nationwide crime syndicate known as the Mafia. . . . Its leaders are usually found in control of the most lucrative rackets in their cities. There are indications of a centralized direction and control of these rackets. . . . The Mafia is the cement that helps to bind the Costello-Adonis-Lansky syndicate of New York and the Accardo-

Guzik-Fischetti syndicate of Chicago. . . . These groups have kept in touch with Luciano since his deportation from the country."

Unfortunately for a good story—and the existence of the Mafia would be a whale of a story—neither the Senate Crime Committee in its testimony, nor Kefauver in his book, presented any real evidence that the Mafia exists as a functioning organization. One finds police officials asserting before the Kefauver committee their *belief* in the Mafia; the Narcotics Bureau *thinks* that a worldwide dope ring allegedly run by Luciano is part of the Mafia; but the only other "evidence" presented—aside from the incredulous responses both of Senator Kefauver and Rudolph Halley when nearly all the Italian gangsters asserted that they didn't know about the Mafia—is that certain crimes bear "the earmarks of the Mafia."

The legend of the Mafia has been fostered in recent years largely by the peephole writing team of Jack Lait and Lee Mortimer. In their *Chicago Confidential,* they rattled off a series of names and titles that made the organization sound like a rival to an Amos and Andy Kingfish society. Few serious reporters, however, give it much credence. Burton Turkus, the Brooklyn prosecutor who broke up the "Murder, Inc." ring, denies the existence of the Mafia. Nor could Senator Kefauver even make out much of a case for his picture of a national crime syndicate. He is forced to admit that "as it exists today [it] is an elusive and furtive but nonetheless tangible thing," and that "its organization and machinations are not always easy to pinpoint." His "evidence" that many gangsters congregate at certain times of the year in such places as Hot Springs, Arkansas, in itself does not prove much; people "in the trade" usually do, and as the loquacious late Willie Moretti of New Jersey said, in explaining how he had met the late Al Capone at a race track, "Listen, well-charactered people you don't need introductions to; you just meet automatically."

Why did the Senate Crime Committee plump so hard for its theory of the Mafia and a national crime syndicate? In part, they may have been misled by their own hearsay. The Senate Committee was not in the position to do original research, and its staff, both legal and investigative, was incredibly small. Senator Kefauver had begun the investigation with the attitude that with so much smoke there must be a raging fire. But smoke can also mean a smoke screen. Mob activities is a field in which busy gossip and exaggeration flourish even more readily than in a radical political sect.

There is, as well, in the American temper, a feeling that "somewhere," "somebody" is pulling all the complicated strings to which this jumbled world dances. In politics the labor image is "Wall Street," or "Big Business"; while the business stereotype was the "New Dealers." In the field of crime, the side-of-the-mouth low-down was "Costello."

The salient reason, perhaps, why the Kefauver Committee was taken in by its own myth of an omnipotent Mafia and a despotic Costello was its failure to assimilate and understand three of the more relevant sociological facts about institutionalized crime in its relation to the political life of large urban communities in America, namely: (1) the rise of the American Italian community, as part of the inevitable process of ethnic succession, to positions of importance in politics, a process that has been occurring independently but almost simultaneously in most cities with large Italian constituencies—New York, Chicago, Kansas City, Los Angeles; (2) the fact that there are individual Italians who play prominent, often leading roles today in gambling and in the mobs; and (3) the fact that Italian gamblers and mobsters often possessed "status" within the Italian community itself and a "pull" in city politics. These three items are indeed related—but not so as to form a "plot."

The Italian community has achieved wealth and political influence much later and in a harder way than previous immigrant groups. Early Jewish wealth, that of the German Jews of the late nineteenth century, was made largely in banking and merchandising. To that extent, the dominant group in the Jewish community was outside of, and independent of, the urban political machines. Later Jewish wealth, among the East European immigrants, was built in the garment trades, though with some involvement with the Jewish gangster, who was typically an industrial racketeer (Arnold Rothstein, Lepke and Gurrah, etc.) Among Jewish lawyers, a small minority, such as the "Tammany lawyer" (like the protagonist of Sam Ornitz's *Haunch, Paunch* and *Jowl*) rose through politics and occasionally touched the fringes of crime. Most of the Jewish lawyers, by and large the communal leaders, climbed rapidly, however, in the opportunities that established and legitimate Jewish wealth provided. Irish immigrant wealth in the northern urban centers, concentrated largely in construction, trucking and the waterfront, has, to a substantial extent, been wealth accumulated in and through political alliance, e.g. favoritism in city contracts. Control of the politics of the city thus has been crucial for the continuance of Irish political wealth. This alliance of Irish immigrant wealth and politics has been reciprocal; many noted Irish political figures lent their names as important window-dressing for business corporations (Al Smith, for example, who helped form the U.S. Trucking Corporation, whose executive head for many years was William J. McCormack, the alleged "Mr. Big" of the New York waterfront) while Irish businessmen have lent their wealth to further the careers of Irish politicians. Irish mobsters have rarely achieved status in the Irish community, but have served as integral arms of the politicians, as strong-arm men on election day.

The Italians found the more obvious big city paths from rags to riches pre-empted. In part this was due to the character of the early Italian immigration. Most of them were unskilled and from rural stock. Jacob Riis could remark in the '90's, "the Italian comes in at the bottom and stays there." These dispossessed agricultural laborers found jobs as ditchdiggers, on the railroads as section hands, along the docks, in the service occupations, as shoemakers, barbers, garment workers, and stayed there. Many were fleeced by the "padrone" system, a few achieved wealth from truck farming, wine growing, and marketing produce; but this "marginal wealth" was not the source of coherent and stable political power.

Significantly, although the number of Italians in the U.S. is about a third as high as the number of Irish, and of the 30,000,000 Catholic communicants in the United States, about half are of Irish descent and a sixth of Italian, there is not one Italian bishop among the hundred Catholic bishops in this country, or one Italian archbishop among the 21 archbishops. The Irish have a virtual monopoly. This is a factor related to the politics of the American church; but the condition also is possible because there is not significant or sufficient wealth among Italian Americans to force some parity.

The children of the immigrants, the second and third generation, became wise in the ways of the urban slums. Excluded from the political ladder—in the early '30's there were almost no Italians on the city payroll in top jobs, nor in books of the period can one find discussion of Italian political leaders—finding few open routes to wealth, some turned to illicit ways. In the children's court statistics of the 1930's, the largest group of delinquents were the Italian; nor were there any Italian communal or social agencies to cope with these problems. Yet it was, oddly enough, the quondam racketeer, seeking to become respectable, who provided one of the major supports for the drive to win a political voice for Italians in the power structure of the urban political machines.

This rise of the Italian political bloc was connected, at least in the major northern urban centers to another important development which tended to make the traditional relation between the politician and the protected or tolerated illicit operator more close than it had been in the past. This is the fact that the urban political machines had to evolve new forms of fund-raising since the big business contributions, which once went heavily into municipal politics, now—with the shift in the locus of power—go largely into national affairs. (The ensuing corruption in national politics, as recent Congressional investigations show, is no petty matter; the scruples of businessmen do not seem much superior to those of the gamblers.) One way urban political machines raised their money resembled that of the large corporations which are no longer dependent on Wall Street: by self-financing—that is, by "taxing" the large number of municipal employees who bargain collectively with City Hall for their wage increases. So the firemen's union contributed money to O'Dwyer's campaign.

A second method was taxing the gamblers. The classic example, as *Life* reported, was Jersey City, where a top lieutenant of the Hague machine spent his full time screening applicants for unofficial bookmaking licenses. If found acceptable, the applicant was given a "location," usually the house or store of a loyal precinct worker, who kicked into the machine treasury a high proportion of the large rent exacted. The one thousand bookies and their one thousand landlords in Jersey City formed the hard core of the political machine that sweated and bled to get out the votes for Hague.

A third source for the financing of these machines was the new, and often illegally earned, Italian wealth. This is well illustrated by the career of Costello and his emergence as a political power in New York. Here the ruling motive has been the search for an entrée—for oneself and one's ethnic group—into the ruling circles of the big city.

Frank Costello made his money originally in bootlegging. After repeal, his big break came when Huey Long, desperate for ready cash to fight the old-line political machines, invited Costello to install slot machines in Louisiana. Costello did, and he flourished. Together with Dandy Phil Kastel, he also opened the Beverly Club, an elegant gambling establishment just outside New Orleans, at which have appeared some of the top entertainers in America. Subsequently, Costello invested his money in New York real estate (including 79 Wall Street, which he later sold), the Copacabana night club, and a leading brand of Scotch whiskey.

Costello's political opportunity came when a money-hungry Tammany, starved by lack of patronage from Roosevelt and La Guardia, turned to him for financial support. The Italian community in New York has for years nursed a grievance against the Irish and, to a lesser extent, the Jewish political groups for monopolizing political power. They complained about the lack of judicial jobs, the small number—usually one—of Italian Congressmen, the lack of representation on the state tickets. But the Italians lacked the means to make their ambitions a reality. Although they formed a large voting bloc, there was rarely sufficient wealth to finance political clubs. Italian immigrants, largely poor peasants from Southern Italy and Sicily, lacked the mercantile experience of the Jews, and the political experience gained in the seventy-five-year history of Irish immigration.

During the Prohibition years, the Italian racketeers had made certain political contacts in order to gain protection. Costello, always the compromiser and fixer rather than the muscle-man, was the first to establish relations with Jimmy Hines, the powerful leader of the West Side in Tammany Hall. But his rival, Lucky Luciano, suspicious of the Irish, and seeking more direct power, backed and elected Al Marinelli for district leader on the Lower West Side. Marinelli in 1932 was the only Italian leader inside Tammany Hall. Later, he was joined by Dr. Paul Sarubbi, a partner of Johnny Torrio in a large, legitimate liquor concern. Certainly, Costello and Luciano represented no "unified" move by the Italians as a whole for power; within the Italian community there are as many divisions as in any other group. What is significant is that different Italians, for different reasons, and in various fashions, were achieving influence for the first time. Marinelli became county clerk of New York and a leading power in Tammany. In 1937, after being blasted by Tom Dewey, then running for district attorney, as a "political ally of thieves . . . and big-shot racketeers," Marinelli was removed from office by Governor Lehman. The subsequent conviction by Dewey of Luciano and Hines, and the election of La Guardia, left most of the Tammany clubs financially weak and foundering. This was the moment Costello made his move. In a few years, by judicious financing, he controlled a block of "Italian" leaders in the Hall—as well as some Irish on the upper West Side, and some Jewish leaders on the East Side—and was able to influence the selection of a number of Italian judges. The most notable incident, revealed by a wire tap on Costello's phone, was the "Thank you, Francisco" call in 1943 by Supreme Court nominee Thomas Aurelio, who gave Costello full credit for his nomination.

It was not only Tammany that was eager to accept campaign contributions from newly rich Italians, even though some of these *nouveaux riches* had "arrived" through bootlegging and gambling. Fiorello La Guardia, the wiliest mind that Melting Pot politics has ever produced, understood in the early '30's where much of his covert support came from. (So, too, did Vito Marcantonio, an apt pupil of the master: Marcantonio has consistently made deals with the Italian leaders of Tammany Hall—in 1943 he supported Aurelio, and refused to repudiate him even when the Democratic Party formally did.) Joe Adonis, who had built a political following during the late '20's, when he ran a popular speakeasy, aided La Guardia financially to a considerable extent in 1933. "The Democrats haven't recognized the Italians," Adonis told a friend. "There is no reason for the Italians to support anybody but La Guardia; the Jews have played ball with the Democrats and haven't gotten much out of it. They know it now. They will vote for La Guardia. So will the Italians."

Adonis played his cards shrewdly. He supported La Guardia, but also a number of Democrats for local and judicial posts, and became a power in the Brooklyn area. His restaurant was frequented by Kenny Sutherland, the Coney Island Democratic leader; Irwin Steingut, the Democratic minority leader in Albany; Anthony DiGiovanni, later a Councilman; William O'Dwyer, and Jim Moran. But, in 1937, Adonis made the mistake of supporting Royal Copeland against La Guardia, and the irate Fiorello finally drove Adonis out of New York.

La Guardia later turned his ire against Costello, too. Yet Costello survived and reached the peak of his influence in 1942, when he was instrumental in electing Michael Kennedy leader of Tammany Hall. Despite the Aurelio fiasco, which first brought Costello into notoriety, he still had sufficient power in the Hall to swing votes for Hugo Rogers as Tammany leader in 1945, and had a tight grip on some districts as late as 1948. In those years many a Tammany leader came hat in hand to Costello's apartment, or sought him out on the golf links, to obtain the nomination for a judicial post.

During this period, other Italian political leaders were also coming to the fore. Generoso Pope, whose Colonial Sand and Stone Company began to prosper through political contacts, became an important political figure, especially when his purchase of the two largest Italian-language dailies (later merged into one), and of a radio station, gave him almost a monopoly of channels to Italian-speaking opinion of the city. Through Generoso Pope, and through Costello, the Italians became a major political force in New York.

That the urban machines, largely Democratic, have financed their heavy campaign costs in this fashion rather than having to turn to the "moneyed interests," explains in some part why these machines were able, in part, to support the New and Fair Deals without suffering the pressures they might have been subjected to had their source of money supply been the business groups. Although he has never publicly revealed his political convictions, it is likely that Frank Costello was a fervent admirer of Franklin D. Roosevelt and his efforts to aid the common man. The basic measures of the New Deal, which most Americans today agree were necessary for the public good, would not have been possible without the support of the "corrupt" big-city machines.

There is little question that men of Italian origin appeared in most of the leading roles in the high drama of gambling and mobs, just as twenty years ago the children of East European Jews were the most prominent figures in organized crime, and before that individuals of Irish descent were similarly prominent. To some extent statistical accident and the tendency of newspapers to emphasize the few sensational figures gives a greater illusion about the domination of illicit activities by a single ethnic group than all the facts warrant. In many cities, particularly in the South and on the West Coast, the mob and gambling fraternity consisted of many other groups, and often, predominantly, native white Protestants. Yet it is clear that in the major northern urban centers there was a distinct ethnic sequence in the modes of obtaining illicit wealth, and that uniquely in the case of the recent Italian elements, the former bootleggers and gamblers provided considerable leverage for the growth of political influence as well. A substantial number of Italian judges sitting on the bench in New York today are indebted in one fashion or another to Costello; so too are many Italian district leaders—as well as some Jewish and Irish politicians. And the motive in establishing Italian political prestige in New York was generous rather than scheming for personal advantage. For Costello it was largely a case of ethnic pride. As in earlier American eras, organized illegality became a stepladder of social ascent.

To the world at large, the news and pictures of Frank Sinatra, for example, mingling with former Italian mobsters could come somewhat as a shock. Yet to Sinatra, and to many Italians, these were men who had grown up in their neighborhoods, and who were, in some instances, bywords in the community for their helpfulness and their charities. The early Italian gangsters were hoodlums—rough, unlettered, and young (Al Capone was only twenty-nine at the height of his power). Those who survived learned to adapt. By now they are men of middle age or older. They learned to dress conservatively. Their homes are in respectable suburbs. They sent their children to good schools and had sought to avoid publicity. Costello even went to a psychiatrist in his efforts to overcome a painful feeling of inferiority in the world of manners.

As happens with all "new" money in American society, the rough and ready contractors, the construction people, trucking entrepreneurs, as well as racketeers, polished up their manners and sought recognition and respectability in their own ethnic as well as in the general community. The "shanty" Irish became the "lace curtain" Irish, and then moved out for wider recognition. Sometimes acceptance came first in established "American" society, and this was a certificate for later recognition by the ethnic community, a process well illustrated by the belated acceptance in established Negro society of such figures as Sugar Ray Robinson and Joe Louis, as well as leading popular entertainers.

Yet, after all, the foundation of many a distinguished older American fortune was laid by sharp practices and morally reprehensible methods. The pioneers of American capitalism were not graduated from Harvard's School of Business Administration. The early settlers and founding fathers, as well as those who "won the west" and built up cattle, mining and other fortunes, often did so by shady speculations and a not inconsiderable amount of violence. They ignored, circumvented or stretched the law when it stood in the way of America's destiny, and their own—or, were themselves the law when it served their purposes. This has not prevented them and their descendants from feeling proper moral outrage when under the changed circumstances of the crowded urban environments later comers pursued equally ruthless tactics.

Ironically, the social development which made possible the rise to political influence sounds, too, the knell of the Italian gangster. For it is the growing number of Italians with professional training and legitimate business success that both prompts and permits the Italian group to wield increasing political influence; and increasingly it is the professionals and businessmen who provide models for Italian youth today, models that hardly existed twenty years ago. Ironically, the headlines and exposés of "crime" of the Italian "gangsters" came years after the fact. Many of the top "crime" figures long ago had forsworn violence, and even their income, in large part, was derived from legitimate investments (real estate in the case of Costello, motor haulage and auto dealer franchises in the case of Adonis) or from such quasi-legitimate but socially respectable sources as gambling casinos. Hence society's "retribution" in the jail sentences for Costello and Adonis was little more than a trumped-up morality that disguised a social hypocrisy.

Apart from these considerations, what of the larger context of crime and the American way of life? The passing of the Fair Deal signalizes, oddly, the passing of an older pattern of illicit activities. The gambling fever of the past decade and a half was part of the flush and exuberance of rising incomes, and was characteristic largely of new upper-middle class rich having a first fling at conspicuous consumption. This upper-middle class rich, a significant new stratum in American life (not rich in the nineteenth century sense of enormous wealth, but largely middle-sized businessmen and entrepreneurs of the service and luxury trades—the "tertiary economy" in Colin Clark's phrase—who by the tax laws have achieved sizable incomes often much higher than the managers of the super-giant corporations) were the chief patrons of the munificent gambling casinos. During the war decade when travel was difficult, gambling and the lush resorts provided important outlets for this social class. Now they are settling down, learning about Europe and culture. The petty gambling, the betting and bingo which relieve the tedium of small town life, or the expectation among the urban slum dwellers of winning a sizable sum by a "lucky number" or a "lucky horse" goes on. To quote Bernard Baruch: "You can't stop people from gambling on horses. And why should you prohibit a man from backing his own judgment? It's another form of personal initiative." But the lush profits are passing from gambling, as the costs of coordination rise. And in the future it is likely that gambling, like prostitution, winning tacit acceptance as a necessary fact, will continue on a decentralized, small entrepreneur basis.

But passing, too, is a political pattern, the system of political "bosses" which in its reciprocal relation provided "protection" for and was fed revenue from crime. The collapse of the "boss" system was a product of the Roosevelt era. Twenty years ago Jim Farley's task was simple; he had to work only on some key state bosses. Now there is no longer such an animal. New Jersey Democracy was once ruled by Frank Hague; now there are five or six men each top dog, for the moment, in his part of the state or faction of the party. Within the urban centers, the old Irish-dominated political machines in New York, Boston, Newark, and Chicago have fallen apart. The decentralization of the metropolitan centers, the growth of suburbs and satellite towns, the break-up of the old ecological patterns of slum and transient belts, the rise of functional groups, the increasing middle-class character of American life, all contribute to this decline.

With the rationalization and absorption of some illicit activities into the structure of the economy, the passing of an older generation that had established a hegemony over crime, the general rise of minority groups to social position, and the break-up of the urban boss system, the pattern of crime we have discussed is passing as well. Crime, of course, remains as long as passion and the desire for gain remain. But big, organized city crime, as we have known it for the past seventy-five years, was based on more than these universal motives. It was based on certain characteristics of the American economy, American ethnic groups, and American politics. The changes in all these areas means that it too, in the form we have known it, is at an end.

5. The Management of Status

The search for admiration in the eyes of one's peers is so common a human motive that we almost take it for granted. The adolescent no less than the businessman feels its force, but in the case of some adolescents, aggressiveness and bravery in gang fighting have come to be marked off as the path to high status. "You were great, baby," says one of the boys described by James F. Short and Fred L. Strodtbeck. It is delinquency that is being praised, however, not conformity to the law.

Big Jake, leader of the Potentates, had been "cooling it" over the fall and winter. However Guy, leader of the Vice Kings, with whom the Potentates were often at war, warned: "Better watch Big Jake—he has to do *something.*" Why? "He's *got* to build that rep again. He's been gone—now he's got to show everybody he's *back!*"

—report from a director of detached workers with juvenile gangs

Like Big Jake, Duke, of the King Rattlers, had also been in jail. Before his internment he had been known for his self-possession—for being a "cool" leader. Although a capable and active fighter when he thought it necessary, he never lost his head and was very effective in negotiation, conciliation, and control. When he came out of jail his leadership and his personal future were threatened and uncertain, and he became belligerent, aggressive, and apparently reckless—with the approval of his gang. Once things settled down for him, however, he reverted to the cool behavior that had made him such an effective leader.

As with leaders of nations, the qualities that raise boys to the tops of juvenile gangs are not necessarily those that best qualify them to stay there, or to rule. "A good suitor may not make a good husband, or a good campaigner a good president." Moreover gangs, though they may admire the fighting campaigner, are often more difficult to control than nations; members who feel abused can sometimes simply drop out, as citizens cannot.

These restrictions, however, do not limit fighting between gangs. Here a leader can work off his aggressions, show off his fighting prowess, and win

From James F. Short and Fred L. Strodtbeck, "Why Gangs Fight," **Trans-action,** 1 (Sept.–Oct., 1964), pp. 25–29.

prestige and popularity with his gang, making his position more secure. As with nations, tyrannizing outsiders is always more acceptable. A despot is someone who abuses his own people; if he attacks and tyrannizes other groups, he is a great and victorious leader, leading enthusiastic followers on to glory.

Juvenile gang leaders invest a great deal in their fighting reputations. Leadership and delinquency must therefore go together. In nearly all gangs we studied, over a three year period, we found that skill in fighting was highly valued, whether or not the gang itself had a fighting "rep." A fight often occurred because a gang, or its leaders, simply could not tolerate a real or implied threat to whatever reputation they had.

Some gangs are definitely "conflict oriented." Fighting is a major and necessary activity for them and a means of acquiring respect, admiration, and prestige within them. They must and do fight often. They have a heavy investment in—and therefore motivation toward—combat. Their leadership, reputation, and status are under constant challenge—anytime they falter some other gang will try to make them fall. They must be prepared for defense—indeed, they believe they must attack from time to time before others attack them, and to remind possible enemies to beware. "We are the mighty Vice Kings!" a leader will shout in challenge—much as Beowulf, using other names, might have done. The very titles and roles they create for themselves reflect the warlike stance—"war counselor," "armorer." These offices need not be clearly or formally defined or even performed; but they are recognized and given deference, and competition for them is fierce.

"Conflict" of course need not always involve major war—the primary purpose of battle is to prove oneself, not to capture anything. The kind of guerilla combat such gangs engage in was well illustrated in the following abstract of a detached worker's incident report:

I was sitting talking to the Knights, re-emphasizing my stand on guns, because they told me they had collected quite a few and were waiting for the Vice Kings to start trouble. I told them flatly that it was better that I got the gun than the police. They repeated that they were tired of running from the Vice Kings and that if they gave them trouble they were fighting back.

I looked out of the car and noticed two Vice Kings and two girls walking down the street. William then turned around and made the observation that there were about fifteen or twenty Vice Kings across the street in the alley, wandering up the street in ones or twos.

The Vice Kings encountered Commando (the leader) Jones, and a couple of other Knights coming around the corner. The Vice Kings yelled across to Commando and his boys, and Commando yelled back. I got out to cool Commando down, since he was halfway across the street daring them to do something. I grabbed him and began to pull him back.

But the Vice Kings were in a rage, and three came across the street yelling that they were mighty Vice Kings. At this point, along came Henry Brown with a revolver, shooting. Everybody ducked and the Vice Kings ran. I began to throw Knights into my car because I knew that the area was "hot."

In the car the boys were extremely elated. "Baby, did you see the way I swung on that kid?" "Man, did we tell them off?" "Did you see them take off when I leveled my gun?" "You were great, baby . . ."

The tension was relieved. They had performed well and could be proud . . .

No doubt the Vice Kings too felt the thrill of having faced conflict and come off well. They had met great danger bravely, and had a good alibi for not having won unquestioned victory—the enemy had a gun. The Knights, on their part also had an alibi—the worker had intervened. Both sides therefore won, and could mutually share satisfaction and enhanced reputation. Gang combat is not necessarily a winner-take-all game. No one need be defeated. The two gangs had "played the game" according to the standards of their "community"; they had been rewarded, and law and order were now restored. The larger society too profits from a no-loser game. Of course, results are not always so harmless. Boys and gangs are often beaten and people and property often injured in this "game."

Threats to the status of a leader can result in violence to whole gangs; but the process is more complicated than it seems. Threat to leadership is merely a special case of "status management," which involves all gang boys. How can high status best be achieved and maintained in the continuing and risky give and take of gang life?

Several kinds of threats to status are covered by the broad conception of status management. They are well illustrated in the elements involved in a "humbug"—a general brawl—that our workers witnessed and recorded.

Jim, the detached worker, had taken his gang, the North Side Vice Kings, to a professional basketball game at the Chicago Amphitheater. The boys were in good spirits, but restless and volatile. Duke, the strongest leader, had been drinking. He sat near a younger group, the Junior Chiefs. He was friendly to them but obnoxious to venders and others, and was generally putting on a show for the younger boys.

Duke announced that he was going to buy some beer—he had recently turned twenty-one. The worker told him that beer was out when they were on an officially sponsored activity. Duke bought it anyway, and after an argument in which Duke kept mentioning his age, Jim took the beer from him. Duke became abusive to the worker and other spectators; and the other Vice Kings also acted up. Jim then announced that the entire group had to leave immediately.

On the way out they met another group, the South Side Rattlers. As they passed, Duke "fat-mouthed" one of them and blows were exchanged. The Rattlers, at first confused, retaliated and the humbug was on, while their workers, caught off guard, tried vainly to separate them.

A third group, the Cherokees, now happened on the scene. Having a grudge against the Vice Kings, they waited for no further invitation. "No one stopped to get an explanation of what was going on. The fellows just looked up, saw the fighting, and joined in." The Rattlers, apparently frightened by a couple of knives and a pistol, had started to run, and the fighting might have died had the Cherokees stayed out.

The police partially broke up the battle, but a new round of insults started it again. A fourth group, the Midget Vice Kings arrived; hearing challenge and counter-challenge, they too gave battle, siding with the Vice Kings.

After the combat, the detached workers reported that all three major groups involved talked about going home to get their "stuff" (weapons) and preparing to fight. The Rattlers, having been forced to retreat, were especially disturbed and made many threats. However, when the police came up and escorted them to their car, eliminating all possibility of further humbugs, they acted relieved and happy. On the way home they teased each other about running.

One group—the Junior Chiefs—had not been challenged, or otherwise received any "status threats." Not very surprisingly, they did not fight, and stayed and watched the basketball game.

The other gangs, however, did feel their reputations and "manhood" threatened. Elements of threat included:

- The worker publicly ignored and down-graded Duke's newly achieved adulthood.
- Following this, he degraded him in the eyes of his special, younger, audience, the Junior Chiefs—and of his own gang, of which he was supposed to be a leader.
- He publicly humiliated and degraded all the rest of the Vice Kings by ordering them to leave, like a bunch of kids who could not be trusted to behave in public. This too he did before the Junior Chiefs—an act which immediately downgraded them in the gang world—and before adults, who could immediately identify them as "kids."
- Searching for an outlet for rage and frustration, and for a means to rebuild their shattered "reps," the Vice Kings encountered the Rattlers. They attacked them. Now the reputations of the Rattlers (and later of the Cherokees) were threatened, and *they* counter retaliated.

Yet, for all the ferocity, the fights were short-lived. Every group except the Vice Kings, who had been most threatened, were brought under control fairly quickly and stayed to see the basketball game—only the Vice Kings missed it. Moreover, despite talk of retaliation, the humbug was self-contained; in the following months there was no more humbugging between these groups. The fight served the usual purpose of upholding reputations and preserving the images of street warriors ready for combat.

Closer analysis, however, reveals more to the story. What happened to the ferocious warrior image after the fights were stopped? And why so easily stopped? Also, not all the boys fought. Except for the Vice Kings, each group contained some boys who stayed out. Careful review suggests that those most deeply involved in the fighting were the core gang-members—the leaders and those who wanted to be leaders. Not all gang members—and not all gangs—have the same investment in rep and status. Certainly no gang rules or standards, spoken or implied, require that *all* boys fight every time, even under these provocative circumstances.

Gang rules and expectations do influence the behavior of members; but that influence is not clear cut, and depends mostly on the situation. Gangs are fluid; members change; boys come and go for days or weeks at a time, and unless they are leaders, or important core members, they are hardly missed. Under such circumstances, the group leaders cannot make members—especially fringe members—conform or give obedience by threatening expulsion or withdrawal of privileges. Most of the gang leaders we studied were surprisingly conciliatory within the group. But they had a special interest in making members want to belong to a gang with a good reputation.

This article is concerned primarily with juvenile gangs whose status is built around conflict. But it must be emphasized that, despite prevalent stereotypes, juvenile gangs are not all conflict oriented, and value systems may vary among them as among other human groupings. A "retreatist" gang, which built its value system around the effect of dope, provides a dramatic contrast.

Although criticized and ridiculed repeatedly by other gangs for their cowardice and lack of manhood, the retreatists seldom responded to taunts, and always retreated from combat. They did not worry about their reputations as fighters—they had none—and did not think them important—in fact, they thought the conflict oriented gangs to be "square." Directly challenged to join other white gangs in repelling Negro "wade-in" demonstrators on a beach in Chicago, they got "high" on pills and unconcernedly played cards during the entire incident.

The basis of camaraderie—what was important—to the drug users was "kicks." Past and present exploits—their legends of valor—continually recounted, concerned "high" experiences and "crazy" behavior rather than bravery or toughness. "You get the feeling," a member of the team of research observers said, "that whatever the activity of the moment, the guys will talk about it in relation to dope—how taking dope affects their participation in the activity."

Even their humor revolved around the effect of dope—the antics of friends under the influence. They laughed about the boy who kept trying to start a junked car that had no motor. Another one, beaten by a Chinese laundryman he tried to rob, "was so doped out of his mind" that he asked the arriving police to arrest the other for beating him so. Some others climbed to a bedroom window and grabbed the leg of a girlfriend to wake her, but got the wrong window and the wrong leg—both of them her father's!

Not all gangs value combat. But each will protect what it does value. When the retreatists find what they value threatened, they withdraw, protectively. When a conflict oriented gang feels its status threatened, it fights.

"Status threat" is a special case of the general status thesis—that people will tend to do what gives them standing and respect in society. But with adolescent boys in a gang "what gives them standing and respect" is contained in the limited compass of the face-to-face relationships within the gang, not—except indirectly—with the social class structure of society at large. Of course, directly and indirectly, pressures from outside do affect the gang boys. They come from at least three levels.

Adult sponsored and controlled institutions of the larger society. Schools, places of employment, social agencies, police, and other officials represent adult "authority." Their orientation is middle-class; they preach and perhaps believe that worth and success come from hard work, deferred gratification, self control, good grades, good behavior, saving money, and becoming a "leader" in approved organizations. Gang boys fail to achieve according to these standards. The hypothesis that, with legitimate channels closed to them they will choose the illegitimate, therefore does not disagree with our findings. But how this works precisely is not very clear, and other research indicates that these boys may not be as alienated as many think. Other pressures must also affect them more directly.

The lower classes have their own adult community institutions, which make their own patterns and exert their own pressures. There are poolrooms, parties, informal neighborhood gatherings, and the obvious social and political power manifested by the adults in rackets and politics.

At this level, standards of adult behavior most appropriate to everyday life for the boys are inferred and directly inculcated. Observation strongly suggests that the gang boys recognize and respect the exercise of power in their neighborhoods, whether from legitimate or illegitimate sources. But there is no demonstration of legitimate power they know that compares in drama and impact with the evidence of the power of organized crime—the numerous gang slayings of hoodlums, and even of politicians. Both Negro and white gang boys repeat as a by-word: "You can't beat the syndicate."

But modeling behavior after adults in order to "achieve adulthood" seems not to be as important a factor among Negroes as among whites. Lower class Negro communities differ; there are fewer sharp age distinctions; all ages compete for excitement wherever it may be found—a bottle, a battle, or a broad. Poolhalls are frequented by young and old alike.

The adoption of adult lower class standards therefore cannot be the only, or even the major, cause of delinquency among adolescents. In the conflict prone gangs especially, the next level must be the most important.

The Adolescent Gang World. The juvenile "delinquent"—especially the gang leader—is faced with a condition, not a theory. He must daily act out his role under the eyes of his fellow gang members, and the members and leaders of other gangs. Almost by definition, the destiny of a warlike gang is controlled by the actions, real or expected, of other gangs. How a gang defends or enhances its status depends on its judgment of the whole fluid situation. What is the state of peace or war with rival gangs? What old gangs are feuding? What new gangs are trying to carve out niches for themselves?

Even a group organized for criminal purposes, as one of ours was, will shift its goals to fighting if under threat or attack from outside—even though this might, for a criminal gang, bring on risk of exposure.

The interrelationships in the gang world are extensive. A gang will have "branches" across neighborhood lines (East Side Cobras and West Side Cobras); it will have Senior, Junior, and Midget divisions within a neighborhood, with the younger members modeling themselves on the older, and expecting model behavior from them.

Even where pressures from outside make themselves manifest, they must filter down into and be expressed within the values of the gang itself. In fact the gang owes much of its reason for existence to its need to face and cope with such pressures, not losing status in the process—as would certainly happen if the adolescents had to face, nakedly, the censures, criticisms, and punishments of a middle-class or adult world they do not understand, and which does not understand them.

Each outside level represents forces which affect status within the gang—a boy can acquire "rep" by defiance of police, by vandalism of a neighborhood institution, or by showing "heart" in a gang fight. Whether or not the threat originated inside or outside the group, recognizing the existence of the gang and its internal dynamics is crucial to understanding how gang boys maintain status. The larger society is remote and abstract; even the neighborhood has indirect contact; the gang provides the face-to-face audience, the most direct and meaningful rewards and punishments.

Problems of status management are not confined to adolescent gangs. They affect us all—they rain on the just and the unjust alike, on parents, on delinquents, on corporation vice-presidents. And they rouse many besides juvenile gangs to violence.

In our work we noted that often merely assigning a worker to a gang, even before he had a chance to do anything, made the gang more docile, because being important enough to rate your own worker was such a mark of prestige that more energetic proof was not as necessary. Learning the techniques of status management—understanding the dynamics and importance of status considerations within juvenile gangs—provides a powerful lever by which gang behavior and delinquency can be grasped—and, perhaps, controlled.

6. Playing It Cool

As Short and Strodtbeck have shown, not all delinquents use violence as the way of achieving esteem. There are some who retreat into the passivity of narcotics, and the ability to "play it cool" is the most admired pattern of behavior. In the following article by Harold Finestone, the use of drugs is analyzed as part of a life style that renounces that which cannot be achieved.

Growing recognition that the most recent manifestation of the use of opiates in this country has been predominantly a young peoples' problem has resulted in some speculation as to the nature of this generation of drug users. Is it possible to form an accurate conception as to what "manner of man" is represented by the current species of young drug addict? Intensive interviews between 1951 and 1953 with over fifty male colored users of heroin in their late teens and early twenties selected from several of the areas of highest incidence of drug use in Chicago, served to elicit from them the expression of many common attitudes, values, schemes of behavior, and general social orientation. Moreover, since there was every reason to believe that such similarities had preceded their introduction to heroin, it appeared that it was by virtue of such shared features that they had been unusually receptive to the spread of opiate use. Methodologically, their common patterns of behavior suggested the heuristic value of the construction of a social type. The task of this paper is to depict this social type, and to present a hypothetical formulation to account for the form it has taken.

No special justification appears to be necessary for concentrating in this paper on the social type of the young colored drug user. One of the distinctive properties of the distribution of drug use as a social problem, at least in Chicago, is its high degree of both spatial and racial concentration. In fact, it is a problem which in this city can be pinpointed with great accuracy as having its incidence preponderantly among the young male colored persons in a comparatively few local community areas. The following delineation of the generic characteristics of young colored drug users constitutes in many respects an ideal type. No single drug addict exemplified all of the traits to be depicted but all of them revealed several of them to a marked degree.

Harold, Finestone, "Cats, Kicks and Color" **Social Problems,** v (July, 1957), 3–13. Permission also granted by The Society for the Study of Social Problems.

The young drug user was a creature of contrasts. Playing the role of the fugitive and pariah as he was inevitably forced to do, he turned up for interviews in a uniformly ragged and dirty condition. And yet he talked with an air of superiority derived from his identification with an elite group, the society of "cats." He came in wearing a nonfunctional tie clip attached to his sport shirt and an expensive hat as the only indications that he was concerned with his appearance and yet displayed in his conversation a highly developed sense of taste in men's clothing and a high valuation upon dressing well. He came from what were externally the drabbest, most overcrowded, and physically deteriorated sections of the city and yet discussed his pattern of living as though it were a consciously cultivated work of art.

Despite the location of his social world in the "asphalt jungle" of the "Blackbelt" he strictly eschewed the use of force and violence as a technique for achieving his ends or for the settling of problematic situations. He achieved his goals by indirection, relying, rather, on persuasion and on a repertoire of manipulative techniques. To deal with a variety of challenging situations, such as those arising out of his contacts with the police, with his past or potential victims, and with jilted "chicks," etc., he used his wits and his conversational ability. To be able to confront such contingencies with adequacy and without resort to violence was to be "cool." His idea was to get what he wanted through persuasion and ingratiation; to use the other fellow by deliberately outwitting him. Indeed, he regarded himself as immeasurably superior to the "gorilla," a person who resorted to force.

The image of himself as "operator" was projected onto the whole world about him and led to a complete scepticism as to other persons' motives. He could relate to people by outsmarting them, or through openhanded and often ruinous generosity, but his world seemed to preclude any relationship which was not part of a "scheme" or did not lend itself to an "angle." The most difficult puzzle for him to solve was the "square," the honest man. On the one hand the "square" was the hard-working plodder who lived by routine and who took honesty and the other virtues at their face value. As such, he constituted the prize victim for the cat. On the other hand, the cat harbored the sneaking suspicion that some squares were smarter than he, because they could enjoy all the forbidden pleasures which were his stock in trade and maintain a reputation for respectability in the bargain.

The cat had a large, colorful, and discriminating vocabulary which dealt with all phases of his experience with drugs. In addition, he never seemed to content himself with the conventional word for even the most commonplace objects. Thus he used "pad" for house, "pecks" for food, "flicks" for movies, "stick hall" for pool hall, "dig the scene" for observe, "box" for record player, "bread" for money, etc. In each instance the word he used was more concrete or earthier than the conventional word and such as to reveal an attitude of subtle ridicule towards the dignity and conventionality inherent in the common useage.

His soft convincing manner of speaking, the shocking earthiness and fancifulness of his vocabulary, together with the formidable gifts of charm and ingratiation which he deployed, all contributed to the dominant impression which the young drug user made as a person. Such traits would seem to have fitted naturally into a role which some cats had already played or aspired to play, that of the pimp. To be supported in idleness and luxury through the labors of one or more attractive "chicks" who shoplifted or engaged in prostitution or both and dutifully handed over the proceeds was one of his favorite fantasies. In contrast with the milieu of the white underworld, the pimp was not an object of opprobrium but of prestige.

The theme of the exploitation of the woman goes close to the heart of the cat's orientation to life, that is, his attitude towards work. Part of the cat's sense of superiority stems from his aristocratic disdain for work and for the subordination of self to superiors and to the repetitive daily routine entailed by work, which he regards as intolerable. The "square" is a person who toils for regular wages and who takes orders from his superiors without complaint.

In contrast with the "square," the cat gets by without working. Instead he keeps himself in "bread" by a set of ingenious variations on "begging, borrowing, or stealing." Each cat has his "hustle," and a "hustle" is any non-violent means of "making some bread" which does not require work. One of the legendary heroes of the cat is the man who is such a skillful con-man that he can sell "State Street" to his victim. Concretely, the cat is a petty thief, pickpocket, or pool shark, or is engaged in a variety of other illegal activities of the "conning" variety. A very few cats are actually living off the proceeds of their women "on the hustle."

The main purpose of life for the cat is to experience the "kick." Just as every cat takes pride in his "hustle," so every cat cultivates his "kick." A "kick" is any act tabooed by "squares" that heightens and intensifies the present moment of experience and differentiates it as much as possible from the humdrum routine of daily life. Sex in any of its conventional expressions is not a "kick" since this would not serve to distinguish the cat from the "square," but orgies of sex behavior and a dabbling in the various perversions and byways of sex pass muster as "kicks." Some "cats" are on an alcohol "kick," others on a marihuana "kick," and others on a heroin "kick." There is some interchangeability among these various "kicks" but the tendency is to select your "kick" and stay with it. Many of these young drug users, however, had progressed from the alcohol to the marihuana to the heroin "kick." Each "kick" has its own lore of appreciation and connoisseurship into which only its devotees are initiated.

In addition to his "kick" the cat sets great store on the enjoyment of music and on proper dress. To enjoy one's "kick" without a background of popular music is inconceivable. The cat's world of music has a distinctive galaxy of stars, and the brightest luminaries in his firmament are performers such as "Yardbird" (the late Charlie Parker) and disc jockeys such as Al Benson. Almost every cat is a frustrated musician who hopes some day to get his "horn" out of pawn, take lessons, and earn fame and fortune in the field of "progressive music."

The cat places a great deal of emphasis upon clothing and exercises his sartorial talents upon a skeletal base of suit, sport shirt, and hat. The suit itself must be conservative in color. Gaiety is introduced through the selection of the sport shirt and the various accessories, all so chosen and harmonized as to reveal an exquisite sense of taste. When the cat was not talking about getting his clothes out of pawn, he talked about getting them out of the cleaners. With nonchalant pride one drug user insisted that the most expensive sport shirts and hats in the city of Chicago were sold in a certain haberdashery on the South Side. The ideal cat would always appear in public impeccably dressed and be able to sport a complete change of outfit several times a day.

The cat seeks through a harmonious combination of charm, ingratiating speech, dress, music, the proper dedication to his "kick," and unrestrained generosity to make of his day to day life itself a gracious work of art. Everything is to be pleasant, and everything he does and values is to contribute to a cultivated aesthetic approach to living. The "cool cat" exemplifies all of these elements in proper balance. He demonstrates his ability to "play it cool" in his unruffled manner of dealing with outsiders such as the police, and in the self-assurance with which he confronts emergencies in the society of "cats." Moreover, the "cat" feels himself to be any man's equal. He is convinced that he can go anywhere and mingle easily with anyone. For example, he rejects the type of music designated "the blues" because for him it symbolizes attitudes of submission and resignation which are repugnant and alien to his customary frame of mind.

It can be seen now why heroin use should make such a powerful appeal to the cat. It was the ultimate "kick." No substance was more profoundly tabooed by conventional middle-class society. Regular heroin use provides a sense of maximal social differentiation from the "square." The cat was at last engaged, he felt, in an activity completely beyond the comprehension of the "square." No other "kick" offered such an instantaneous intensification of the immediate moment of experience and set it apart from everyday experience in such spectacular fashion. Any words used by the cat to apply to the "kick," the experience of "being high," he applied to heroin in the superlative. It was the "greatest kick of them all."

In the formulation now to be presented, the cat as a social type is viewed as a manifestation of a process of social change in which a new type of self-conception has been emerging among the adolescents of the lower social-economic levels of the colored population in large urban centers. It is a self-conception rooted in the types of accommodation to a subordinate status achieved historically by the colored race in this country, a self-conception which has become increasingly articulated as it responded to and selected various themes from the many available to it in the milieu of the modern metropolis. Blumer's classification of social movements into general, specific, or expressive, appears to provide a useful framework for the analysis of the social type of the cat.

In terms of these categories the cat as a social type is the personal counterpart of an expressive social movement. The context for such a movement must include the broader community, which, by its policies of social segregation and discrimination, has withheld from individuals of the colored population the opportunity to achieve or to identify with status positions in the larger society. The social type of the cat is an expression of one possible type of adaptation to such blocking and frustration, in which a segment of the population turns in upon itself and attempts to develop within itself criteria for the achievement of social status and the rudiments of a satisfactory social life. Within his own isolated social world, the cat attempts to give form and purpose to dispositions derived from but denied an outlet within the dominant social order.

What are these dispositions and in what sense may they be said to be derived from the dominant social order? Among the various interrelated facets of the life of the cat, two themes are central, those of the "hustle" and the "kick." It is to be noted that they are in direct antithesis to two of the central values of the dominant culture, the "hustle" versus the paramount importance of the occupation for the male in our society, and the "kick" versus the importance of regulating conduct in terms of its future consequences. Thus, there appears to be a relationship of conflict between the central themes of the social type of the cat and those of the dominant social order. As a form of expressive behavior, however, the social type of the cat represents an indirect rather than a direct attack against central conventional values.

It is interesting to speculate on the reasons why a type such as the cat should emerge rather than a social movement with the objective of changing the social order. The forces coercing the selective process among colored male adolescents in the direction of expressive social movements are probably to be traced to the long tradition of accommodation to a subordinate status on the part of the Negro as well as to the social climate since World War II, which does not seem to have been favorable to the formation of specific social movements.

The themes of the "hustle" and "kick" in the social orientation of the cat are facts which appear to be overdetermined. For example, to grasp the meaning of the "hustle" to the cat, one must understand it as a rejection of the obligation of the adult male to work. When asked for the reasons underlying his rejection of work the cat did not refer to the uncongenial and relatively unskilled and low paid jobs which, in large part, were the sole types of employment available to him. He emphasized rather that the routine of a job and the demand that he should apply himself continuously to his work task were the features that made work intolerable for him. The self-constraint required by work was construed as an unwarranted damper upon his love of spontaneity. The other undesirable element from his point of view was the authoritarian setting of most types of work with which he was familiar.

There are undoubtedly many reasons for the cat's rejection of work, but the reasons he actually verbalized are particularly significant when interpreted as devices for sustaining his self-conception. The cat's feeling of superiority would be openly challenged were he to confront certain of the social realities of his situation, such as the discrimination exercised against colored persons looking for work and the fact that only the lowest status jobs are available to him. He avoided any mention of these factors which would have forced him to confront his true position in society and thus posed a threat to his carefully cherished sense of superiority.

In emphasizing as he does the importance of the "kick" the cat is attacking the value our society places upon planning for the future and the responsibility of the individual for such planning. Planning always requires some subordination and disciplining of present behavior in the interest of future rewards. The individual plans to go to college, plans for his career, plans for his family and children, etc. Such an orientation on the part of the individual is merely the personal and subjective counterpart of a stable social order and of stable social institutions, which not only permit but sanction an orderly progression of expectations with reference to others and to one's self. Where such stable institutions are absent or in the inchoate stages of development, there is little social sanction for such planning in the experience of the individual. Whatever studies are available strongly suggest that such are the conditions which tend to prevail in the lower socio-economic levels of the Negro urban community. Stable family and community organization is lacking in those areas of the city where drug use is concentrated. A social milieu which does not encourage the subordination and disciplining of present conduct in the interests of future rewards tends by default to enhance the present. The "kick" appears to be a logical culmination of this emphasis.

Accepting the emergence of the self-conception of the cat as evidence of a developing depressive social movement, we may phrase the central theoretical problem as follows: What are the distinctive and generic features of the cat's social orientation? Taking a cue from the work of Huizinga as developed in *Homo Ludens,* we propose that the generic characteristics of the social type of the cat are those of play. In what follows, Huizinga's conception of play as a distinctive type of human activity will be presented and then applied as a tool of analysis for rendering intelligible the various facets of the social orientation of the cat. It is believed that the concept of play indicates accurately the type of expressive social movement which receives its embodiment in the cat.

According to Huizinga the concept of play is a primary element of human experience and as such is not susceptible to exact definition.

"The *fun* of playing resists all analysis, all logical interpretation. . . . Nevertheless it is precisely this fun-element that characterizes the essence of play." The common image of the young colored drug addict pictures him as a pitiful figure, a trapped unfortunate. There is a certain amount of truth in this image but it does not correspond to the conception which the young colored addict has of himself or to the impression that he tries to communicate to others. If it were entirely true it would be difficult to square with the fact that substantial numbers of young colored persons continue to become drug users. The cat experiences and manifests a certain zest in his mode of life which is far from self-pity. This fun element seemed to come particularly to the fore as the cat recounted his search for "kicks," the adventure of his life on the streets, and the intensity of his contest against the whole world to maintain his supply of drugs. Early in the cycle of heroin use itself there was invariably a "honeymoon" stage when the cat abandoned himself most completely to the experience of the drug. For some cats this "honeymoon" stage, in terms of their ecstatic preoccupation with the drug, was perpetual. For others it passed, but the exigencies of an insatiable habit never seemed to destroy completely the cat's sense of excitement in his way of life.

While Huizinga declines to define play, he does enumerate three characteristics which he considers to be proper to play. Each one of them when applied to the cat serves to indicate a generic feature of his social orientation.

a) *First and foremost . . . all play is a voluntary activity.*

"Here we have the first main characteristic of play: that it is free, is in fact freedom." The concept of an expressive social movement assumes a social situation where existing social arrangements are frustrating and are no longer accepted as legitimate and yet where collective activity directed towards the modification of these limitations is not possible. The cat is "free" in the sense that he is a pre-eminent candidate for new forms of social organization and novel social practices. He is attempting to escape from certain features of the historical traditions of the Negro which he regards as humiliating. As an adolescent or young adult, he is not fully assimilated into such social institutions as the family, school, church, or industry which may be available to him. Moreover, the social institutions which the Negroes brought with them when they migrated to the city have not as yet achieved stability or an adequate functioning relationship to the urban environment. As a Negro, and particularly as a Negro of low socio-economic status, he is excluded from many socializing experiences which adolescents in more advantaged sectors of the society take for granted. He lives in communities where the capacity of the population for effective collective action is extremely limited, and consequently there are few effective controls on his conduct besides that exercised by his peer group itself. He is fascinated by the varied "scenes" which the big city spreads out before him. Granted this setting, the cat adopts an adventurous attitude to life and is free to give his allegiance to new forms of activity.

b) . . . A second characteristic is closely connected with this (that is, the first characteristic of freedom), namely, that play is not "ordinary" or "real" life. It is rather a stepping out of "real" life into a temporary sphere of activity with a disposition all of its own. Every child knows perfectly well that he is "only pretending," or that it was "only for fun." . . . This "only pretending" quality of play betrays a consciousness of the inferiority of play compared with "seriousness," a feeling that seems to be something as primary as play itself. Nevertheless . . . the consciousness of play being "only a pretend" does not by any means prevent it from proceeding with the utmost seriousness, with an absorption, a devotion that passes into rapture and, temporarily at least, completely abolishes that troublesome "only" feeling.

It is implicit in the notion of an expressive social movement that, since direct collective action to modify the sources of dissatisfaction and restlessness is not possible, all such movements should appear under one guise, as forms of "escape." Persons viewing the problem of addiction from the perspective of the established social structure have been prone to make this interpretation. It is a gross oversimplification, however, as considered from the perspective of the young drug addict himself. The emergence of the self-conception of the cat is an attempt to deal with the problems of status and identity in a situation where participation in the life of the broader community is denied, but where the colored adolescent is becoming increasingly sensitive to the values, the goals, and the notions of success which obtain in the dominant social order.

The caste pressures thus make it exceedingly difficult for an American Negro to preserve a true perspective of himself and his own group in relation to the larger white society. The increasing abstract knowledge of the world outside—of its opportunities, its rewards, its different norms of competition and cooperation—which results from the proceeding acculturation at the same time as there is increasing group isolation, only increases the tensions.

Such conditions of group isolation would appear to be fairly uniform throughout the Negro group. Although this isolation may be experienced differently at different social levels of the Negro community, certain features of the adaptations arrived at in response to this problem will tend to reveal similarities. Since the struggle for status takes place on a stage where there is acute sensitivity to the values and status criteria of the dominant white group, but where access to the means through which such values may be achieved is prohibited, the status struggle turning in on itself will assume a variety of distorted forms. Exclusion from the "serious" concerns of the broader community will result in such adaptations manifesting a strong element of "play."

Frazier in *Black Bourgeoisie* discusses the social adaptation of the Negro middle class as "The World of Make-Believe."

The emphasis upon "social" life or "society" is one of the main props of the world of make-believe into which the black bourgeoisie has sought an escape from its inferiority and frustrations in American society. This world of make-believe, to be sure, is a reflection of the values of American society, but it lacks the economic basis that would give it roots in the world of reality.

In the Negro lower classes the effects of frustrations deriving from subordination to the whites may not be experienced as personally or as directly as it is by the Negro middle class, but the massive effects of residential segregation and the lack of stable social institutions and community organization are such as to reinforce strong feelings of group isolation even at the lowest levels of the society.

It is here suggested that the function performed by the emergence of the social type of the cat among Negro lower class adolescents is analogous to that performed by "The World of Make-Believe" in the Negro middle class. The development of a social type such as that of the cat is only possible in a situation where there is isolation from the broader community but great sensitivity to its goals, where the peer group pressures are extremely powerful, where institutional structures are weak, where models of success in the illegitimate world have strong appeals, where specific social movements are not possible, and where novel forms of behavior have great prestige. To give significance to his experience, the young male addict has developed the conception of a heroic figure, the "ideal cat," a person who is completely adequate to all situations, who controls his "kick" rather than letting it control him, who has a lucrative "hustle," who has no illusions as to what makes the world "tick," who is any man's equal, who basks in the admiration of his brother cats and associated "chicks," who hob-nobs with "celebs" of the musical world, and who in time himself may become a celebrity.

The cat throws himself into his way of life with a great deal of intensity, but he cannot escape completely from the perspective, the judgments, and the sanctions of the dominant social order. He has to make place in his scheme of life for police, lockups, jails, and penitentiaries, to say nothing of the agonies of withdrawal distress. He is forced eventually to confront the fact that his role as a cat with its associated attitudes is largely a pose, a form of fantasy with little basis in fact. With the realization that he is addicted he comes only too well to know that he is a "junky," and he is fully aware of the conventional attitudes towards addicts as well as of the counter-rationalizations provided by his peer group. It is possible that the cat's vacillation with regard to seeking a cure for his addiction is due to a conflict of perspectives, whether to view his habit from the cat's or the dominant social order's point of view.

c) Play is distinct from "ordinary" life both as to locality and duration. This is the third main characteristic of play: its secludedness, its limitedness. It is "played out" within certain limits of time and place. It contains its own course and meaning.

It is this limited, esoteric character of heroin use which gives to the cat the feeling of belonging to an elite. It is the restricted extent of the distribution of drug use, the scheming and intrigue associated with underground "connections" through which drugs are obtained, the secret lore of the appreciation of the drug's effects, which give the cat the exhilaration of participating in a conspiracy. Contrary to popular conception, most drug users were not anxious to proselyte new users. Of course, spreading the habit would have the function of increasing the possible sources of supply. But an equally strong disposition was to keep the knowledge of drug use secret, to impress and dazzle the audience with one's knowledge of being "in the know." When proselyting did occur, as in jails or lockups, it was proselyting on the part of a devotee who condescended to share with the uninitiated a highly prized practice and set of attitudes.

As he elaborates his analysis of play, Huizinga brings to the fore additional aspects of the concept which also have their apt counterpart in the way of life of the cat. For instance, as was discussed earlier, the cat's appreciation of "progressive music" is an essential part of his social orientation. About this topic Huizinga remarks, "Music, as we have hinted before, is the highest and purest expression of the *facultas ludend.*" The cat's attitude toward music has a sacred, almost mystical quality. "Progressive music" opens doors to a type of highly valued experience which for him can be had in no other way. It is more important to him than eating and is second only to the "kick." He may have to give up his hope of dressing according to his standards but he never gives up music.

Huizinga also observes, "Many and close are the links that connect play with beauty." He refers to the "profoundly aesthetic quality of play." The aesthetic emphasis which seems so central to the style of living of the cat is a subtle elusive accent permeating his whole outlook but coming to clearest expression in a constellation of interests, the "kick," clothing, and music. And it certainly reaches a level of awareness in their language. Language is utilized by the cat with a conscious relish, with many variations and individual turns of phrase indicating the value placed upon creative expression in this medium.

It is to be noted that much of the description of the cat's attributes did not deal exclusively with elements unique to him. Many of the features mentioned are prevalent among adolescents in all reaches of the status scale. Dress, music, language, and the search for pleasure are all familiar themes of the adolescent world. For instance, in his description of the adolescent "youth culture" Talcott Parsons would appear to be presenting the generic traits of a "play-form" with particular reference to its expression in the middle class.

It is at the point of emergence into adolescence that there first begins to develop a set of patterns and behavior phenomena which involve a highly complex combination of age grading and sex role elements. These may be referred to together as the phenomena of the "youth culture." . . .

Perhaps the best single point of reference for characterizing the youth culture lies in its contrast with the dominant pattern of the adult male role. By contrast with the emphasis on responsibility in this role, the orientation of the youth culture is more or less irresponsible. One of its dominant roles is "having a good time." . . . It is very definitely a rounded humanistic pattern rather than one of competence in the performance of specified functions.

Such significant similarities between this description and the themes of the social type of the cat only tend to reinforce the notion that the recent spread of heroin use was a problem of adolescence. The cat is an adolescent sharing many of the interests of his age-mates everywhere but confronted by a special set of problems of color, tradition, and identity.

The social orientation of the cat, with its emphasis on nonviolence, was quite in contrast to the orientation of the smaller group of young white drug users who were interviewed in the course of this study. The latter's type of adjustment placed a heavy stress upon violence. Their crimes tended to represent direct attacks against persons and property. The general disposition they manifested was one of "nerve" and brashness rather than one of "playing it cool." They did not cultivate the amenities of language, music, or dress to nearly the same extent as the cat. Their social orientation was expressed as a direct rather than an indirect attack on the dominant values of our society. This indicates that the "youth culture" despite its generic features may vary significantly in different social settings.

In his paper, "Some Jewish Types of Personality," Louis Wirth made the following suggestive comments about the relationship between the social type and its setting.

A detailed analysis of the crucial personality types in any given area or cultural group shows that they depend upon a set of habits and attitudes in the group for their existence and are the direct expressions of the values of the group. As the life of the group changes there appears a host of new social types, mainly outgrowths and transformations of previous patterns which have become fixed through experience.

What are some of the sources of the various elements going to make up the social type of the cat which may be sought in his traditions? The following suggestions are offered as little more than speculation at the present time. The emphasis upon nonviolence on the part of the cat, upon manipulative techniques rather than overt attack, is a stress upon the indirect rather than the direct way towards one's goal. May not the cat in this emphasis be betraying his debt to the "Uncle Tom" type of adjustment, despite his wish to dissociate himself from earlier patterns of accommodation to the dominant white society? May not the "kick" itself be a cultural lineal descendant of the ecstatic moment of religious possession so dear to revivalist and store-front religion? Similarly, may not the emphasis upon the exploitation of the woman have its origin in the traditionally greater economic stability of the colored woman?

W. I. Thomas, in one of his references to the problems raised by the city environment, stated, "Evidently the chief problem is the young American person." In discussing the type of inquiry that would be desirable in this area he states that it should

. . . lead to a more critical discrimination between that type of disorganization in the youth which is a real but frustrated tendency to organize on a higher plane, or one more correspondent with the moving environment, and that type of disorganization which is simply the abandonment of standards. It is also along this line . . . that we shall gain light on the relation of fantastic phantasying to realistic phantasying. . . .

Posed in this way the problem becomes one of evaluating the social type of the cat in relation to the processes of social change. This social type is difficult to judge according to the criterion suggested by Thomas. Since many of the cat's interests are merely an extreme form of the adolescent "youth culture," in part the problem becomes one of determining how functional the period of adolescence is as preparation for subsequent adult status. However, the central phases of the social orientation of the cat, the "hustle" and the "kick," do represent a kind of disorganization which indicates the abandonment of conventional standards. The young addicted cat is "going nowhere." With advancing age he cannot shed his addiction the way he can many of the other trappings of adolescence. He faces only the bleak prospect, as time goes on, of increasing demoralization. Although the plight of the young colored addict is intimately tied to the conditions and fate of his racial group, his social orientation seems to represent a dead-end type of adjustment. Just as Handlin in *The Uprooted* suggests that the first generation of immigrant peoples to our society tends to be a sacrificed generation, it may be that the unique problems of Negro migrants to our metropolitan areas will lead to a few or several sacrificed generations in the course of the tortuous process of urbanization.

The discussion of the social type of the cat leads inevitably to the issue of social control. Any attempt to intervene or modify the social processes producing the "cat" as a social type must have the objective of reducing his group isolation. For instance, because of such isolation and because of the cat's sensitivity to the gestures of his peers, the most significant role models of a given generation of cats tend to be the cats of the preceding age group. Where, in a period of rapid change, the schemes of behavior of the role models no longer correspond to the possibilities in the actual situation, it is possible for attitudes to be transmitted to a younger generation which evidence a kind of "cultural lag." Thus the condition of the labor market in Chicago is such as to suggest the existence of plentiful employment opportunities for the Negro in a variety of fields. But because such openings are not mediated to him through role models it is possible that the cat is unable to take advantage of these opportunities or of the facilities available for training for such positions.

The social type of the cat is a product of social change. The type of social orientation which it has elaborated indicates an all too acute awareness of the values of the broader social order. In an open class society where upward mobility is positively sanctioned, an awareness and sensitivity to the dominant values is the first stage in their eventual assimilation. Insofar as the social type of the cat represents a reaction to a feeling of exclusion from access to the means towards the goals of our society, all measures such as improved educational opportunities which put these means within his grasp will hasten the extinction of this social type. Just as the "hoodlum" and "gangster" types tend to disappear as the various more recently arrived white ethnic groups tend to move up in the status scale of the community, so it can confidently be expected that the cat as a social type will tend to disappear as such opportunities become more prevalent among the colored population.

7. Good Old Boys

The delinquent behavior of the young narcotic addicts described by Finestone is rooted in the conditions of the urban ghetto. But rural areas also have their quota of crime—areas where moonshining, eluding the police in souped-up cars, and casual violence are accepted as normal pursuits. Tom Wolfe, creating a literary style to match a lawlessness recalled with nostalgia, tells the legend of Junior Johnson and shows how crime can become a sport.

The legend of Junior Johnson! In this legend, here is a country boy, Junior Johnson, who learns to drive by running whiskey for his father, Johnson, Senior, one of the biggest copperstill operators of all time, up in Ingle Hollow, near North Wilkesboro, in northwestern North Carolina, and grows up to be a famous stock car racing driver, rich, grossing $100,000 in 1963, for example, respected, solid, idolized in his hometown and throughout the rural South. There is all this about how good old boys would wake up in the middle of the night in the apple shacks and hear a supercharged Oldsmobile engine roaring over Brushy Mountain and say, "Listen at him—there he goes!" although that part is doubtful, since some nights there were so many good old boys taking off down the road in supercharged automobiles out of Wilkes County, and running loads to Charlotte, Salisbury, Greensboro, Winston-Salem, High Point, or whatever, it would be pretty hard to pick out one. It was Junior Johnson specifically, however, who was famous for the "bootleg turn" or "about-face," in which, if the Alcohol Tax agents had a roadblock up for you or were too close behind, you threw the car up into second gear, cocked the wheel, stepped on the accelerator and made the car's rear end skid around in a complete 180-degree arc, a complete about-face, and tore on back up the road exactly the way you came from. God! The Alcohol Tax agents used to burn over Junior Johnson. Practically every good old boy in town in Wilkesboro, the county seat, got to know the agents by sight in a very short time. They would rag them practically to their faces on the subject of Junior Johnson, so that it got to be an obsession. Finally, one night they had Junior trapped on the road up toward the bridge around Millersville, there's no way out of there, they had the barricades up and they could hear this souped-up car roaring around the bend, and here it comes—but suddenly they can hear a siren and see a red light flashing in the grille, so they think it's another agent, and boy, they run out like ants and pull those barrels and boards and sawhorses out of the way, and then—Ggghhzzzzzzzhhhhhhgggggzzzzzzzeeeeeong!—gawdam! there he goes again, it was him, Junior Johnson! with a gawdam agent's si-reen and a red light in his grille!

I wasn't in the South five minutes before people started making oaths, having visions, telling these hulking great stories, all on the subject of Junior Johnson. At the Greensboro, North Carolina, Airport there was one good old boy who vowed he would have eaten "a bucket of it" if that would have kept Junior Johnson from switching from a Dodge racer to a Ford. Hell yes, and after that—God-almighty, remember that 1963 Chevrolet of Junior's? Whatever happened to that car? A couple of more good old boys join in. A good old boy, I ought to explain, is a generic term in the rural South referring to a man, of any age, but more often young than not, who fits in with the status system of the region. It usually means he has a good sense of humor and enjoys ironic jokes, is tolerant and easygoing enough to get along in long conversations at places like on the corner, and has a reasonable amount of physical courage. The term is usually heard in some such form as: "Lud? He's a good old boy from over at Crozet." These good old boys in the airport, by the way, were in their twenties, except for one fellow who was a cabdriver and was about forty-five, I would say. Except for the cabdriver, they all wore neo-Brummellian clothes such as Lacoste tennis shirts, Slim Jim pants, windbreakers with the collars turned up, "fast" shoes of the winkle-picker genre, and so on.

. . .

Cars and bravery! The mountain-still operators had been running white liquor with hopped-up automobiles all during the thirties. But it was during the war that the business was so hot out of Wilkes County, down to Charlotte, High Point, Greensboro, Winston-Salem, Salisbury, places like that; a night's run, by one car, would bring anywhere from $500 to $1000. People had money all of a sudden. One car could carry twenty-two to twenty-five cases of white liquor. There were twelve half-gallon fruit jars full per case, so each load would have 132 gallons or more. It would sell to the distributor in the city for about ten dollars a gallon, when the market was good, of which the driver would get two dollars, as much as $300 for the night's work.

The usual arrangement in the white liquor industry was for the elders to design the distillery, supervise the formulas and the whole distilling process and take care of the business end of the operation. The young men did the heavy work, carrying the copper and other heavy goods out into the woods, building the still, hauling in fuel—and driving. Junior and his older brothers, L. P. and Fred, worked that way with their father, Robert Glenn Johnson, Sr.

Johnson, Senior, was one of the biggest individual copperstill operators in the area. The fourth time he was arrested, the agents found a small fortune in working corn mash bubbling in the vats.

"My Daddy was always a hard worker," Junior is telling me. "He always wanted something a little bit better. A lot of people resented that and held that against him, but what he got, he always got h'it by hard work. There ain't no harder work in the world than making whiskey. I don't know of any other business that compels you to get up at all times of night and go outdoors in the snow and everything else and work. H'it's the hardest way in the world to make a living, and I don't think anybody'd do it unless they had to."

Working mash wouldn't wait for a man. It started coming to a head when it got ready to and a man had to be there to take it off, out there in the woods, in the brush, in the brambles, in the muck, in the snow. Wouldn't it have been something if you could have just set it all up inside a good old shed with a corrugated metal roof and order those parts like you want them and not have to smuggle all that copper and all that sugar and all that everything out here in the woods and be a coppersmith and a plumber and a copper and a carpenter and a pack horse and every other goddamned thing God ever saw in this world, all at once.

And live decent hours—Junior and his brothers, about two o'clock in the morning they'd head out to the stash, the place where the liquor was hidden after it was made. Sometimes it would be somebody's house or an old shed or some place just out in the woods, and they'd make their arrangements out there, what the route was and who was getting how much liquor. There wasn't anything ever written down. Everything was cash on the spot. Different drivers liked to make the run at different times, but Junior and his brothers always liked to start out from 3 to 4 A.M. But it got so no matter when you started out you didn't have those roads to yourself.

"Some guys liked one time and some guys liked another time," Junior is saying, "but starting about midnight they'd be coming out of the woods from every direction. Some nights the whole road was full of bootleggers. It got so some nights they'd be somebody following you going just as fast as you were and you didn't know who h'it was, the law or somebody else hauling whiskey."

And it was just a business, like any other business, just like a milk route—but this funny thing was happening. In those wild-ass times, with the money flush and good old boys from all over the country running that white liquor down the road ninety miles an hour and more than that if you try to crowd them a little bit—well, the funny thing was, it got to be competitive in an almost aesthetic, a pure sporting way. The way the good old boys got to hopping up their automobiles—it got to be a science practically. Everybody was looking to build a car faster than anybody ever had before. They practically got into industrial espionage over it. They'd come up behind one another on those wild-ass nights on the highway, roaring through the black gulches between the clay cuts and the trees, pretending like they were officers, just to challenge them, test them out, race . . . *pour le sport,* you mothers, careening through the darkness, old Carolina moon. All these cars were registered in phony names. If a man had to abandon one, they would find license plates that traced back to . . . nobody at all. It wasn't anything, particularly, to go down to the Motor Vehicle Bureau and get some license plates, as long as you paid your money. Of course, it's rougher now, with compulsory insurance. You have to have your insurance before you can get your license plates, and that leads to a lot of complications. Junior doesn't know what they do about that now. Anyway, all these cars with the magnificent engines were plain on the outside, so they wouldn't attract attention, but they couldn't disguise them altogether. They were jacked up a little in the back and had 8.00 or 8.20 tires, for the heavy loads, and the sound—

"They wasn't no way you could make it sound like an ordinary car," says Junior.

God-almighty, that sound in the middle of the night, groaning, roaring, humming down into the hollows, through the clay gulches—yes! And all over the rural South, hell, all over the South, the legends of wild-driving whiskey running got started. And it wasn't just the plain excitement of it. It was something deeper, the symbolism. It brought into a modern focus the whole business, one and a half centuries old, of the country people's rebellion against the Federals, against the seaboard establishment, their independence, their defiance of the outside world. And it was like a mythology for that and for something else that was happening, the whole wild thing of the car as the symbol of liberation in the postwar South.

"They was out about every night, patroling, the agents and the State Police was," Junior is saying, "but they seldom caught anybody. H'it was like the dogs chasing the fox. The dogs can't catch a fox, he'll just take 'em around in a circle all night long. I was never caught for transporting. We never lost but one car and the axle broke on h'it."

8. $4,000,000 a Day

Crime as a commonplace event that is accep by one's peers is by no means confined to adolescent hipsters or Good Old Boys looking for excitement. The man in the white collar—the middle-class citizen working in a store or office—has all too often come to accept breaking the law as an ordinary part of the day's routine, according to Norman Jaspan and Hillel Black. The individual acts of thievery, they argue, may not amount to much, but the sum of this sort of larceny far exceeds the losses of society due to such crimes as robbery.

According to insurance company figures, white collar employees, rank and file, supervisory and executive, are stealing about four million dollars in cash and property from their employers each working day. By the end of 1960, such thefts will reach the astronomical figure of more than one billion dollars per year. Compared to the white collar crook, the professional criminal is an amateur. The F.B.I. reports that the nation's burglars, pickpockets, armed robbers and auto robbers and auto thieves managed to steal 479 million dollars in 1957. This is considerably less than half the amount stolen by the country's white collar embezzlers.

Not only are the losses severe, but the rate of white collar crime is increasing ominously. And there is no sign of abatement. Indeed, the amount of loss is rising much faster than the amount of money in actual circulation. From 1946 to 1956 fidelity or "honesty" insurance increased about seventy per cent. During the same period "honesty" insurance losses climbed 250 per cent. Just consider banks, one of the largest sites of white collar crime. In the last two decades 105 were forced to close their doors because of embezzlement, and an average of one out of five has experienced at least one embezzlement in the past five years. Right now it is estimated that between ten and twenty-five million dollars is missing in thefts that haven't even been discovered.

The harm growing out of white collar crime cannot be measured. For the consumer it means higher prices, and for the worker decreased earnings. For numerous businesses it means the difference between success and failure. And in some instances it can mean bankruptcy for an entire community. But perhaps most dangerous of all, white collar crime portends the pse of our ethical code of fair play and honesty. Indeed, the implica- n is that we are becoming a nation of thieves and embezzlers. If this atement seems too strong, consider the following facts.

In 1960 an estimated five billion dollars will probably change hands in kickbacks, payoffs and bribes. But that isn't the only area where dishonesty is an accepted fact of life. You will grant that most people try to cheat on their income tax if they think they can get away with it. To give you some idea of how many people try, and incidentally do not succeed, consider the amount paid in penalties, interest and back taxes for 1957, a record year. According to the Commissioner of Internal Revenue Service, the most recent figure reported comes to a whopping $1,661,354,000, an eighteen per cent increase over the previous year.

Frank Gibney, writing in *Life* recently on white collar crooks, took a look at an active, if somewhat compact, day of a reputable New York state businessman. During the day, the businessman bribed a cop, cheated on his income tax, entertained his wife at the expense of his company, bribed a building inspector, took a kickback in the form of a TV set, juggled his books, issued a misleading ad, lifted an office desk set for his personal use and advised his wife to forget the maid's social security tax. Writes Gibney: "Laying aside the cares of the day, he settles down to watch the news on his souvenir TV set—and fulminates about the dishonesty of the 'union racketeers' he sees on the screen."

If this solid and respected member of the community had been successfully prosecuted for his day's activities, he could have received thirty-three years in jail and a fine of $26,500. Yet, if he had been brought to court on any of these charges, he undoubtedly would have been filled with righteous indignation. You can hear his wail. "Why pick on me? Everybody else is doing it." Frankly, he would have been right.

This apparent national indifference to dishonesty is not limited to our private lives. It extends to the very life blood of our society, the nation's market places. The core of our independence is the free enterprise system under which a businessman is supposed to compete fairly and honestly with his competitors. But does he? Of course, in many cases he does. But in too many instances his only aim is a quick and easy profit, no matter what ethics are involved. His methods of gaining such profit have degenerated into a nefarious activity called business espionage.

The purpose of business spying is to steal secrets from your competitor without regard to fair play or the law. The result is subterfuge, lies, hypocrisy and dishonesty. Richard Austin Smith, writing in *Fortune,* says that in the opinion of some business spies, "there is more industrial espionage going on in the U.S. today than in any other period in our history." He notes that their operations range from spying out a competitor's multimillion-dollar bid on a government contract to paying a supermarket clerk five dollars a week for an advance copy of the Thursday

Specials. Business espionage helps mold an atmosphere in which stealing from the competitor leads to the next step, embezzling from one's own employer.

This atmosphere of dishonesty and ethical laxity is not limited to the business world. During just the first year of its investigations the Select Senate Committee unearthed outright theft or misuse of $10,000,000 by the leaders of seven international labor unions, an average of $5 out of the pocket of each rank and file member. Government, our most sacrosanct area of public trust, has witnessed the departure of nearly a dozen top federal officials during the Democratic and Republican administrations of Truman and Eisenhower. These officials have either been jailed, fired, or they resigned under charges ranging from fraud and influence peddling to conflict of interest.

These facts and figures, as shocking as they may appear, only skim the surface of white collar crime. Examine, for a moment, just one case from our files, that of a large private hospital. The institution's pharmacist decided to go into business for himself. His stock, the hospital's drugs. His clients, neighborhood druggists. His yearly profit, $40,000. Nurses and volunteer service workers not only stole thousands of dollars' worth of sheets and pillow cases but sent all their dirty linen to the hospital's laundry. Members of the staff bilked their own hospital of thousands of dollars in drugs. They simply had the drugs requisitioned in the names of the welfare patients who were supposed to get them free. It reached the point where the family of a paying patient was billed for drugs that had been prescribed ten days after the patient died.

The tragedy of white collar crime is not just the cost in dollars and cents, but the corruption of our most respected citizens, the professional worker, the executive, the top government and union official.

The final irony is this: With the threatened obliteration of our standards of honesty and fair play, it actually has become easier for the dishonest white collar worker to steal. Since World War II, business has expanded tremendously. This growth has made it increasingly difficult for management to know what is going on in its own house. The days when the boss knew everyone in his plant or office are well past. As a result, those who are prone to steal have more opportunity to do so.

Indeed, the dishonest employee is literally given the opportunity to steal. Unlike the burglar, he doesn't have to jimmy his way into the office and blow the safe. He already has the key and the right combination. Often he handles company merchandise, records and funds as part of his job. There's no chance that he will be shot while committing his crime, and he has the time and opportunity to falsify records and cover up. Many dishonest employees have fooled their employers for more than ten years, and some for as long as twenty-five years while pocketing loot well into the seven-figure bracket.

To sum up: With the rapid and extensive increase in white collar crime and the abasement of our ethics of fair play and honesty, we are inexorably heading toward that final denouement, a nation of embezzlers.

But who is this thief in the white collar? What does he look like? What are his motives? Where and how does he operate?

PART III

WHAT CAN BE DONE?

INTRODUCTION[1]

Donald R. Cressey

Social control involves all the mechanisms by which a society secures conforming behavior from its members. It includes all the means of child rearing, all the devices for assimilating newcomers into a society, and all the forms of governmental power that either directly or indirectly ensure that individuals conform to the demands of the law.

In this broad sense, a parent or another adult who teaches a child the words "cat," "chair," and "cup" is participating in the process of social control, for as the child learns the meaning of words, he also learns to behave toward designated objects in prescribed ways. The entire socialization process involves social control of this kind, and there are many different mechanisms by which such control is accomplished. Similarly, when adults seek membership in a society or a group, various formal and informal methods are used to inspire them to learn new ways of behaving and, at the same time, to unlearn old ways of behaving. The assimilation of immigrants, the induction of children into the adult "age of responsibility," and the process of "prisonization" of prison inmates are all examples of this kind of social control.[2]

Our concern here is with the governmental devices we have established for enacting criminal laws and for maintaining conformity to them. These devices are aimed at maximizing the amount of conformity in our society. They are, obviously, mechanisms of social control. Viewed from a narrow perspective, social control in the process of government includes only the *formal* devices a society uses to control its members. When we consider measures for control of crime, we usually are concerned with these formal devices—enactment of precise laws and enforcement of these laws by the police, prosecuting attorneys, judges, probation officers, prison wardens, and parole workers.

In a broader view, however, crime is controlled by the use of *all* the techniques of social control, including those used in child rearing and in the assimilation of newcomers. A person who teaches a child that "honesty" means respect for the property rights of others is engaging in the governmental process, for he is inspiring the child to conform to the laws prohibiting larceny, burglary, and robbery, among others. As a child learns the word "cat" he in effect "consents" to follow the rules, developed over the years by his elders, for behavior with reference to cats. As he learns more complex concepts pertaining to "duty," "morality," and "decency," he in effect learns to give his consent to be governed by the persons defining these concepts for him. Developing this consent to be governed is a fundamental political control device, because if it were completely successful, coercive enforcement of laws would be unnecessary. The formal machinery of justice is, then, a mechanism of last resort. The matter is complicated, however, by the fact that criminal law and the various cogs in the machinery of justice—legislatures, police, courts, prisons, and so on—are, as well as being mechanisms for coercive enforcement, also mechanisms for establishing and maintaining consent to be governed. Moreover, the activities of enforcement agencies, like the criminal law itself, are based on two basic alternative and conflicting notions about the most effective system for maximizing the amount of conformity to criminal laws.

Government and Criminal Law

The governing of persons who have some degree of freedom is no easy task even in a small organization, such as a family, a business firm, a university, a police department, or a prison. In a larger organization, such as an army or a nation, it is even more difficult. Just as parents are confronted with the problem of ensuring that their children adhere to family rules and prison wardens necessarily have the problem of ensuring that inmates adhere to prison rules, so the more general governmental authorities have the problem of ensuring that citizens adhere to those social rules codified in criminal law.

Two basic problems confront all persons who would ensure that others follow rules. One is the problem of obtaining consent to be governed. The "governors" must somehow get the governed to agree, usually unwittingly, to the governors' definition of morality, deviance, and deficiency. In this sense, at least, it is correct to say that whoever controls the definition of the situation controls the world.

The second problem is one of maintaining the consent of the governed once it has been obtained. Those who are attempting to exercise social control must be prepared to cope with nonconformity. This means that they must constantly be seeking appropriate measures for control of those members whose conduct indicates that they have withdrawn, at least partially or temporarily, their consent to be governed. In utilizing these measures, the governors must not inadvertently take actions that significantly diminish the degree of consent that has been given. In child rearing, to take a simple example, parents must not punish their disobedient children so severely that the children lose respect for the parents and again become disobedient. In crime control, governments must not take actions that alienate the respectable citizen.

The first line of defense against crime, then, is to inspire the citizenry with a sense of morality or a sense of decency that, if completely successful, would make it impossible for a person even to *think* about criminality as a behavioral alternative. Control in this sense lies in group pressure rather than in the direct fear of punishment. Not the fear of legal penalties, as such, but the fear of loss of status in the group is the most effective deterrent. What occurs, therefore, is that the person learns and feels that doing a specified thing in violation of a group standard, which also happens to be in violation of the law, would not be in harmony with his personality: it would lower him; it would not occur to him to do such a thing. He would feel uncomfortable in violating the law and would secure no satisfaction from it. This is the principal method of controlling behavior, whether the behavior is regulated by law or not. One who has a sense of duty to his government, a sense of loyalty about the political order of his society, or a sense of decency about his own conduct has given his consent to be governed. Perhaps this is what Sir James F. Stephen, the noted English jurist, meant when he said with reference to capital punishment:

> *Some men, probably, abstain from murder because they fear that, if they committed murder, they would be hung. Hundreds of thousands abstain from it because they regard it with horror. One great reason why they regard it with horror is that murderers are hung with the hearty approbation of all reasonable men.*[3]

Richard H. McCleery noted that this system of control by definition of the situation is basic even in maximum-security prisons. It is commonly believed that control of inmates in such institutions is accomplished by concrete walls, steel bars, and guns. But this belief is in error, for such devices become important only when there is a failure in control of definitions of what is "proper behavior": ". . . the heart of custodial controls in traditional prisons lies in the daily regimentation, routines, and rituals of domination which bend the subjects into a customary posture of silent awe and unthinking acceptance."[4]

A "customary posture of silent awe and unthinking acceptance" is, similarly, the fundamental basis of conformity to criminal law. It is this "posture" that constitutes consent to be governed. But a society must *maintain* the consent of the governed once it has been obtained. If a high degree of conformity is to be obtained, those being governed must *like* to be governed, because either a reward is given for cooperation due to a sense of duty, loyalty, or decency, or for some other reason. The process of crime control must consist in part of actions designed to prevent deviation and in part of actions designed to correct deviation, but without causing the wholesale withhrawal of the consent to be governed.

It often is said that force is used to maintain conformity, but this oversimplifies the case. Force might be used to expel the deviant.[5] Force might be used to restrain the deviant while attempts are made to "rehabilitate" him. But the principal use of force is not for the physical control of deviants. It is for the ex post facto infliction of pain on wrongdoers. Such ex post facto infliction of pain, deliberately imposed by the state acting in its corporate capacity, is punishment. The pain may be either physical, as in the case of whipping, or psychological, as in the case of imprisonment. In either event, it is assumed to have some value in correcting the deviant ("I cannot make you follow the rules, but I can make you wish you had followed them, and this will make you want to follow them in the future") or in inspiring others with a sense of decency ("Look what happens to indecent people").

But even official punishment of criminals, like other correctional devices, must be executed with caution. All these actions must be taken in a manner such that the behavior of the criminal is changed but the consent of the governed is not lost. If such intentional infliction of suffering is to be accepted by the criminal and by the citizenry in general, it must be imposed justly in measures suitable to correcting deviation without stimulating rebellion. Maintaining consent of the governed, then, requires that punishments for law violation be accepted as legitimate by those being governed. In our society, for example, punishments of criminals are accepted as legitimate, as fair and just, only if there is some evidence that the violators were given sufficient *advance notice* that deviation from agreed-upon rules will have punishment as its consequence. Especially in Western societies, with long traditions of barring ex post facto legislation, punishment of criminals probably would result in loss of consent of the governed—in the form of revolt, rebellion, or passive resistance—if governments did not maintain rather elaborate systems for warning citizens that nonconformity of certain kinds will be punished.[6] In other words, democratic states operate on the basic assumption that conformity can be maximized only if the punitive system has a rational base. If punishments were imposed irrationally or capriciously, the citizen would be unable to determine which rules he should conform to. Moreover, the infliction of punishments in an apparently arbitrary way would be widely viewed as unjust and would, accordingly, contribute to divisiveness in the society. Stated in reverse, the principle is: Punishments can be inflicted on criminals without danger of revolt, rebellion, or passive resistance if sufficient advance notice is given in the form of precise rules.

The rules themselves provide some of the necessary elements of warning. An important function of criminal law, as far as maintaining consent of the governed is concerned, is providing the advance notice necessary for justice. The carefully formulated and precisely stated prohibitions stipulated in criminal laws give advance notice that wrongdoers will be punished.[7] We shall see later that, consistently, one function of police, courts, prisons, electric chairs, and gas chambers is to provide advance notice that those who violate the law will have pain deliberately imposed on them. Police, courts, prisons, and parole boards administer punishments, but they also help make punishment acceptable as a social policy. They effectively make us docile witnesses to actions involving the infliction of pain, actions that we would regard as horrendous if they occurred out of context. They do this by virtue of the fact that their very presence teaches us that one who has been warned about the punitive consequences of his criminal conduct has no right to complain if his criminal conduct is, in fact, punished. The epitome of the effectiveness of this system occurs among professional criminals who, as an expression of manliness, advise each other that risking official punishment is one of the facts of life: "If you can't pay, don't play."

The governors who would maximize the consent of the governed and, thus, the amount of conformity, also give another form of advance notice that whoever violates a criminal law risks punishment. Because it is not correct to assume that *all* criminal laws are perfectly clear, advance notice is given in the form of warnings that *further* violations of certain kinds of laws will have punishment as a consequence. This is one of the basic purposes of the discretion officially or unofficially granted to criminal justice administrators. When discretion is exercised, the rules regarding punishment for specified offenses are modified. They are modified, basically, because not doing so would lead to withdrawal of some degree of the citizenry's consent to be governed, thus increasing the amount of criminality. It is sometimes necessary to retreat from a battle in order to win the war. The machinery of justice is designed to negotiate agreements to "maintain a posture of silent awe and unthinking acceptance." It is sometimes essential, for a maximum number of successful negotiations of this kind, that the stipulated penalties be modified and even that some harmful conduct be ignored.

Legislative Contradictions

The rule-making bodies of social groups seldom have a unified ideology regarding the procedures to be used for inspiring and maintaining conformity. A father, for example, may at one time spank his son for violating family rules and at another time overlook such violations—and in both cases he may argue that whatever action he takes is "for the good of the child" or "for the good of the family." In a nation, comparable inconsistencies in implementing a desire for a maximum amount of conformity are found in criminal laws and in law enforcement agencies due to contradictions in the theory that lies behind them.

One body of theory maintains that conformity to criminal laws is maximized by swift, certain, and uniform punishment of those who break the rules. The "classical school" of criminology that developed during the last half of the eighteenth century in England, and later spread to other European countries and the United States, popularized this notion. The objective of the leaders of this school was to provide advance notice that crime would have punishment as its consequence; and according to the ideology popularized by these men, all persons who violate a specific law should receive identical punishments regardless of age, sanity, social position, or other conditions or circumstances. The underlying principle of behavioral and social control developed here is the idea of deterrence. People conform only when the pleasures of conforming are greater than the pleasures of committing crimes. If crime results in certain punishment, the amount of conformity will be maximized because the pains of nonconformity will make conformity more pleasant than deviation. By means of a rational, closely calculated system of justice, including the uniform imposition of swift and certain punishments, the undesirability and impropriety of certain behavior is emphasized to such a degree that it simply does not occur to people to engage in such behavior.

Although this theory is not, and never was, used in its pure form, it is one of the pillars of our contemporary system for the administration of justice. This fact becomes apparent whenever legislators demand an increase in the severity of the penalty for some offense, whenever police are criticized for not enforcing the law, and whenever the very existence of probation and parole systems is attacked. Such actions are all based on the assumption that the legislature knows best and that any deviation from its program is a corruption of authority.[8]

There is, however, a second body of theory based on the belief that law violations and law violators must be handled individually as far as punishment is concerned. In fact, the extreme idea of equality promoted by the classical school was almost immediately modified at two points. First, children and "lunatics" were exempted from punishment on the ground that they are unable to calculate pleasures and pains intelligently. Second, judges were allowed to set penalties within limits, so that a small amount of judicial discretion was possible. These modifications of the classical doctrine were the essence of what came to be called the"neoclassical school." The principle behind these modifications remains as another of the pillars of our contemporary system for administering criminal justice. The basic idea was, and is, that the entire set of circumstances of the offense and the entire character of the offender are to be taken into account when deciding what the punishment, if any, shall be. Individualization of punishment has extended the principle of exemptions to persons other than children and the insane, and this means, of course, that judicial discretion is to be exercised officially.[9]

Underlying these two principal sets of penal theory are basic attitudes about the justice of deliberately imposing pain and suffering on people who break the law. The principle of strict enforcement rests on the idea that each crime has its price. The ideas of the classical school developed concurrently with development of the price system in economic affairs, and the monetary implications of punishments are apparent in such phrases as "debt to society" and "pay the price of his crime." Just as price is assumed to bear a constant relation to a commodity, so, it is assumed, should the penalty bear a constant relationship to the crime. There is to be no bargaining or haggling. The legislative body determines the price once and for all. But from the viewpoint of the neoclassical school and the individualization of punishment, it is argued that an injustice is done if the price of a crime does not vary with the conditions under which it is perpetrated. For example, it is sometimes considered unjust to impose identical sentences on two murderers who have committed their offenses under quite different circumstances.

Attitudes about intention and purposiveness also are involved. There are in our culture two principal reactions to violations of the law. Clearly, the reaction to illegal acts perceived as *deliberate* or *purposive* is usually one of punishment and close surveillance—and the classical school was apt to assume that all criminal behavior is intentional. Just as clearly, however, we believe that when deviation is unintentional, due to ignorance or inability to conform, it should have education (in its broadest sense) as its consequence, rather than punishment—and the neoclassical school argued that some harmful behavior is not deliberate and, therefore, is not criminal.[10]

Enforcing the Law and Maintaining Consent

Our basic conceptions of justice, then, are closely allied with two contradictory sets of penal theory. These conceptions of justice are also intermingled with our ideologies about efficient programs for securing and maintaining the consent of the governed. When implemented, the theories and ideologies become directives for action on the part of criminal law administrators. But since the theories and ideologies are contradictory, we cannot logically expect police, prosecuting attorneys, judges, wardens, parole officials, and others to be consistent in their methods of dealing with lawbreakers and potential lawbreakers. The agencies represented by such officials are microcosms of the society supporting them, at least in regard to problems of maximizing the amount of conformity. All are concerned with the administration of justice, not with punishment of law violators. We want such personnel to administer the law strictly by invoking procedures that make it certain that violators of criminal laws pay the price for doing so. We also want such personnel to administer the law fairly by modifying these procedures in such a way that the consent of the governed is not lost. Implementing the latter, however, necessarily means that we fail in the former, and vice versa.

Administrators of justice, in effect, are called upon to play a game they cannot win. We are confident that swift, certain, and uniform punishments of intentional deviations will maximize the amount of conformity in the society. We also are confident that if the punishments so imposed are either too lenient or too severe the degree of conformity will diminish. If the price of a crime is set too low, everyone will buy it. But if the price is set too high, then exacting it will result in loss of control of both the offenders and the public at large. When punishments are too severe or otherwise unjust, it is true that citizens will not necessarily revolt or withdraw their consent to be governed, but they may well shield criminals from the law enforcement process. Even if they do not themselves commit crimes, they may learn to overlook crimes, with the result that the law's effectiveness in maximizing conformity diminishes. We assign to administrators of justice the difficult task of striking the delicate balance between severity and leniency of punishments and between imposing punishments uniformly and imposing them irregularly.

Unless one understands the various duties assigned to criminal justice administrators, their everyday behavior appears as incoherent and topsy-turvy as the court procedures in Wonderland appeared to Alice.[11] Actually, these officials have been assigned at least four interrelated functions—but these functions are not explicitly listed in any set of rules. In fact, it is doubtful that even a majority of the personnel involved have thought much about them. Nonetheless, they operate according to basic assumptions they have learned to make about the proper and efficient ways of maximizing the amount of law obedience in the society they represent. It is in this sense that agencies for the administration of justice are microcosms of their society. Without thinking about it, administrators of justice bring to bear on the persons they encounter the same social control mechanisms that have been brought to bear on them as members of the society.

First, it is the duty of criminal justice administrators, like parents and theologians, to attempt to inspire conformity to proper standards, as defined in criminal law. In any society, the formal legal apparatus consisting of police, courts, and prisons is principally an apparatus of last resort to be used when more informal processes of inspiring conformity have failed. Thus, if the family were completely successful in socializing children in the values that lawmakers view as right and proper, then the need for a formal apparatus to punish persons who do not adhere to those values would be minimal. But because the family cannot be completely successful in this regard, officials of other social institutions, including the government, also are expected to participate in the socialization process. As a policeman "shows the flag," for example, by parading his beat in uniform, he symbolizes the idea that citizens must conform or be punished, and in this "law enforcement officer" role he symbolizes the punitive and deterrent conception of justice in his society. But, at the same time, he also symbolizes what is right and proper in society, and, stated in exaggerated form, he is the epitome of morality.[12] In a general sense, he does this by *participating* in the society rather than by standing outside the society and "policing" the behavior of the members.

Similarly, the courts and all the other cogs in the machinery of justice are designed in part with a view toward inspiring conformity in citizens. The drama of the courtroom and the dignity of the procedures and the officials are designed in part to stimulate so much respect for the law that court procedures will be necessary in a minimum number of instances. The habit of mind that makes for conformity is established in part by the legal apparatus itself.

Second, it is the duty of officials involved in the administration of justice to implement the notion that the pains of retribution for nonconformity will be distributed equally among the persons who deserve them. This is the basis of the expectation, stemming from the principle of strict enforcement, that the police will make arrests or issue summonses for any violations of criminal law that come to their attention. A Michigan statute, for example, provides:

> *It shall be the duty of the police . . . to apprehend any and all persons in the act of committing any offense against the laws of the state . . . and to take the offender forthwith before the proper court or magistrate, to be dealt with for the offense; to make complaints to the proper officers and magistrates of any person known or believed by them to be guilty of the violation of the ordinances of the city or the penal laws of the state; and at all times diligently and faithfully to enforce all such laws . . .*[13]

Justice and fairness require that punishments for similar deviations and rewards for similar kinds of conformity be distributed uniformly, without regard for the social status or other characteristics of the offender. The police and other officials implement this system of justice by being honest and incorruptible, which means that they do not take into account the social characteristics of the offender or the circumstances of the offense and then, on the basis of them, make adjustments by deciding not to invoke the penal process. If they were not to treat people equally and enforce the law by uniformly and dispassionately invoking the penal process (that is, arrest-trial-punishment) whenever a violation occurred, we would have an undesirable system of government by men rather than a desirable system of government by law.

However, this duty to distribute punishments equally is complicated by the implication that the rules to be enforced by the police and courts, at least, are clear and of equal importance. If the police were only to enforce the law, in contrast to *interpreting* or *administering* the law, they could ignore no crimes; they would make arrests or issue summonses in all instances of observed law violation. Further, the police could not forestall the commission of crimes; they only issue summonses and make arrests of persons observed in the process of breaking the law. However, the assumptions underlying the conception of the policeman as a law enforcement officer and nothing else are not warranted. These assumptions would include the premises that all laws are perfectly clear, that lawmakers actually want all violators brought into court, and that the police are not necessarily to be alert to potential violations. As Frank J. Remington has said:

It is obvious that arrests are not made for every offense which comes to the attention of the police. So great has been the proliferation of criminal statutes that arrest of all violators would cause a breakdown of the criminal justice system. There must therefore be a limitation upon the number of persons subjected to the criminal process. As a practical matter, this limitation must take place, in large part, at the arrest stage since this is ordinarily the first official decision relating to the offender's conduct. The power and responsibility which this discretion gives the police is immense. Too often the existence of discretion is denied and its exercise is, therefore, left without guidance and control from the legal system.[14]

Third, it is the duty of criminal justice administrators to symbolize a system of justice stipulating that officially prescribed punishments should, in specific cases, be mitigated in various ways, depending upon the circumstances of the offense or the characteristics of the offender. They implement this system of justice by being "just," "honest," "kind," "helpful," "fair," and "understanding." The "real" offense committed by the defendant must, in fact, be similar to the "real" offense committed by defendants who received the same punishment in the past. It is important to note in this connection that the power of discretion officially granted to courts was not officially extended to the police when police systems were invented. It still has not officially been extended to them.[15] Nevertheless, the police must constantly adjust criminal law, despite the fact that they also have a duty to enforce the law. The policeman is being just when he behaves in terms of his duty to invoke the penal process whenever he observes a violation, regardless of the consequences to the offender, for punishments are to be distributed equally. But he also is being just when he overlooks offenses by using discretion, for in doing so he takes mitigating circumstances into account, thus attempting to maximize the consent of the governed.

The authority for such use of discretion probably lies in the laws and police department regulations that stipulate that the police have a duty to maintain peace and order, as well as a duty to make arrests. As he goes about maintaining order, the policeman must engage in crime prevention and must attempt to maximize conformity by using discretion as to whether or not the penal process will be invoked.[16] A rule for the policemen working in the Intelligence Division of the Portland, Maine, police department quite explicitly indicates that the danger of losing consent of the governed is to be carefully considered when making arrests for gambling:

He [the intelligence officer] shall guard himself against being forced into ill-advised action against minor non-commercial violators that may result in arousing public indignation; raids on church buildings, homes, and privately occupied hotel rooms not used for commercial purposes are occasional examples.[17]

In correctional work, the idea that punishment should be individualized is ordinarily justified in the name of treatment. This notion grew out of arguments against the practice of attempting to impose uniform punishments on all persons violating a particular law. Attention, it is said, is to be focused on the criminal rather than on the crime. It is argued that a strictly equal application of penalties is as obviously ineffective as would be a policy calling for uniform treatment of medical patients no matter what their ailments. Generally, an attempt is made to diagnose the cause of criminality and to base the techniques of reformation upon the diagnosis. An analogy with the method of diagnosis, prescription, and therapy for medical patients is apparent. It is correctly pointed out that two or three centuries ago diseases were not differentiated from each other. Bloodletting was almost the only treatment, varying in amount with the seriousness of the ailment. Since then the germ theory of disease and experimental methods have produced a variety of treatment methods adapted to particular diseases. By analogy, if criminality is looked upon as a set of diseases, then the idea of complete uniformity must be modified.

If there is one key to understanding present-day practices in correctional agencies, it is the conflict between the notion that criminals should be punished and the notion that they should be treated. One approved reaction to crime is hostility, with insistence that the criminal be made to suffer. Another approved reaction is that of nonpunitive treatment.[18] The former is the "official" reaction of society, as reflected in the principle of strict enforcement. The latter has come into correctional work somewhat unofficially, for the same reasons that discretion has come into police work rather unofficially.

Fourth, policemen, judges, wardens, and other administrators of criminal justice are obligated to give advance notice that deviants will be made to suffer. The simple presence of such authorities, and of the institutions they represent, stimulates conformity by reminding potential wrongdoers of the likelihood of punishment. Just as the prohibitions stipulated in criminal laws give advance notice that wrongdoers will be punished, so law enforcement personnel give advance notice that whoever violates a criminal law risks punishment. But, as we have already noted, it is not correct to assume that all criminal laws are perfectly clear or that all offenders will be ordered into court by police. Discretion, specifically in the form of warnings that *further* violations will have punishment as a consequence, is necessary.

The breadth of the discretion we entrust to the police and prosecuting attorneys transfers "from the legislature to enforcement officials the de facto power of determining what the criminal law in action shall be."[19] Since this is the case, there is a diminished warning function of the criminal law as written by legislatures. Police and prosecuting attorneys, then, must substitute unofficial warnings for the official ones with the result that discretion leads to discretion. Suppose that a policeman is granted the power to decide whether or not a law applies to a specific piece of observed conduct. If in exercising this discretion he decides that the conduct is, in fact, a crime, he must inform the offender of this fact before he invokes the penal process. If he does not do so, his "criminal law in action" becomes unjust ex post facto legislation. Informing the offender that his conduct is going to be handled as a crime means both that the present act is overlooked and that fair warning is given that further violations will be punished. Reporting on British and American police, Michael Banton says:

> *In many situations the police are heavily dependent upon the public for information concerning crime and criminals; people will not collaborate in such inquiries if they feel that they are not getting a fair deal from the police. Consequently, police forces everywhere trade pardons in return for better public relations: first offenders and others are regularly let off in the belief that they will feel they have been given a fair chance.*[20]

Consent of the governed is not lost, then, when further violations are later punished. This is essentially the same process used when the magistrates presiding over "drunk courts" rather routinely dismiss the cases of all first offenders in order to save time.[21]

In the courts, such discretion, together with its warning function, has been legitimated by laws, making it permissible for judges to suspend sentences, to grant probation, and to impose a mild sentence as a warning that further violations will be punished more severely. The principal controversies about probation, which is administered by courts, arise because the judge need not explicitly make public his reasons for mitigating penalties and granting probation and because revocation of probation is subject to the discretion of the probation officer. The development of "plea bargaining," in which the defendant pleads guilty in exchange for a lighter sentence than he would receive if convicted of the offense charged, has unofficially extended the area of court discretion even further. There are many reasons for engaging in plea bargaining. A basic one, ordinarily overlooked, is that such bargaining warns the defendant that the *next* offense will bring down the wrath of society upon his head.

Summary and Conclusions

Administrators of justice are expected to implement contradictory legal theories for establishing and maintaining consent of the governed and, thus, for maximizing the amount of conformity in a society. On the one hand, they are to implement the idea that swift, certain, and uniform punishment of law violators will both reform the violators and deter others. On the other hand, they are to implement the idea that consent of the governed can be established and maintained, and conformity maximized, only if punishments are justly imposed, which means that the citizenry will be warned in advance that violations will be punished and that the circumstances of the offense and the characteristics of the offender will be taken into account before punishments are allocated. Sometimes officially, but sometimes unofficially, policemen, court personnel, and correction workers have been instructed to use discretion but at the same time to enforce the law. These personnel administer, in their daily work, justice according to a concept that sometimes makes it seem unfair to do anything but invoke the penal process and sometimes makes it seem unfair to invoke that process. Variations depend, at least in part, on the kinds of specific duties and obligations the personnel have been assigned for securing consent to be governed and for maximizing conformity among the citizens they encounter in their routine work activities.

Notes

1. This essay is an extensive revision and elaboration of Donald R. Cressey and Elg Elgesem, "The Police and Social Control," in Nils Christie (ed.), *Scandinavian Studies in Criminology* (forthcoming).
2. See Joseph P. Fitzpatrick, "Crime and the Immigrant," in Gus Tyler (ed.), *Organized Crime in America* (Ann Arbor: University of Michigan Press, 1962), pp. 415–421; Donald L. Garrity, "The Prison as a Rehabilitation Agency," in Donald R. Cressey (ed.), *The Prison: Studies in Institutional Organization and Change* (New York: Holt, Rinehart and Winston, 1961), pp. 358–380; and Stanton H. Wheeler, "Socialization in Correctional Communities," *American Sociological Review*, 26 (October 1961), 697–712.
3. James F. Stephen, *A General View of the Criminal Law of England* (London: Macmillan, 1863), p. 99.
4. Richard H. McCleery, "The Governmental Process and Informal Social Control," in Cressey, *op. cit.*, p. 154. See also Gresham M. Sykes, *The Society of Captives: A Study of a Maximum Security Prison* (Princeton, N.J.: Princeton University Press, 1958), pp. 52–53.
5. See A. Radcliffe-Brown, *The Adaman Islanders* (Cambridge, England: The University Press, 1922); and Hans von Hentig, *Punishment, Its Origin, Purpose and Psychology* (London: William Hodge, 1937).
6. The French penal law written in 1791, immediately following the revolution, followed principles set down in a declaration written only a month after Bastille Day. Among these principles was the idea that no one should be punished except for an act that has previously been declared an offense: *"Nul ne peut être puni qu'en vertu d'une loi établie et promulguée antérieurement au délit et légalement appliqûee"* ("No one can be punished except by virtue of a law that has been established and promulgated in advance of the crime, and legally applied"). See Leon Radzinowicz, *A History of the English Criminal Law and Its Administration from 1750* (New York: Macmillan, 1948), I, 293–295. The Constitution of the United States, submitted by Congress to the states for ratification on September 28, 1787, says in Article I: "No Bill of Attainder or ex post facto Law should be passed." (Bills of attainder were special legislative acts directed against a designated person, pronouncing him guilty of an alleged crime [usually treason] and sentencing him to death and extinction of civil rights [attainder]. Legislative acts of this kind inflicting punishment other than death were called "bills of pains and penalties," but they are included in the constitutional prohibition.)
7. In reference to the more traditional crimes, knowledge of wrongfulness can be fairly assumed. Almost everyone is aware that murder, rape, and the obvious forms of theft are wrong. If one intentionally murders without knowing that the act is criminal, we proceed on the further assumption that he is blameworthy for his lack of knowledge. "This seems to be the

essential rationale of the maxim, *Ignorantia legis neminem excusat,* which has been so misunderstood and abused in relation to regulatory crimes, involving conduct which is not intrinsically wrongful." Henry M. Hart, Jr., "The Aims of the Criminal Law," *Law and Contemporary Problems,* 23 (Summer 1958), 413–414. See also Jerome Hall, "Ignorance and Mistake in Criminal Law," *Indiana Law Journal,* 33 (Fall 1967), 27–34; and Jerome Hall, *General Principles of Criminal Law,* 2nd ed. (Indianapolis: Bobbs-Merrill, 1960), pp. 360–414.

8. See Gresham M. Sykes, "The Corruption of Authority and Rehabilitation," *Social Forces,* 34 (March 1956), 257–262.
9. We cannot here discuss the arguments of the "positive school" of criminology. The leaders of this school, in the nineteenth century, popularized individualization by denying individual responsibility and advocating an essentially nonpunitive reaction to crime and criminality. See George B. Vold, *Theoretical Criminology* (New York: Oxford University Press, 1958), pp. 27–40; and Donald R. Cressey and Edwin H. Sutherland, *Principles of Criminology,* 7th ed. (Philadelphia: Lippincott, 1966), pp. 313, 354–355, 683. The idea of individualization had elements of novelty in its formulation, but to a considerable degree "it was but a reassertion of the old idea of equity (*epieikia*) as the correction of the undue rigor of the law, a corrective to the injustice which results from the fact that the abstract rule cannot take into account all the specific circumstances that are relevant to the case. It assumes its simplest and oldest form in the pardoning power . . . Some religions, indeed, make God's forgiveness His most glorious attribute." Morris R. Cohen, *Reason and Law* (New York: Free Press, 1950), p. 53.
10. The injustice, from this perspective, of "strict liability" statutes cannot be considered here. (The English call "strict responsibility" what Americans call "strict liability.") Such statutes hold actors criminally responsible regardless of their intentions. For example, in statutory rape a man who has sexual intercourse with a girl beneath a specified age of consent, set by the legislature, has committed a crime even if he is entirely convinced that she is above the age of consent. Similarly, one who remarries after his spouse has been presumed dead following a fixed period of unexplained absence risks the peril of conviction of bigamy. If the missing spouse is alive, the one who remarries is a bigamist, regardless of his intentions. In effect, the courts say, "Good faith and reasonable inquiry have nothing to do with this . . . We attribute to the legislature, a purpose to discourage the remarriage of abandoned spouses as socially impolitic, by requiring those who attempt it to take a gambler's chance of becoming a criminal." Hart, *op. cit.,* p. 430. See the discussion in Hall, *General Principles of Criminal Law, op. cit.,* pp. 325–359; and Colin Howard, *Strict Responsibility* (London: Sweet and Maxwell, 1963).
11. See "Off With Their Heads," below.
12. British police perform this role more effectively than do American police. See Michael Banton, *The Policeman in the Community* (London: Tavistock, 1964), pp. 123–125.
13. Annotated Michigan Statutes, 5.1752, 1949; quoted in Joseph Goldstein, "Police Discretion Not to Invoke the Criminal Process: Low Visibility

Decisions in the Administration of Justice," *Yale Law Journal,* 69, No. 4 (March 1960), 557.

14. Frank J. Remington, "The Law Relating to 'On the Street' Detention, Questioning and Frisking of Suspected Persons and Police Arrest Privileges in General," in Claude R. Sowle (ed.), *Police Power and Individual Freedom: The Quest for Balance* (Chicago: Aldine, 1962), p. 20.
15. Apparently exceptional are the police of New Mexico, where a statute provides that police must investigate all violations of criminal laws that are called to their attention but are allowed to use discretion as to enforcement.
16. We are not directly concerned here with the "servant of the public" activities of the police—activities such as issuing licences, directing traffic, and rendering first aid. See Elaine Cumming, Ian Cumming, and Laura Edell, "Policemen as Philosopher, Guide and Friend," *Social Problems,* 12 (Winter 1965), 276–286. See also "The Policeman's Lot," below.
17. Quoted by Goldstein, *op. cit.,* pp. 561–562, note 33.
18. For discussion of the relationship of correctional institutions to community interest groups, see Lloyd E. Ohlin, "Conflicting Interests in Correctional Objectives," in Richard A. Cloward, *et al.* (eds.), *Theoretical Studies in Social Organization of the Prison* (New York: Social Science Research Council, 1960), pp. 111–129; and Donald R. Cressey, "Prison Organization," in James G. March (ed.), *Handbook of Organizations* (New York: Rand-McNally, 1965), pp. 1030–1032.
19. Hart, *op. cit.,* p. 428.
20. Banton, *op. cit.,* p. 137.
21. See "Mass Production" and "The Negotiated Plea," below.

Suggestions for Further Reading

Banton, Michael. *The Policeman in the Community*. London: Tavistock, 1964.

Clemmer, Donald. *The Prison Community*. Reissued ed. New York: Holt, Rinehart and Winston, 1958.

Cloward, Richard A., *et al. Theoretical Studies in Social Organization of the Prison*. New York: Social Science Research Council, 1960.

Cohen, Morris R. *Reason and Law*. New York: Free Press, 1950.

Cressey, Donald R. (ed.). *The Prison: Studies in Institutional Organization and Change*. New York: Holt, Rinehart and Winston, 1961.

Douglas, William O. *An Almanac of Liberty*. New York: Doubleday, 1954.

Gibbons, Don C. *Changing the Lawbreaker: The Treatment of Delinquents and Criminals*. Englewood Cliffs, N.J.: Prentice-Hall, 1965.

Ginsberg, Morris. *On Justice in Society*. Baltimore: Penguin, 1965.

Glaser, Daniel. *The Effectiveness of a Prison and Parole System*. Indianapolis: Bobbs-Merrill, 1964.

Goffman, Erving. *Asylums: Essays on the Social Situations of Mental Patients and Other Inmates*. New York: Anchor Books, 1961.

Goldfarb, Ronald. *Ransom: A Critique of the American Bail System*. New York: Harper & Row, 1965.

Hoebel, E. Adamson. *The Law of Primitive Man: A Study in Comparative Legal Dynamics*. Cambridge, Mass.: Harvard University Press, 1954.

LaFave, Wayne R. *Arrest: The Decision to Take a Suspect into Custody*. Boston: Little, Brown, 1965.

Mayers, Lewis. *The American Legal System*. Rev. ed. New York: Harper & Row, 1964.

Morris, Terence, and Pauline Morris. *Pentonville: A Sociological Study of an English Prison*. London: Routledge and Kegan Paul, 1963.

Newman, Donald J. *Conviction: The Determination of Guilt or Innocence Without Trial*. Boston: Little, Brown, 1966.

Ohlin, Lloyd E. *Selection for Parole*. New York: Russell Sage Foundation, 1951.

Schur, Edwin M. *Crimes Without Victims: Deviant Behavior and Public Policy*. Englewood Cliffs, N.J.: Prentice-Hall, 1965.

Sellin, Thorsten (ed.). *Capital Punishment*. New York: Harper & Row, 1967.

Skolnick, Jerome H. *Justice Without Trial: Law Enforcement in Democratic Society*. New York: Wiley, 1966.

Sykes, Gresham M. *The Society of Captives: A Study of a Maximum Security Prison*. Princeton, N. J.: Princeton University Press, 1958.

Szasz, Thomas S. *Law, Liberty, and Psychiatry*. New York: Macmillan, 1963.

Vold, George B. *Theoretical Criminology*. New York: Oxford University Press, 1958.

Ward, David A., and Gene G. Kassebaum. *Women's Prison: Sex and Social Structure*. Chicago: Aldine, 1965.

Yablonsky, Lewis. *Synanon: The Tunnel Back*. Baltimore: Penguin, 1967.

1 THE POLICE

The United States has about 420,000 policemen and they probably have as efficient technology at their disposal as any law enforcement group in the world. Nonetheless, crime in the United States continues to increase more rapidly than the population. Why? It should be clear by now that there are many reasons that are quite independent of the police themselves and the legal structure within which they operate. Yet the police and the courts are sometimes seen as having the sole responsibility for the control of crime in a highly oversimplified picture of society versus the criminal.

American society, of course, has long been distrustful of police authority, and distrust continues to be perpetuated through many social mechanisms. A certain antipathy is often instilled at an early age that is then reinforced by an unfortunate encounter with the law, by newspaper stories of corruption and brutality, and so on. Also, the public frequently neutralizes police authority by stereotyping the police as stupid or tyrannical or even criminal.

In any event, to understand the police fully it is first essential to learn what they actually do. It is equally important to recognize the constraints on police powers and the reasons for the existence of such constraints, because then we can better assess some of the proposals that have been offered to increase police effectiveness.

1. The Average Cop

Public ambivalence toward the police is reflected in the images evoked by the word "cop"—a word that is much disliked by the police themselves. As with other terms used to reinforce stereotypes, the word carries a derogatory sting. The police officer, after all, is the man who enforces the law—rules that not everyone agrees with, understands, or sees the need for.

St. Clair McKelway takes us behind the stereotype. Although the piece is perhaps a bit overly sentimental and somewhat dated (salaries have increased), McKelway presents a sympathetic portrait of the officer as a hard-working bureaucrat trapped in a highly inconsistent structure.

By all ordinary standards, Albert Moran Williams is something of an eccentric. He takes long walks six days a week, sometimes strolling for eight hours with scarcely a rest. He is often lonely during these jaunts through the city streets, yet when he speaks to a fellow-man, it is almost always to upbraid him. He is constantly getting himself embroiled in other people's affairs. If he passes a store at night, he tries the door to see if it is unlocked, but if he finds anybody else doing this, he chases him. He sleeps irregularly, and often has breakfast at 3 P.M. and lunch at midnight. Because of a sense of duty inordinately strong for a man of his years and upbringing, he hardly ever relaxes as other men do. He is young and healthy-looking, yet he clothes himself in a bag and, in winter, a benny as well; he always carries with him, among other things, a roscoe, a potsie, and a biscuit, and he is constantly on the lookout for shoo-flies. He is rather deeply preoccupied with death and he is more religious than any of the boys he grew up with on the West Side, except the one who became a Catholic priest. He has acquired a realistic, almost cynical conception of the human species, and he, in turn, is regarded with a certain animosity by the average citizen. Most of his friends are men of his own calling, and shop talk dominates his conversation at work and at play. He has been on the force four and a half years now; soon he will be a first-grade patrolman.

You would be puzzled by many of the words he uses. What most of us call his beat he refers to as his post, and when he is on it, he is working his tour, not his shift. His uniform is his bag and his winter overcoat his benny. A complaint against a law-breaker he calls a diddo. If he has an influential friend—a politician, a prominent banker, a big lawyer—this friend is his rabbi. His shield is his potsie and his gun is his roscoe. His watch, of course, is his biscuit. Bullets, to him, are liver pills. The sergeant is the boss, the captain is the skipper, and the lieutenants who supervise patrols and spy on patrolmen are shoo-flies. The telephone he uses to call his station house is the box. His wife, even to her face, is usually the cook.

Williams, at the moment, is a second-grade patrolman. Behind him is his work as third- and fourth-grade patrolman and probationary patrolman, or rookie. His first day on a regular tour is far in the past, and the rookie of twenty-five who stepped out of the detail for the first time and watched the squad of broad, blue backs go marching down the street away from him, leaving him alone to keep the peace on East Fifty-third Street, seems almost unrecognizable to him now. But the memory of that first day is vivid. He had had the uniform on before at home. While his wife was in the kitchen, he had looked at it appreciatively in the mirror in their bedroom. That first day on tour he thought that everybody must be looking at him, and felt desperately uncomfortable. As he walked along, his temples throbbing, he underwent the most devastating emotional experience of his life. All of his thoughts had been thrown inward and he had been seeing only himself in this blue uniform; and all at once he thought of bandits, of women stabbed in the throat and children kidnapped, of collisions and ambulances and fires, and of thieves dodging into areaways; he thought of crime and catastrophe and realized, all in a flash, what he was and what he was there for. He felt giddy and hysterical, and he remembers now that he stopped suddenly in his tracks, like a thoroughbred setter, and looked about him searchingly. That was all. In a few moments he was all right again. "It was the Goddamn'est thing ever happened to me," he says. "You know what? I almost fainted—would you believe it?"

Before his probationary period began, Williams had spent two years of part-time study at Delehanty's police preparatory school on East Fifteenth Street, where he had listened to one lecture a week and learned enough to pass the preliminary examination which made him eligible for the Police Academy of the Department. There followed a six months' intensive course, during which his mind was introduced to the intricacies of the penal code and his body subjected to scientific building and strengthening exercises. He learned, for instance, that garbage cans must be covered when placed on the sidewalk and that known pickpockets may be arrested for jostling if proof of a specific theft is lacking. He also learned to shoot 85 per cent accurately at life-size targets. Long before the course was ended, he had begun inevitably to think of professional criminals as his personal adversaries rather than as mere foes of society. The lectures on the sanitary code, traffic regulations, simple and felonious assault, forgery, larceny and juvenile delinquency produced in him a similarly specialized attitude toward the public at large. He became intimately acquainted in theory with all manner of crimes and misdemeanors of profit and passion. The average citizen began to appear to Williams as a potential criminal, holding within him the capabilities of arson, thievery, sexual degeneracy, homicide and a thousand variations of unsocial conduct. As he rode home to his flat in the Bronx in those days of preparation, he found himself scrutinizing the strap-hangers on the subway with a frank and uninhibited suspicion. "That fellow there," he would say to himself cheerfully, "looks like a cheap forger to me."

His encounters with ordinary citizens since he began to patrol a post have made him aware of the citizen's grave misunderstanding of the patrolman's problems. He remembers with a sense of injury one of the first emergencies with which he was confronted while on his tour in the East Fifties. The hood of a taxicab occupied by two well-dressed businessmen burst into flames and the driver pulled up at the curb. Williams, still a bit overzealous, perhaps, dashed to a fire-box and turned in an alarm. But before the engines had time to get there, the fire was out, the motor running again, and the occupants of the cab were urging the driver to proceed.

"You got to wait," Williams told the driver, placing a restraining hand on the steering wheel. "The fire engines are coming."

"That's absurd," said one of the businessmen, leaning out of the window. "We are in a hurry; the first is out. Go ahead, driver."

"No you don't," repeated Williams tensely.

In about five long minutes, the engines arrived; the firemen inspected the taxi, threw away some charred bits of cotton waste, got back in their engines, and departed, bells clamoring. Only then did Williams permit the cab to proceed on its way with its impatient occupants.

"Did they think I was going to let the damn cab go, and me standing there with nothing to show the firemen?" Williams demanded after relating this incident to his wife. "You'd think they'da seen that. But all they thought about was how they had to get wherever the hell they were going."

"Of course, dear," said Mrs. Williams.

The gulf is widened by other elements as well. From time to time he runs across references in the newspaper editorials to the "stupidity of the police force" and "graft in the police force." Once in his favorite popular magazine he was reading an entertaining story and enjoying it very much until he came to a terse simile: "as dumb as a cop." This infuriated him, and he has never bought that magazine again.

Then one afternoon, a couple of years ago, Williams shouldered his way through a crowd on Third Avenue in the Fifties and dragged the broken body of a young boy from under the wheels of a truck. A hysterical woman grabbed the policeman's arm as the ambulance was about to depart, and he had to show her the body; it was her son. The woman did not collapse, but she seemed so frail and helpless and forlorn that Williams walked with her to the tenement across the street, where she lived. He answered her distracted questions about having the body removed to an undertaker's. He promised to attend to this for her and so accompanied her into the little parlor of the flat, getting out his fountain pen and memorandum pad. Just then the father, who ran a bakery shop down the block, came through the front door and into the parlor—an anxious little Serbian immigrant with an apron around his waist and a dusty derby on his head.

"He's dead," the woman told her husband.

The baker uttered no word but stood there a moment and slowly sank into a chair with his hat still on his head. Then he became aware of the presence of Williams. He took off his derby hurriedly, and, looking up at the tall figure in uniform, he said, "Excuse me, Officer, I didn't see you."

Williams finds it difficult to explain his reactions to this incident.

"It sounds goofy, telling about it like that," he says. "But it made me feel kind of—well, lonely as hell, if you know what I mean."

As he grows older, Williams's outlook grows almost mellow; he approaches thirty with a more kindly feeling for the citizens who are his wards, but he retires deeper and deeper into the separate sphere of city life which is the Police Department. Having served four and a half years, he will become a first-grade patrolman in another six months and his salary, already increased three times, will be raised to four thousand, one hundred and fifty dollars a year. He knows he possesses a pecuniary security not enjoyed by most of the boys he used to play with on the western extremity of Twenty-third Street. He has even gone so far as to count off a group of ten of these boys on his fingers. One, as has been mentioned, became a priest. One is a taxi-driver; two progressed from petty thievery to gangdom, and one of these died in a gang fight two years ago; one is a doctor, overworked, poor, but cheerful; two studied law at night, and one of these is climbing rapidly—the other died in a Saranac sanitarium last winter of tuberculosis; another is a petty officer in the Navy; another is a saloon keeper; and the tenth is Williams, who feels he is doing pretty well.

He has a six-room flat in the Bronx and two kids thus far, both boys, one six and the other four. He thinks probably one more child would be sufficient and he hopes it will be a girl. He owns a Chevrolet and, although there is a Department regulation against it, he drives it to work and parks it on the street all day. He is buying a shack, as he calls it, up in Westchester. Next door on one side is a patrolman who went through the Police Academy with Williams. Williams's credit is automatically good at real-estate and automobile agencies and at department stores; they know policemen can be removed from the force for credit delinquency, and they know most of them are responsible fellows anyway.

His hours of work are trying: six eight-hour days of from 8 A.M. to 4 P.M., then thirty-two hours off; then six days of from 12 midnight to 8 A.M., then thirty-two hours off; then six days of from 4 P.M. to midnight, then thirty-two hours off, and the cycle commences again.

He has not fired his gun at any person yet. He has not been shot at yet, either, but he knows that a score of patrolmen are killed or maimed by bullets every year and, while he does not brood over this, it has given him an unnatural awareness of death. He is a Catholic. He swears conventionally and uses the names of God, the Saviour and some of the saints in vain, but he goes to Mass fairly regularly and has shadowy convictions concerning a personal God whom he sometimes pictures patting him on the back. If ever he has to chase a brace of killers into a dark alleyway, he will in all probability risk a sudden ending without a second's hesitation, with his potsie—an excellent target—shining on his breast.

He has been called into innumerable family squabbles, has warned hundreds of householders about garbage cans, has discovered, by trying all the store doors at night, numerous burglaries after the loot has been taken. A glance at the statistics piled up by Williams and his comrades of the police force for an average year shows that the vast majority of arrests are for violations of the sanitary laws, the traffic laws, the gambling laws and other unexciting statutes. Williams actually chased a burglar once and caught him merely by grabbing him, and he has stopped many street fights between toughs who needed firm handling. On the whole, however, he has had few dealings with professional criminals and gangsters, and often doesn't know the most notorious of the latter when he sees them. He has accepted, in all, perhaps three hundred dollars of what he calls honest graft from persons who have insisted on paying him not to do something that he probably wouldn't have done anyway, and Christmas presents from merchants amount sometimes to fifty dollars a year all together, but he has never viciously extorted any money from anybody. He knows the risk of detection is great and, besides, he is no greedier than any other wage earner and he has more personal pride, perhaps, than most. He has contributed to poor people on his post and to organized charities at least as much as he has accepted in graft and gratuities.

When he is on an evening tour, drunks become one of his chief concerns; he has sent some of these home in taxicabs, consoled others with philosophical reflections, complied with the insistent conversational demands of many, and arrested still others and taken them to Night Court. He likes his liquor himself, but he doesn't often get tipsy while on duty and never gets really drunk even when off duty.

Walking the tour isn't so bad, he thinks, except on muggy days, and then it is downright terrible. He's not supposed to smoke, and so he has to duck into a store or someplace to get a few puffs every now and then. He has to watch the time closely, though, for his periodic calls from the street boxes to the sergeant at the station house must be made on the minute, or else the sergeant grows irate and tells him to have his biscuit overhauled. His feet never bother him any more, but they did at first. The thick soles he affects are sensible—the pavements are broiling in summer and icy in winter. He gets a soft assignment once in a while, a prize fight or a political meeting. The Department parades bore him—just another long walk, he says.

During his first year on the force—he had been married then about three years—he got in pretty deep with a dumb Italian girl on his tour, and later on he had quite an affair with a rather swell lady, but he couldn't talk to either of them and finally gave up that sort of thing as too troublesome, too risky, and unsatisfactory all round. His wife seems to understand him and his boys are young enough to worship him. Every now and then, he takes his wife to Broadway, and they go to a show and maybe a chop-suey joint afterward, to give her a vacation from the kitchen. He has to carry his roscoe and his potsie even on these occasions, but when he is out with the cook like that, he wouldn't think of hitting anybody up for free grub or free drinks. He takes off his benny and his bag, of course, when his tour is over, and dresses in civilian clothes when off duty.

Williams's father was half Scotch and half English—a foreman in a lumber yard when he died four years ago. His mother was all Irish. Williams went through one year of high school and quit to go to work in the lumber yard where his father was foreman. He had a trivial tiff with his father there and left home for a while, traveling as far west as Newark and as far north as Yonkers, working as a bus boy in a lunchroom, as a timekeeper for a building contractor, and in lumber yards where his father was not the foreman. After a year and a half of this, he came home, got to going around with the girl he later married, and with the help of her father, who was a clerk in a big dairy company, obtained a steady job as a driver of a milk wagon. He made friends with one of the other drivers, whose brother was a cop—and that was how Williams happened to decide to become a cop himself.

He has no particular bent for deduction, though he sometimes imagines he has, and consequently he is unlikely to be chosen for the detective branch, where the pay is higher. The four thousand, one hundred and fifty dollars a year which he will achieve soon is the most he can make unless he becomes a sergeant, in which case he would receive about five hundred more dollars a year. He cannot get this promotion through influence alone, but his rabbi has been able to have some of the routine complaints of shoo-flies erased, thus making his next step up a little less difficult. Williams's rabbi is the boyhood friend who is now a rising lawyer and a Tammany worker. If Williams becomes a sergeant, he may rise later on to be a lieutenant, and he may even become a captain some day. But even if he remains a patrolman, as the great majority of patrolmen do, he will be eligible for retirement on half pay after twenty-five years' service. He has no desire to get in the traffic division because he thinks the traffic man has a solitary job, harder and more confining than his, and the pay is the same.

Williams is five feet, nine and one-half inches in height and he weighs one hundred and sixty-five pounds, which is the precise average for a New

York patrolman. He possesses that comforting conviction most of us have: he thinks he is not quite like anybody else, or even quite like any other policeman. The New York police force includes seventeen thousand-odd patrolmen, who are variously slimmer, fatter, taller, shorter, and more or less greedy, intelligent and ambitious than he is. But as these things go, Williams is the average patrolman whom one may see on the streets of New York any day one chooses to look for him.

2. The Policeman's Lot

It is clear from McKelway's portrait that police are called into many highly unusual situations. But most people have no idea of how diverse and varied police work is. Officers find themselves dispensing legal, medical, and psychiatric counseling in their effort to maintain public order. An understanding of the highly varied and personal character of police work is essential to an analysis or appreciation of police problems.

"Police work" is a phrase that conjures up in some minds a dramatic contest between a policeman and a criminal in which the party with the stronger arm or the craftier wit prevails. To be sure, when a particularly desperate or guileful criminal must be hunted down and brought to justice, there are heroic moments in police work.

The situations that most policemen deal with most of the time are of quite another order, however. Chapters 2 and 3 of this report have shown that much of American crime, delinquency, and disorder is associated with a complex of social conditions: Poverty, racial antagonism, family breakdown, or the restlessness of young people. During the last 20 years these conditions have been aggravated by such profound social changes as the technological and civil rights revolutions, and the rapid decay of inner cities into densely packed, turbulent slums and ghettos.

It is in the cities that the conditions of life are the worst, that social tensions are the most acute, that riots occur, that crime rates are the highest, that the fear of crime and the demand for effective action against it are the strongest. It is in the cities that a large proportion of American policemen work and that a large proportion of police money is spent. Though there are 40,000 separate law enforcement agencies in the Nation, 55 of them, the police departments of the cities of more than 250,000 population, employ almost one-third of all police personnel. Policing a city of more than one million population costs $27.31 per resident per year; policing a city of less than 50,000 costs less than one-third as much, or $8.74.

A great majority of the situations in which policemen intervene are not, or are not interpreted by the police to be, criminal situations in the sense

From the President's Commission on Law Enforcement and Administration of Justice, **The Challenge of Crime in a Free Society** (Washington, D.C.: U.S. Government Printing Office, 1967).

that they call for arrest with its possible consequences of prosecution, trial, and punishment. This is not to say that the police intervene in these situations mistakenly. Many of them are clear public nuisances that the community wants stopped: Radios blaring or dogs barking at 3 o'clock in the morning, more or less convivial groups obstructing sidewalks, or youths throwing snowballs at passing motorists.

Many situations involve people who need help whether they want it or not: Helpless drunks out in freezing weather, runaway boys who refuse to go home, tourists in search of exciting night life in a dangerous neighborhood. Many of them involve conduct that, while unlawful, cannot be prevented or deterred to any great degree by means now at the disposal of the criminal justice system: Using narcotics, prostitution, gambling, alcoholism. Many situations, whether or not they involve unlawful conduct, may be threatening: A sidewalk orator exercising the right of free speech in the midst of a hostile crowd, a midnight street corner gathering of youths whose intentions are questionable, an offer by a belligerent drunk to lick any man in the house.

All of these situations could involve the violation of some ordinance or statute. All of them could lead to a serious breach of public order, or for that matter to a serious crime. Much of police work is seeing to it they do not lead to this extreme. This means becoming involved in the most intimate, personal way with the lives and problems of citizens of all kinds.

It is hard to overstate the intimacy of the contact between the police and the community. Policemen deal with people when they are both most threatening and most vulnerable, when they are angry, when they are frightened, when they are desperate, when they are drunk, when they are violent, or when they are ashamed. Every police action can affect in some way someone's dignity, or self-respect, or sense of privacy, or constitutional rights. As a matter of routine policemen become privy to, and make judgments about, secrets that most citizens guard jealously from their closest friends: Relationships between husbands and wives, the misbehavior of children, personal eccentricities, peccadilloes and lapses of all kinds. Very often policemen must physically restrain or subdue unruly citizens.

A common kind of situation that illustrates the complexity, delicacy—and frustration—of much police work is the matrimonial dispute, which police experts estimate consumes as much time as any other single kind of situation. These family altercations often occur late at night, when the only agency available to people in trouble is the police. Because they occur late at night, they can disturb the peace of a whole neighborhood. And, of course, they can lead to crime; in fact, they are probably the single greatest cause of homicides. Yet the capacity of the police to deal effectively with such a highly personal matter as conjugal disharmony is, to say the least, limited. Arresting one party or both is unlikely to result in either a prosecution or a reconciliation. Removing one of the parties from the scene, an expedient the police often resort to, sometimes by using force, may create temporary peace, but it scarcely solves the problem. An order to see a family counselor in the morning is unenforceable and more likely to be ignored than obeyed. And mediating the difficulty of enraged husbands and wives ad hoc is an activity for which few policemen—or people in any other profession—are qualified by temperament or by training. Again no statistics are available, but there is a strong impression in police circles that intervention in these disputes causes more assaults on policemen than any other kind of encounter.

Since police action is so often so personal, it is inevitable that the public is of two minds about the police: Most men both welcome official protection and resent official interference. Upon the way the police perform their duties depends to a large extent which state of mind predominates, whether the police are thought of as protectors or oppressors, as friends or enemies. Yet policemen, who as a rule have been well trained to perform such procedures as searching a person for weapons, transporting a suspect to the stationhouse, taking fingerprints, writing arrest reports, and testifying in court, have received little guidance from legislatures, city administrations, or their own superiors, in handling these intricate, intimate human situations. The organization of police departments and the training of policemen are focused almost entirely on the apprehension and prosecution of criminals. What a policeman does, or should do, instead of making an arrest or in order to avoid making an arrest, or in a situation in which he may not make an arrest, is rarely discussed. The peacekeeping and service activities, which consume the majority of police time, receive too little consideration.

Finally, more than public attitudes toward the police and, by extension, toward the law, are influenced by the way any given policeman performs his duties. Every Supreme Court decision that has redefined or limited such important and universal police procedures as search and seizure, interrogation of suspects, arrest, and the use of informants has been a decision about the way a specific policeman or group of policemen handled a specific situation. Most of the recent big-city riots were touched off by commonplace street encounters between policemen and citizens. In short, the way any policeman exercises the personal discretion that is an inescapable part of his job can, and occasionally does, have an immediate bearing on the peace and safety of an entire community, or a long-range bearing on the work of all policemen everywhere.

3. The Need for Discretion

Should all suspected offenders be arrested? A number of studies have shown that if caught in a delinquent act a conservatively dressed, well-mannered, white juvenile is much less likely to be arrested than a tough, swearing Negro boy in the slums. The injustice here is readily apparent, but it is only part of the larger and more complex issue of police discretion.

In Wayne La Fave's analysis of the debate about police discretion, he points out that obviously no person should be arrested for a crime of which he is not suspected. Yet at times justice may best be served by a decision not to make the arrest despite clear evidence of legal violation. The problem then is who should have the responsibility for the choice.

Perhaps the most significant feature of current criminal justice administration is the great amount of discretion which is exercised by police. Decisions not to arrest because of the nature of the offense, the circumstances of its commission, or some other factor are made routinely. The use of judgment in deciding whether one apparently guilty of criminal conduct should be subjected to the criminal justice process is an obviously important exercise of governmental power. Arrest is the usual intake point for persons who are channeled into the criminal justice system. Therefore, the police to a large extent define the outer limits of law enforcement by the way in which they make this decision.

There is a common stereotype of police as ministerial officers whose only function is that of gathering evidence and making an arrest whenever sufficient evidence exists. This is illustrated by the assumption, frequently made, that police and firemen are similar since both are uniformed and are concerned with the safety of persons and property. Police themselves tend to reinforce this conception of their function by denying that they exercise discretion and by failing to specify the standards or criteria upon which they base their decisions.

A wide gulf thus separates theory and practice. Discretion is exercised by the police but this takes place largely without the knowledge of the general public, without the concerted efforts of police administrators to

From Wayne R. La Fave, **Arrest: The Decision to Take a Suspect Into Custody** (Boston: Little, Brown and Company, 1965). Reprinted by permission.

insure that it is exercised properly, and without adequate attention from legislatures and courts.

Whatever one may conclude about the necessity or desirability of the exercise of discretion by police, it is apparent that this is an issue deserving a great deal more attention than it has traditionally been given in the past.

Because the exercise of discretion involves decision-making not strictly governed by legal rules, but rather with a significant element of personal judgment, it is sometimes said to be totally improper in criminal law enforcement, where the consequences of official action directly affect a citizen's freedom and property.

No one would assert that law enforcement agencies have a right to exercise discretion beyond the outer boundaries of the law defining criminal conduct, such as by arresting for conduct which the legislature has not declared to be a crime. The issue is rather whether discretion within these boundaries, exemplified by the common police decision not to arrest in some situations where criminal conduct has occurred, i[s] proper. Some assert that the two situations are essentially the same and that both involve an abuse of power: "[T]he rule of law [means] . . . that the citizen should be free from arbitrary power. A discretion to withhold a punishment may result in just as much arbitrary power as discretion to use extra-legal punishment."

Whatever their status in principle, it is clear that the two situations are dealt with differently in current practice. It is not common to arrest a person unless he is at least suspected of having engaged in criminal conduct. It is common for some persons not to be arrested even though it can easily be proved that they have engaged in criminal conduct.

. . .

It is obvious that in practice some discretion must be employed somewhere in the existing criminal justice system. The exercise of discretion in interpreting the legislative mandate is necessary because no legislature has succeeded in formulating a substantive criminal code which clearly encompasses all conduct intended to be made criminal and which clearly excludes all other conduct. Poor draftsmanship and a failure to revise the criminal law to eliminate obsolete provisions have contributed to existing ambiguities. However, even where care has been taken, it has not been possible to draft substantive provisions which are entirely free from ambiguity. This is a result not only of limitations upon the effectiveness of language but also of the inability of a legislature to envisage all of the day-to-day law enforcement problems which may arise.

Even more important is the fact that not enough financial resources are allocated to make possible enforcement of all the laws against all offenders. The legislative body responsible for granting appropriations makes a general decision as to how much it is willing to pay for law enforcement, but usually provides no guidance as to how this sum is to be expended.

Allocation of resources to enforcement agencies is ordinarily decided by a municipal legislative body, while the criminal law is defined by the state legislature, which often leaves the administrator subject to conflicting legislative mandates. The same conflict occurs when the state legislature appropriates money to a state police unit, since the crime-defining and budget decisions are essentially unrelated even within the same unit of government. Because of the obvious dilemma created by limited resources and lack of established priorities for enforcement, the necessity of discretionary enforcement on this basis has received some recognition. Yet there are no suggested principles to guide the exercise of such discretion.

Finally, the exercise of discretion seems necessary in the current criminal justice system for reasons unrelated to either the interpretation of criminal statutes or the allocation of available enforcement resources. This is because of the special circumstances of the individual case, particularly the characteristics of the individual offender which "differentiate him from other offenders in personality, character, sociocultural background, the motivations of his crime, and his particular potentialities for reform or recidivism." The infinite variety of individual circumstances complicates administration by mere application of rules. Justice Charles D. Breitel, who has had extensive administrative, legislative, and judicial experience, stresses this point:

If every policeman, every prosecutor, every court, and every post-sentence agency performed his or its responsibility in strict accordance with rules of law, precisely and narrowly laid down, the criminal law would be ordered but intolerable.

Individualized treatment of an offender, based upon the circumstances of the particular case, is well recognized at the sentencing stage, where discretion is provided. These same circumstances may be apparent at the arrest stage and may seem to the police to dictate that the criminal process not be invoked against a particular offender. While sentence discretion is widely recognized, arrest discretion is not. This may reflect an assumption that, while individual circumstances may justify mitigation, the individualization of criminal justice should never go so far as to result in the complete exoneration of a particular offender. The contrary view is that the individual circumstances sometimes make conviction and even arrest excessive, so that proper administration requires the exercise of discretion at the early as well as at subsequent stages in the process.

It has been traditional to give explicit recognition to the propriety of discretion on the part of the prosecutor and either to deny or, more commonly, to ignore the issue of police discretion. To some extent this attitude is based upon an assumption that the prosecutor is qualified to exercise discretion while the average police agency is not. This may result from the fact that the prosecutor has ordinarily been better educated than most police officers and, unlike most police, is directly responsible to the electorate.

The effect upon traditional attitudes of assumptions about the comparative competence of the prosecutor and the police is difficult to assess. Different educational requirements may be the result rather than the cause of the different attitudes about their respective responsibilities. There is, however, reason to believe that the assumption that the average municipal police agency lacks any special competence to make policy decisions is an important current factor. For example, the United States Supreme Court held it proper for the Federal Trade Commission to follow a policy of proceeding criminally against only major violators because there were insufficient resources to proceed against all violators. This kind of judgment was said to be within the expertness of the enforcement agency, which is familiar with the economic problems being dealt with. Under similar circumstances, a Philadelphia court held an identical policy of the Philadelphia Police Commissioner to be improper. The Philadelphia court gave no indication that it believed that the police commissioner was particularly qualified to decide how best to allocate the limited enforcement resources made available to him.

Although it is theoretically possible to have a system in which all discretion is exercised by the prosecutor, this would be difficult, perhaps impossible, to implement in practice. There are a number of alternatives:

(a) The police could make no arrests until the matter had been reviewed by the prosecutor. Referrals often are made in doubtful cases, but the feasibility of doing so is limited by the need to make an immediate arrest in some cases and the fact that prior consultation in all cases would place a considerably greater strain on police resources than does the current practice.

(b) The police could arrest all violators, leaving to the prosecutor the responsibility for exercising discretion when he decides whether to charge the suspect. Carried to its extreme, this would require the police to construe all criminal statutes liberally, leaving it to the prosecutor to decide whether ambiguity ought to be resolved in favor of prosecution or release. As a consequence, more persons would be arrested and later determined not to have violated the statute than is the case under current practice. The police would thus be liable for damages, at least in theory, because current tort law seems clearly to hold the officer liable for any mistake in the determination of the meaning of a criminal statute. The imposition on the persons arrested would be great, particularly in cases where arrest in itself is damaging to reputation. To the extent that such a practice would require more arrests to be made, it would necessitate the allocation of greater resources to law enforcement, an expense which municipalities would probably not be willing to incur for the purpose of eliminating police discretion.

(c) Police could confine their decisions to policies made known in advance by the prosecutor and courts. The formulation of self-executing policies presents the same kind of difficulty as is presented by the effort to draft self-executing statutes. The range of individual variations is so great that it is difficult to deal with all of them in a brief verbal formulation. If the policy statements are elaborate, police training would need to be greatly improved to communicate effectively these statements to the individual officer. Most important, perhaps, is the fact that the prosecutor's policies may not adequately take account of limited police resources, particularly since the prosecutor, a county officer, is not directly concerned with the fiscal policies of the cities in the country, upon which most police departments in the area must rely for their support .

4. The Right of Silence

American society has a long tradition of limiting police powers that began with the Bill of Rights. One example is that most of us would not condone physical abuse as a method of obtaining confessions regardless of the suspected offense.

But what of the use of psychological pressure? Is it unfair, for example, to hire an actor to identify the suspect and accuse him of a serious crime in order to increase the likelihood that he will confess?

Confessions and resulting guilty pleas are reported to be obtained for nearly 90 percent of those convicted in court. In 1964, however, the United States Supreme Court ruled in the case of Escobedo v. Illinois *that defendants were entitled to lawyers in the police station, as well as the courtroom, because most suspects were unaware of their right of silence as guaranteed in Article 5 of the Constitution. This ruling generated a good deal of controversy because many persons (especially police officials) thought it would seriously hamper the control of crime, whereas others saw it as giving reality to a right that already existed.*

Two years later the Supreme Court granted certiorari, that is, the right of appeal, to the case of Miranda v. Arizona, *in an effort to further specify the limits of police discretion regarding the interrogation of suspects. In the latter part of these brief selections from the lengthy Miranda decision, Chief Justice Earl Warren quotes from police training manuals in an effort to clearly specify why many current practices will henceforth be regarded as a violation of the suspect's constitutional rights.*

The cases before us raise questions which go to the roots of our concepts of American criminal jurisprudence: the restraints society must observe consistent with the Federal Constitution in prosecuting individuals for crime. More specifically, we deal with the admissibility of statements obtained from an individual who is subjected to custodial police interrogation

From "Miranda v. Arizona," **United States Supreme Court Reports,** Vol. 384 (Washington, D.C.: U.S. Government Printing Office, 1966).

and the necessity for procedures which assure that the individual is accorded his privilege under the Fifth Amendment to the Constitution not to be compelled to incriminate himself.

We dealt with certain phases of this problem recently in *Escobedo v. Illinois,* 378 U.S. 478 (1964). There, as in the four cases before us, law enforcement officials took the defendant into custody and interrogated him in a police station for the purpose of obtaining a confession. The police did not effectively advise him of his right to remain silent or of his right to consult with his attorney. Rather, they confronted him with an alleged accomplice who accused him of having perpetrated a murder. When the defendant denied the accusation and said "I didn't shoot Manuel, you did it," they handcuffed him and took him to an interrogation room. There, while handcuffed and standing, he was questioned for four hours until he confessed. During this interrogation, the police denied his request to speak to his attorney, and they prevented his retained attorney, who had come to the police station, from consulting with him. At his trial, the State, over his objection, introduced the confession against him. We held that the statements thus made were constitutionally inadmissable.

This case has been the subject of judicial interpretation and spirited legal debate since it was decided two years ago. Both state and federal courts, in assessing its implications, have arrived at varying conclusions. A wealth of scholarly material has been written tracing its ramifications and underpinnings. Police and prosecutor have speculated on its range and desirability. We granted certiorari in these cases, 382 U.S. 924, 925, 937, in order further to explore some facets of the problems, thus exposed, of applying the privilege against self-incrimination to in-custody interrogation, and to give concrete constitutional guidelines for law enforcement agencies and courts to follow.

We start here, as we did in *Escobedo,* with the premise that our holding is not an innovation in our jurisprudence, but is an application of principles long recognized and applied in other settings. We have undertaken a thorough re-examination of the *Escobedo* decision and the principles it announced, and we reaffirm it. That case was but an explication of basic rights that are enshrined in our Constitution—that "No person . . . shall be compelled in any criminal case to be a witness against himself," and that the "the accused shall . . . have the Assistance of Counsel"—rights which were put in jeopardy in that case through official overbearing. These precious rights were fixed in our Constitution only after centuries of persecution and struggle. And in the words of Chief Justice Marshall, they were secured "for ages to come and . . . designed to approach immortality as nearly as human institutions can approach it," *Cohens v. Virginia,* 6 Wheat. 264, 387 (1821).

Over 70 years ago, our predecessors on this Court eloquently stated:

The maxim nemo tenetur seipsum accusare *had its origin in a protest against the inquisitorial and manifestly unjust methods of interrogating accused per-*

sons, which has long obtained in the continental system, and, until the expulsion of the Stuarts from the British throne in 1688, and the erection of additional barriers for the protection of the people against the exercise of arbitrary power, was not uncommon even in England. While the admissions or confessions of the prisoner, when voluntarily and freely made, have always ranked high in the scale of incriminating evidence, if an accused person be asked to explain his apparent connection with a crime under investigation, the ease with which the questions put to him may assume an inquisitorial character, the temptation to press the witness unduly, to browbeat him if he be timid or reluctant, to push him into a corner, and to entrap him into fatal contradictions, which is so painfully evidenced in many of these earlier state trials, notably in those of Sir Nicholas Throckmorton, and Udal, the Puritan minister, made the system so odious as to give rise to a demand for its total abolition. The change in the English criminal procedure in that particular seems to be founded upon no statute and no judicial opinion, but upon a general and silent acquiescence of the courts in a popular demand. But, however adopted, it has become firmly embedded in English, as well as in American jurisprudence. So deeply did the inequities of the ancient system impress themselves upon the minds of the American colonists that the States, with one accord, made a denial of the right to question an accused person a part of their fundamental law, so that a maxim, which in England was a mere rule of evidence, became clothed in this country with the impregnability of a constitutional enactment. Brown v. Walker, *161 U.S. 591, 596–597* (*1896*).

. . .

Our holding will be spelled out with some specificity in the pages which follow but briefly stated it is this: the prosecution may not use statements, whether exculpatory or inculpatory, stemming from custodial interrogation of the defendant unless it demonstrates the use of procedural safeguards effective to secure the privilege against self-incrimination. By custodial interrogation, we mean questioning initiated by law enforcement officers after a person has been taken into custody or otherwise deprived of his freedom of action in any significant way. As for the procedural safeguards to be employed, unless other fully effective means are devised to inform accused persons of their right of silence and to assure a continuous opportunity to exercise it, the following measures are required. Prior to any questioning, the person must be warned that he has a right to remain silent, that any statement he does make may be used as evidence against him, and that he has a right to the presence of an attorney, either retained or appointed. The defendant may waive effectuation of these rights, provided the waiver is made voluntarily, knowingly and intelligently. If, however, he indicates in any manner and at any stage of the process that he wishes to consult with an attorney before speaking there can be no questioning. Likewise, if the individual is alone and indicates in any manner that he does not wish to be interrogated, the police may not question him. The mere fact that he may have answered some questions or volunteered some statements on his own does not deprive him of the right to refrain from answering any further inquiries until he has consulted with an attorney and thereafter consents to be questioned.

. . .

Again we stress that the modern practice of in-custody interrogation is psychologically rather than physically oriented. As we have stated before, "Since *Chambers v. Florida,* 309 U.S. 227, this Court has recognized that coercion can be mental as well as physical, and that the blood of the accused is not the only hallmark of an unconstitutional inquisition." *Blackburn v. Alabama,* 361 U.S. 199, 206 (1960). Interrogation still takes place in privacy. Privacy results in secrecy and this in turn results in a gap in our knowledge as to what in fact goes on in the interrogation rooms. A valuable source of information about present police practices, however, may be found in various police manuals and texts which document procedures employed with success in the past, and which recommend various other effective tactics. These texts are used by law enforcement agencies themselves as guides. It should be noted that these texts professedly present the most enlightened and effective means presently used to obtain statements through custodial interrogation. By considering these texts and other data, it is possible to describe procedures observed and noted around the country.

The officers are told by the manuals that the "principal psychological factor contributing to a successful interrogation is *privacy*—being alone with the person under interrogation." The efficacy of this tactic has been explained as follows:

If at all practicable, the interrogation should take place in the investigator's office or at least in a room of his own choice. The subject should be deprived of every psychological advantage. In his own home he may be confident, indignant, or recalcitrant. He is more keenly aware of his rights and more reluctant to tell of his indiscretions of criminal behavior within the walls of his own home. Moreover his family and other friends are nearby, their presence lending moral support. In his own office, the investigator possesses all the advantages. The atmosphere suggests the invincibility of the forces of the law.

To highlight the isolation and unfamiliar surroundings, the manuals instruct the police to display an air of confidence in the suspect's guilt and from outward appearance to maintain only an interest in confirming certain details. The guilt of the subject is to be posited as a fact. The interrogator should direct his comments toward the reasons why the subject committed the act, rather than to court failure by asking the subject whether he did it. Like other men, perhaps the subject has had a bad family life, had an unhappy childhood, had too much to drink, had an unrequited attraction to women. The officers are instructed to minimize the moral seriousness of the offense, to cast blame on the victim or on society. These tactics are designed to put the subject in a psychological state where his story is but an elaboration of what the police purport to know already—that he is guilty. Explanations to the contrary are dismissed and discouraged.

The texts thus stress that the major qualities an interrogator should possess are patience and perseverance. One writer described the efficacy of these characteristics in this manner:

In the preceding paragraphs emphasis has been placed on kindness and stratagems. The investigator will, however, encounter many situations where the sheer weight of his personality will be the deciding factor. Where emotional appeals and tricks are employed to no avail, he must rely on an oppressive atmosphere of dogged persistence. He must interrogate steadily and without relent, leaving the subject no prospect of surcease. He must dominate his subject and overwhelm him with his inexorable will to obtain the truth. He should interrogate for a spell of several hours pausing only for the subject's necessities in acknowledgment of the need to avoid a charge of duress that can be technically substantiated. In a serious case, the interrogation may continue for days, with the required intervals for food and sleep, but with no respite from the atmosphere of domination. It is possible in this way to induce the subject to talk without resorting to duress or coercion. This method should be used only when the guilt of the subject appears highly probable.

The manuals suggest that the suspect be offered legal excuses for his actions in order to obtain an initial admission of guilt. Where there is a suspected revenge-killing, for example, the interrogator may say:

Joe, you probably didn't go out looking for this fellow with the purpose of shooting him. My guess is, however, that you expected something from him and that's why you carried a gun—for your own protection. You knew him for what he was, no good. Then when you met him he probably started using foul, abusive language and he gave some indication that he was about to pull a gun on you, and that's when you had to act to save your own life. That's about it, isn't it, Joe?

Having then obtained the admission of shooting, the interrogator is advised to refer to circumstantial evidence which negates the self-defense explanation. This should enable him to secure the entire story. One text notes that "Even if he fails to do so, the inconsistency between the subject's original denial of the shooting and his present admission of at least doing the shooting will serve to deprive him of a self-defense 'out' at the time of trial."

When the techniques described above prove unavailing, the texts recommend they be alternated with a show of some hostility. One ploy often used has been termed the "friendly-unfriendly" or the "Mutt and Jeff" act:

. . . In this technique, two agents are employed, Mutt, the relentless investigator, who knows the subject is guilty and is not going to waste any time. He's sent a dozen men away for this crime and he's going to send the subject away for the full term. Jeff, on the other hand, is obviously a kindhearted man. He has a family himself. He has a brother who was involved in a little scrape like

this. He disapproves of Mutt and his tactics and will arrange to get him off the case if the subject will cooperate. He can't hold Mutt off for very long. The subject would be wise to make a quick decision. The technique is applied by having both investigators present while Mutt acts out his role. Jeff may stand by quietly and demur at some of Mutt's tactics. When Jeff makes his plea for co-operation, Mutt is not present in the room.

The interrogators sometimes are instructed to induce a confession out of trickery. The technique here is quite effective in crimes which require identification or which run in series. In the identification situation, the interrogator may take a break in his questioning to place the subject among a group of men in a line-up. "The witness or complainant (previously coached, if necessary) studies the line-up and confidently points out the subject as the guilty party." Then the questioning resumes "as though there were now no doubt about the guilt of the subject." A variation on this technique is called the "reverse line-up":

The accused is placed in a line-up, but this time he is identified by several fictitious witnesses or victims who associated him with different offenses. It is expected that the subject will become desperate and confess to the offense under investigation in order to escape from the false accusations.

The manuals also contain instructions for police on how to handle the individual who refuses to discuss the matter entirely, or who asks for an attorney or relatives. The examiner is to concede him the right to remain silent. "This usually has a very undermining effect. First of all, he is disappointed in his expectation of an unfavorable reaction on the part of the interrogator. Secondly, a concession of this right to remain silent impresses the subject with the apparent fairness of his interrogator." After this psychological conditioning, however, the officer is told to point out the incriminating significance of the suspect's refusal to talk:

Joe, you have a right to remain silent. That's your privilege and I'm the last person in the world who'll try to take it away from you. If that's the way you want to leave this, O.K. But let me ask you this. Suppose you were in my shoes and I were in yours and you called me in to ask me about this and I told you, "I don't want to answer any of your questions." You'd think I had something to hide, and you'd probably be right in thinking that. That's exactly what I'll have to think about you, and so will everybody else. So let's sit here and talk this whole thing over.

Few will persist in their initial refusals to talk, it is said, if this monologue is employed correctly.

In the event that the subject wishes to speak to a relative or an attorney, the following advice is tendered:

[T]he interrogator should respond by suggesting the subject first tell the truth to the interrogator himself rather than get anyone else involved in the matter. If the request is for an attorney, the interrogator may suggest that the subject save

himself or his family the expense of any such professional service, particularly if he is innocent of the offense under investigation. The interrogator may also add, "Joe, I'm only looking for the truth, and if you're telling the truth, that's it. You can handle this by yourself."

From these representative samples of interrogation techniques, the setting prescribed by the manuals and observed in practice becomes clear. In essence, it is this: To be alone with the subject is essential to prevent distraction and to deprive him of any outside support. The aura of confidence in his guilt undermines his will to resist. He merely confirms the preconceived story the police seek to have him describe. Patience and persistence, at times relentless questioning, are employed. To obtain a confession, the interrogator must "patiently maneuver himself or his quarry into a position from which the desired object may be obtained." When normal procedures fail to produce the needed result, the police may resort to deceptive stratagems such as giving false legal advice. It is important to keep the subject off balance, for example, by trading on his insecurity about himself or his surroundings. The police then persuade, trick, or cajole him out of exercising his constitutional rights.

Even without employing brutality, the "third degree" or the specific stratagems described above, the very fact of custodial interrogation exacts a heavy toll on individual liberty and trades on the weakness of individuals. This fact may be illustrated simply by referring to three confession cases decided by this Court in the Term immediately preceding our *Escobedo* decision. In *Townsend v. Sain,* 372 U.S. 293 (1963), the defendant was a 19-year-old heroin addict, described as a "near mental defective," *id.,* at 307–310. The defendant in *Lynumn v. Illinois,* 372 U.S. 528 (1963), was a woman who confessed to the arresting officer after being importuned to "cooperate" in order to prevent her children from being taken by relief authorities. This Court similarly reversed the conviction of a defendant in *Haynes v. Washington,* 373 U.S. 503 (1963), whose persistent request during his interrogation was to phone his wife or attorney. In other settings, these individuals might have exercised their constitutional rights. In the incommunicado police-dominated atmosphere, they succumbed.

. . .

In order fully to apprise a person interrogated of the extent of his rights under this system then, it is necessary to warn him not only that he has the right to consult with an attorney, but also that if he is indigent a lawyer will be appointed to represent him. Without this additional warning, the admonition of the right to consult with counsel would often be understood as meaning only that he can consult with a lawyer if he has one or has the funds to obtain one. The warning of a right to counsel would be hollow if not couched in terms that would convey to the indigent—the person most often subjected to interrogation—the knowledge that he too has a right to have counsel present. As with the warnings of the right to remain silent and of the general right to counsel, only by effective and express explanation to the indigent of this right can there be assurance that he was truly in a position to exercise it.

Once warnings have been given, the subsequent procedure is clear. If the individual indicates in any manner, at any time prior to or during questioning, that he wishes to remain silent, the interrogation must cease. At this point he has shown that he intends to exercise his Fifth Amendment privilege; any statement taken after the person invokes his privilege cannot be other than the product of compulsion, subtle or otherwise. Without the right to cut off questioning, the setting of in-custody interrogation operates on the individual to overcome free choice in producing a statement after the privilege has been once invoked. If the individual states that he wants an attorney, the interrogation must cease until an attorney is present. At that time, the individual must have an opportunity to confer with the attorney and to have him present during any subsequent questioning. If the individual cannot obtain an attorney and he indicates that he wants one before speaking to police, they must respect his decision to remain silent.

. . .

To summarize, we hold that when an individual is taken into custody or otherwise deprived of his freedom by the authorities and is subjected to questioning, the privilege against self-incrimination is jeopardized. Procedural safeguards must be employed to protect the privilege, and unless other fully effective means are adopted to notify the person of his right of silence and to assure that the exercise of the right will be scrupulously honored, the following measures are required. He must be warned prior to any questioning that he has the right to remain silent, that anything he says can be used against him in a court of law, that he has the right to the presence of an attorney, and that if he cannot afford an attorney one will be appointed for him prior to any questioning if he so desires. Opportunity to exercise these rights must be afforded to him throughout the interrogation. After such warnings have been given, and such opportunity afforded him, the individual may knowingly and intelligently waive these rights and agree to answer questions or make a statement. But unless and until such warnings and waiver are demonstrated by the prosecution at trial, no evidence obtained as a result of interrogation can be used against him. [Many of the quotations in this decision are from Fred Edward Inbau and John E. Reid, *Criminal Interrogations and Confessions* (Baltimore: Williams and Wilkins, 1962).]

5. Cost and Effectiveness

The police act within a set of constraints established through their relationships with other legal and social structures. But, in addition to establishing constraints for police, other parts of society may also furnish mechanisms by which police effectiveness might be improved. For example, what has come to be called systems analysis and cost-effectiveness techniques were first applied in large manufacturing organizations and then in the reorganization of the Department of Defense. Some writers have argued that these modern administrative tools, developed for other organizations, might be used to greatly increase the effectiveness of the police.

The report of the Space-General Corporation describes an application of systems analysis to California's Agencies of Criminal Justice. However, the benefit of the application of these methods to the crime problem has yet to be demonstrated; and, although the idea appears promising on paper, rather obvious conclusions are apt to be presented as significant breakthroughs.

Under contract to the State of California through the Youth and Adult Corrections Agency, Space-General Corporation has undertaken a systems analysis and cost/effectiveness study of the California system of criminal justice. Of six-months duration, this study represents the initial attempt to apply the techniques of systems engineering to the problems of crime and delinquency. The study was defined to cover the broad spectrum of criminal justice, including local law enforcement, the courts, probation, juvenile and adult institutions, and parole.

One disclosure of the analysis was in the area of crime statistics. Upon reviewing all aspects of the statistics from the past five years, it became apparent that a substantial percentage of the committed group were between the ages of 14 and 29 years. It was reasonable then, in an attempt to learn as much as possible about the phenomenon of crime, to form a new

From Space-General Corporation, **Final Report, Prevention and Control of Crime and Delinquency** (El Monte, Calif.: Space-General Corporation, 1965). Reprinted by permission.

crime rate statistic based not upon the total population, but upon the population in this age group. The result of this analysis was a relatively constant crime rate for both juvenile and adult groups over the past five years. This was true in spite of the fact that the 14 to 29 age group in the overall population had increased by more than 35 percent. If the crime rate calculated in this way remains constant over the next ten years, the number of crimes will show an increase in that time of 55 percent. In fact, from 1960 to 1975, this crime susceptible age group in California is expected to increase 110 percent, almost twice the expected 60% increase of the total population. Crime is indeed increasing faster than is population, but primarily as a result in the increase in the number of members of the crime susceptible age group.

One of the new findings emerging from this study was the introduction of the concept of "career costs." These costs represent the total costs of the entire system required to process an average offender over his entire lifetime. Using mathematical modeling techniques and computer solutions it has been possible to calculate the career costs of offenders in several crime and delinquency categories. Examination of some of these career costs shows what appear to be startling discrepancies between system expenditures and the seriousness of the offense. For example, the analysis indicated that the average cost of an adult homicide offender is $5,800 while that of a forgery and check offender is $16,900.

Another new development achieved by use of the computer simulation was the calculation of the cost/effectiveness of system policies or other operating conditions. An analysis was made of the effect on the total system cost of changing the values of certain relevant conditions, as sentence length, parole violation rate, and others.

The study has also resulted in an increased understanding of the interrelations existing between the functions of various jurisdictions. For example, an analytic model was used to show that the rate of parole violation should increase (and was also used to predict the magnitude of the increase) as the relative use of probation increases. Another analysis showed that the average inmate behavior in prisons will deteriorate over a period of time, due to the continued selection for parole of those inmates who exhibit acceptable behavior.

There presently exists a lack of information which must be overcome if complete understanding of the objectives and operations of the system of criminal justice is to be achieved. This lack is in the understanding of relations existing between system expenditures and system performance. It is primarily because of this gap in our knowledge that certain programs are being proposed. In a sense, we do not accurately know how to allocate resources to reduce crime.

California now spends about $600 million per year for the prevention and control of crime and delinquency, combining state and local costs. The program which is recommended here will require an estimated annual expenditure of less than three percent of that amount. Cost offsets expected to occur over the duration of the program will reduce the total cost to the state at the end of five years to less than that required for the continuation of present policy.

6. Some Immediate Steps

Although new administrative methods, such as systems analysis, might help in the future reorganization of the police, are there any specific things that can be done now?

The President's Commission on Law Enforcement and Administration of Justice listed many recommendations, but let us consider four that have the possibility of immediate application. First, technology is currently available that could be used to improve alarm systems and public callboxes so that crimes could be reported more rapidly. Second, simple standardization of a single police telephone number would increase reporting speed. Third, so-called simulation studies—which have proved to be effective in space flight training—could be used to improve internal police communication. Fourth, the Commission suggested that the use of nonlethal weapons might solve many of the officer's problems in apprehending suspects.

Such concrete, limited proposals are probably useful. It is important to recognize, however, that all such innovations will have to be carried out within a fundamental framework of social and legal institutions; and possible changes in these institutions, as well as minor additions, need to be considered.

Devices for sounding an alert with no human intervention would have advantages both as a deterrent to criminals and in facilitating the response to an incident. Many devices are available: silver-tape electric alarms, pressure and acoustic sensors, radar, and ultrasonic, infrared, and ultraviolet beams. These devices can protect unattended premises from intrusion by detecting movement in a room or motion across a perimeter.

False alarms are a problem for any alarm system. In Washington, D.C., in 1965, 4,450 alarms were received by the police; 98 percent of them were false. Since answering each false alarm takes an average of about 30 minutes and since patrol cars tend to spend about half their time answering calls, this was approximately equivalent to full-time duty of one patrol car.

From the President's Commission on Law Enforcement and Administration of Justice, **The Challenge of Crime in a Free Society** (Washington, D.C.: U.S. Government Printing Office, 1967).

New, low-cost private alarm systems are being developed and may become widely installed. These devices can automatically send prerecorded messages directly to the police. As a consequence, the police should expect a significant increase in the number of false alarms. To prevent this increase from seriously disrupting police operations, police departments should establish minimum standards for direct-calling alarm installations. On-site inspection should be required to assure that the alarm itself is mechanically and electrically reliable (usually not a serious problem), that its installation is not subject to simple accidental failure as from blowing wind, and that it is not subject to accidental triggering by the occupants.

Various kinds of street alarm or surveillance networks have been proposed to detect crime in the streets. The proposals range from simple pushbutton alarms to sophisticated pattern-recognizing devices that detect cries of "help." Other sensors include closed-circuit TV cameras (fed to a console at the police station), simple microphones, and magnetic sensors triggered by specially coded devices carried by individuals. To explore these suggestions, the task force has examined several system designs. The automatic systems cost over $1 million per square mile, far too much for most communities. Furthermore, they may pose an insoluble false-alarm problem and so are not recommended. Accessible street emergency communication facilities, discussed below, can serve many of the same functions, and can be developed much more readily.

The apprehension process can respond only after it gets a call, and a number of things can be done to modify existing street communications equipment to make it easier for a victim or a witness to reach the police.

The victim of a robber careful enough to steal the last dime cannot now use the public telephone. Public telephones can be adapted so that the operator can be reached without using money, as was demonstrated in a recent test in Hartford, Conn. The Bell Telephone System is now planning to extend this capability widely.

Most major cities have a network of police callboxes that are usually inconspicuous and locked. Washington, D.C., has 920 such boxes, or about one every one-fourth mile. During World War II these boxes were painted red, white, and blue, and made available to the public in case of air raids and other emergencies.

The Commission recommends:

Police callboxes should be designated "public emergency callboxes," should be better marked and lighted, and should be left unlocked.

The false-alarm rate for such callboxes would probably be far less than from a mechanical alarm, since a potential prankster would have to reveal his voice. While experience with a police callbox may not turn out to be fully comparable, one metropolitan fire department estimates the false alarm rate for calls received over the telephone to be less than 3 percent, far less than the false-alarm rate for an automatic or a mechanically-actuated alarm.

In trying to call the police from an ordinary telephone, a person may be bewildered by the many police jurisdictions and the various telephone numbers associated with them. In the Los Angeles area alone, there are 50 different telephone numbers that reach police departments within Los Angeles County. It should be possible to have a single telephone number to reach the police directly. England has such a universal emergency number.

The Commission recommends:

Wherever practical, a single police telephone number should be established, at least within a metropolitan area and eventually over the entire United States, comparable to the telephone company's long-distance information number.

This is difficult but feasible with existing telephone switching centers; it appears practical with the new electronic switching systems being installed by the Bell System, and should be incorporated. In the interim, telephone companies should print on each telephone number disc the number of the police department serving that telephone's location.

Once a call reaches the police, the facts must be sent to the police officers who will respond. This linkage occurs in the police communications center, which performs what the military calls the command-and-control function. Military analysts have given extensive attention to this function.

The communications center's role has increased as the telephone has become the common access to the police, and as more police officers have been equipped with radios. Even though the communications center is the nerve center controlling the minute-by-minute deployment of the police force, it has received surprisingly little attention. It is often squeezed into a spare corner of police headquarters under the command of a sergeant or a patrolman. It operates with obsolete or poorly designed equipment and procedures that have tended to evolve by chance rather than through careful design. A notable exception in Chicago, which invested $2 million in modernizing its center in 1961.

When a person calls the police, a complaint clerk takes the call, decides on the police reaction and its priority, passes the information to a radio dispatcher who then dispatches a car. This gathering, evaluating, and disseminating of information normally takes from 1 to 5 minutes, and occupies 20–50 percent of the total response time. It can take much longer during periods of intense congestion.

Even before considering major new technology, improving such simple aspects of command and control as floor layouts, design of headsets and microphones, and location of control switches and time stamps can improve a center's performance under heavy load. In some centers, the same person serves as the complaint clerk and the dispatcher; in others, the functions are separated. Some centers have a dispatcher handling part of a city; others have several dispatchers all handling calls for the whole city. Such differences, which can affect performance significantly under critical loads, have evidently evolved more from tradition and physical restrictions than as the result of planning. Each of the different possible configurations can be experimentally measured, both in operating centers and under laboratory control in a simulation laboratory. In this manner, standard and emergency plans and procedures can be tested, decision rules can be evaluated, and training and experience can be provided police officers under simulated extreme conditions.

In a riot or other general emergency, the communications center must transform a police department from a loose collection of independent units to a cohesive, co-ordinated force. Means must be provided to collect and display, rapidly and continuously, all the varieties of tactical intelligence relating to the location of events and the disposition of forces. The communications center staff must be headed by a commander who can assimilate this information and who has the authority to command the available forces. Contingency plans for situations that might arise must be developed and stored in a readily accessible form. These plans can be tested in a simulation laboratory.

. . .

A patrol officer, in meeting the diverse criminal situations he must face, has a limited range of weaponry—either the short-range nightstick or the potentially lethal handgun. If an officer feels that his life is threatened, he may have to shoot, with the attendant risk that the suspect or innocent bystanders may be killed. If a suitable nonlethal weapon were made available, it could supplement the officer's present arsenal and possibly serve as a replacement for the handgun.

In the past 100 years, 180 New York City policemen have been killed while apprehending suspects. A study of these 180 cases revealed that in every instance the combat range was 21 feet or less and that in most cases it was 10 feet or less. Since 1960, 96 percent of the murders of police officers have been with firearms, and of those 78 percent were with handguns. Thus, in most emergency situations, the officer does not have an opportunity to make a careful weapon selection—nonlethal or lethal—and he should have the services of one weapon or a combined weapon. The weapon should be immediately available and ready for instant use.

For a nonlethal weapon to be an acceptable replacement for a handgun, it must incapacitate its victim at least as fast as a gun. Even then there might be opposition to it. A criminal knowing that he cannot be killed might act more aggressively than he would facing a gun.

The qualities that must be sought in a general purpose nonlethal weapon are almost immediate incapacitation and little risk of permanent injury to the individual who is the target. Survey of a wide range of possibilities leads to the conclusion that these requirements are incompatible with current technology. For example, darts have been used to inject tranquilizing drugs into animals. However, the drugs presently available offer too great a risk, because of the close correspondence between the dose required to incapacitate quickly and a lethal dose. No nonlethal weapon is presently available that could serve as a replacement for the handgun, but a continuing effort to achieve such a weapon should be pursued. In this connection the products of military research should be continually examined for possible applicability.

When a nonlethal weapon is considered as a supplement to the policeman's gun, the requirements for immediate incapacitation can be relaxed. Supplemental nonlethal weapons, such as tear gas or CS gas dispensers in various forms, might be used in circumstances in which an officer's life was not threatened, but it would be necessary for police departments to set careful guidelines specifying the circumstances under which they could be used. Evaluation of public reaction to the use of various nonlethal weapons under various circumstances would be an essential part of research into this subject.

2 THE COURTS

When the general public pictures the courtroom in his mind, he is likely to conjure up an image of verbal combat and impassioned speeches. The picture, however, is somewhat misleading—it is largely based on the drama of trials by jury that actually account for only a small portion of the criminal court's time. Most defendants plead guilty, often on the basis of negotiations with the prosecuting attorney as described by Donald Newman in his selection.

If this were not true, our criminal courts would be even more overcrowded than they are at the present time. A jury trial can be a long, involved business because our legal system has painstakingly created a body of rules and procedures that pursues two goals—the punishment of the guilty and *the protection of the innocent.*

There are those writers who feel that the criminal court today is grossly ineffective as it goes about its dual tasks; others, more kindly disposed, argue that we are doing the best that can be done in the complicated effort to secure justice. Both would probably agree, however, that there is one aspect of the criminal court that sorely needs improvement—namely, the procedure of sentencing, which is all too apt to remain a hit-or-miss affair.

1. Off with Their Heads

To the layman, courtroom procedures sometimes seem unduly complex and as likely to subvert the truth as to secure it. One hundred years ago this was perhaps even more true than it is today, for procedural rules had reached a peak of elaboration. Lewis Carroll expressed an ironical view that adults as well as children could appreciate.

The twelve jurors were all writing very busily on slates. "What are they doing?" Alice whispered to the Gryphon. "They ca'n't have anything to put down yet, before the trial's begun."

"They're putting down their names," the Gryphon whispered in reply, "for fear they should forget them before the end of the trial."

"Stupid things!" Alice began in a loud indignant voice; but she stopped herself hastily, for the White Rabbit cried out "Silence in the court!" and the King put on his spectacles and looked anxiously round, to make out who was talking.

Alice could see, as well as if she were looking over their shoulders, that all the jurors were writing down "stupid things!" on their slates, and she could even make out that one of them didn't know how to spell "stupid," and that he had to ask his neighbour to tell him. "A nice muddle their slates'll be in, before the trial's over!" thought Alice.

. . .

"Let the jury consider their verdict," the King said, for about the twentieth time that day.

"No, no!" said the Queen. "Sentence first—verdict afterwards."

"Stuff and nonsense!" said Alice loudly. "The idea of having the sentence first!"

"Hold your tongue!" said the Queen, turning purple.

"I won't!" said Alice.

"Off with her head!" the Queen shouted at the top of her voice. Nobody moved.

"Who cares for *you?*" said Alice (she had grown to her full size by this time). "You're nothing but a pack of cards!"

From Lewis Carroll, **The Complete Works of Lewis Carroll** (New York: Random House, n.d.). Reprinted by permission.

2. Guilty or Not Guilty

There are many defendants, we would suppose, who wish that they too could grow like Alice in Wonderland and disperse the court like a pack of cards. But the rules of evidence, the assigned roles of the prosecuting attorney and the defense attorney, and the procedures of examination and cross-examination are all designed, in theory, to further the search for the truth, the whole truth, and nothing but the truth. The following selection is a television script from a series designed to inform the public on the workings of the court. The case is a hypothetical one, but it still gives us a fair view of what happens in the courtroom.

At or about 10:00 P.M. on August 12, 1948, George Winters and Arthur Hoffman were standing at the bar and drinking at Finnegan's Tavern in Philadelphia. They had been there, drinking steadily, since about 8:30 P.M.

Winters and Hoffman, who had known each other for several years and who had served together in the Army overseas, were discussing their wartime experiences. The discussion turned to the morality of the European women whom the men had met during the tour of foreign duty. Hoffman, who was obviously showing the effects of his liquor, stated that in his opinion European women were a loose and immoral lot, far more so, in fact, than American women. Winters, relatively sober, disagreed, declaring that women were the same the world over. An argument ensued, growing increasingly more bitter. In the heat of the argument, Winters said, "The trouble with you, Hoffman, is that when you were overseas the only kind of woman that you ever looked for was the loose and easy kind. You never looked for the decent kind. That's why you have such a low opinion of them."

Enraged at Winters' remark, Hoffman lunged drunkenly at Winters and attempted to strike him. Hoffman was restrained by a number of men at the bar and was ordered by O'Leary, the bartender, to leave the Tavern immediately. Hoffman obeyed, but as he was going out the door, he turned and shook his fist in Winters' direction, stating, "It's a good thing those guys were there to help you. Next time I catch you alone though you had better watch out. If I ever get you alone, they'll put you away in a pine box."

Shortly thereafter Winters left the Tavern and went home.

On the day following, at about 7:00 P.M., Winters was walking alone along Grays Ferry Avenue, between 30th and 31st Streets. The sky was overcast and a light drizzle was falling. As Winters was walking along, he glanced up and saw, in the light of a street light, Hoffman walking toward him. At about the same time Winters saw Hoffman look up in his direction and immediately reach with his right hand toward his back pocket. Winters, as he stated later, fearful that Hoffman was reaching for a gun, instantly drew a gun from his own pocket and shot and killed Hoffman, who was about thirty feet away.

It subsequently developed that Hoffman was unarmed and was apparently reaching for a handkerchief in the right rear pocket of his trousers.

The shooting was witnessed by Charles Hawley who happened to be walking along Grays Ferry Avenue, about twenty-five feet behind Winters.

Immediately after the shooting, Winters turned himself in at the police station and announced that he had shot and killed Hoffman, but stated that he had done so in self-defense and that he had been afraid that Hoffman was about to carry out his threat of the preceding evening.

Winters was subsequently indicted for the murder of Arthur Hoffman.

. . .

As the trial is about to begin, the jury, the attorneys, and all the participants are in their respective places. The Judge enters and the Crier opens Court, after which the Judge calls the case of the Commonwealth v. Winters.

JUDGE: Gentlemen, are you ready in the case of Commonwealth v. Winters?

BOTH ATTYS: Yes, your Honor.

JUDGE: Very well, you may proceed.

The District Attorney makes his opening address to the jury, at the conclusion of which he asks for a verdict of first degree murder, with the penalty fixed at death.

The District Attorney calls his first witness, Dr. Wadsworth, to the stand and he is sworn.

SPEISER: Dr. Wadsworth, you are the Coroner's physician, are you not?

WADSWORTH: Yes.

SPEISER: In your official capacity did you examine the body of Arthur Hoffman, the deceased in this case?

WADSWORTH: Yes.

SPEISER: Where and when did you make the examination?

WADSWORTH: At the Philadelphia County morgue at about 10:30 P.M. on August 13, 1948.

SPEISER: In the presence of whom, if anyone?

WADSWORTH: In the presence of Alice Hoffman, the widow, and Albert Ricci, a friend of the deceased.

SPEISER: Did Mrs. Hoffman and Mr. Ricci identify the body of the deceased as that of Arthur Hoffman?

WADSWORTH: Yes.

SPEISER: Dr. Wadsworth, did you conduct a post mortem on the body of Arthur Hoffman?

WADSWORTH: Yes.

SPEISER: What did you determine to be the cause of death?

WADSWORTH: A gunshot wound of the chest. The bullet entered the body between the seventh and eighth ribs on the left side and pierced the left ventricle of the heart.

SPEISER (*Advancing to witness stand*): Dr. Wadsworth, I show you this spent bullet and ask if you can identify it.

MCBRIDE (*Rising and addressing the court*): If the Court please, the defendant concedes that Hoffman's death was caused by a bullet fired from defendant's gun.

SPEISER (*Returning to his table*): Very well, I have no further questions.

MCBRIDE: No cross-examination.

Dr. Wadsworth leaves the stand and resumes his place in the courtroom. Mr. Speiser calls his next witness, Charles Hawley, who takes the stand and is sworn.

SPEISER: Mr. Hawley, where were you on August 13, 1948, at about 7:00 P.M.

HAWLEY: I was walking east on Grays Ferry Avenue, on the south side between 31st and 32nd Streets.

SPEISER: Tell us what, if anything, you noticed.

HAWLEY: Well, as I was walking along, I noticed this fellow—(*Nodding toward Winters.*)—walking ahead of me. I was looking straight ahead, not paying much attention to anything in particular, when I saw Winters suddenly reach into his raincoat pocket, pull out a gun and shoot down the street.

SPEISER: Could you see at what he was shooting?

HAWLEY: Yes. Just as I saw him pull the gun, I noticed another fellow walking toward us. He was the fellow that Winters was going to shoot. I yelled to stop him, but he didn't pay any attention to me.

MCBRIDE: I object to the witness testifying as to what he did. The answer is not responsive, it's immaterial, and I move that it be stricken out.

JUDGE: Objection sustained. (*Turning to Hawley.*) Just answer the questions.

SPEISER: You testified that Winters was wearing a raincoat. Was it raining?

HAWLEY: It was sort of drizzling.

SPEISER: Was it raining so hard that it was difficult to make out Hoffman's features?

MCBRIDE: Objection.

JUDGE: Overruled.

HAWLEY: Yes, it was.

SPEISER: Did you see Hoffman just before he was shot?

HAWLEY: Yes, sir.

SPEISER: Where was he at that time with respect to the nearest street lamp?

HAWLEY: He was just under a light.

SPEISER: At the time of the shooting, where was Winters with respect to the nearest street light?

HAWLEY: Well, as best I can remember, he was about forty feet away from Hoffman—that would be pretty near just in the middle, in the dark space between two lights.

SPEISER: In view of the fact that Winters was in the dark space, would you say that he could be seen or recognized by Hoffman?

MCBRIDE: Objection.

JUDGE: Sustained.

SPEISER: Cross-examine.

MCBRIDE: When you saw Hoffman, he was under the street lamp and you could see him pretty well, couldn't you?

HAWLEY: Yes, sir.

MCBRIDE: And at that time Winters was a lot closer to Hoffman than you were, wasn't he?

HAWLEY: Well, he was about twenty or thirty feet in front of me—Winters, that is—so I guess he was pretty much closer.

MCBRIDE: Now, when you saw Hoffman, you saw him reach into the back pocket of his pants, is that correct?

HAWLEY: Yes, with his right hand, reaching into the back pocket of his pants.

MCBRIDE: As though he were reaching to pull something from that pocket?

HAWLEY: Yes, sir.

MCBRIDE: That's all.

SPEISER: That is the Commonwealth's case, your Honor.

The Defense Attorney makes his initial address to the jury and calls his first witness, Albert Ricci, who takes the stand and is sworn.

MCBRIDE: Mr. Ricci, you were a friend of Arthur Hoffman, the deceased in this case?

RICCI: Yes, sir.

MCBRIDE: How long had you known him?

RICCI: Ever since we were kids. Art and I grew up together and went to the same schools, through high school, that is. Lots of times before he got married we used to go out on double dates or maybe we'd just go out and drink a few beers. I guess Art was just about my best friend. We even enlisted together back in 1942, but we got separated in the Army—he got shipped to E.T.O. and I was out in the Pacific.

McBride: Mr. Ricci, you were with Winters and Hoffman on August 12, 1948, weren't you?

Ricci: Yes, sir.

McBride: You were at the taproom with them.

Ricci: Yes, sir.

McBride: Did Hoffman threaten to kill Winters next time he saw him?

Ricci: I heard Art say something about their putting George in a pine box, but Art had been drinking and—

McBride (*Interrupting*): Please just answer my questions. You did hear Hoffman threaten Winters, did you not?

Ricci: If you call that a threat, yes.

McBride: Prior to that threat, did you see or hear Winters do anything to provoke such a threat?

Ricci: No, sir.

McBride: Cross-examine.

Speiser: You say that you knew Arthur Hoffman for years and that you would occasionally drink with him. Did he ever get drunk?

Ricci: Well, I don't know that you'd exactly call it drunk. But sometimes he'd get to feeling his drinks.

Speiser: Was the defendant Winters ever with you and Hoffman on any of those occasions?

Ricci: Sure. The three of us would go out together lots of times, before Art got married.

Speiser: When Hoffman was feeling his drinks, how would he act?

Ricci: Different ways. Sometimes he'd be awfully funny, giving imitations and singing and things. Other times he'd sort of get belligerent and threaten to punch people in the nose.

Speiser: Did he ever threaten you?

McBride: I object. That question is completely irrelevant to the question of whether Hoffman threatened the life of this defendant.

Speiser: I am trying to show that these so-called threats were not threats at all, as Winters knew, and that he had no ground for fearing his life was in danger.

Judge: I'll overrule the objection provided the Commonwealth shows that the threats were made in Winters' presence.

Speiser: Very well.

Judge (*To Mr. McBride*): And grant an exception to defendant.

Speiser: Did Hoffman ever threaten you?

Ricci: Yes, often.

Speiser: In Winters' presence?

Ricci: Sure, lots of times. (*Talking rapidly.*) Listen, I can tell you lots about that—Art was always talking like that when he'd been drinking, making threats, I mean, and we all took it like a joke. He didn't mean nothing by it. And if Winters tries to tell you that he was scared—

MCBRIDE (*Jumping to his feet*): I object to that uncalled-for speech by the witness and I move that it be stricken from the record and the jury instructed to disregard it.

JUDGE: Sustained. And I will so instruct the jury. (*To Ricci.*) Hereafter just answer the question that is asked you and don't give way to such an outburst again.

RICCI: Yes, sir.

SPEISER: Did Hoffman ever carry out any of his so-called threats?

RICCI: Not that I knew of.

SPEISER: That's all.

MCBRIDE: You testified that Hoffman was a peaceful person, I believe?

RICCI: That's right.

MCBRIDE: And that his threats to punch people in the nose and so forth were regarded as sort of a joke?

RICCI: That's right.

MCBRIDE: But you never heard him threaten to kill anyone except Winters, did you?

RICCI: No.

MCBRIDE: And you wouldn't regard a threat like that as a joke, would you?

RICCI: No, sir.

SPEISER: Objection.

MCBRIDE: No further questions.

Mr. McBride calls George Winters to the stand, where he is sworn.

MCBRIDE: Mr. Winters, you're the defendant in this case, are you not?

WINTERS: Yes, sir.

MCBRIDE: You don't deny that you fired the shot that killed Arthur Hoffman, do you?

WINTERS: No, sir, I don't.

MCBRIDE: Why did you shoot Hoffman?

WINTERS: I was afraid he was going to kill me if I didn't shoot him first. You see, just the day before he threatened to kill me the next time he saw me.

MCBRIDE: Will you please tell us the circumstances leading up to and surrounding the threat?

WINTERS: Well the night before, August 12 that would be, Art and I went to a taproom for a few beers. We got there about 8:30 P.M. After we'd been drinking there for an hour or so we got to talking about our wartime experiences. We talked about this and that and then we got to reminding each other of some of the women we'd known overseas. Art said he thought all European women were an immoral bunch and that he'd never met a decent one. I told him he was all wrong and that he got that idea just because the only girls he ever looked for over there were the immoral ones. I guess that got him mad because he jumped at me and tried to poke me.

MCBRIDE: Did you do or say anything to Hoffman, other than what you've just told us, to provoke that assault?

WINTERS: No, sir. That was all there was to it.

MCBRIDE: As Hoffman attempted to strike you, did you hit back at him?

WINTERS: Of course not. I'd seen Art like that before, so I just kind of leaned away from him and some fellows at the bar held his arms.

MCBRIDE: What happened after that?

WINTERS: Well, the bartender told Art to get out of the taproom, and as he started to go he turned around and shook his fist at me and said something like, "It's lucky for you that those guys stopped me, but next time I see you they'll put you away in a pine box."

MCBRIDE: What did you understand by that remark?

WINTERS: That Art would kill me next time he saw me.

MCBRIDE: Had he ever threatened you in that manner before.

WINTERS: No, sir. He never said anything like that before.

MCBRIDE: What was your reaction to that threat?

SPEISER: Objection. The question is too vague and irrelevant.

JUDGE: Overruled.

MCBRIDE: Will you please answer the question.

WINTERS: Well, first I was surprised, 'cause I'd never seen Art like that before. Then I began to worry. You see, I was with Art in Normandy and I knew he was pretty quick with a gun. So that's why I decided to carry a gun with me next day, just in case Art wasn't kidding. That's why I had the gun with me.

MCBRIDE: Did you always carry a gun?

WINTERS: No.

MCBRIDE: Now will you please tell us the events leading up to the shooting.

WINTERS: Well, the next evening, August 13, I was walking along Grays Ferry Avenue, heading east between 30th and 31st Streets. It was about seven o'clock and kind of drizzly. I happened to look up and there was Art about thirty to forty feet away walking toward me. As I looked up I saw him look up, and then I saw him reach for his rear trouser pocket. I got panicky. I remembered what he'd said the night before and I was scared he was going to shoot me, so I pulled out my gun and shot him first. Later on I found out that he didn't have a gun with him, but only a handkerchief in his pocket. But I thought he was going to kill me.

MCBRIDE: After you shot Hoffman what did you do.

WINTERS: I went to the police station and gave myself up.

MCBRIDE: Cross-examine.

SPEISER: Mr. Winters, did you know whether Hoffman usually carried a gun?

WINTERS (*After a pause*): Yes, he did.

SPEISER: What kind of a gun was it?

WINTERS (*Again pausing*): I don't know, I never saw it but I guess he carried one.

SPEISER: Then when you just said that you knew Hoffman carried a gun you weren't telling the truth, were you?

WINTERS: I guess he carried one.

SPEISER: When you first saw Hoffman walking toward you, he was under a street lamp, wasn't he?

WINTERS: Yes, sir.

SPEISER: And you were in the darker or shadowed portion of the sidewalk?

WINTERS: Yes, sir.

SPEISER: So that although you could see Hoffman, it's quite possible that he couldn't see you?

MCBRIDE: I object to that question. He can't testify to what Hoffman could or couldn't see.

JUDGE: Objection sustained.

SPEISER: You testified that when Hoffman lunged at you in the taproom you weren't particularly afraid. That you'd seen him like that before.

WINTERS: I guess that was why.

SPEISER: And you knew that he didn't mean the things he did or said while he was drinking, didn't you?

WINTERS (*After a pause*): I don't know what I thought. I just know that I wasn't particularly scared when he hit at me, but I was scared next day when I thought he was going to shoot me.

SPEISER: But you knew that Hoffman used to get belligerent when he'd been drinking.

WINTERS: Sometimes, yes.

SPEISER: And sometimes he'd threaten to punch people, or knock them down, or make them wish they'd never been born, didn't he?

WINTERS: Yes, sir.

SPEISER: In fact, he sometimes threatened you like that.

WINTERS: Sometimes he did.

SPEISER: But he never carried out any of those threats, did he?

WINTERS: No, sir.

SPEISER: So that you weren't particularly worried by them, were you?

WINTERS: Not until he threatened me that last time.

SPEISER: By the way, Hoffman was married, wasn't he?

WINTERS: Yes, sir.

SPEISER: When did he marry?

WINTERS: A couple of months after he got out of the service. He married Alice on September 8, 1946.

SPEISER: You remember the date pretty well, don't you? (*No answer.*)

Before Hoffman was married, you used to have dates with Alice, didn't you?

WINTERS: A few times, yes.

SPEISER: And as a matter of fact you were in love with Alice Hoffman, and in August, 1946, you asked her to marry you, didn't you?

MCBRIDE: I object to that as irrelevant.

JUDGE: It might be relevant on the question of motive. Objection overruled.

SPEISER: Now please answer the question, Mr. Winters.

WINTERS (*In a low voice*): Yes.

SPEISER: You still love her, don't you? (*No answer.*) And you hated the thought of her being married to a man with Hoffman's views of women, didn't you? (*Long pause, no answer.*) No further questions.

MCBRIDE: Did your feeling toward Alice have anything to do with this shooting?

WINTERS: No, sir.

MCBRIDE: That's all. The defense rests.

JUDGE: Very well, gentlemen, you may go to the jury.

The attorneys deliver their summations to the jury. If there are to be only two speeches, the Defense Attorney speaks first and then the District Attorney. After the last speech the Judge delivers his charge and the jury thereupon retires to deliberate. When a verdict has been reached, the jury returns to the jury box.

CRIER: Members of the jury, have you agreed upon a verdict?

FOREMAN: We have.

CRIER: Prisoner, rise. (*Winters stands.*) The jury will stand during the rendition of the verdict. Prisoner, look upon the jury. Jurors, look upon the prisoner. How say you, guilty or not guilty?

FOREMAN: We find the prisoner . . .

If the prisoner is acquitted the Crier adjourns Court. If he is guilty, his attorney asks that sentence be deferred, and the request is granted. Court is then adjourned.

Comment

This case involves the question of self-defense. If a killing is committed in defense of one's life, it is not murder or any other crime. If the killing is committed in the reasonable but mistaken belief that one's life is being threatened, the killing is not a crime. If the killing is done in the mistaken belief that the killer's life is threatened, but there is no reasonable ground for the belief, the killing is manslaughter. If the killing is intentional and without any real belief in danger, the killing is murder. These are the issues involved here. The defense contends that Winters had reasonable grounds to believe that Hoffman was going to kill him. The Commonwealth contends that Winters killed Hoffman out of malice and frustrated love for Alice Hoffman, and that in any event he had no basis for killing, that his life was not in danger.

3. A Meeting of Adversaries

How successful is the court in its attempt to discover the truth? Could a jury tell from the information in the preceding selection whether Winters was innocent or guilty? David Dressler argues that the task is almost impossible under our present system of "trial by combat." The major fault lies in turning lawyers into adversaries rather than making them impartial seekers after truth, and he suggests some changes.

The average criminal trial, said the late Judge Jerome Frank, is a "sublimated brawl." A decade ago, few of Judge Frank's colleagues bothered to defend their profession when he made the charge in his crusading book, *Courts on Trial;* today many progressive lawyers and judges are battling for the very reforms he championed, and in some Federal and state courts the ancient rituals are changing. But even now in the United States, despite our prevailing respect for the scientific search for truth, trial techniques are as unscientific as an appendectomy performed with a tomahawk. With the sensational Finch murder trial in court for the *third* time in California, the law is still "a ass, a idiot," as Mr. Bumble put it—if not worse.

Unfortunately for advocates of reform, most lawyers are proud of this instance of cultural lag. Our so-called adversary theory against which judge Frank inveighed sets the rules of trial procedure. It stems from medieval trial by combat and is basic both to English common law and to American legal codes. In the old days accuser and accused met on the field of battle and had at each other with sword or lance. If the accused fell, he was guilty. If the accuser died, that proved he didn't have a just cause to begin with. Thus was "truth" revealed.

Today, instead of fighting with lethal weapons, we use legal arguments. Where combatants formerly met face to face, they now have surrogates—attorneys—who fight for them. The judge acts as referee, theoretically protecting the contenders against foul blows. The jury decides which "side" fought the better fight. But fight it is and the object is to win, not necessarily to reveal the truth.

The heart of the adversary system—and the source of many of the evils which the reforms now in progress aim to eliminate—is "surprise," a tech-

Dressler, David, "Trial by Combat in American Courts," **Harper's Magazine**, CCXXII (April, 1961), 31–36.

nique which some lawyers call "trial from ambush." The intent of surprise is to time a sudden blow so as to throw the opposition off balance and overwhelm it before it can recover.

An example of a successful surprise is the following: A Chicago attorney, Luis Kutner, was in Federal Court defending William Henderson, who had been charged with piracy on the high seas. Henderson had boarded a sight-seeing motor launch operating on Lake Michigan and, when it left its moorings, pulled a pistol and robbed the passengers. At trial, thirty erstwhile passengers positively identified the defendant as their assailant. Kutner cross-examined diffidently, as if his cause were hopeless. He presented no evidence on his own, and listened respectfully as United States Attorney Al Bosworth summed up and rested his case, by which time Henderson's guilt was plain as a wart.

Then Kutner addressed Judge James H. Wilkerson: "Your Honor, the defense moves for a directed verdict of acquittal, on grounds this court lacks competent jurisdiction." Under Federal law, counsel pointed out, the port of registry of a vessel determines jurisdiction. "The boat in question is registered out of Milwaukee. Chicago is therefore not the venue of the crime."

The judge ordered acquittal.

Now, as he told me in an interview, Kutner knew all along that the case belonged in a Milwaukee court. He could have moved for change of venue before the trial opened in Chicago. Instead, he let it run its course. He allowed the prosecution to rest its case, confident it had won. Then he sprang his trap. In the eyes of the law, Kutner's conduct was entirely ethical. Under the adversary theory he was an advocate, which is to say he was obliged to be strictly partisan. As a partisan, he was entitled to use surprise.

Tongue in cheek, attorneys insist that the adversary system guarantees revelation of all facts bearing on an issue, and so it furthers the scientific method in trial practice. A lawyer buried beneath a mountain of books in the Los Angeles County Law Library told me, "I am here seeking the matter that will win a certain action. My opponent is here, too, with the same purpose. I search with fervor and frenzy. Nothing favorable to my position will escape me. The same is true of my opponent, dammit! He and I will search and together we will bring in facts so plain that even a jury of potato peelers and peanut vendors will understand them."

Maybe. But when I headed the New York State Division of Parole, I had been in and out of courts for seventeen years and most of the time I felt those potato peelers and peanut vendors were licked. They would not get at the truth because it lay hidden behind a curtain of flimflam and obfuscation. Each attorney was out to help his side and his side only, at almost any cost. Each wanted the jury to believe that he and he alone was the bearer of the Holy Grail, while his opponent was a knave out to suppress the truth. Each witness swore he was telling nothing but the truth, even when his story was directly contrary to what a witness for the other side swore was true. No witness was permitted to tell all he knew, although under oath to tell "the whole truth." No witness could tell what he did tell in his own way. The attorney on his side suggested by his questions what the witness should say. In cross-examination the opposing lawyer tried to trap him into saying something else. Each counselor hoped to cajole the jury into disregarding everything the other lawyer or witnesses said. The net outcome, all too often, probably was that the talesmen agreed with the wag who said that cases are decided only "according to the preponderance of the perjury." They voted for the side that seemed to tell fewer lies.

Juries might get at the truth if counsel researched cases scientifically. When two research men investigate causes of cancer they make a hypothesis and check it with an open mind. They may pursue different courses but they clear their findings with each other.

Not so in criminal trial practice. According to the late eminent attorney, Charles P. Curtis, the counsel who sets out to build evidence "will waste a lot of time if he goes with an open mind." Unlike a scientist, he will not sit down with his opposite number and say, "Here is what I found. What did you find? We are both after the same thing—truth. What can we agree on, in the interest of justice?" Instead, he squirrels away his evidence, citations, and arguments—his putative "facts"—hoping his opponent will be overwhelmed by them in the courtroom.

An attorney told a Bar Association audience: "Of course surprise elements should be hoarded. Your opponent should not be educated as to matters concerning which you believe he is still in the dark. Obviously, the traps should not be uncovered. Indeed, you may cast a few more leaves over them so that your adversary will step more boldly on the low ground believing it is solid."

The leaves over the low ground are yellowed pages of musty law books containing ancient trial decisions, which serve as precedents. Precedents are hallowed. What was good enough for great-great-grandpappy is all the better today because it is aged-in-the-book. The contemporary counselor who has a talent for digging these vintage morsels becomes a scholar in the law, highly respected and extravagantly paid. More important, he gains an advantage. The older a precedent, the less likely it is his adversary will find it, too. In court, before an amused jury, the opposing lawyer is trapped and the victory may go to the legal scholar.

What makes such tactics more deplorable is that the precedents often fail to go to the heart of a matter. They award a decision, not on the essence of a case—that is, whether the defendant is guilty or not—but more frequently on mere technicality. If, as happened in one Florida case, the judge simply has to leave the bench to answer the call of nature while counsel is summing up for the jury, the opposing lawyer will make no demur. He has an early precedent up his sleeve that holds if a judge has to go, the trial should be recessed, even though all the evidence is in and only summation is in progress. Then, if the verdict is against his side, the lawyer will jostle the precedent loose and demand a new trial.

There are literally hundreds of thousands of technicalities that have won cases in the past. Many of them are contradictory. The lawyer who can't find the special one that fits his case had better turn in his diploma.

In one case, the advocate found just what he needed to defend his client, a North Carolinian who had fired across the state line and killed a man in Tennessee. When North Carolina attempted to charge him, the attorney cried foul. The act, he pointed out, was completed in Tennessee, and the law requires a man be tried where the act was completed. North Carolina had to agree. Tennessee then tried to extradite the killer as a fugitive from justice. Impossible, counsel fumed. Since his client had never been in Tennessee how could he be a fugitive from that state? Tennessee gave up. Thus, remarks Roscoe Pound, dean of legal philosophers, "The state which had him could not try him, while the state which could try him did not have him and could not get him."

If, by amazing mischance, a counselor finds no precedent, *circa* 1800, to prove his case, he might try another form of surprise, the hit-run tactic. He may fire an improper question at a witness, knowing it must be withdrawn. It will be expunged from the record but not from the recollection of the jurors.

When the Teamsters' president James R. Hoffa was tried for bribery in 1957, his attorney, Edward Bennett Williams, was content to have eight Negroes on the jury. I was an observer in the court and saw John Cye Cheasty, a prosecution witness, come up for cross-examination. Out of a clear sky, Williams asked him if he had not once been engaged by a bus line to investigate the National Association for the Advancement of Colored People during a Florida labor dispute.

The horrified prosecutor jumped to his feet, protesting that the question was altogether immaterial to the matter at issue. The judge sustained the objection and ordered the jury to disregard the question—one of many neat legal fictions is that jurors can forget what they have heard. Actually, the damage was done. It seems reasonable to assume that at least eight veniremen considered Cheasty's testimony as the biased mouthings of an enemy of labor and minorities.

Soon after, another dramatic surprise staggered the prosecution. Ex-champion Joe Louis sauntered into the courtroom, put an arm around Hoffa, and explained to newsmen, "I just came over to say hello to my friend Jimmy." Acquittal for the friend of the oppressed followed.

While in the Hoffa case surprise benefited the defense in court, the prosecution usually has a distinct advantage in preparing certain surprises before trial. For example, the findings of the police laboratory are available to it, rarely to the defense.

In one Los Angeles case, a defendant charged with murder convinced his attorney he was absolutely innocent. Although some attorneys consider it their duty to defend guilty clients, and the canons of the bar hold that this is the one way to assure that mitigating circumstances will be put before a jury, this particular attorney prefers not to handle such cases. He feels he cannot win unless he goes into court convinced in his own mind he is defending an innocent man. At trial, the state produced a police witness who testified he photographed the latent print of the palm of a hand, found on the window sill over which the slayer climbed to gain entrance. The print was the defendant's. Had defense been apprised of this before trial, it might have prepared a better argument in favor even of a guilty client. Taken by surprise, it surrendered the decision to the prosecution. Almost certainly a guilty man was convicted in this instance, but it is our theory that even a guilty man is entitled to the best possible defense.

A case which is still moot as this is written offers another illustration, this time in a situation where we do not know whether the defendant was guilty or innocent. In the first trial early last year of Dr. R. Bernard Finch and Carole Tregoff Pappa for the murder of the physician's wife, the district attorney let Dr. Finch, called by the defense, testify to details of the fatal struggle. He alleged his wife came at him with a gun, he seized it in self-defense and it was accidentally discharged, killing Mrs. Finch. Thereupon the prosecutor on the seventy-first day of the trial brought in tape recordings of an interview between the physician and police shortly after his arrest. On the tape, Dr. Finch gave testimony directly contrary to what he had just given on the stand. Neither the accused nor his counsel knew the interview was recorded. The prosecutor had hoarded the tapes for just such a purpose. It would seem that if a trial is intended to discover truth, both sides should have known of the existence of the tapes. Each side would insist that the truth ought to be brought into court. How could it hurt, then, to reveal it before the trial?

Nevertheless, when I asked a Los Angeles police official whether police findings should not be shared with the defense, he replied, "Do the Dodgers give the Giants their signals?" No, but human beings are not baseballs, trials are not baseball games, and the stakes are not pennants. The liberty and perhaps the life of a defendant is at stake in every criminal trial. Police science should be employed in the interest of truth and justice, not to win a battle for one side.

Because adversary methods sanction a battle of wits rather than a search for truth, a few leaders in the law have become restive. They know that we have at hand methods of finding evidence scientifically, that trials can be made more truthful and just than they usually are at present. Largely as a result of their efforts, the American Bar Association has at long last instituted reforms in the adversary method, though much more remains to be done. The first attack was on surprise. To minimize the unfairness and inefficiency of this technique, the American Bar Association produced what it calls "discovery."

Judge Frank likened surprise to a cat-and-mouse game. He thought the mouse should at least have "a peek at the cat's claws." That peek is now provided by discovery. This is, in essence, legal machinery by which one side is required to inform the other, in advance of trial or sufficiently in advance during trial, that certain evidence will be introduced. Forewarned, the other side has time to prepare its case.

As far back as 1848, England provided a first step in discovery. By changes in procedure, the prosecution was obliged to place before a magistrate all the evidence it planned to produce at trial. The defense was to be present and thus would have the information and could prepare adequately. The U.S. waited almost a century to follow suit. But in 1946, Federal Courts began operating under revised Rules of Criminal Procedure, developed under the sponsorship of the American Bar Association. For the first time, some discovery was officially sanctioned in criminal cases before Federal tribunals. Under the new Rules, defense may move, and the court order, that the Government shall show to the defendant's counsel specific documents and tangible objects material to preparation of the case for the accused.

Suppose John Smith is charged with kidnaping a child in violation of Federal statutes. The father is to be the principal Government witness. He has given the United States Attorney a sworn statement that the kidnaper sent him a ransom note. The note itself is in the prosecutor's possession. Defense counsel goes before a Federal judge, in the presence of the U.S. Attorney, and asks to see the statement. He also wants a photostat of the ransom note, so the handwriting may be compared with his client's.

The requested data would be essential to a reasonable defense in this instance, and would probably be furnished. This would not always be the case. It is not the purpose of discovery to facilitate "fishing expeditions" that will give away the Government's case in each and every respect. The buckshot approach to discovery will not be permitted. Counsel must satisfy the judge that the requested information is material to building a defense and that denial would place the defendant in an untenable position at trial. Only then will discovery be ordered.

Because it is and undoubtedly should remain discretionary with the court, discovery was rarely granted in the first decade under the revised Rules. Beginning about the late 1950s Federal Courts became more liberal, but even now discovery is the exception rather than the rule.

But the trend has begun. The American Law Institute has stimulated the states to follow the Federal example. California, Delaware, Florida, Maryland, Michigan, New Jersey, and Ohio have enacted statutes authorizing some degree of discovery, and in the past several years the effects are being felt in state courts. In the majority of jurisdictions the prosecution must provide the defense with a list of its witnesses. In some states the substance of the expected testimony must also be revealed before trial.

Most discovery is in the interest of the defense, since it is the prosecution that brings the charge and believes it has evidence to sustain it. But some disclosure favors the prosecution. In several states the defense is required to notify the prosecutor when it plans to plead not guilty by virtue of insanity. Michigan, Arizona, Ohio, Kansas, Wisconsin, require that the prosecution be notified if the defense claims an alibi.

The disclosure of alibi was required by law even before 1946 in at least one state—Ohio. Its value is illustrated by the case of "Roaring Bill" Potter, a politician murdered in Cleveland. Racketeer Hymie Martin was arrested in Pittsburgh for the offense, and extradited. He would have escaped conviction but for the Ohio law which specified that the defendant must give three days' notice of a proposed alibi. County Prosecutor Ray T. Miller, was so notified and, checking, learned that at the extradition hearing in Pittsburgh, Martin's attorney brought witnesses who swore the accused was in that city when Potter was murdered. The testimony apparently failed to convince.

At the trial in Cleveland, the same attorney presented different witnesses who testified Martin was in Akron the day of the murder. All the County Prosecutor had to do was place in evidence the testimony given at the extradition hearing. Since the defendant could not have been in Pittsburgh and Akron simultaneously, the conflict was obvious. The credibility of the alibi was destroyed and Martin was convicted.

Does discovery make it harder to convict the guilty? Not so, says Maryland's Supreme Court. "We are not impressed by the fear. . . . It apparently has not had that effect."

Professor Abraham S. Goldstein, of Yale Law School, in an article prepared for *The Yale Law Journal* this winter, suggests a safeguard if it be feared that discovery will tip the balance to the side of the defense. In return for discovery the accused could be required to waive immunity from self-incrimination. He could be required to take the stand. That would give the prosecution an opportunity for its own discovery, direct from the man who, by the prosecution's presumption, knows most about the crime. Professor Goldstein holds the law could be so written as not to conflict with the Constitutional guarantee that a defendant may not be forced to testify against himself.

The trend toward discovery is impressive but as yet limited. It continues to meet with resistance by a majority of attorneys. Professor W. T. Morgan, of Harvard Law School, has explained why: "Some of the finest legal minds today are anxious for revolutionary changes in procedure, but they are as voices crying in the wilderness compared to the great unleavened mass of lawyers who are abundantly satisfied with things as they are. With even a slight modification of procedure in civil and criminal cases the

United States could dispense with half her lawyers. The average citizen, therefore, need not expect the legal profession to commit hari-kari."

It will take an entirely new generation of lawyers, trained in a loftier philosophy, to bring a more effective justice into our courts. Most attorneys today come from law schools that imbue them with the theory of winning decisions at almost any cost. They have been taught to use not only surprise but every other questionable advantage which a complacent judge, himself a product of such schools, will allow.

Logic argues that a witness belongs to neither side. He should mount the stand to tell what he knows, whatever the outcome. But budding lawyers study textbooks that teach them to consider witnesses either "friendly" or "hostile." According to such texts, the hostile witness is an outsider and, as Charles P. Curtis says in *The Ethics of Advocacy,* "A lawyer is required to treat outsiders as if they were barbarians and enemies."

Is the hostile witness honest but egotistic? One text advises the cross-examiner he might "deftly tempt the witness to indulge in his propensity for exaggeration, so as to make him 'hang himself.' " A truthful but irascible fellow? "Make him lose his temper and seem spiteful." One recent text by Lewis W. Lake has a section titled "How to Humiliate and Subdue a Recalcitrant Witness." Not a dishonest witness, mind you, but merely one who is recalcitrant, meaning he won't go along with the cross-examiner. The neophyte is instructed:

When you have forced the witness into giving you a direct answer to your question you really have him under control; he is off-balance, and usually rather scared. This advantage should be followed up with a few simple questions such as, "You did not want to answer that question, did you?" If the witness says that he wanted to answer it, ask him in a resounding voice, "Well, why did you not answer it when I first asked you?" Whatever his anwer is you then ask him, "Did you think that you were smart enough to evade answering the question?" Again, whatever the answer is you ask him, "Well, I would like for the jurors to know what you have behind all this dodging and ducking you have done." . . . This battering and legal-style "kicking the witness around" not only humiliates but subdues him.

We have barely emerged from the era of the self-made lawyer, who needed only a mail-order law book and a fireplace in front of which to study. That was good enough in Abe Lincoln's day, but we can do better today. This is an age of specialization, but one in which we believe the specifics of professional practice should be superimposed on a foundation of general education. Yet over half of today's attorneys are trained in the law without learning to understand the society for which law is created. They do not have college degrees. The majority attended schools of a type which a Columbia University dean called "vocational bargain basements." An investigator for the American Bar Association reported in 1954 that of nine law schools he inspected, six "showed no impact of the modern world whatsoever."

But a measure of improvement is on the way. The great universities now require a liberal art base for the law degree. They teach law as an institution of society, as a philosophy, a science and a craft. When enough of their students have been graduated, law will be practiced with a sense of responsibility for the ethics of modern life. At any rate, there is a chance that lawyers will accept the obligation to make law serve society.

A Daumier print shows a lawyer arguing in court. Nearby sit a woman and child. The caption reads: "He defends the widow and orphan unless he is attacking the orphan and the widow." That's trial by combat under adversary rules. We require much better in our time.

4. Mass Production

Actually, as we have pointed out, a trial is a rarity in the administration of criminal justice. Most defendants enter a plea of guilty and the major business of the criminal court is to decide what to do next. Even so, the court is very likely to be overwhelmed by the flood of cases, as described by Judge Robert Clifton. He raises the serious question of whether or not our ideals of justice can be maintained in the face of such pressure.

Superior Judge Robert Clifton, presided over the intoxication arraignment court in Los Angeles for many years. He became deeply interested in the problem of how vast numbers of cases might be handled in ways that would help reduce the burden of alcoholism on the community, and he accomplished a great deal in devising methods for individualizing the treatment of offenders while still handling enormous volume. Here is a portion of his description of the procedures in his court (which "processed" 200 to 250 persons per day, with occasional days running as high as 400):

If the defendant pleads guilty (some 95 per cent or more do plead guilty) the judge immediately fixes the fine or sentence, or in a few cases continues the case to get a report from the probation officer. The judge may summarily, or later upon getting a report, put the defendant on probation and suspend the imposition of all or part of the sentence or fine, or suspend the imposition of any sentence and place the defendant upon probation upon reasonable terms and conditions. . . .

You say, "How can one judge handle 60,000 cases a year—250 a day?" "What do you do with them?" Well, first we have the "make sheet," a teletyped report from the Police Record and Identifiction Bureau, showing the date of arrest, the date of the last previous arrest for intoxication, the number of such arrests in the past six months, and the total intoxication arrests, plus a summary of the defendant's other arrests. . . . Then we have the defendant himself, and at a glance you can have some information as to whether he is in good shape or a physical wreck or on the verge of d.t.'s; whether he is well dressed or in rags, etc. . . . All this, the make sheet, the officer's arrest report and a glance at the defendant, give a world of information before he opens his mouth. Then, if he wishes, the defendant may make a statement of matters which might affect the sentence, and in addition, of course, the court may ask questions concerning his employment, family, what steps he has taken about alcoholism, etc. [From a speech given to the Health and Hospital Committee of the Los Angeles Chamber of Commerce in 1958.]

Judge Clifton went on to describe in detail the various types of dispositions made in the cases. First offenders usually had their cases dismissed. Persons with records showing a number of arrests in recent weeks or months might be told that they have a very serious problem and put on summary probation, with the condition that they attend three meetings of Alcoholics Anonymous within 30 days. Others might be directed to a rehabilitation clinic to work out an out-patient treatment which the court would require be carried out as a condition of probation. Drunks who came off "Skid Row" might receive sentences of up to 120 days, to be spent at a rehabilitation center specially devised for such persons, who might otherwise spend most of their time in jail because of repetitive arrests.

Judge Clifton's description is eloquent testimony of the pressures imposed by mass production criminal justice on a thoughtful and conscientious magistrate. In a recent letter to the author, he made these further comments:

When you have a large number of defendants to handle, it is easy to develop techniques which could be criticized, such as: upon a defendant entering a plea of guilty, the judge could easily snap out "30 days" or some other disposition of the case and immediately call the next defendant's name while the last defendant was being hustled off, instead of asking the defendant, after his plea, about the offense. If the defendant were asked why he stole something or did something or other, and he made an explanation, this would slow down the procedure, because the next man, of course, would do the same thing, and the court in each case would have to listen to lengthy explanations beside the plea. Where there are here a large number of cases to handle, it is easy to develop a technique of quick sentences to avoid explanations. . . .

In courts where there are large numbers of cases, it is seldom that probation reports are obtained, That is, the judges sentence the prisoners without probation reports. Let me give you an example of that. I can recall very well one of our judges stating that in every drunk driving case he got a probation report. This procedure could be literally impossible in our drunk driving courts where I sat some ten years ago, when we had 65 arraignments on Monday, 50 on Tuesday, and 35 on the other days of the week. The probation officer wouldn't have time to handle many cases excepting drunk driving cases if we asked for probation reports in all cases.

These are the volume-processing techniques forced on our lower court magistrates by mass production criminal justice.

5. The Negotiated Plea

Why does an accused criminal enter a guilty plea? One large part of the answer, as Donald Newman points out, lies in the bargaining between the defendant and the prosecuting attorney, in which the defendant pleads guilty in return for a less serious charge or a lighter sentence. It is a process that undoubtedly speeds the administration of criminal law, but there are many who have qualms about such "bargain justice."

A major characteristic of criminal justice administration, particularly in jurisdictions characterized by legislatively fixed sentences, is charge reduction to elicit pleas of guilty. Not only does the efficient functioning of criminal justice rest upon a high proportion of guilty pleas, but plea bargaining is closely linked with attempts to individualize justice, to attain certain desirable conviction consequences, and to avoid undesirable ones such as "undeserved" mandatory sentences.

If, as one Michigan judge put it, "all law is compromise," then compromise in the conviction process is neither surprising nor less desirable than compromise exercised at other stages in the criminal justice process. Certainly the negotiated plea is only one of a series of discretionary decisions that characterize the administration of criminal justice. From the initial decision of whether to investigate a crime to the final decision of whether to revoke a parole, the entire administrative process rests upon discretionary choices, formally recognized or not, of men who must fit law to cases. A police officer may decide not to arrest a suspect for reasons unrecognized, perhaps, in the general legislative mandate to the police. A prosecutor may choose not to charge a suspect at all or to charge him with a crime less serious than his conduct objectively warrants in order to accomplish some end that a more accurate charge might prevent. The same process, somewhat more visible, occurs at the conviction stage when a defendant is allowed to plead guilty to a lesser offense than the one of which he is actually guilty, or where, in exchange for his plea, he is promised a less serious sentence than would otherwise be imposed.

In large part, the negotiated plea is motivated by a desire to individualize the consequences of conviction for deserving defendants. But this is not the sole reason for the practice. As the term implies, plea negotiation involves

From Donald J. Newman, **Conviction: The Determination of Guilt or Innocence Without Trial** (Boston: Little, Brown, and Company, 1966). Reprinted by permission.

an exchange of concessions and advantages between the state and the accused. The defendant who pleads guilty is treated less severely than he would be if he were convicted of the maximum charge and assessed the most severe penalty. At the same time, he waives his right to trial, thereby losing his chance, no matter how slight, for outright acquittal. The state, at the relatively small cost of charge reduction or sentence leniency, gains the numerous administrative advantages of the guilty plea over a long, costly, and always uncertain trial. In this way the negotiated plea in a real sense answers two important objectives of criminal justice administration: the individualization of justice and the maintenance of the guilty plea system.

. . .

Most criminal cases, from very serious felonies to minor, common misdemeanors, are processed through the court stages of the criminal justice system without formal contest, without the procedures of an open, adversary trial. It is fair to say that the major forms of nontrial adjudication—the guilty plea, the negotiated plea, and summary acquittal of certain guilty defendants by the trial judge—together form one of the most important processes in day-by-day criminal justice administration, and yet one that has been largely neglected in professional literature, by researchers, and by lawmaking bodies. Most informed and even general public attention has turned to the trial, particularly the jury trial, as a means of determining guilt or innocence in criminal matters. Perhaps this is as it should be: the nature and conduct of a criminal trial is vitally important in a democratic society. The philosophy, the objectives, the procedures, and the protections of the trial set standards of criminal justice administration that influence all other stages of the process from arrest to correctional treatment.

Yet this strong focus on trial has resulted in relative neglect of the other forms of adjudication. The guilty plea process, frequently occurring and of great administrative significance, has grown without much formal attention, with very little legislative or appellate court guidance. Plea bargaining, while long known to those familiar with criminal courts, has remained largely unrecognized at the legislative and appellate court levels and generally invisible to all but direct participants. Likewise the trial judge's exercise of discretion in acquitting certain of the guilty has been mainly ignored until such recent developments as the American Law Institute's Model Penal Code.

. . .

Observation of practice indicates that downgrading charges and promising lenient sentences in exchange for guilty pleas are common and are widely supported by both prosecutors and trial judges as necessary to maintain the guilty plea system. This practice of plea negotiation, while quasi-routine in certain cases, is basically an active bargaining process in which both sides, the state and the accused, make explicit concessions in order to "settle" a case without going to trial. Because the bargaining process is informal, commonly without a record of any agreements, there are often misunderstandings about whether promises were really made, and accusations by defendants of unfilled bargains and of unkept promises by the prosecutor or court. These are essentially problems of the application of plea bargaining, of the internal workings of a process that is otherwise accepted as common practice. However, a major unresolved question in regard to plea bargaining is simply whether such bartering in criminal cases is a proper form of criminal justice administration in a democratic society. This is not a question of the shortcomings of bargaining procedures but of the appropriateness of this practice even assuming that concessions are made in honorable fashion by the prosecutor or judge, the bargains are kept, and that only the actually guilty trade their pleas for leniency. Neither is this a question of unequal bargaining opportunities or of deception by failing to honor agreements or even of fear of inducing the actually innocent to plead guilty. It is instead an issue of informality versus formal and fixed procedures, of an open adversary test of guilt versus out of court settlement of criminal cases, of discretion versus full enforcement.

This practice of bargaining for guilty pleas and the basic question of its propriety are receiving increasing attention by appellate courts. A number of recent cases in which bargains have been made and kept have reached the appellate level, an unusual occurrence because, in effect, there is no truly injured party in such actions. In these cases the propriety of bargaining as a practice in and of itself has come under consideration and, although with some strong dissent, it has been upheld as proper and administratively realistic. These cases by no means provide the final answer to the question, and no doubt the propriety of this practice will be considered and reconsidered in the future.

Whatever the final outcome of the propriety question, whether plea bargaining is eventually forbidden or is given formal recognition, at present it is clearly a major characteristic of nontrial adjudication. Currently informal and sporadic, it raises a number of problems of application and consequences that deserve further attention. Charge reduction as one form of plea negotiation, for example, is directly related to the problem of sentence disparity, a matter of current concern to defendants, trial judges, and corrections personnel. Disparity has traditionally been viewed as solely a sentencing problem, yet it is apparent that downgrading at adjudication not only is closely related to sentencing differentials but is determinative of whatever disparity exists in fixed sentence jurisdictions.

Plea negotiation has consequences for correctional determinations that go beyond disparity as such. There has traditionally been a keen interest on the part of correctional personnel with sentencing practices of judges and on the part of judges with correctional programs and alternatives. Virtually no attention has been paid, however, to the relationship between post-conviction processes and adjudication practices of trial courts. Sentencing in its own right, as a joint responsibility of legislature, court, and correctional agency, has been called a "numbers game" because legislative maximum and minimum sentences can be and are commonly modified by the judge, and in turn his sentence can be and is modified by parole practices or reduced time for good behavior provisions of the law. Plea bargaining infinitely complicates this whole process, and where charge reduction is common it makes sentencing a "labeling game" as well as a manipulation of numbers. Sophisticated interpretation is needed not only for the formal sentence of an offender to determine its actual value but also for an official conviction record to determine the offender's actual criminality.

The process of plea negotiation affects both the length of correctional control and the determination of who is incarcerated and who placed on probation. To the extent that a major correctional objective is the treatment and rehabilitation of criminal offenders, the existence of plea bargaining makes the selection for major treatment alternatives and the time under correctional control a matter of skill in negotiation rather than solely a function of the treatment needs of the offender. While there is some evidence of correctional compensation for leniency or label changes as a result of negotiation, this is also largely sporadic and informal. This relationship of adjudication and correctional programs has not received much attention on the part of either correctional authorities or judges.

. . .

The exercise of discretion by agencies which apply the law is a characteristic common to all stages in the criminal justice process. This is also true at the adjudication stage, where trial judges frequently acquit certain obviously guilty defendants in an effort to individualize justice, to introduce an element of equity in what otherwise would be a quasi-automatic, unfeeling process. But discretion exercised here, as at all stages of the process, raises questions of its propriety, of its dimensions and consequences, and of controls on it.

In theory and in common expectation, the proper function of the judge in his adjudicatory capacity is to evaluate evidence of guilt or innocence, to make an impartial finding as his assessment of the evidence leads him. Here, as at the police level of the process, discretion is neither traditional nor specifically delegated as it is with the prosecutor in the charging decision, the judge at sentencing, and correctional authorities in postconviction determinations. A judge's desire to distinguish degrees of criminality and individualize the consequences of conviction is customarily provided by sentencing alternatives, by his ability to set variable lengths of incarceration or to place certain defendants on probation. In practice, however, judges commonly confront cases where guilt is clear but in which it seems to them conviction itself and any sentence whatsoever would be unduly harsh, unnecessary, or ineffective. In these cases, usually minor crimes or minor variations of more serious crimes, judges ignore evidence of guilt and order the defendants acquitted.

Judicial power to acquit in this manner is obvious; double jeopardy protections prevent appellate reversal of these cases even in those states, like Wisconsin, with a broad right of state appeal. But, in general, the practice has been viewed as inconsistent with the traditional stress on evidentiary requirements in the guilt or innocence decision, and as improper, even "reprehensible," in certain cases. There is, however, some current recognition of both the frequency and the desirability of this practice in cases of minor law violation. The American Law Institute's Model Penal Code proposes authority for the trial judge to acquit in certain cases of de minimis law infraction in spite of evidence sufficient to convict. The propriety of this practice, the basic nature of the trial judge's adjudicatory role, however, remains in dispute. Appropriate criteria for such acquittals, including the question of which types of conduct constitute de minimis violations, remain worthy of further study and analysis. Likewise the question of whether formal controls on the acquittal practices of trial courts are possible and, if so, how effective such controls can be, also deserves more attention than has been the case.

Too little is presently known about the consequences of judicial acquittal practices on other stages of the criminal justice process. On the one hand, these acquittals keep certain of the guilty, primarily those who are viewed as sick rather than criminal, from correctional agencies. In general this type of screening is supported by postconviction agencies on the grounds that the alternative of conviction and sentencing would flood correctional agencies with minor offenders, many of whom are chronically disturbed and largely untreatable. On the other hand, acquittal of the guilty in effect acts in review of prior arrest and charging decisions. Because the judge views a case with a certain perspective which is quite possibly different from that of the police and prosecutor, and yet, because he rarely adequately communicates his reasons for acquittal to these agencies or fully considers their purposes in bringing the case to court, uncertainty about the purpose of the practice is common. In some cases, acquittal is used in frank discipline of the police, but in others it in no way reflects an opinion that earlier stages were improperly handled. The difference between these is not always clear. There is no doubt, however, that in both instances repetitive acquittal of guilty defendants has an impact on both police and prosecutor practices. This points up the continuing need to view the exercise of judicial discretion in nontrial adjudication in the context of the overall criminal justice process.

. . .

A major issue in American criminal justice, still to be resolved, is the importance of counsel in nontrial adjudication, particularly in the guilty plea process. Certainly there is room for the lawyer here. There is little doubt that he can contribute to certain major objectives of the guilty plea system if he is aware of his own potential and sufficiently informed and skilled to do so. A capable defense counsel can help make the guilty plea process more accurate and fair, can assist by providing full and complete records of court proceedings, can help in achieving correctional treatment objectives, and at the same time can serve the best interests of his client by advice in regard to the plea decision and by negotiating the plea. The basic question is whether most lawyers are sufficiently aware of the importance of these contributions and sufficiently informed to carry them out.

By both traditional formal training and by public acclaim a lawyer is prepared to be an advocate at trial of a contested case. While many of the skills and most of the knowledge which make a good trial lawyer are also applicable in the guilty plea process, the ground rules are different, the client's needs are different, and some additional knowledge and skills are required for effective representation in this largely informal process. In bringing his professional competence to bear on the guilty plea decision, the attorney's knowledge of the substantive law, of defenses to criminal liability, and of evidence and standards of proof is comparable to knowledge required to go to trial. But in the case of a guilty plea, if the lawyer is to achieve maximum effectiveness he must also be familiar with informal procedures and with bargaining possibilities and avenues, must be able to explain the whole process to his client, including an accurate assessment of likely sentencing consequences, and must have awareness of the importance of records not only for immediate purposes but for the future needs of his client as well. In this respect, he must know court practices and common plea bargaining patterns. He must be familiar with sentencing structure and sentencing practices and with correctional programs, policies, and practices. In short, he must have knowledge and skills that relate the conviction process to other stages in the total system of criminal justice, to the informal, discretionary handling of cases from the prosecutor's level onward to the correctional stage.

The problem is that many lawyers lack the knowledge and skills to really make effective contributions either to their clients or to the courts and other agencies in the guilty plea system. Furthermore, the typical lawyer is commonly unaware of the range of his possible contributions once he confronts a client who neither needs nor wants a trial. A large majority of defendants are also ignorant of the facts of the process. In waiving their right to trial they usually also waive their right to counsel almost as a matter of course. As long as counsel is considered important only at trial by defendants and by lawyers themselves the contribution of the practicing bar to the nontrial system will be likely to remain minimal. Realization of the contributions lawyers can make and the skills necessary to function effectively in the guilty plea process should provide a major and important challenge to law schools and to local bar associations.

6. A Time for Change

"Let the punishment fit the crime," said Cesare Beccaria in 1764; and society, agreeing, designed neat schedules of crimes and appropriate punishments. There are many people today, however, who think that we might begin to consider the possibility of making the punishment fit the criminal, in light of our growing knowledge about human behavior. James Bennett, Director of the Federal Bureau of Prisons for twenty-five years, suggests that the time for change is now.

A quaint old custom which still prevails in the courts of England contains an interesting lesson for those who ponder all aspects of the criminal law. It seems that on certain ceremonial days the English judges carry with them as they proceed to the bench a little bouquet of gay flowers surrounded by a frill of white lace paper. Sometimes, also, just before the judge ascends the dias, flowers are strewn on the floor before him. The charming effect produced by this ceremony and by a dignified, bewigged judge tripping to the bench with what really is a corsage can well be imagined. An English wit said this custom was to "temper the severe dignity of the judges with a certain Arcadian charm." But, as a matter of fact, this bit of pageantry originated at the time when the jail at "Old Bailey" adjoined the courtroom. About 1750 a severe visitation of "gaol fever" carried off at one fell swoop a lord mayor, an alderman, several learned counsel, and two judges. The recorder of the court and other officers of the court narrowly escaped disaster. An eminent physician of that day reported that the "closeness and stench" of the jail were the causes of the disaster. He ordered that the courts be provided with bunches of rue and sweet-smelling flowers and that the prisoners be thoroughly disinfected with vinegar before being brought into court. The "posies" English judges carry even to this day as they proceed to the bench are reminders of a time when the courts tried to ward off disease by smelling nosegays of sweet flowers instead of going to the heart of the difficulty and thoroughly overhauling the criminal law and making it serve its mission.

One of the reasons for this failure to be more constructive about the ultimate objectives of the criminal law is that we persist in keeping out of sight and putting behind us such disquieting subjects. It is always something that is of no importance to the "good" people, the people who govern us, because they are confident they won't ever come in conflict with the law

From **Correctional Processes,** Bennett, I Va L. Weekly *DICTA* Compilation 73 (1949).

or go to prison. So they press a nosegay to their lips and pass by on the other side.

It is curious that the problem of crime and the understanding of the criminal has not kept pace with the growth of scientific knowledge or the seeming increase in the number of those who violate our laws. The problem grows and yet we, with all our knowledge, with all our effort, make such a slight impress upon the total problem. Certainly the time has now come for us to turn our energies and our knowledge to the solution of some of these problems which had had to stand aside while the prosecution of the war took precedence.

But now we can begin to overhaul some of the social and legal concepts which have delayed progress. Among the first to be tackled is a revision of our law school curriculum. All too much attention is paid in most law schools to the opinions of the appellate courts and the technicalities of law, and too little time and effort are spent on studying human beings and the problems that come before the courts. As has been repeatedly pointed out the concept which most people have of the law comes through the criminal courts. It is surprising to know, for instance, that one out of every six people in the District of Columbia had some contact last year either with the traffic courts, the municipal court or the district court. Most of these people, of course, do not have or need a lawyer to present their case, but it is of the utmost importance that this great grist of business be handled with understanding, dignity, and dispatch. The curriculum of law students ought to contain some clinical training in these courts so that when the day arrives that the lawyer becomes the judge he will have had some practical experience.

It is remarkable how few lawyers have anything more than the most casual acquaintanceship with the emotional and psychological forces which lie behind the behavior of the men and women and young people who come into conflict with the law. Many a lawyer becomes so engrossed in fine legal distinctions that he doesn't have time to learn how to recognize mental deviations. Few lawyers give thought to whether in fact the doctrine of free will and individual moral responsibility has any meaning today. The "law of the tooth and the claw" still has many strongholds in our thinking.

For any lawyer to try to apply the doctrine of free will to the typical psychopath who gets into court is sheer nonsense and no lawyer would do so if he knew how to recognize such an individual. The psychopath is usually an intelligent, attractive, affable, and seemingly sincere person and yet he possesses a fundamentally defective personality which is characterized by a less than normal ability to control primitive drives and to refrain from antisocial behavior. He is unable to abide by the tenets and customs of society. Thus he finds himself in continuous conflict with the law and the standards of the majority. He is seriously deficient in judgment and because he is unable to profit from past experience he repeats today an action for which he was punished yesterday. The aggressive psychopath, and especially the sexual psychopath, presents a grave threat to the peace and order of society, one substantially more serious than that presented by the frankly neurotic, psychotic or feeble-minded individual and yet legal concepts make it impossible to handle his case in a way that would fully protect the public.

And if courts and correctional institutions are fully to protect the public there must be a closer coordination. At present those who plan, administer, and apply correctional treatment have little to say concerning how much time is needed in specific cases to bring about a cure. They are in the curious position of a doctor who diagnoses a case, administers the treatment, and yet has no say as to when the patient may be discharged. No one can say how many men who have learned their lesson and are ready to return to the status of full citizens cannot be released because some judge 2 or 7 or 10 years before believed on the basis of the vague and hurried information he had, and on the basis of sometimes hasty judgment, that the defendant required a minimum of 10 or 20 or 30 years before he could be entrusted again to society. This is bad, surely, and excites our pity. But it is far worse to see a man who must be released from prison and returned to society when we know that he will again commit crime. Certainly penology has now reached a point where there are men who can select with almost unfailing accuracy the men who again will commit crime. We have data enough, for instance, to predict the future of certain sex or constitutional psychopaths. It is true that there are a great many borderline cases in which the penologists cannot predict with certainty the future behavior pattern of some of the men in their custody, but even for these they can in most cases do a better job than is now being done. And if we save one crime, one robbery or one violent death through preventing the premature release of a vicious criminal the effort would assuredly be well worthwhile.

One of the ways to see that the criminal law and legal processes more adequately fulfill their responsibilities is to change our system of sentencing. Our present sentencing procedure is ineffectual. Almost every judge of a criminal court will agree that the factors to be taken into consideration in determining the amount of time a prisoner should serve are nebulous. We have not yet decided whether men go to prison for punishment or as punishment. Nor do we know to what extent a sentence can deter others from committing crime or whether the sole purpose of the sentence is for expiation of the offense. It seems to be difficult for many judges and attorneys to recognize those criminals whose offense demands the prompt and public imposition of penal and protective custody, or those who for the good of society must be held up as an example, or those whose rehabilitation is to be the paramount consideration.

If one thinks about the paradoxes and inconsistencies of our whole criminal law and correctional processes he almost inevitably comes to the conclusion that some changes in the ordinary sentencing procedures are necessary. Many proposals have been made to change the methods by which punishment is meted out to the offender. They vary all the way from having the jury determine the exact sentence to the system that prevails in California at present where a board determines, within statutory limitations, the amount of time that a convicted offender should serve. Some 39 States have some variation of the so-called indeterminate sentence applying to one or more types of offenders. Yet the Federal system and some State systems cling to a procedure where the judge has sole responsibility for determining the length of the sentence. The Youth Correction Authority idea which has been previously explained in "Dicta" is one suggestion for providing greater flexibility for a particular type of offender. Another suggestion is that some sort of a board should either determine the sentence or advise the courts as to the length of time which a particular offender should serve. The purpose here, of course, is to permit observation and examination of the prisoner by experts and thus secure greater uniformity and consistency of sentencing in the light of the character of the criminal rather than the crime he has committed.

Another suggestion has been that the courts initially pronounce merely a tentative sentence which would become the maximum and after examination of the defendants a board submit their recommendations to the court. The court would then be authorized to accept the recommendation or reject it or pronounce a different sentence so long as it would not exceed the maximum sentence pronounced tentatively. This latter suggestion also presumes that in certain instances where exemplary punishment is required the court could pronounce the final sentence at the time the accused is before it.

Almost everyone admits that some such procedure would be an improvement over present methods, but these plans meet opposition because of the fears that the sentencing board will be political or not properly qualified or not alert to the crime problem of particular areas, but these are administrative problems which could be solved. In fact, they are being solved for some or all offenders in California, New York, New Jersey, Massachusetts, and, of course, in almost all larger jurisdictions with juveniles.

Modernizing the criminal law must be founded upon closer cooperation between the courts and the correctional processes. Also, it must be based on broader education and training of the lawyer. A knowledge of psychiatry, for instance, is far more important to the ordinary practitioner than admiralty law. Actual clinical training in the criminal courts, visits to prisons, brief reviews of police training school manuals, and sponsorship of some discharged prisoner will do far more toward fitting one for handling the problems of people in the toils of the law than reading *McNaughton's* case or common law forms of pleading and practice. An up-to-date criminal law also would seem to assume the necessity for a change in sentencing methods. But most of all it would call for a rededication of lawyers to the cause of justice, human beings, and equal justice under law.

3 THE PRISON

Prior to the nineteenth century, men were beaten, branded, deported, or killed as a penalty for their criminal behavior. Only in the last 150 years has imprisonment emerged as a major weapon of the state for dealing with the criminal.

To assess current proposals for changes in our penal policy, it is essential to recognize that there are now at least four major objectives that society hopes to achieve through the use of imprisonment. First, there is the goal of retribution, for society still believes that the criminal must be made to suffer for his wrongdoing. Second, there is the goal of deterrence, either for the man who is in prison or for those on the outside who have not yet broken the law. Third, it is hoped that somehow imprisonment can lead to rehabilitation so that in the future the law is obeyed gladly rather than from fear. Fourth, there is the idea that if we accomplish nothing else we can at least keep the criminal out of circulation. Unfortunately, these goals are often in conflict and their inconsistencies are reflected in the operation of the prison.

Eventually, of course, the prison doors must be opened, the prisoner released, for there are very few criminals who receive—or serve—a life sentence. There are those penologists who have hoped that the careful supervision of parole would be more effective in preventing crime than time spent in a cell—and they are typical of those who have hoped somehow to find a just and humane way of preventing crime.

1. A World Apart

On January 23, 1850, Fyodor Dostoevsky arrived at the fortress of Omskin, Siberia, to begin serving his sentence for revolutionary activities. He stayed there for years with thieves, murderers, rapists, and political prisoners as his daily companions. His experience there provided the basis for one of the great books in literature, The House of the Dead, *which still stands as a classic statement of what it means to serve a prison term.*

Our prison stood at the edge of the fortress grounds, close to the fortress wall. One would sometimes, through a chink in the fence, take a peep into God's world to try and see something; but one could see only a strip of the sky and the high earthen wall overgrown with coarse weeds, and on the wall sentries pacing up and down day and night. And then one would think that there are long years before one, and that one will go on coming to peep through the chink in the same way, and will see the same wall, the same sentries and the same little strip of sky, not the sky that stood over the prison, but a free, far-away sky. Imagine a large courtyard, two hundred paces long and a hundred and fifty wide, in the form of an irregular hexagon, all shut in by a paling, that is, a fence of high posts stuck deeply into the earth, touching one another, strengthened by cross-way planks and pointed at the top; this was the outer fence of the prison. On one side of the fence there is a strong gate, always closed, always, day and night, guarded by sentries; it is opened on occasion to let us out to work. Outside the gate is the world of light and freedom, where men live like the rest of mankind. But those living on this side of the fence picture that world as some unattainable fairyland. Here there is a world apart, unlike everything else, with laws of its own, its own dress, its own manners and customs, and here is the house of the living dead—life as nowhere else and a people apart. It is this corner apart that I am going to describe.

When you come into the enclosure you see several buildings within it. On both sides of the large inner court run two long log-houses of one storey. These are the prison barracks. Here the convicts live, distributed in divisions. Then at the farther end of the enclosure another similar log-house: this is the kitchen, divided in two for the use of two messes. Beyond it another building, where are the cellars, the storehouses and stables, all under one roof. The middle of the courtyard is empty and forms a fairly large level square. Here the convicts fall in, here they are mustered, and their names are called over in the morning, at midday, and in the evening, and on occasion several times a day as well—if the sentries are suspicious and not very clever at counting. A fairly wide space is left all round between the buildings and the fence. Here behind the buildings prisoners of an unsociable and gloomy disposition like to walk in their spare time, to think their own thoughts, hidden from all eyes. Meeting them as they walked there, I used to like looking into their grim, branded faces, and guessing what they were thinking about. There was a prisoner whose favourite occupation in his spare time was counting the posts in the fence. There were fifteen hundred of them, and he had counted and noted them all. Every post stood for a day with him: he marked off one post every day, and in that way could see at a glance from the number of posts uncounted how many days he had left in prison before his term was out. He was genuinely glad every time one side of the hexagon was finished. He had many years yet to wait, but one had time in prison to learn patience. I once saw a convict who had been twenty years in prison and was being released take leave of his fellow prisoners. There were men who remembered his first coming into the prison, when he was young, careless, heedless of his crime and his punishment. He went out a grey-headed, elderly man, with a sad sullen face. He walked in silence through our six barrack-rooms. As he entered each room he prayed to the ikons, and then bowing low to his fellow prisoners he asked them not to remember evil against him. I remember too how a prisoner who had been a well-to-do peasant in Siberia was one evening summoned to the gate. Six months, before, he had heard that his former wife had married again, and he was terribly downcast about it. Now she herself had come to the prison, asked for him, and given him alms. They talked for a couple of minutes, both shed tears and parted for ever. I saw his face when he returned to the barracks. . . . Yes, in that place one might learn to be patient.

When it got dark we used all to be taken to the barracks, and to be locked up for the night. I always felt depressed at coming into our barrack-room from outside. It was a long, low-pitched, stuffy room, dimly lighted by tallow candles, full of a heavy stifling smell. I don't understand now how I lived through ten years in it. I had three planks on the wooden platform; that was all I had to myself. On this wooden platform thirty men slept side by side in our room alone. In the winter we were locked up early; it was fully four hours before everyone was asleep. And before that—noise, uproar, laughter, swearing, the clank of chains, smoke and grime, shaven heads, branded faces, ragged clothes, everything defiled and degraded. What cannot man live through! Man is a creature that can get accustomed to anything, and I think that is the best definition of him.

There were two hundred and fifty of us in the prison, and the number scarcely varied. Some came, others completed their sentence and went away, others died. And there were some of all sorts. I imagine every province, every region of Russia had some representative there. There were some aliens, and there were some prisoners even from the mountains of Caucasus. They were all divided according to the degree of their criminality, and consequently according to the number of years they had to serve. I believe there was no sort of crime that had not sent some prisoner there. The bulk of the prison population were exiled convicts or *sylno-katorzhny* of the civilan division (the *silno-katorzhny,* or heavily punished convicts, as the prisoners naïvely mispronounced it).

These were criminals entirely deprived of all rights of property, fragments cut off from society, with branded faces to bear witness for ever that they were outcasts. They were sentenced to hard labour for terms varying from eight to twelve years, and afterwards they were sent to live as settlers in some Siberian village. There were prisoners of the military division, too, who were not deprived of rights, as is usual in Russian disciplinary battalions. They were sentenced for brief terms; at the expiration of their sentence they were sent back whence they had come, to serve in the Siberian line regiments. Many of them returned almost at once to the prison for some second serious offence, this time not for a short term, but for twenty years: this division was called the "lifers." But even these "lifers" were not deprived of all rights. Finally there was one more, fairly numerous, special division of the most terrible criminals, principally soldiers. It was called "the special section." Criminals were sent to it from all parts of Russia. They considered themselves in for life, and did not know the length of their sentence. According to law they had to perform double or treble tasks. They were kept in the prison until some works involving very severe hard labour were opened in Siberia. "You are in for a term, but we go onwards into servitude," they used to say to other prisoners. I have heard that this class has since been abolished. The civilian division, too, has been removed from our prison also, and a single disciplinary battalion of convicts has been formed. Of course, the officials in control of the prison were all changed at the same time. So I am describing the past, things long bygone.

It was long ago; it all seems like a dream to me now. I remember how I entered the prison. It was in the evening, in January. It was already dark, the men were returning from their work, and they were getting ready for the roll-call. A non-commissioned officer with moustaches at last opened for me the door of this strange house in which I was to spend so many years, and to endure sensations of which I could never have formed the faintest idea if I had not experienced them. I could never have imagined, for instance, how terrible and agonising it would be never once for a single minute to be alone for the ten years of my imprisonment. At work to be always with a guard, at home with two hundred fellow prisoners; not once, not once alone! Yet this was not the worst I had to get used to!

There were here men who were murderers by mischance and men who were murderers by trade, brigands and brigand chiefs. There were simple thieves, and tramps who were pickpockets or burglars.

There were people about whom it was difficult to guess why they had come. Yet each had his own story, confused and oppressive as the heaviness that follows a day's drinking. As a rule they spoke little of their past, they did not like talking about it and evidently tried not to think of bygone days. I knew some among them, even murderers, so gay, so heedless of everything that one might bet with certainty that their consciences never reproached them. But there were gloomy faces, too, men who were almost always silent. As a rule it was rare for anyone to talk of his life, and curiously was not the fashion; it was somehow not the custom and not correct. Only on rare occasions, from want of something better to do, some prisoner would grow talkative, and another would listen coldly and gloomily. No one could astonish anyone here. "We are men who can read," they would often say with strange satisfaction. I remember how a robber began once when he was drunk (it was sometimes possible to get drunk in prison) telling how he had murdered a boy of five, how he had enticed him at first with a toy, led him away to an empty shed, and there had murdered him. The whole roomful of men, who had till then been laughing at his jokes, cried out like one man, and the brigand was forced to be silent; it was not from indignation they cried out, but simply because there is no need to talk *about that,* because talking *about that* is not the correct thing. I may mention in parenthesis that they were "men who could read," and not in the slang, but in the literal sense. Probably more than half of them actually could read and write. In what other places in which Russian peasants are gathered together in numbers could you find two hundred and fifty men, half of whom can read and write? I have heard since that someone deduces from such facts that education is detrimental to the people. That is a mistake; there are quite other causes at work here, though it must be admitted that education develops self-reliance in the people. But this is far from being a defect.

The divisions were distinguished from one another by their dress: some had half their jackets brown and half grey, and the same with their trousers —one leg dark brown and one grey. One day when we were at work a girl who was selling rolls looked at me intently for some time and then suddenly burst out laughing. "Ugh, how horrid," she cried, "they had not enough grey cloth and they had not enough black!" There were others whose jackets were all grey, and only the sleeves were blackish-brown. Our heads were shaved in different ways too; some had half the head shaved lengthways and others transversely.

At the first glance one could discover one conspicuous trait, common to all this strange family; even the most prominent and original personalities, who unconsciously dominated the others, tried to adopt the common tone of the prison. Speaking generally, I may say that, with the exception of a few indefatigably cheerful fellows who were consequently regarded with contempt by everyone, they were all sullen, envious, dreadfully vain, boastful people, prone to take offence and great sticklers for good form. Not to be surprised at anything was regarded as the greatest merit. They were all mad on keeping up to their standard of good form. But often the most aggressive conceit was followed in a flash by the most cringing feebleness. There were some genuinely strong characters; they were simple and unaffected. But strange to say, among these really strong people there were some who were vain to the most exaggerated degree, to a morbid point. As a rule vanity and regard for appearances were most conspicuous. The majority of them were corrupt and horribly depraved. Slander and backbiting went on incessantly; it was hell, outer darkness. But no one dared to rebel against the self-imposed rules and the accepted customs of the prison; all submitted to them. There were exceptional characters who found it hard and difficult to submit, but still they did submit. Some who came to the prison were men who had lost their heads, had become too reckless when at liberty, so that at last they committed their crimes as it were irresponsibly, as it were without an object, as it were in delirium, in intoxication, often from vanity excited to the highest pitch. But they were quickly suppressed, though some had been the terror of whole villages and towns before they came to prison. Looking about him, the newcomer soon realised that he had come to the wrong place, that there was no one he could impress here, and he gradually submitted and fell in with the general tone. This general tone was apparent externally in a certain peculiar personal dignity of which almost every inmate of the prison was acutely conscious. It was as though the status of a convict, of a condemned prisoner, was a sort of rank, and an honourable one too. There was no sign of shame or repentance! Yet there was an external, as it were official, resignation, a sort of philosophic calm. "We are a lost lot," they used to say; "since we didn't know how to get on in freedom now we must walk the Green Street, and count the ranks." "Since we disobeyed our fathers and mothers, now we must obey the drum tap." "We wouldn't embroider with gold, so now we break stones on the road." Such things were often said by way of moral reflections and proverbial sayings, but never seriously. They were all words. I doubt whether one of the convicts ever inwardly admitted his lawlessness. If anyone, not a prisoner, were to try reproaching the criminal for his crime, upbraiding him (though it is not the Russian way to reproach a criminal), an endless stream of oaths would follow. And what masters of abuse they were! They swore elaborately, artistically. Abuse was carried to a science with them; they tried to score not so much by insulting words as by insulting meaning, spirit, ideas—and that is subtler and more malignant. This science was developed to a higher point by their incessant quarrels. All these people were kept at work by force, consequently they were idle, consequently they were demoralised; if they had not been depraved beforehand, they became so in prison. They had all been brought together here apart from their own will; they were all strangers to one another.

2. Cellhouse *A*, Cellhouse *C*

"It would seem worthwhile from a historical standpoint to have a report on a fairly typical American prison in the present decade," said Donald Clemmer in the Preface to his sociological study of an American prison in the 1930s. The cellblocks were relatively clean, there was little sadistic brutality among the guards—but it seems doubtful that the prison had advanced very much toward its goal of building a program for the rehabilitation of the criminal.

A house has 400 cells. This building is of the block type in which the block containing the 400 cells stands in the center of a long, rectangular building. There are four galleries, one of which is on the ground floor, and the others directly above. In *A* house the cells are 7 feet long, 6½ feet high, and 4 feet and 8 inches wide. Between each cell is a solid stone and cement partition of 8½ inches. The back and sides of the cell are of solid concrete, painted gray. The steel-barred gate constitutes the front part of the cell. Each cell is equipped with a double deck, gas-pipe-frame bed which is moveable. The mattresses for the beds are of cheap construction and filled with excelsior. Two blankets, a pillow and slip, and one sheet are provided. The cells also contain two stools, a wash basin, a can of water, and a covered bucket used for toilet purposes. In each cell is one 25-watt light. In this oldest building ventilation is provided by blower fans which are not very effective. The narrow windows are also opened on occasions. The heating system operates effectively except for the cells on the ground floor and the "monkey-cages." The cells are scrubbed once each week, and the mattresses are aired and sunned about once in six days. By use of an insecticide and by blow torches, an effort is made to keep the cells free from cockroaches and bed bugs. The so-called "monkey-cages" are steel-barred, moveable cells which are placed on the ground floor and used because of over-crowding. They contain the same equipment as the cells of the regular block, but are even smaller and more reminiscent of early penology at its worst than is the cell block proper. In general, *A* house is a miserable domicile. The toilet buckets, in spite of daily care and disinfecting, lend a putrid odor. The small windows and the antiquated ventilating system do little to cleanse the atmosphere from 420 toilet cans and 850 male bodies which are not too frequently bathed. In summer the walls collect moisture. On cold winter nights the air is warm and stuffy, as the few guards on duty object to opening the windows completely as the cold air would make them uncomfortable. The mattresses are generally lumpy. The 25-watt bulbs are so weak that a yellowish gloom pervades the cellhouse and reading is difficult. More than any other place in the prison, one gets here the impression of caged animals in cramped quarters.

Cellhouse *C,* completed in 1932, is a less unhappy place for the 1,000 men who occupy its 500 cells. It is also of the cellblock construction, being 5 galleries high. The cells here are 7½ feet high, 10 feet, 3 inches long, and 6 feet, 5 inches wide. The cells are of solid concrete construction except for the "front door" which consists of strong steel bars. The partitions between cells are 9 inches thick. Ventilation in this newer building is modern and the large glass windows admit light and air. The cell equipment consists of a modern toilet with running water and a small wash stand. The two beds in each cell are attached to the wall with iron chains and may be swung upright and parallel with the wall to provide more room. The bed equipment is otherwise the same as in *A* house. Two stools and a shelf for storing necessary articles are also included. In general, the living conditions of *C* house are hygienic.

The inside dormitory, a building formerly used as a shop, has two stories and holds 180 men on the first floor and 190 on the second. There are no cells here, although the windows and doors are barred. The beds are double-decked cots which are placed in long rows. Each inmate has a locker which is stored under the bed. Every man is also provided with a stool. At one end of each floor an open space is left for recreational purposes. A wash room contains toilets, showers, and wash stands of modern type but insufficient in number to care properly for the number of men who must use the facilities at one time. The inmates who live here have no special privileges other than the fact that they are not confined to cells. In general, the dormitory is clean, hygienic, and furnishes a fairly decent physical environment. The 120 men who live and work on the Honor Farm are provided with good living conditions in a new domitory.

. . .

Another factor affecting the relations among prisoners is the apparent existence of social classes. In an artificial and highly controlled group of 2,300 men, class distinctions cannot be clear cut, but the attitudes of certain types who are more or less alike in orientation toward other types of men, give indication that some stratification exists. From our study we feel warranted in designating three general categories: the élite class, the middle class, and the "hoosier" class.

The three classes are not definitely demarcated. The criteria used in the formulation of three classes refer to the attitudes the men hold regarding who is the equal of whom. These attitudes towards others are built upon not only individual complex psycho-social items, but also on the reputation men have before they come to prison, their behavior while in prison, especially in reference to officials, and certain other personality traits. In the class which we have termed the "élite," are the more intelligent, urbanized, sophisticated offenders who, for the most part, do not toady to officials, and who set themselves apart, and have their relations chiefly with each other. Criminal experience and anti-administration attitudes will generally be found among them, although there are some who are not basically criminalistic and who behave neutrally toward officials. Intelligent, quiet, and dignified prisoners as well as those with money, who are otherwise not too objectionable, may be included. The élite are aloof from the "hoosiers" but not from the middle class. They have no particular or strong loyalty to each other as members of a class, nor are all of them aware of a class distinction in the population. They may sometimes rub shoulders with the "hoosiers" at work, but they maintain a social distance. The social distance is maintained, not as a specific awareness of their belonging to a class, but more as consciousness of whom they feel, as isolated individuals, are their social equals.

The middle class is composed of the great mass of the men who are generally not outstanding as criminals or as "characters." They are scarcely aware that some prisoners feel, and occasionally act, superior to them. They are not aware that they constitute a class except that they dislike the "hoosiers" and do not voluntarily associate with them. In the great middle class are persons qualified for inclusion in the élite group but the circumstances of work assignment or individual wishes to have none but necessary contacts with any prisoner, prohibits mixing. The "hoosiers" are designated as such by the other two classes. They are unaware that they compose a class and there is no proletarianism among them. When they are subjected to snobbery by the élite, they refer to the élite as "big-shot hoosiers." This third, or lowest class, includes practically all the abnormal sex offenders, the dull, backward, and provincial persons, the lower range of the feeble-minded, some of the known stool pigeons, the persons who show a marked lack of physical courage, the confirmed "suckers," the extremely pious, the habitual braggarts, and some sexual perverts.

Marked inconsistencies in the assignment of certain men to their class become apparent in such instances as the following: A man accepted as a member of the élite class may be continually acting as a stool pigeon, but in so clever a way as to avoid detection; a man may be designated as a "hoosier" because of a rural background, little knowledge of crime, gullibility, or for other reasons, while in the basic character values which are held in esteem by the prisoners he should classify as a member of the élite; the élite may include as a social equal a person with considerable money, who, otherwise, would be termed a "hoosier." It is quite possible for a man in the middle group to rise to the upper group through behavior which bears the stamp of the prisoners' approval, such as assaulting an officer or refusing to give information to authorities, even though punished. Similarly, a member of the élite class may lose caste and no longer be treated as a social equal by his former companions through behavior which is contrary to the class code. Likewise, a person once classed as a "hoosier" does not always remain one. A twenty-two-year-old feeble-minded boy was released after serving a three-year sentence. While in prison he had been used for sex purposes and had been a stool pigeon. Immediately upon his release he was committed to a feeble-minded colony. While there he piled a number of mattresses together and set fire to them. Considerable damage was done by the fire and newspaper publicity followed with the result that he was returned to prison for *Malicious Mischief*. Upon his return he was at first accepted as a social equal by some of the élite and middle-class men because of his belligerent rebelliousness, but as months passed he gravitated again to the lowest class.

As has already been stated, the prison community should not be thought of as having a strict social stratification since the classes are not sufficiently clear cut. While there is some assumption of superiority by the élite it is not shared by all, and though a few in the "hoosier" class are aware of their rank, most are not. In a community where free choice of work, residence, and associates does not operate as in an unrestricted community, some of the customary processes do not occur. This lack of freedom prohibits the formation of distinct social classes but even in a loosely stratified society, relationships are influenced thereby.

The relations among the prisoners are further influenced by certain responses of personalities to the culture. The behavior of individuals in any society is determined not only by personal-social relationships which are non-standardized and non-conventional, but also by the conventionalized, group-accepted forms of conduct commonly called "cultural patterns." To these two types of influences operative among prisoners may be added a third, the "prison culture." The so-called "prison culture" is too complex and too little understood to admit of analysis here. However, it is important to show how these three determinants affect the behavior of men in prison. For example: Prisoners *A* and *B* had an argument as to whose duty it was to clean the cell, and a fight ensued. *A* whipped *B* and, as a result, *B* nursed a grudge. So far the behavior was determined by personal-social determinants. For revenge, *B* mutilated *A*'s Bible and while *A* knew that *B* had done it, and hated him for it, yet he did not inform the officials. In not giving information against *B*, *A* was responding to an item of the prison culture, an item which prescribes that one inmate shall not inform officials about another. In possessing a Bible (which few prisoners do), *A* was responding to an item of the general culture, i.e., the institution of religion. Inmates who learned of the affair began to admire *A* whom they had considered, up to this time, merely a religious fanatic. Thus, through conforming to the code of prisoners he lessened the social distance between himself and certain other prisoners, and contributed to the development of positive relations. Another man is in the habit of leaving a group immediately when vulgar or indecent jokes are being told. This behavior is partly a personal-social response, and partly a response to the general culture of the inmate's background. It is, however, a response which develops negative relations with the group of inmate story tellers. In general, the responses which are in harmony with the prison culture develop positive relations with the majority of inmates, and responses to the general culture develop negative relationships on those levels (usually the mores) where the two cultures clash. The personal-social contacts may stimulate either positive or negative relations, depending on circumstances.

Some men become integrated into the prison culture and some do not. In either case, such men have no particular conflicts. However, a portion of the men become only partially assimilated and may be said to be on the border, or in the shadows of, two cultures, and not acculturized to either. These men may reject some standards or items of the penal culture and adopt others, but they will not reject all the items of the general culture, nor accept all the items of the prison culture. They are thus in the shadows of both cultures, and their behavior seems confused and illogical to those other inmates who have become assimilated and cling tenaciously to the precepts of one culture or the other. The conflicts and difficulties arise, of course, on the level of the mores, customs of conduct, and matters of right and wrong, and do not refer to habits of sleeping, eating, or dressing, for example, which are essentially the same for both the penal and the non-penal cultures. For example, a man on the border of the two cultures may approve of some crimes against property and not of others; in one circumstance he will condone cheating at gambling and not at another; in one instance he would not divulge and peddle information to officials, and in another instance he would. Behavior of this sort is incomprehensible to men who are completely in and of one culture or the other. "You can't be both ways," the inmates say over and over again, and this attitude stressing conformity is an important force in the development of positive or negative relationships.

3. The Dumping Ground

It is all too easy for the general public to think that it has somehow solved the crime problem when it places the criminal behind bars and then forgets about him. Prison administrators, however, cannot afford the luxury of such naïveté, and they are painfully aware of the overcrowding, the lack of resources and staff, and the difficulties of maintaining order, which often turn the hope of rehabilitation into a bitter joke. In James Bennett's comments on the nature of imprisonment, his optimism about the future of the prison is tempered by his long experience as director of the Federal Bureau of Prisons and his awareness of what society has been able to accomplish in the past.

Yesterday a State penal administrator sought my advice on the problems of his State's bulging institutions. This morning I received a letter from a worried Philadelphian who wanted to find some way of spending hard-earned tax moneys on badly needed schools instead of the new jail for which they were budgeted.

There might be a solution to both problems, I had to respond, if someone would take a look at the men confined in prison and jail and weed out those who do not belong there.

The average citizen seems to have the impression that our jails are inhabited chiefly by thieves and our prisons by murderers, rapists, and kidnapers—and therefore they belong where they are. If his impression were correct, there might be some justification for his conclusion. But unfortunately he is wrong to begin with.

More than half the persons committed to our jails are drunks and vagrants. Two-thirds of all offenders who are sent to prison every year are convicted of such nonviolent acquisitive crimes as burglary, larceny, forgery, and automobile theft. Less than 10 percent have been convicted of homicide, rape, or kidnaping. Robberies account for another 10 percent and an assortment of miscellaneous crimes for the remainder.

Every big city has its skid-row character who has been sent to jail for short terms on 80, 90, or 100 occasions. He is even greeted by the police, the magistrate, and the jailer as an "old friend." He is hardly a serious

From James V. Bennett, **Of Prisons and Justice** (Washington, D.C.: U.S. Government Printing Office, 1964). Reprinted by permission of North American Newspaper Alliance, Inc.

menace to society, but he is herded behind the bars of justice and forgotten, for a time.

Some of the men in prison are unquestionably the vicious, unregenerate enemies of society. But a much larger number are the physically and mentally handicapped. Some are social misfits, and there are some who look upon work as the white man's burden. Some are the disadvantaged of our teeming cities and our distress areas of the mountains, blighted railroad or mining towns, or the victims of alcohol, drugs, and barbiturates.

The dubious distinction of having received the most severe sentence in the entire Federal prison system belongs to a prisoner who is serving a term of natural life without eligibility for parole. Other lifers, who may have been convicted of multiple murders or other heinous crimes, are eligible for parole at the end of 15 years. This prisoner, you say, must be a desperado of the worst sort, a homicidal maniac, a compulsive rapist, or a violently dangerous bank robber.

He is, on the contrary, a mentally retarded youth, an epileptic and a drug addict, convicted of selling drugs to support his addiction. His habit, incidentally, was acquired when he was committed to a State hospital for treatment of his epilepsy and his seizures were controlled over a long period of time by the administration of drugs.

The resident population of our jails and prisons can be thinned out if we look to the intelligence and resources of our communities for a solution. In Denver, Judge William H. Burnett and his associates in the municipal court cut the "drunk" population of the city jail by 60 percent in recent years. They did it by marshaling community resources, turning some of these persons over to a medical commission for treatment in a State hospital, and encouraging those with some constructive motivation left to join Alcoholics Anonymous or a similar organization. Judge Roy Harrison, of Des Moines, has reduced the rate of arrests for drunkenness in his city by more than 30 percent through similar efforts.

Our Nation's prisons can also be made less crowded. Many of the alcoholics, it has been already demonstrated, can be diverted to community programs more fitted to deal with their problems. Addiction should be treated as a medical matter and subject to civil commitment to hospitals rather than criminal commitment to prisons. Senator Keating of New York has already introduced legislation which would accomplish this objective. The mentally retarded belong in State institutions equipped and staffed to give them the training they will need to get along in life. The mentally ill should be in State mental hospitals. There are only a handful of psychiatrists scattered among the Nation's prisons and professional treatment is simply not available for those who need it. There would not be so many check forgers, "paperhangers" and "no funds" checkwriters if businessmen were less eager for the stranger's dollar.

Then there are the incidental or early offenders convicted of minor crimes who could get along under probation supervision in the community. An evenhanded use of properly administered probation would go far to reduce prison populations without in the least handicapping law enforcement. Yet statistics indicate that its use depends on local court practices and funds for supervisory officers rather than the fitness of defendants for probation grants. In the Federal courts of South and North Carolina as many as two-thirds of all convicted defendants are placed on probation. In western Tennessee as few as 8 percent. This great variation is very largely the reflection of local court practice in the same States.

Who then should be sent to prison, one might ask.

Send there the men who repeatedly commit serious offenses or deliberately choose crime as a way of life. The prison staffs can expose them to higher and more worthwhile values and perhaps change them. Send the youthful offenders who commit crimes because they do not have the maturity or the education or vocational skills to earn their way in modern society. The prison can equip them with those skills, give them the guidance and discipline they lack usually for want of a stable home. Send the men whose presence in the community would risk the lives and welfare of our citizens. The prisons are admirably designed to restrain their antisocial drives.

The prison can serve useful purposes in the fight against crime. And it should be permitted to fulfill those purposes, rather than used as a dumping ground by communities who choose to evade their own responsibilities.

Early in 1960 a 32-year-old man was committed to a Federal prison upon his conviction of forging a $58.40 check. He was unemployed at the time of his offense, his wife had just suffered a miscarriage, and they needed money for food and rent. He was a veteran who had been honorably discharged from the Army in 1952. He had been in trouble only once before, when he received a summary court-martial for a minor act of misconduct.

At about the same time there was also committed to prison a 36-year-old man, who had been convicted of forging a check for $35.20. He was also unemployed, and his wife left him. He had been honorably discharged from the Navy in 1946. A year prior to his forgery charge he had been committed to jail for 30 days for drunk driving, and shortly thereafter sentenced to 6 months in the county jail for failing to provide for the child that had been born to his marriage.

Our records disclose that the histories and offenses of these two men are practically identical. Yet the first man received 15 years in the penitentiary, the second man received 30 days. Why? Simply because they appeared before two different judges.

The statistics tend to conceal the extremes in leniency or severity, but they still vary sufficiently to demonstrate that the kind of justice dispensed to an offender depends upon the judge before whom he is convicted. For the crime of forgery, an offense involving remarkably similar circumstances and individuals, the Federal courts of western Arkansas and western Oklahoma in 1959 gave average terms of 58 and 63 months, respectively, while Maine and southern New York imposed an average of 9 months. For auto theft, again an offense which involves similar factors in most cases, southern Iowa imposed terms averaging more than 46 months, but western New York imposed terms averaging about 11 months.

The same situation exists in the State courts. The time served by all persons sentenced to prison for felonies in Vermont averages 9 months, but in Illinois it averages 31 months. The average rapist serves 19 months in New Jersey, but he serves 40 months in the neighboring State of New York. Those convicted of homicide, on the average, serve less than 3 years in Texas, but more than 12 years in Ohio.

Needless to say, these inequities fail to stimulate a respect for the law among the very persons whom the law is supposed to teach that respect. The prisoner who must serve his excessively long sentence with other prisoners who receive relatively mild sentences under the same circumstances cannot be expected to accept his situation with equanimity. And the more fortunate prisoners do not attribute their luck to a sense of fairness and justice on the part of the law but to its whimsies. The existence of such disparities is among the major causes of prison riots, and it is one of the reasons why prisons so often fail to bring about an improvement in the social attitudes of its charges.

The United States, except for Massachusetts and Connecticut, is the only nation in the Western World where the sentence, as long as it remains within legal limits, can be imposed by a single judge without any review of its fairness by a higher court. And it is no wonder that our country is the only Western nation where sentences are characterized by extreme and widespread inequities. Considering the many adverse effects of such disparities on law enforcement it is hardly strange that although our prison sentences are on the whole the most severe in the world, we also continue to have one of the highest crime rates. The deterrent and rehabilitative purposes of the law are largely frustrated and nullified by sentences of an inconsistent and unjust nature.

The problem has not been totally neglected. Every Attorney General of the United States for the past 30 years has expressed his concern over this problem. The Federal judiciary has had it under continuous study since 1938. The anxiety of the bar and the public has been mirrored in repeated articles in law journals and the press.

But it was not until 1958 that the first meaningful action was taken. Representative Emanuel Celler, chairman of the powerful House Judiciary Committee, introduced remedial legislation in the lower Chamber, and the late Senator Thomas C. Hennings, the great humanitarian and student of constitutional law, sponsored it in the upper Chamber. In a survey made by Chairman Celler the proposed legislation received the endorsement of a majority of the Federal and State judges, law school deans and professors, and other interested groups from whom the committee solicited views.

The new legislation was enacted unanimously by both Chambers of the Congress in August 1958. In this omnibus act the Congress recognized that despite present shortcomings the function of sentencing was inherently judicial and should remain in the hands of the judges. But it sought to improve sentencing practices by urging the judges to get together periodically to develop a more consistent approach to their duties. The judges have followed this cue and have already held nearly a dozen seminars in which many of the issues accounting for inconsistent sentencing have been identified and studied.

The new law also gave the courts a practicable means of minimizing disparities. It simply authorized the courts to fix a maximum term within legal limits and to vest in the parole board the responsibility of determining when the individual offender could be considered eligible for parole. Sentencing consistency was therefore sought, not by any impossible attempt to measure the seriousness of the crime in terms of months and years, but by trying to keep the offender in prison until such time as he convincingly demonstrates his readiness for a law-abiding life in the community and he has served sufficiently long to deter others from similar crimes. The Congress foresightedly admitted that some defendants presented perplexing problems to the sentencing court and authorized the court to commit such defendants for an extended period of observation and study in a correctional institution before fixing the ultimate term.

Not all judges have yet attended a sentencing seminar. Not all judges are yet using the new discretionary sentencing procedures. But gradually the entire Federal judiciary is being drawn into the new programs. State legislatures are also studying the advisability of similar statutes. Newly appointed judges are preparing themselves more conscientiously for their sentencing duties. Individual courts are putting forth a concrete effort to make their sentencing actions consistent with those of their colleagues. California has taken from the courts the determination of how long a prisoner shall serve and placed it in the hands of a special seven-man tribunal. Other States allow the courts to fix only the maximum and leave the exact time to be served to special boards. Contrary to what some prosecutors predicted, the time actually served is longer when the fixing of the sentence is left to experts than when it remains in the hands of a single judge.

The problem of sentence disparities, however, is still serious. But the courts, encouraged by the lawmakers, are traveling down the road toward its resolution. Perhaps we shall some day reach the point where the principle of equal justice shall have achieved a reasonable semblance of reality.

The 118-year-old State penitentiary had just experienced a riot. Five persons had died, 60 had been injured, a number of buildings had been burned, and wanton damage exceeded $3 million. The Governor asked me to find out what was wrong.

There was a great deal wrong in the ancient and overcrowded prison. For example, I found six men jammed indiscriminately into a dirt-encrusted cell originally built for a single prisoner. Light and air struggled into the cell through a minuscule window and seeped through a strap-iron door so low and narrow that I had to crouch to enter. The cell itself was so cluttered with sweaty clothes, dirty blankets, and old papers that there was room enough for only one prisoner to move about at a time. Conditions throughout the penitentiary were equally bad. "If anyone is rehabilitated here," the warden commented, "it is entirely by accident."

That State is now building another institution to take the population pressure off the old penitentiary. But it has no plans for scrapping it and substituting more adequate facilities for a modern rehabilitation program. Apparently prisons are destined to be used forever. More than a hundred prisons still in operation today were built before Grant took Richmond. When Grant entered Richmond he found there a prison still in use today which was opened in 1797. The following year, 1798, New Jersey opened its Trenton Prison, now standing as a disgrace to American penology and periodically erupting in violence, bloodshed, and escape plots.

The old prisons cannot even be crowded out by burgeoning urbanism. Built in 1811, a day when space and traffic presented no problems, the Maryland Prison stagnates yet in the heart of Baltimore. The Ohio Penitentiary, opened in 1834, is a civic eyesore in downtown Columbus.

In 1956 I had heartfelt hopes that an era of infamy in American penology had closed. A New Jersey Governor had the funds to replace the Trenton Penitentiary, which had long shamed the consciences of professional penologists. But now I learn that old prisons do not die so easily. An effort is to be made to patch it up, so I am told, and worry along with it under the delusion it can be modernized.

These long-outworn prisons are given a seemingly perpetual lease on life because of the dramatic rise in the national prisoner population since World War II. Penal administrators must seek out every available facility, no matter how old or inadequate, to house their increasingly numerous charges.

The prisoners in Federal institutions have increased by 35 percent during the postwar period. New York and Ohio have experienced a similar increase. In Texas the prisoner population has nearly tripled. In California the number of prisoners has gone up from 7,363 in 1946 to more than 22,000 in 1960. The State is now engaged in a frantic new construction and improvisation program to find accommodations for the men which now crowd its instituions, nearly 6,000 over design capacities.

Legislatures are slow to authorize funds for new institution construction, but the courts continue to send men to prison in an everengulfing stream. The administrator must find the space somehow. In our Atlanta Penitentiary, 8 or 10 men are now occupying cells intended for 4. The single cells each hold two men. Beds are strung closely together in dingy basement areas. And prisoners still arrive daily.

Although the prison warden may find a place, however, unsatisfactory, for the prisoners to sleep, the rest of the prison facilities fall hopelessly behind. Men stand in line at the toilets and washbowls. They go to the dining room in shifts; the dining room of the Atlanta Penitentiary is in continuous use throughout the day. But the effects of overcrowding are even more destructive in terms of the prison's purpose in salvaging men. The classrooms cannot accommodate all the men who need even basic education. The shops, industries, and maintenance work of an overcrowded prison cannot provide jobs for all.

Overcrowding means idleness, and in some prisons as many as 50 percent of the prisoners can only sit vacantly in their cells or mill aimlessly in the prison yard. What should be a time for preparation in anticipation of a fresh start in life turns out instead to be a stultifying, soul-deadening interim. And yet the prison warden is told, when such men leave prison and return again to crime, "You failed to rehabilitate them." The warden was never given a chance.

Most of the wardens I know are charged with running an overcrowded prison. And many of the wardens I know are nervous men. They pace the floor in their offices. They order the steward to put more meat in the stew. They tour the prison daily, and concealing their anxiety, search the faces of the men.

With the aid of their skimpy staffs, they can try only to keep the lid on. But experience tells them it is only a matter of time. It may be today, or tomorrow. It is no accident that the decade of the 1950's has seen the most overcrowding in the history of American prisons—and also the most unrest, violence, and disorder among American prisoners. In the first 3 years of the decade there were more destructive prison riots than in the previous 50 years. The unrest broke out again in 1959, raged for a time, and then subsided.

American prison systems are now trying desperately to construct enough new facilities to contain and treat the mounting prisoner populations. But the present rate of prison commitments suggests that the effort is not enough. Prison populations continue to multiply faster than prison facilities. Despite a rise in the number of prisoners that should warrant the construction of a new institution annually, the Federal prison system, for example, has been authorized only one new institution since 1940.

Until the public recognizes that more adequate institutional facilities are needed if the role of prisons in crime control is to be fully realized, our wardens seem destined to remain nervous and sleepless for yet another decade. And perhaps yet another.

. . .

A prison administrator is repeatedly reminded how widely our citizens disagree as to the fundamental purposes of a prison. On the one hand, there are those who accuse him of running country clubs, coddling prisoners, and otherwise removing the sting from the punishment meted out to those miscreants who have at great expense been caught and convicted.

On the other hand are the armchair psychologists and amateur criminologists who tell the administrator that the total effect of a prison is to brutalize those persons unfortunate enough to land in one. They say that only the ignorant and untalented would work in a prison, and that behind its walls brutality, apathy, and worse are rampant.

Both charges may be made although the persons making them may never have stepped foot inside a prison. In my 30 years with the Bureau of Prisons, I have learned that a prison administrator does not lack for suggestions on how to run his prisons.

Actually, at least as far as many American prisons are concerned, both viewpoints are wrong. The day when brutality was common has long since gone, and the inherent nature of a prison prevents it from becoming a country club.

Make no mistake about it, a prison sentence is tough medicine. It imposes a stigma that will linger with the offender long after he has served his time. It takes a man away from his loved ones for what is now becoming a longer and longer period. It confines him to a few acres of land during that time. Inevitably it enforces monotonously regular hours upon him. It clothes him in a cheap uniform completely lacking in any sartorial elegance. And it deprives him of any normal sex outlet. For most, the latter is more refined torture than the cruelest of corporal punishment.

During the 30 years of my association with prison work I have known of only two men who wanted to be in prison. One was an old man, 83 years of age, friendless, arthritic, and crippled, who had been in prison so long that he had lost contact with all friends and relatives. Another was a middle-aged mental incompetent who was so homesick for the Medical Center for Federal Prisoners where he had served two previous sentences that he arranged his recommitment to that institution by the desperate expedient of sending a crude bomb through the mail to a Bureau of Prisons official.

The prison administrator walks the tightrope between softness and harshness by making a prison purposeful and by providing a program of training and constructive work. He can do this only if he can keep the numerical population of the prison within manageable limits and he is not frustrated by shortsighted laws. The prisoner is there to learn the moral values of society and the prison is punishment enough, the regime he follows there has the higher purpose of salvaging his social usefulness.

To relieve the hardships of a prison which would otherwise become inhuman the prisoner is accorded such privileges as correspondence and visits with his family, weekly movies, a recreation program. Religious instruction is made available and as attractive as possible so that those inner changes so essential to true reform actually occur. To appeal to his legitimate aspirations and talents there are the talent shows, the educational and vocational training programs, the prison newspaper, human relations groups. And modestly paid jobs and productive work are furnished in order to give the prisoner a basis for self-respect, without which prison rehabilitation programs would founder.

It is not coddling to make a socialized human being out of a criminal. A deliberately punitive prison program would have vastly destructive effects on the public welfare. For with the exception of the three or four, out of a hundred, who die in prison, the rest all come out some day. They come right back into the community, and it is to make this day filled with hope, not hate, that prison programs should point.

The recognition of this principle does not solve the prison administrator's dilemma. The society whom he serves, or at least the representatives of that society, do not yet give full support to that principle.

I read in the newspaper the other day that a judge had given a tax accountant a term of 31 years and 31 days on tax fraud charges. As I read the item I wondered what the judge expects us to do with this man when he reaches one of our institutions. His crime, as crimes go in this country, does not warrant a punishment which exceeds that usually given to armed bank robbers. He is educated and has employable skills. He raised a family and kept out of trouble for most of his life, his offense apparently stemming from a temporary lapse in his sense of values.

How, I asked myself, can we be expected to keep hope, drive, and ambition alive in this prisoner over the long years of his sentence? How can we prevent him from hating and attempting to get even with a society that permits that sort of thing?

Not long ago we had to release a prisoner who had reecived a term of 98 days for armed bank robbery and he is now on probation. When he left us he was about as unskilled, emotionally unstable, and lacking in social values as when he entered. I sincerely hope that he manages to keep out of trouble, but if he fails, the whole machinery of justice—the courts and the prisons—will stand indicted for his failure. As for the prison warden who released this man, I know that he has already experienced a deep sense of frustration. The youngster might have been straightened out more enduringly before he was exposed to further serious temptation. Whether the judge's leniency has truly served the welfare both of this youngster and society remains for the future to determine.

The warden does his best to deal with problems the individual prisoner poses, even within the limitations of such capricious sentences. But in the meantime he must tend to his knitting. He has a plant worth many millions of dollars to run. He has to find housing and work for the prisoners who crowd in on him from the courts. He has to run a large prison industry and perhaps an agriculture program that would rank among the largest in Iowa or Kansas. And he must be quick to answer the phone—it might be a disturbance, an escape, anything.

He really cannot solve his dilemma. Society must do it for him. Society must decide what kind of individual it wants to come out of prison. An unreconstructed rebel, ready to rob another bank! Or a trained mechanic who wants a job in a garage! There is, obviously, but one choice.

4. Future Directions

The picture presented by James Bennett is not very encouraging. The prison problem in the United States may, indeed, get a good deal worse unless substantial changes are made, for a growing population of offenders is placing ever greater demands on limited resources. The Task Force on Corrections of the President's Commission on Law Enforcement and Administration of Justice views more research as one of the great hopes for the future—but we need to remember that more research and more knowledge are useless if the public is unwilling to take the steps that will translate them into action.

The most conspicuous problems in corrections today are lack of knowledge and unsystematic approach to the development of programs and techniques. Changes in correctional treatment have been guided primarily by what Wright calls "intuitive opportunism," a kind of goal-oriented guessing.

If the range of alternatives for solving correctional problems were narrow, well-organized, and familiar, the best approach might be this intuitive and pragmatic one. But this is not the case. Failure to attempt really systematic research and evaluation of various operational programs has led to repetitive error. Even more, it has made it impossible to pinpoint the reasons for success when success did occur.

The possibility has not been adequately considered, for example, that the impact of new techniques may be overwhelmed by negative influences already existing in correctional systems, or the possibility that introduction of new techniques may produce negative effects upon procedures already present. Individual practices which by themselves might have been helpful often seem to generate conflict when joined irrationally with other practices. For example, the tendency for custody and treatment people to be at odds with each other in correctional institutions (a schism reinforced by organizing them as separate divisions) often contributes to the cynicism, rather than the reformation, of offenders. Inmates are encouraged to concentrate on means for exploiting the rift among staff members rather than working with staff to resolve common problems.

The beginnings of correctional research stemmed from several different

From Task Force on Corrections, the President's Commission on Law Enforcement and Administration of Justice, **Task Force Report: Corrections** (Washington, D.C.: U.S. Government Printing Office, 1967).

interests. Correctional administrators have required population accounting procedures for budget and capital outlay planning. Theoreticians began studying correctional populations because of their interest in the causes of criminality and the processes of correctional change. Some research was instigated to demonstrate to legislatures and others the cost-effectiveness of the various treatment alternatives born of increasing emphasis on rehabilitation.

From these beginnings, the scope of research expanded after World War II, with increasing emphasis on scientific management and operations research in other fields. Since universities were unable to provide systematic, on-going evaluation services, university-trained research persons were employed by correctional organizations to evaluate programs. During the 1950's, correctional research divisions were created in several States.

Initially, research activities in correctional agencies tended to be isolated. The creation of an ongoing research activity did not mean that the correctional organization utilized research for program formulation and policy decisions. There were two reasons for this. First, researchers tended to approach organizational problems from an academic frame of reference and were not acquainted with operational problems of correctional organizations. They used mysterious language, and their techniques for evaluation were alien to correctional administrators. Second, correctional administrators were not versed in a social science approach to problem solving and did not know how to incorporate an ongoing research program into the correctional program of their departments.

The contemporary trend is toward the integration of research and action. Researchers are becoming increasingly acquainted with correctional organizations and correctional managers with the uses of social science research in the development of action programs.

The role of research demands a close integration of these two concerns. Broadly characterized, research can provide basic information about offenders, such as number, rates, trends, and individual characteristics. Researchers can contribute information on research findings and theoretical developments that have implications for correctional program development and thus help assure that program formulations are in accord with the strongest evidence and best theorizing. And researchers can participate in planning programs to help frame hypotheses for the testing of program claims and devise experimental designs to test them. Researchers must cooperate too in program operation, to observe and record implementation and insure that results are substantiated.

If various program strategies are to be evaluated in terms of their effectiveness in achieving objectives, it is necessary to designate criteria of outcome and instruments of measurement. This procedure is complicated if goals for different populations of offenders differ, as is usually the case. Moreover, at the present time it is not possible to compare outcomes from different correctional populations or systems because of the lack of comparability or the simple unavailability of outcome data. This handicap must be reduced through attempts to secure greater comparability of standards and definitions. Better communication of results is also needed.

The first requirement for an efficient use of research in correctional program development is an organizational arrangement that calls for integration of the functions of administration, treatment, and evaluation. Prior to the introduction of research, there was only one communicational channel within the system: the channel between administration and treatment. With the advent of research, the channels of communication increase to three.

There is a need to overcome such barriers through the development of a common commitment subscribed to by administrators, program operators, and researchers. The gap between administrator and treater could be substantially lessened if management committed itself to specific treatment strategies which would be given adequate tests and if it shared program decisions with treatment personnel. The gap between administrator and researcher could be narrowed through adoption of a common frame of reference as to the role of evaluation in the total management process. The gap between treaters and researchers could be lessened through mutual commitment to the goal of improving treatment by evaluation. Treaters would be called upon to enter actively into the evaluation process and would be seen as indispensable collaborators in research. Research would be seen as an aid rather than a threat to the treatment of the offender.

Correctional decision-making is characteristically handicapped by several deficiencies. First, data essential to the making of sound decisions often are not available. In determining whether to grant parole, for example, decisions usually are based on scanty information collected at the time the offender was committed to the institution. Information on changes that have occurred during confinement is not usually available or is inadequate.

Second, information that is available may be irrelevant to the outcomes which determine whether the decision was sound. It is characteristic of any decision-making process that those involved often are not aware of the particular bits of information they employ in arriving at a judgment. Moreover, the information they do use may, by empirical standards, be unrelated to the judgment being made. The question of relevance cannot be answered by argument but only by careful research.

Studies of the decisions made by juvenile court judges indicate that, while some judges are interested primarily in psychological information, others are equally fixed in their orientation to social background items. This raises a question as to the types of information which should be employed. Some studies have suggested that if information believed by the decision-makers to be extremely important is arbitrarily withheld, there appears to be no significant change in the decisions made. Although he may vigorously deny it, the decision-maker tends to make the same decisions whether or not he has access to the information desired.

There is an even more interesting finding from such studies. By withholding certain items of information from the directors of juvenile institutions in England, decisions regarding the prognosis of inmate performance could often be improved. In other words, certain items of information tended to mislead the officials because they attached greater weight to them than was warranted.

A final and related problem is that the volume of information often overloads human capacity for analysis and utilization. The sheer number of offenders under correctional supervision is staggering and is growing rapidly each year. Adequate disposition of these offenders may require tens or hundreds of items of information of each offender at each step in the correctional cycle. Computerized information systems have a potential for simplifying access to these data.

A core responsibility found in all phases of the correctional process is the requirement of gathering and analyzing information about the offender that will provide an adequate basis on which to predicate the series of correctional decisions.

Whether the decision is to invoke the judicial process, to choose between probation or imprisonment, to select the appropriate degree of security in a correctional institution, or to determine the timing for release from incarceration or the necessity for revocation of parole, judicial and administrative decision-makers are concerned with very similar issues:

1. The degree or extent of threat to the public posed by the individual. Significant clues will be provided by the nature of the present offense and the length of any prior record.
2. The nature of the response to any earlier correctional programs.
3. The kind of personal stability and responsibility evidenced in his employment record, residential patterns, and family support history.
4. The kind of personal deficiences apparent, including educational and vocational training needs.
5. The personal psychological characteristics of the offender that determine how he perceives the world and his relationship to it.

A few correctional research programs are seeking to test the way in which these personal dimensions can be subjected to objective analyses and used as the basis for predicting the probable response of given offenders to alternative correctional programs. Some progress is evident in both statistical and psychological research experiments.

Paralleling these general needs is the need for professional clinical personnel to assist in the evaluation of the bizarre-acting, seriously disturbed, and mentally deficient offenders and to provide consultation and advice to the line staff who must deal on a day-to-day basis with this special group.

Central to such evaluation is the necessity for identifying those dangerous or habitual offenders who pose a serious threat to the community's safety. They include those offenders whose personal instability is so gross as to erupt periodically in violent and assaultive behavior and those individuals whose long-term exposure to criminal influences has produced a thoroughgoing commitment to criminal values that is resistive of superficial efforts to effect change. For these persons the still primitive state of treatment methodologies can only offer some long-term confinement followed by the kind of parole supervision that will provide maximum possible control.

There is a clear need for an improved capability in the information gathering and analysis process and continued experimental development to improve the predictive power of the information gathered. These needs imply increased manpower and the training requisite to the development of sophistication and skill in the investigative-diagnostic process.

There are many problems to be solved. The technological ones are perhaps the least difficult since we have entered an area when rapid processing, communication, and display of information are possible.

A much more difficult problem lies in developing data which are sufficiently exact, relevant, and reliable to place into an automated system. Much of the existing information about offenders consists of "soft" descriptions (e.g., "aggressive" or "dependent") which are highly impressionistic and unreliable. The most sophisticated data-processing systems can do nothing to improve the quality of the information fed in. Indeed, there is a danger of creating an illusion of scientific omniscience through premature use of advanced methods for handling data.

Painstaking efforts are needed to define which data are relevant to particular decisions, to "harden" the data through scaling and through standardization and validation techniques, to obtain improved criteria on the basis of which judgments are made as to success and failure of various types of offenders and correctional programs. None of these tasks is impossible, but each is extremely complex. Much pilot work is needed before major financial and organizational commitment is made to new techniques and equipment.

The administrative and jurisdictional fragmentation that characterizes corrections in this country has had some significant advantages. Diversity has been important in a period of development when no one aim or method could lay claim to infallibility, and a monolithic system might well have discouraged experiment and innovation. With increasing official recognition for research and demonstration efforts, fragmentation no longer is essential to this process, and a greater degree of consolidation and coordination seem to afford offsetting advantages in the efficient utilization of resources and in the elimination of irrational disparities and contradictions in policy and treatment.

One such need is for the consolidation or pooling of services and facilities where this would result in their improvement or significant gains in efficiency. Tiny county jails, for example, cannot begin to meet necessary standards or provide effective rehabilitative programs; neighboring jurisdictions need to group together to do this. Indeed the entire split in most jurisdictions between misdemeanant facilities (under local control, usually of law enforcement officials) and those for felons (usually handled by State correctional authorities) has operated generally to hinder advances in misdemeanant systems. To a lesser extent, the administrative separation of the juvenile and adult systems has created anomalies. At another level, specialized services for offender groups such as women, the mentally ill, the dangerous inmate, and long-term prisoners cannot in most States be provided as well as they could be in regional or even Federal facilities.

The development of close cooperation between institution and community programs is another essential organizational need, touched on above in connection with discussion of reintegration strategy. Institutional programing must point toward preparing the offender to reenter the community rather than isolating him from it, as has predominantly been the case in the past. This requires close and constant attention to the interaction between the two worlds and underscores problems arising from the separate administration of institutions and field services.

In heavily populated jurisdictions, combined authority could be regionalized to keep the management function close to operations and to encourage creative leadership and program development. Such an arrangement would be consistent with the concept of a small, multipurpose institution serving as a center for community treatment as well as handling offenders who are either moving toward or returning from specialized and higher custody facilities.

Corrections also needs to collaborate with employment services, mental health, social welfare, public works, and other agencies as well as with other parts of the criminal justice system. There are offenders—mentally ill criminals and drunks, for example—for whom it is difficult to determine which system should assume primary responsibility for handling. Joint or multi-agency task forces could contrive programs to improve education, work, family services, mental health, and many other services directed toward offenders. Adjustments could be worked out in law, policy, and financing to facilitate such collaborative approaches to solving problems. And this could be done without diminishing (indeed it could strengthen by more sharply defining) the special capacity of corrections to supply needed controls over the behavior of offenders.

Changes are also needed in the internal organization of most correctional agencies. Their bureaucratic structure is typically hierarchical, with rigid chains of communication and command. Official directives tend to lose their rationale and justification as they filter down through the system. For every official directive there are likely to be many unofficial interpretations which occur in discussions outside of the official channels of communication. Many subordinate officials have to depend upon unofficial versions of policy in order to gain any sense of what is expected of them.

Steps can be taken to minimize these problems of management. Offender advisory bodies and group discussion programs are needed to create a more significant role for offenders and for rank-and-file staff. The trend towards smaller institutions and "flatter" tables of organization have the same general objective. In some places, teams of staff and offenders are assigned responsibilities for program planning, implementation, and assessment.

Another approach to revitalizing correctional administration is to categorize the staff according to broad program functions instead of the positions occupied in the table of organization. Its aim is to seek a true collaboration instead of a mechanistic division of effort. Thus, groups of staff working in a unit of an institution might collectively be given responsibility for guiding, disciplining, and training inmates, rather than sharply separating these functions between counselors, guards, and teachers.

This model of functional collaboration assumes that, whatever the worker's special skills or major responsibilities, he will devote some time and energy to the performance of other functions. Treatment personnel would participate in the collection and analysis of research data, researchers would be involved in program planning and in direct contact with offenders. Hopefully, such sharing of experience might broaden the perspectives of staff members, communicate the interdependence of the organization's various functions and roles, and encourage the development of common goals and expectations.

5. The Back Door of the Prison

The idea that the criminal can be reformed by locking him up for years on end in the distorted environment of the prison, with nothing but other criminals for company, has seemed absurd to some observers. Supervision and counseling in the free community is far superior, they have argued, in the form of either probation or parole. It is the latter that is discussed by Wilber La Roe. If parole has not been as successful a technique as its adherents hoped it would be, the fault may lie with oppressive caseloads and lack of community support rather than with the idea itself.

In a metropolitan newspaper there appeared a cartoon picturing the law enforcement agencies sending criminals into the front door of a prison, while at the same time the board of parole opened the back door and let them out. The inference was plain: the realists were making a serious attempt to enforce the law, while the sentimental exponents of parole were nullifying their efforts by extending leniency to offenders. A humorous column in the *Washington Times–Herald* suggests that all prisons be equipped with revolving doors, thus facilitating parole administration.

Dr. Wilcox denies that parole is synonymous with leniency but says that, on the contrary, "It is to be commended because it is at once the most severe and the safest method by which prisoners may be released." He reaches the inescapable conclusion that "most reasonable men will agree that society will be better protected by such a system of conditional, supervised release than by a system which permits the criminal to go scot-free."

As a matter of fact, criminals are more apt to obtain leniency as such from some other source. It is an everyday occurrence for a prosecuting attorney to accept a plea of guilty to a lesser offense than that charged in the indictment in order to avoid a trial and save expense. There probably does not exist a district attorney who has not accepted a plea of manslaughter when the offense charged is really murder, or a plea of simple assault where the crime is far more serious. Every day the courts are extending "leniency" when they impose short sentences because of some mitigating circumstance, or when they place convicted persons on probation, completely avoiding a prison sentence, where it appears that putting

From Wilber La Roe, Jr., **Parole with Honor** (Princeton, N.J.: Princeton University Press, 1939). Reprinted by permission.

them on their good behavior will be more effective than the degradation of incarceration.

These forms of leniency it is not intended to criticize—each of them serves a useful purpose, and the assumption that they are contrary to the public interest is erroneous. But the point to be made here is that parole, which releases a man under restrictions instead of releasing him as a free agent, is not in reality a form of leniency, the truth being that the kind of release which the prisoner obtains under parole is far more severe, and subjects him to far greater obligations, than the release which he obtains if permitted to go his way at the expiration of his term.

Furthermore, it would appear that parole does not in fact reduce the length of time served inside the prison by prisoners. In a recent study [Attorney General's *Survey of Release Procedures,* Vol. IV, "Parole," p. 4] made by the Department of Justice it is said: "Comparative studies in recent years show that parole has resulted in longer terms of imprisonment than those exacted under definite sentences in which parole was not granted. The reports of the Census Bureau for 1933 indicate that the average time served prior to parole (17.4 months) was longer than the average time served on definite sentences in which parole was not granted (17 months)." While it may seem incredible to the reader that this should be so, the explanation lies in the fact that longer sentences are usually imposed in the jurisdictions having parole systems, and in the further fact that where there is no parole system the offender is released automatically at the end of his sentence, which is usually a "flat" sentence, whereas under the parole system, which is normally accompanied by the indeterminate sentence, the prisoner is held in custody until he is ready to be released.

The same judge who, under a system where flat sentences are imposed without parole, would hesitate to sentence a seventeen-year-old boy to a longer term than two years, would probably not hesitate, under a parole system accompanied by the indeterminate sentence, to sentence the same boy to a term of one to five years. The board of parole would thus be enabled to release him at any time between the minimum and maximum, in which event he might remain in custody for one, two, three, four or five years, depending on the extent of his response to institutional training and on the ability of the parole authorities to work out a plan for his resumption of normal life in the community.

A vivid contrast between the conventional method of releasing prisoners without restrictions, on the one hand, and the parole method, on the other hand, is given by Winthrop D. Lane, formerly director of the New Jersey parole system, and one of the nation's leading experts in this field:

Fundamentally there are two ways by which an offender can leave an institution. One of these is for an official to conduct him to the front door and say: "You have served your time. You have paid your price. The penalty exacted by society has been met. From now on we have no interest in you. This institution has done its best. If we have failed to make a man of you, that is your fault. We wish you well but, there being nothing further we can do, we wash our hands of the matter. Keep out of mischief—and here is ten dollars." The offender, with a suit of prison-made clothes on his back, walks off. He may or may not be met by friends. He may or may not have a job. Not infrequently the only thing he knows to do is to return to his old associations and to criminal ways.

The other way in which an offender may be released is for the official to say to him: "We have tried to make a man of you. If we have failed, we are sorry, but we have no intention of quitting the job now. We shall keep an interest in you. We shall do our level best to help you get on your feet and to live usefully within the law in your community. This means that you will be on parole. You will have a parole officer, who will be your friend. He will help you get a job. He will help to straighten out your family difficulties and be of assistance in all other ways possible. You are to feel free to call upon him, and he will often call upon you. You must observe the conditions of your parole, which have been explained to you. We may as well be frank with you and tell you that we are doing this for two reasons: first, in order that we may help you; and, second, in order that we may bring you back to the institution if you disappoint us. We have no intention of letting you commit additional crimes. Our supervision will be close and, so long as you permit it, friendly. It will become unfriendly only when you show evidence of going wrong. Now, go ahead, keep out of trouble, and make a man of yourself."

Commenting on the practical difference between these two methods, Mr. Lane says: "In the one case society is protected and the offender helped, and in the other case neither happens." Frankly conceding that there are types of prisoners "for whom permanent custodial care is necessary," Mr. Lane contends, and with unanswerable logic, that *if* a prisoner is to be released, it is in the interest of the community to release him *with* supervision rather than *without* it. He quotes with approval a statement made by the Rev. William S. Beal, formerly chaplain of Maryland Penitentiary, that "every man ought to serve a period of his sentence on the outside." And he reminds us that Sanford Bates, in addressing the Massachusetts Legislature in 1928, said: "We stand here today to make the statement that in the light of modern penology no man should ever be turned from prison directly into the community without the help, the safeguard, and the protection of parole supervision."

Every week the author sits as a member of a board of parole, passing upon the parole applications of more than a score of prisoners. In every group of prisoners will be found men of widely different characteristics and backgrounds: the young fellows who are by no means hardened felons; the average who have had some experience in crime; and finally the hardened criminals of various ages who would be, except for their incarceration, a real menace to the community. Usually parole is granted to the young men who are not definitely antisocial, and it is denied to the "hard-boiled" offenders. But the author constantly feels, as do also his colleagues on a board of parole, that the mere denial of parole to the hardened criminals is by no means a solution of the problem. Before very long they will be handed ten dollars and released anyway—is it sentimentality to face the stark fact that these men are a grave menace to society? What will happen when the ten dollars has been spent? Would not the community be better protected if even these hardened offenders could be released under such conditions and restrictions as would at least prevent them from rejoining their old gangs?

THE HOPE OF REFORM

The desire for revenge has been a constant stumbling block in the efforts to prevent crime, for it has meant that we have sharply restricted ourselves in the search for new and more effective techniques. It has meant that we are not yet ready to pay the financial cost of necessary experimentation, as Fritz Redl and David Wineman point out. Even when we discover techniques of rehabilitation that appear promising, such as those described by Lloyd McCorkle and Rita Volkman and their co-workers, we are not prepared to make the social and emotional commitments that will carry us beyond the experimental stage.

Yet it is perfectly clear that if we are ever going to deal effectively with the problem of crime we will need to overcome the simple demand for retribution, the distorted fears, and the public apathy delineated in the report of the President's Commission on Law Enforcement and Administration of Justice. We can be sure that any solution to the problem of crime will involve more than the cure of known offenders; we will certainly need to concern ourselves with the prevention of crime, and this will entail far-reaching changes in the structure of society. The control of crime is not merely a matter of reaching into the individual's psyche, for the sources of human behavior also lie in the social environment, as illustrated by Jane Jacobs' discussion of street life in American cities. The changes needed in this environment, Paul Goodman suggests, are part of our "missed revolution," and the fact that we have not yet achieved a just, humane, and decent social order is a part of not only the crime problem but a host of other social problems as well.

Can we control crime more effectively than we do at the present time? We think so—but it will require far more money, far more knowledge, far more enthusiasm for social changes than we have brought to bear on the problem up to now. There is no cheap and easy solution; mere declarations of indignant concern are useless.

Can we combat crime and still maintain extended civil liberties? We think we can and we must, for if we gain in one at the expense of the other, we lose the game altogether. Crime, it has been said, is part of the price of a free society. We can reduce crime and deal with it more effectively and more justly, but we cannot expect to eliminate it without destroying an ideal of society that is of far greater import than our difficulties with crime.

1. The Cost of Rehabilitation

"Who Mislaid Santa Claus?" ask Fritz Redl and David Wineman, for they argue that the public expects a solution for crime and delinquency as an inexpensive gift when no such gift is possible. Our society, veering erratically between a punitive harshness and a sentimental indulgence, looks for an easy out and refuses to confront the fact that large amounts of money will be needed to deal more effectively with the man who breaks the law.

Our trouble is that we don't know enough about Hate. Consequently, we don't take it seriously enough. Just consider the Juvenile Delinquency issue in the United States at this time of writing as an example. Public opinion allows itself the most ridiculous display of cheap denial mechanisms, which surpass anything we might have been subjected to eighty years ago on issues like Tuberculosis or Venereal Disease. Remember the time when "consumption" became something akin to a fad? It made one "ethereal looking," made one "interesting," made one not exactly cute but respectable. Withering away from it became the subject of poetic compositions, and was contrasted as the nobility of the weak against the crude red-cheekedness of unthinking muscular health. There also was a time when diseases like syphilis were allowed to destroy thousands of victims unchallenged because looking at the causes might imply some kind of morbidity. And, after all, those as yet unafflicted could still enjoy, over their morning coffee, the sweet taste of triumph over the fact that the wicked got their just deserts.

We wouldn't display such an attitude today toward any disease. TB has been sobered down to the status of an unfortunate affliction which we had better fight with laborious and expensive scientific efforts instead of getting enthralled about it and romanticizing its aesthetic aspects. And VD has become just another disease. We have separated the moral disgust about the way in which some people contract it from the problem of research into its causes and into techniques for cure. We have asked the preacher, the teacher, the public health educator, to see what they can do about the moral side of the picture. The physician will approach the person afflicted with the objectivity assured all matters of medical seriousness. Whatever feelings of shame, embarrassment, and guilt the public originally attached to the disease it now reserves for the fact that we still don't know all the answers to problems of prevention, that preventive and curative measures even where known and developed are still not accessible fast enough and cheaply enough in all our communities.

In our thinking about Juvenile Delinquency we have not advanced to nearly so enlightened a stage. We don't really take it seriously. Consider any one of the more shocking crimes, let's say one in which an adolescent sex delinquent murders a younger companion, not exactly in cold blood, but in an anxiety-panic and without much concern for his victim at all. What is the general reaction of the faithful reader of incomplete and usually distorted newspaper reports of a crime like that? It generally wavers between two extremes. The reader is first of all properly shocked and hopes that the criminal will be found soon, will get what he deserves, and will be put away safely so that he can do no more harm. It might be a good idea also, he thinks, to use this opportunity to cut some of the "frills" from the budget of the local reformatory, to admonish the school superintendent to see that the three R's are taught properly instead of allowing youth to be coddled by all sorts of outlandish nonsense like recreational projects and family life discussion groups and the like. It might also be deemed worth while to permit a considerable sum of money to be spent for a few additional "maximum safety rooms" for the institutions of the State. That settles the problem for a while.

The other reaction seems to move along the line of sentimental naïveté. The reader of such a news story may remember what he got out of recent fiction, or from one of those psychiatrically tinged movies, or from that speech the other day in the local PTA, and he now rallies around what he thinks is a "more advanced outlook" on such things. Consequently, he sheds hot tears on the pages of the case history of the delinquent. See, he never had a chance, poor kid. The way he was pushed around! For, after all, who is to blame but the parents and the school? He didn't read the Bible enough, or maybe he read it too much. And, of course, the movies and the comic books, you know. And, maybe we should take great pains to distribute a few more footballs in that bad housing area, and maybe we should send those new curtains to the local detention home after all. Or maybe we should suggest that the parents of delinquent children be sent to jail instead of the children, or should at least "be made" to take classes on child care. Or, perhaps, we should even offer the basement of our church for a project for teenagers, but, of course, let's be sure that only the nice ones get in, for we wouldn't want to have any bad language down there, after all, and who would suggest that the nice kids be expected to mix with the "undesirable element" of our town?

In short, the general attitude of the taxpaying public toward such issues is a pitiful sight to behold. We either "get tough" and take recourse to the most outdated and most obviously stupid defenses against shame, anxiety, and guilt, or we become sentimental and illusional, while we stare at the unfortunate chain of events that ended up in a crime such as this. On two issues, by the way, both camps are agreed. First, that somebody ought to "give us a solution soon" to these problems. Second, that such a solution has to be "simple and inexpensive." For, even though he may know better, who would dare to stand up publicly for high per capita costs for preventive or curative measures? "The taxpayer wouldn't stand for this," we say to ourselves.

Too bad that they mislaid Santa Claus and he isn't playing any more. We think that it is time for the American Community to wake up to the facts of life. We think that delinquency, and especially the phenomenon of Hatred which the more serious crimes invariably involve, is a serious thing. We think that we don't really know enough about it. We think that we ought to find out. It won't do to coddle the delinquent by finding his minor escapades "cute" until the day comes when the whole volume of his hatred bursts into unchecked destruction. And it won't do to keep him in jail, to process him through court hearings, so as to give the general public their show and assure them that "something is being done about it" and to fool them into the illusion that storage or rehabilitative care in some institution solves the problem. In the long run, it comes down to the hard fact that our civilization has grown too sophisticated and decent to resort to the crude measure of simply destroying or removing the individual who doesn't fit in. Unfortunately, it doesn't seem to be wise enough yet or able to show the necessary financial courage to take the steps which would lead to his cure.

There is no doubt in our mind about how the only answer is to be sought. The first step toward a large scale and well organized system of facilities for cure is, of course, adequate and exhaustive research into just what the disturbance is all about to begin with. No, Santa Claus isn't playing any more. There is no escape from the laborious detour by way of patient observation, experiment, and tryout of new treatment designs. And, since psychological reality is as relentless as the physical reality of our gadget world, there is no way out of the fact that the original per capita costs will be high.

2. Milieu Therapy

As the social sciences have developed over the past fifty years or so, the extent to which the social milieu influences behavior has become increasingly evident. Only recently, however, has this knowledge been applied to the rehabilitation of the juvenile delinquent and the adult criminal. In the following description of the Highfields project by Lloyd McCorkle, Albert Elias, and F. Lovell Bixby, we can see how a deliberate effort was made to create a nonpunitive social atmosphere that stands in marked contrast to individual treatment or the usual environment of a penal institution.

While we would prefer in this report to avoid any speculation on the motives behind the delinquent act, and thus avoid the knotty theoretical and practical problems involved in statements on causation, our account would be incomplete without some formulation around the basic problem that any effective program to change attitudes is dependent upon; namely, a reasonably accurate conception of exactly what it is we wish to change and in what direction we wish change to occur. In regard to these issues, rather than make an attempt to explain delinquent conduct, our answer lies in Highfields' response to the kinds of problems that the boys present at the project. These problems seem to stem from the boys' conception of self and others as hostile, aggressive, inadequate persons, and as "hipsters," "wise guys," "squares," and "suckers." The Highfields program is organized to change and modify these distorted images of self and other people. The structure attempts to bring an awareness of the direct relationship between the learning tasks at the project and the immediate psychological problems of the residents, with a conviction that application in carrying out these learning tasks will have a direct and positive effect on the amelioration of these problems. These objectives, we hope, become realities in the lives of the boys in residence as a result of their intimate contacts with the Highfields social system that is maintained by the technique of guided group interaction.

The usage patterns of the Highfields social system are based on the assumption that youthful offenders need an informal, easy, educational experience in a type of social world. The important basic values in the

Highfields social world are security, flexibility, and the absence of punitive or counter-aggressive attitudes on part of staff members.

Highfields is organized to meet the boys' need to feel that it exists to help them during a troubled period in their lives. The emphasis has been to organize and develop a total situation designed to accept and understand the "tough guys," "wise guys," "bad boys," and others, with their present attitudes and ways of relating to others. There is no magic in the proceedings of arrest, detention, or court hearing to transform a confused, anxious, bitter, rebellious delinquent into a boy without aggressions or hostilities; and a necessary initial experience for him is to feel that Highfields does not expect to make him become, almost overnight, a "good boy." If the youthful offender feels he must suddenly become something to get along in a world he has been compelled to enter, experience indicates that he becomes even more anxious, confused, and bitter. Take such a simple matter as eating. Some of the boys who enter Highfields have seldom, if ever, had the opportunity to enjoy a family meal. One such boy was an aggressive, impulsive seventeen-year-old lad who had been engaging in crime almost as a day-by-day occupation for two years prior to residence. This boy had been living in the streets continuously for five years, and at school was a truant and troublemaker. He graduated from selling papers and shining shoes to shoplifting and stealing automobile hubcaps. From this he moved into auto larceny and rolling drunks. He did not have any conception of how people are supposed to behave at a family meal, and would stand up, reach over the table, pile up his plate, and use his fingers instead of knives and forks during the meal. If he had met inflexible rules and regulations around behavior in the dining room, the chances are that instead of feeling Highfields was designed to help him, his feelings of incompetence would have been intensified. Since he was given the opportunity to learn, from experiences with both staff and boys, the greater satisfactions that come from conforming to certain basic rules, he gradually learned to change his style of eating. When he departed from Highfields, while still not an ideal dinner companion for Emily Post, his eating habits were reasonably acceptable. This example is used to illustrate the firm conviction of the Highfields project that youthful offenders need to work up to equality with the outside world by a gradual promotion to those standards, and not by the creation of special standards.

At Highfields, the emphasis has been to create situations where boys can make choices from several possible ways of behaving and then feel secure enough to discuss their particular choices. It cannot be emphasized too strongly that during residence all boys are given opportunities to make choices in situations as much as possible like those they will meet in the community. After making their choices, opportunities to discuss them helps in the learning of new social roles. It should also be pointed out that the emphasis is on their social roles in relation to one another rather than to staff members. For instance, at Highfields, it is relatively simple to steal food from the kitchen. While stealing from the kitchen is disapproved of by both boys and staff, if a boy steals he is not punished. Instead, he is given the opportunity to discuss this behavior with both adults and peers. Since at one time or another practically every boy in residence steals, and the tradition has developed that it is all right to talk this over with the other boys and the adults at the project, most of the boys will discuss such an act. Needless to say, this talking it over with both adults and peers can be a rewarding experience for all.

Flexibility is another indispensable element in the total educational atmosphere developed at Highfields. "Permissiveness" is not used because of the possibility of suggesting the absence of structure. As Kenneth Pray pointed out, "There is no absolute freedom. There must be structure or authority, defining and enforcing the necessary limits upon individual person responsibility and conduct, as a condition of social co-operation and as an indispensable basis of any kind of life in any society." At Highfields the goal has been to develop a structure firm enough to give support and flexible enough to give scope to the boy's individuality. Frequently our boys have lived in a world filled with the "you mustn'ts" so delightfully expressed in one of Lewis Carroll's poems.

"What may I do" at length I cried,
Tired of the painful task.
The teacher quietly replied and said,
"You must not ask."

A world of "you must not" will be challenged by the adolescent, and he will be in more-or-less constant conflict with it. This world orders and forbids, and from his point of view its rules and regulations may have little meaning. He may conform and be coerced into saying, "Yes, sir," but opportunities for him to work out his own rules and regulations are necessary. Consequently, at Highfields, there is not a conventional system of rewards and punishments. It is also important to have as few rules and regulations as possible and not permit them to become fixed, as a result of experience, in a tradition. Therefore, the rules for discipline are simple, easy for all to understand, and include only those which are essential for the maintenance of order. As David Wills observed, "This discipline is conceived as a framework on which to hang the routine services of a community—a device for seeing that those things are done which in any society must be done—that food is made available, cleanliness maintained, health preserved, and the rights of the individual to go about his lawful occupations upheld." This type of discipline is not conceived as character training.

For a community like this to function, it is necessary that all the people who live in it work toward attitudes of greater understanding of one another. It is as important for the boys to understand one another as it is for the staff to understand the boys, or the boys the staff. In this community, people must live together, share experiences, and know one another as persons. The social distance that separates the staff and boys cannot be enforced by rules and regulations, but must be inherent in their reciprocal roles. If the boy can test the adult role, and if he finds it satisfying, he can then, with more knowledge and understanding, accept the adult as a member of the community instead of as a hostile, threatening figure. Consequently, the boy's hostile and aggressive impulses toward both adults and peers are lessened, and he is able to turn to them for guidance and encouragement. In such a situation, there is little need for formal efforts to indoctrinate others, and instruction is by example, not exhortation.

We believe this type of project-design contains what we consider the basic elements indispensable to any program aimed at changing the attitudes or shaping the behavior of delinquent boys. The person must somehow be brought to an awareness that his difficulties are related to motives and patterns of perception within himself. His attempts to account for these difficulties by blaming a hostile or unfavorable human environment must be analyzed as deriving at least in part from a natural human tendency to avoid guilt and self-rejection. He must be assisted in gaining an awareness and a motivation for taking present initiative toward change or growth within himself, and he must be shown the fruitlessness of evading this responsibility by futile attempts to change merely his environment.

This assistance toward understanding comes about through some relationship with the therapist (or therapeutic situation) in which the individual actually attempts to make his faulty modes of perception and behavior work. Repeated demonstrations of this failure may be necessary before he is able to abandon them. It is important that these failures be not interpreted by him as indicating that he is a worthless or helpless person.

Finally, the individual must be provided with opportunities for the learning, testing, and fixating of newer, more effective modes of perceiving and relating to his human environment. As these new patterns emerge and are found rewarding in terms of increased success in relations with the self and others, they tend to become more and more established in the individual's total pattern of adjustment.

3. The Company of Deviants

The idea that a great deal of criminal behavior is learned in much the same fashion as law-abiding behavior is learned has been incorporated under the heading of the theory of differential association, which is the cornerstone of much modern thinking about crime causation. The application of this idea to the reformation of the criminal is still only in its infancy, but in the following article by Rita Volkman and Donald Cressey some of the implications are discussed in detail.

"Synanon," an organization of former drug addicts, was founded in May, 1958, by a member of Alcoholics Anonymous with the assistance of an alcoholic and a drug addict. In December, 1958, Volkman (a non-addict) heard about the two dozen ex-addicts living together in an abandoned store, and she obtained permission of the Synanon Board of Directors to visit the group daily and to live in during the weekends. In July, 1959, she moved into the girls' dormitory of the group's new, larger quarters and continued to reside at Synanon House until June, 1960. Cressey (also a non-addict) visited the House at Volkman's invitation in the spring of 1960; for one year, beginning in July, 1960, he visited the organization on the average of at least once a week. He deliberately refrained from trying to influence policy or program, and his theory about the effects of group relationships on rehabilitation were unknown to the group. Most of the interview material and statistical data reported below were collected by Volkman during her 1959–60 period of residence and were used in the thesis for her Master's degree, prepared under the direction of C. Wayne Gordon. As both a full-fledged member of Synanon and as a participant observer, Volkman attended about three hundred group sessions, a few of which were recorded. She was accorded the same work responsibilities, rights, and privileges as any other member, and she was considered one of Synanon's first "graduates."

. . .

Admission.—Not every addict who knocks on the door of Synanon is given admission. Nevertheless, the only admission criterion we have been able to find is *expressed willingness* to submit one's self to a group that hates drug addiction. Use of this criterion has unwittingly implemented one of Cressey's principles:

From Rita Volkman and Donald R. Cressey, "Differential Association and the Rehabilitation of Drug Addicts," **The American Journal of Sociology,** LXIX (September 1963), 129–142. Reprinted by permission of The University of Chicago Press and the authors.

If criminals are to be changed, they must be assimilated into groups which emphasize values conducive to law-abiding behavior and, concurrently, alienated from groups emphasizing values conducive to criminality. Since our experience has been that the majority of criminals experience great difficulty in securing intimate contacts in ordinary groups, special groups whose major common goal is the reformation of criminals must be created.

This process of assimilation and alienation begins the moment an addict arrives at Synanon, and it continues throughout his stay. The following are two leaders' comments on admission interviews; they are consistent with our own observations of about twenty such interviews.

1. When a new guy comes in we want to find out whether a person has one inkling of seriousness. Everybody who comes here is what we call a psychopathic liar. We don't take them all, either. We work off the top spontaneously, in terms of feeling. We use a sort of intuitive faculty. You know he's lying, but you figure, "Well, maybe if you get a halfway positive feeling that he'll stay. . . ." We ask him things like "What do you want from us?" "Don't you think you're an idiot or insane?" "Doesn't it sound insane for you to be running around the alleys stealing money from others so's you can go and stick something up your arm?" "Does this sound sane to you?" "Have you got family and friends outside?" We might tell him to go do his business now and come back when he's ready to do business with us. We tell him, "We don't need you." "You need us." And if we figure he's only halfway with us, we'll chop off his hair.

It's all in the attitude. *It's got to be positive. We don't want their money. But we may just tell him to bring back some dough next week. If he pleads and begs—the money's not important. If he shows he really cares. If his attitude is good. It's all in the attitude.*

2. Mostly, if people don't have a family outside, with no business to take care of, they're ready to stay. They ain't going to have much time to think about themselves otherwise. . . . Now, when he's got problems, when he's got things outside, if he's got mickey mouse objections, like when you ask him "How do you feel about staying here for a year?" and he's got to bargain with you, like he needs to stay with his wife or his sick mother—then we tell him to get lost. If he can't listen to a few harsh words thrown at him, he's not ready. Sometimes we yell at him, "You're a goddamned liar!" If he's serious he'll take it. He'll do anything if he's serious.

But each guy's different. If he sounds sincere, we're not so hard. If he's sick of running the rat race out there, or afraid of going to the penitentiary, he's ready to do anything. Then we let him right in. . . .

This admission process seems to have two principal functions. First, it forces the newcomer to admit, at least on a verbal level, that he is willing to try to conform to the norms of the group, whose members will not tolerate any liking for drugs or drug addicts. From the minute he enters the door, his expressed desire to join the group is tested by giving him difficult orders—to have his hair cut off, to give up all his money, to sever all family ties, to come back in ten days or even thirty days. He is given expert help and explicit but simple criteria for separating the "good guys" from the "bad guys"—the latter shoot dope. Second, the admission process weeds out men and women who simply want to lie down for a few days to rest, to obtain free room and board, or to stay out of the hands of the police. In the terms used by Lindesmith, and also in the terms used at Synanon, the person must want to give up drug *addiction,* not just the drug *habit.* This means that he must at least *say* that he wants to quit using drugs once and for all, in order to realize his potentials as an adult; he must not indicate that he merely wants a convenient place in which to go through withdrawal distress so that he can be rid of his habit for a short time because he has lost his connection, or for some other reason. He must be willing to give up all ambitions, desires, and social interactions that might prevent the group from assimilating him completely.

If he says he just wants to kick, he's no good. Out with him. Now we know nine out of ten lie, but we don't care. We'd rather have him make an attempt and lie *and then get him in here for thirty days or so—then he might stick. It takes months to decide to stay.*

Most fish [*newcomers*] *don't take us seriously. We know what they want, out in front. A dope fiend wants dope, nothing else. All the rest is garbage. We've even taken that ugly thing called money. This shows that they're serious. Now this guy today was sincere. We told him we didn't want money. We could see he would at least give the place a try. We have to find out if he's sincere. Is he willing to have us cut off his curly locks? I imagine cutting his hair off makes him take us seriously. . . .*

Although it is impossible to say whether Synanon's selective admission process inadvertently admits those addicts who are most amenable to change, no addict has been refused admission on the ground that his case is "hopeless" or "difficult" or that he is "unreachable." On the contrary, before coming to Synanon, twenty-nine of the fifty-two addicts had been on drugs for at least ten years. Two of these were addicted for over forty years, and had been in and out of institutions during that period. The average length of time on drugs for the fifty-two was eleven years, and 56 per cent reported less than one month as the longest period of time voluntarily free of drugs after addiction and prior to Synanon.

Indoctrination.—In the admission process, and throughout his residence, the addict discovers over and over again that the group to which he is submitting is antidrug, anticrime, and antialcohol. At least a dozen times a day he hears someone tell him that he can remain at Synanon only as long as he "stays clean," that is, stays away from crime, alcohol, and drugs. This emphasis is an unwitting implementation of Cressey's second principle:

The more relevant the common purpose of the group to the reformation of criminals, the greater will be its influence on the criminal members' attitudes and values. Just as a labor union exerts strong influence over its members' attitudes toward management but less influence on their attitudes toward say,

Negroes, so a group organized for recreation or welfare purposes will have less success in influencing criminalistic attitudes and values than will one whose explicit purpose is to change criminals.

Indoctrination makes clear the notion that Synanon exists in order to keep addicts off drugs, not for purposes of recreation, vocational education, etc. Within a week after admission, each newcomer participates in an indoctrination session by a spontaneous group made up of four or five older members. Ordinarily, at least one member of the Board of Directors is present, and he acts as leader. The following are excerpts from one such session with a woman addict. The rules indicate the extreme extent to which it is necessary for the individual to subvert his personal desires and ambitions to the antidrug, anticrime group.

Remember, we told you not to go outside by yourself. Whenever anybody leaves this building they have to check in and out at the desk. For a while, stay in the living room. Don't take showers alone or even go to the bathroom alone, see. While you're kicking, somebody will be with you all the time. And stay away from newcomers. You got nothing to talk to them about, except street talk, and before you know it you'll be splitting [*leaving*] *to take a fix together. Stay out of the streets, mentally and physically, or get lost now.*

No phone calls or letters for a while—if you get one, you'll read it in front of us. We'll be monitoring all your phone calls for a while. You see, you got no ties, no business out there any more. You don't need them. You never could handle them before, so don't start thinking you can do it now. All you knew how to do was shoot dope and go to prison.

You could never take care of your daughter before. You didn't know how to be a mother. It's garbage. All a dope fiend knows how to do is shoot dope. Forget it.

There are two obvious illustrations of the antidrug and anticrime nature of the group's subculture. First, there is a strong taboo against what is called "street talk." Discussion of how it feels to take a fix, who one's connection was, where one took his shot, the crimes one has committed, or who one associated with is severely censured. One's best friend and confidant at Synanon might well be the person that administers a tongue lashing for street talk, and the person who calls your undesirable behavior to the attention of the entire group during a general meeting.

Second, a member must never, in any circumstances, identify with the "code of the streets," which says that a criminal is supposed to keep quiet about the criminal activities of his peers. Even calling an ordinary citizen "square" is likely to stimulate a spontaneous lecture, in heated and colorful terms, on the notion that the people who are *really* square are those that go around as bums sticking needles in their arms. A person who, as a criminal, learned to hate stool pigeons and finks with a passion must now turn even his closest friend over to the authorities, the older members of Synanon, if the friend shows any signs of nonconformity. If he should find that a member is considering "sneaking off to a fix somewhere," has kept pills, drugs, or an "outfit" with him when he joined the organization, or even has violated rules such as that prohibiting walking alone on the beach, he must by Synanon's code relinquish his emotional ties with the violator and expose the matter to another member or even to the total membership at a general meeting. If he does not do so, more pressure is put upon him than upon the violator, for he is expected to have "known better." Thus, for perhaps the first time in his life he will be censured for *not* "squealing" rather than for "squealing." He must identify with the law and not with the criminal intent or act.

The sanctions enforcing this norm are severe, for its violation threatens the very existence of the group. "Guilt by association" is the rule. In several instances, during a general meeting the entire group spontaneously voted to "throw out" both a member who had used drugs and a member who had known of this use but had not informed the group. Banishment from the group is considered the worst possible punishment, for it is stressed over and over again that life in the streets "in your condition" can only mean imprisonment or death.

That the group's purpose is keeping addicts off drugs is given emphasis in formal and informal sessions—called "haircuts" or "pull ups"—as well as in spontaneous denunciations, and in denunciations at general meetings. The "synanon," discussed below, also serves this purpose. A "haircut" is a deliberately contrived device for minimizing the importance of the individual and maximizing the importance of the group, and for defining the group's basic purpose—keeping addicts off drugs and crime. The following is the response of a leader to the questions, "What's a haircut? What's its purpose?"

When you are pointing out what a guy is doing. We do this through mechanisms of exaggeration. We blow up an incident so he can really get a look at it. The Coordinators [*a coordinator resembles an officer of the day*] *and the Board members and sometimes an old timer may sit in on it. We do this when we see a person's attitude becoming negative in some area.*

For a real *haircut, I'll give you myself. I was in a tender trap. My girl split. She called me on the job three days in a row. I made a date with her. We kept the date and I stayed out all night with her. Now, she was loaded* [*using drugs*]. *I neglected—or I refused—to call the house. By doing this I ranked everybody. You know doing something like that was no good. They were all concerned. They sent three or four autos looking for me because I didn't come back from work. You see, I was in Stage II.*

X found me and he made me feel real lousy, because I knew he worked and was concerned. Here he was out looking for me and he had to get up in the morning.

Well, I called the house the next morning and came back. I got called in for a haircut.

I sat down with three Board members in the office. They stopped everything to give the haircut. That impressed me. Both Y and Z, they pointed out my absurd and ridiculous behavior by saying things like this—though I did not get loaded, I associated with a broad I was emotionally involved with who was using junk. I jeopardized my own existence by doing this. So they told me, "Well, you fool, you might as well have shot dope by associating with a using addict." I was given an ultimatum. If I called her again or got in touch with her I would be thrown out.

("Why?")

Because continued correspondence with a using dope fiend is a crime against me—it hurts me. It was also pointed out how rank I was to people who are concerned with me. I didn't seem to care about people who were trying to help me. I'm inconsiderate to folks who've wiped my nose, fed me, clothed me. I'm like a child, I guess. I bite the hand that feeds me.

To top that off, I had to call a general meeting and I told everybody in the building what a jerk I was and I was sorry for acting like a little punk. I just sort of tore myself down. Told everyone what a phony I had been. And then the ridiculing questions began. Everybody started in. Like, "Where do you get off doing that to us?" That kind of stuff. When I was getting the treatment they asked me what I'd do—whether I would continue the relationship, whether I'd cut it off, or if I really wanted to stay at Synanon and do something about myself and my problem. But I made the decision before I even went in that I'd stay and cut the broad loose. I had enough time under my belt to know enough to make that decision before I even came back to the house. . . .

Group cohesion.—The daily program at Synanon is consistent with Cressey's third principle, and appears to be an unwitting attempt to implement that principle:

The more cohesive the group, the greater the members' readiness to influence others and the more relevant the problem of conformity to group norms. The criminals who are to be reformed and the persons expected to effect the change must, then, have a strong sense of belonging to one group: between them there must be a genuine "we" feeling. The reformers, consequently, should not be identifiable as correctional workers, probation or parole officers, or social workers.

Cohesion is maximized by a "family" analogy and by the fact that all but some "third-stage" members live and work together. The daily program has been deliberately designed to throw members into continuous mutual activity. In addition to the free, unrestricted interaction in small groups called "synanons," the members meet as a group at least twice each day. After breakfast, someone is called upon to read the "Synanon Philosophy," which is a kind of declaration of principles, the day's work schedule is discussed, bits of gossip are publicly shared, the group or individual members are spontaneously praised or scolded by older members. Following a morning of work activities, members meet in the dining room after lunch to discuss some concept or quotation that has been written on a blackboard. Stress is on participation and expression; quotations are selected by Board members to provoke controversy and examination of the meaning, or lack of meaning, of words. Discussion sometimes continues informally during the afternoon work period and in "synanons," which are held after dinner (see below). In addition, lectures and classes, conducted by any member or outside speaker who will take on the responsibility, are held several times a week for all members who feel a need for them. Topics have included "semantics," "group dynamics," "meaning of truth," and "Oedipus complex."

There are weekend recreational activities, and holidays, wedding anniversaries, and birthdays are celebrated. Each member is urged: "Be yourself," "Speak the truth," "Be honest," and this kind of action in an atmosphere that is informal and open quickly gives participants a strong sense of "belonging." Since many of the members have been homeless drifters, it is not surprising to hear frequent repetition of some comment to the effect that "This is the first home I ever had."

Also of direct relevance to the third principle is the *voluntary* character of Synanon. Any member can walk out at any time; at night the doors are locked against persons who might want to enter, but not against persons who might want to leave. Many do leave.

Holding addicts in the house once they have been allowed to enter is a strong appeal to ideas such as "We have all been in the shape you are now in," or "Mike was on heroin for twenty years and *he's* off." It is significant, in this connection, that addicts who "kick" (go through withdrawal distress) at Synanon universally report that the sickness is not as severe as it is in involuntary organizations, such as jails and mental hospitals. One important variable here, we believe, is the practice of not giving "kicking dope fiends" special quarters. A newcomer kicks on a davenport in the center of the large living room, not in a special isolation room or quarantine room. Life goes on around him. Although a member will be assigned to watch him, he soon learns that his sickness is not important to men and women who have themselves kicked the habit. In the living room, one or two couples might be dancing, five or six people may be arguing, a man may be practicing the guitar, and a girl may be ironing. The kicking addict learns his lesson: These others have made it. This subtle device is supplemented by explicit comments from various members as they walk by or as they drop in to chat with him. We have heard the following comments, and many similar ones, made to new addicts lying sick from withdrawal. It should be noted that none of the comments could reasonably have been made by a rehabilitation official or a professional therapist.

"It's OK boy. We've all been through it before."

"For once you're with people like us. You've got everything to gain here and nothing to lose."

"You think you're tough. Listen, we've got guys in here who could run circles around you, so quit your bull——."

"You're one of us now, so keep your eyes open, your mouth shut and try to listen for a while. Maybe you'll learn a few things."

"Hang tough, baby. We won't let you die."

Status ascription.—Cressey's fourth principle is:

Both reformers and those to be reformed must achieve status within the group by exhibition of "pro-reform" or anti-criminal values and behavior patterns. As a novitiate . . . he is a therapeutic parasite and not actually a member until he accepts the group's own system for assigning status.

This is the crucial point in Cressey's formula, and it is on this point that Synanon seems most effective. The house has an explicit program for distributing status symbols to members in return for staying off the drug and, later, for actually displaying antidrug attitudes. The resident, no longer restricted to the status of "inmate" or "patient" as in a prison or hospital, can achieve any staff position in the status hierarchy.

The Synanon experience is organized into a career of roles that represent stages of graded competence, at whose end are roles that might later be used in the broader community. Figure 1 shows the status system in terms of occupational roles, each box signifying a stratum. Such cliques as exist at Synanon tend to be among persons of the same stratum. Significantly, obtaining jobs of increased responsibility and status is almost completely dependent upon one's attitudes toward crime and the use of drugs. To obtain a job such as Senior Coordinator, for example, the member must have demonstrated that he can remain free of drugs, crime, and alcohol for at least three to six months. Equally important, he must show that he can function without drugs in situations where he might have used drugs before he came to Synanon. Since he is believed to have avoided positions of responsibility by taking drugs, he must gradually take on positions of responsibility without the use of drugs. Thus, he cannot go up the status ladder unless his "attitudes" are right, no matter what degree of skill he might have as a workman. Evaluation is rather casual, but it is evaluation nevertheless—he will not be given a decent job in the organization unless he relinquishes the role of the "con artist" and answers questions honestly, expresses emotions freely, co-operates in group activities, and demonstrates leadership. In a letter to a public official in May, 1960, the founder explained the system as follows:

Continued residence [*at Synanon*], *which we feel to be necessary to work out the problem of interpersonal relationships which underlie the addiction symptom is based on adherence by the individual to standards of behavior, thinking, and feeling acceptable to our culture. There is much work to be done here, as we have no paid help, and each person must assume his share of the burden. Increased levels of responsibility are sought and the experience of self-satisfaction comes with seeking and assuming these higher levels and seems to be an extremely important part of emotional growth.*

An analogy with a family and the development of a child also is used. Officially, every member is expected to go through three "stages of growth," indicated by Roman numerals in Figure 1. Stage I has two phases, "infancy" and "adolescence." In the "infancy" phase (I-A) the

Graduates	Board of Directors
(*Work and live outside*)	(*Policy-makers*)

Stage III

Assistant directors	Office manager
Attend school	Project directors
Business manager	Senior coordinators
Department chiefs	Work outside

Stage II

Hustling crew	Nursery heads
Junior coordinators	Office workers
Kitchen crew chief	Service crew chief

Stage I-B

Automobile crew	Laundry
Barber	Library
Electricity	Maintenance crew
Housecleaning	Plumbing
Kitchen help	Service crew

Stage I-AB

Newcomers Non-workers

Sick, kicking addicts

Stage I-A

member behaves like an infant and is treated as one; as he kicks the habit "cold turkey" (without the aid of drugs) in the living room, he is dependent on the others, and he is supervised and watched at all times. When he is physically and mentally able, he performs menial tasks such as dishwashing and sweeping in a kind of "preadolescent" stage (I-AB) and then takes on more responsible positions (I-B). In this "adolescence" phase he takes on responsibility for maintenance work, participates actively in group meetings, demonstrates a concern for "emotional growth," mingles with newcomers and visitors, and accepts responsibilities for dealing with them. In work activities, for example, he might drive the group's delivery truck alone, watch over a sick addict, supervise the dishwashing or cleanup crews, or meet strangers at the door.

Stage II is called the "young adult stage." Here, the member is in a position to choose between making Synanon a "career," attending school, or going to work at least part time. If he works for Synanon, his position is complex and involves enforcing policy over a wide range of members. In Stage III, "adult," he moves up to a policy-making position in the Board of Directors or moves out of Synanon but returns with his friends and family for occasional visits. He can apparently resist the urge to resort to drugs in times of crisis without the direct help of Synanon members. One man described this stage by saying, "They go out, get jobs, lose jobs, get married, get divorced, get married again, just like everyone else." However, the group does maintain a degree of control. Graduates are never supposed to cut off their ties with their Synanon "family," and they are expected to return frequently to display themselves as "a dope fiend made good."

As time of residence increases, responsibilities to the group, in the forms of work and leadership, tend to increase. In June, 1962, twenty-seven of the 105 members of Synanon were in Stage III. It should be noted that while stage is associated with length of residence, advancement through the stages is not automatic. The longer one lives at Synanon, the "cleaner" he is, the more diffuse the roles he performs, and the higher his status.

It is also important to note that high status does not depend entirely upon one's conduct within the house. Before he graduates to Stage III a member must in some way be accorded an increase in status by the legitimate outside community. This is further insurance that status will be conferred for activities that are antidrug in character. In early 1960, the members began to take an active part in legitimate community activities, mostly in the form of lectures and discussion groups. Since Synanon's inception, more than 350 service groups, church groups, political groups, school and college classes, etc., have been addressed by speakers from Synanon. Such speeches and discussions gain community support for the organization, but they further function to give members a feeling of being important enough to be honored by an invitation to speak before community groups. Similarly, members are proud of those individuals who have "made good" in the outside community by becoming board members of the P.T.A., Sunday-school teachers, college students, and members of civic and service organizations. Over thirty-five Synanon members are now working full or part time in the community, holding a wide range of unskilled (janitor, parking attendant), skilled (truck driver, carpenter, electrician), white-collar (secretary, photographer), and executive (purchasing agent) posts.

Further, the legitimate status of the *group* has increasingly risen during the last two years. Since the summer of 1960, an average of 100–150 guests have attended open-house meetings, and the guests have included distinguished persons from all walks of legitimate life. Well-known psychiatrists, correctional workers, businessmen, newspapermen, and politicians have publicly praised the work of the group. There have been requests for Synanon houses and for Synanon groups from several communities, and Synanon projects are now being conducted at Terminal Island Federal Prison and the Nevada State Prison. Recently, the group has been featured in films, on television and radio shows, and in national magazines. At least two books and a movie are being written about it. Over five hundred citizens have formed an organization called "Sponsors of Synanon." Even strong attacks from some members of the local community and complicated legal battles about zoning ordinances have served principally to unite the group and maximize the *esprit de corps*.

The "synanon."—Synanon got its name from an addict who was trying to say "seminar." The term "Synanon" is used to refer to the entire organization, but when it is spelled with a lower-case *s* it refers only to the meetings occurring in the evenings among small groups of six to ten members. Each evening, all members are assigned to such groups, and membership in the groups is rotated so that one does not regularly interact with the same six or ten persons. The announced aim of these meetings is to "trigger feelings" and to allow what some members refer to as "a catharsis." The sessions are not "group therapy" in the usual sense, for no trained therapist is present. Moreover, the emphasis is on enforcing anti-criminal and anti-drug norms, as well as upon emotional adjustment. These sessions, like the entire program, constitute a system for implementing Cressey's fifth principle, although they were not designed to do so.

> *The most effective mechanism for exerting group pressure on members will be found in groups so organized that criminals are induced to join with noncriminals for the purpose of changing other criminals. A group in which criminal A joins with some noncriminals to change criminal B is probably most effective in changing criminal A, not B; in order to change criminal B, criminal A must necessarily share the values of the anticriminal members.*

In the house, the behavior of all members is visible to all others. What a member is seen to do at the breakfast table, for example, might well be scrutinized and discussed at his synanon that evening. The synanon sessions differ from everyday honesty by virtue of the fact that in these discussions one is expected to *insist on* the truth as well as to tell the truth. Any weapon, such as ridicule, cross-examination, or hostile attack, is both permissible and expected. The sessions seem to provide an atmosphere of truth-seeking that is reflected in the rest of the social life within the household so that a simple question like "How are you?" is likely to be answered by a five-minute discourse in which the respondent searches for the truth. The following discussion is from a tape recording of a synanon session held in June, 1961. It should be noted that an "innocent" question about appearance, asked by an older member who has become a non-criminal and a non-addict, led to an opportunity to emphasize the importance of loyalty to the antidrug, anticrime group.

"What are you doing about losing weight?"

"Why? Is that your business?"

"I asked you a question."

"I don't intend to answer it. It's not your business."

"Why do you want to lose weight?"

"I don't intend to answer it."

"Why?"

"Because it's an irrelevant and meaningless question. You know I had a baby only three weeks ago, and you've been attacking me about my weight. It's none of your business."

"Why did you call your doctor?"

"Why? Because I'm on a diet."

"What did he prescribe for you?"

"I don't know. I didn't ask him."

"What did you ask for?"

"I didn't. I don't know what he gave me."

"Come on now. What kind of pills are they?"

"I don't know. I'm not a chemist. Look the doctor knows I'm an addict. He knows I live at Synanon. He knows a whole lot about me."

"Yeah, well, I heard you also talking to him on the phone, and you sounded just like any other addict trying to cop a doctor out of pills."

"You're a goddamned liar!"

"Yeah, well X was sitting right there. Look, does the doctor know and does the Board know?"

"I spoke to Y [Board member]. It's all been verified."

"What did Y say?"

"I was talking to . . ."

"What did Y say?"

"Well, will you wait just a minute?"

"What did Y say?"

"Well, let her talk."

"I don't want to hear no stories."

"I'm not telling stories."

"What did Y say?"

"That it was harmless. The doctor said he'd give me nothing that would affect me. There's nothing in it. He knows it all. I told Y."

"Oh, you're all like a pack of wolves. You don't need to yell and scream at her."

"Look, I heard her on the phone and the way she talked she was trying to manipulate the doctor."

"Do you resent the fact that she's still acting like a dope fiend and she still sounds like she's conning the doctor out of something? She's a dope fiend. Maybe she can't talk to a doctor any differently."

"Look, I called the doctor today. He said I should call him if I need him. He gave me vitamins and lots of other things."

"Now wait a minute. You called to find out if you could get some more pills."

"Besides, it's the attitude they heard over the phone. That's the main thing."

"Yeah, well they probably projected it onto me."

"Then how come you don't like anyone listening to your phone calls?"

"Are you feeling guilty?"

"Who said?"

"Me. That's who. You even got sore when you found out X and me heard you on the phone, didn't you? You didn't like that at all, did you?"

"Is that so?"

(Silence.)

"I don't think her old man wants her back."

"Well, who would? An old fat slob like that."

"Sure, that's probably why she's thinking of leaving all the time and ordering pills."

"Sure."

(Silence.)

"My appearance is none of your business."

"Everything here is our business."

"Look, when a woman has a baby you can't understand she can't go back to normal weight in a day."

"Now you look. We're really not interested in your weight problem now. Not really. We just want to know why you've got to have pills to solve the problem. We're going to talk about that if we want to. That's what we're here for."

"Look, something's bugging you. We all know that. I even noticed it in your attitude toward me."

"Yeah, I don't care about those pills. I want to know how you're feeling. What's behind all this? Something's wrong. What is it?"

(Silence.)

"Have you asked your old man if you could come home yet?"

(Softly.) *"Yes."*

"What did he say?"

(Softly.) *"He asked me how I felt. Wanted to know why I felt I was ready to come home. . . ."*

(Silence.)

(Softly.) *"I did it out of anger. I wasn't very happy.* (Pause.) *A day before I tried [telephoning him] and he wasn't there.* (Pause.) *Just this funny feeling about my husband being there and me here. My other kid's there and this one's here.* (Pause.) *A mixed-up family."*

"Why do you want to stay then? Do you want to be here?"

"No. I don't want to be here. That's exactly why I'm staying. I need to stay till I'm ready."

"Look, you've got to cut them loose for a while. You may not be ready for the rest of your life. You may not ever be able to be with those people."

(Tears.)

"I know. . . ."

After the synanon sessions, the house is always noisy and lively. We have seen members sulk, cry, shout, and threaten to leave the group as a result of conversation in the synanon. The following comments, every one of which represents the expression of a pro-reform attitude by the speaker, were heard after one session. It is our hypothesis that such expressions are the important ones, for they indicate that the speaker has become a reformer and, thus, is reinforcing his own pro-reform attitudes every time he tries to comfort or reform another.

"Were they hard on you?"

"I really let him have it tonight."

"I couldn't get to her. She's so damned blocked she couldn't even hear what I was trying to tell her."

"Hang tough, man; it gets easier."

"One of these days he'll drop those defenses of his and start getting honest."

"Don't leave. We all love you and want you to get well."

At Synanon, disassociating with former friends, avoiding street talk, and becoming disloyal to criminals are emphasized at the same time that loyalty to non-criminals, telling the truth to authority figures, and legitimate work are stressed. We have no direct evidence that haircuts, synanons, and both formal and spontaneous denunciations of street talk and the code of the streets have important rehabilitative effects on the actor, as well as (or, perhaps even "rather than") on the victim. It seems rather apparent, however, that an individual's own behavior must be dramatically influenced when he acts in the role of a moral policeman and "takes apart" another member. It is significant that older members of Synanon like to point out that the "real Synanon" began on "the night of the big cop out" (confession). In its earliest days, Synanon had neither the group cohesiveness nor the degree of control it now has. Some participants remained as addicts while proclaiming their loyalty to the principle of antiaddiction, and other participants knew of this condition. One evening in a general meeting a man spontaneously stood up and confessed ("copped out") that he had sneaked out for a shot. One by one, with no prompting, the others present rose to confess either their own violations or their knowledge of the violations of their friends. From that moment, the Board of Directors believe, the organization became a truly antidrug group; there has been no problem of drug use since.

. . .

Of the fifty-two residents described earlier, four are "graduates" of Synanon, are living in the community, and are not using alcohol or drugs. Twenty-three (44.2 per cent) are still in residence and are not using alcohol or drugs. Two of these are on the Board of Directors and eleven are working part or full time. The remaining twenty-five left Synanon against the advice of the Board and the older members.

Information regarding the longest period of voluntary abstinence from drugs after the onset of addiction but prior to entering Synanon was obtained on forty-eight of the fifty-two persons. Eleven reported that they were "never" clean, six said they were continuously clean for less than one week, ten were continuously clean for less than one month. Thirty-nine (81 per cent) said they had been continuously clean for less than six months, and only two had been clean for as long as a one-year period. Twenty-seven (52 per cent) of the fifty-two residents have now abstained for a least six months; twelve of these have been clean for at least two years and two have been off drugs continually for over three years.

Between May, 1958 (when Synanon started), and May, 1961, 263 persons were admitted or readmitted to Synanon. Of these, 190 (72 per cent) left Synanon against the advice of the Board of Directors and the older members. Significantly, 59 per cent of all dropouts occurred within the first month of residence, 90 per cent within the first three months. Synanon is not adverse to giving a person a second chance, or even a third or fourth chance: of the 190 persons dropping out, eighty-three (44 per cent) were persons who had been readmitted. The dropout behavior of persons who were readmitted was, in general, similar to first admissions; 64 per cent of their dropouts occurred within the first month, 93 per cent within the first three months after readmission.

Of all the Synanon enrolees up to August, 1962, 108 out of 372 (29 per cent) are known to be off drugs. More significantly, of the 215 persons who have remained at Synanon for at least one month, 103 (48 per cent) are still off drugs; of the 143 who have remained for at least three months, 95 (66 per cent) are still non-users; of the 87 who have remained at least seven months, 75 (86 per cent) are non-users. These statistics seem to us to be most relevant, for they indicate that once an addict actually becomes a member of the antidrug community (as indicated by three to six months of participation), the probability that he will leave and revert to the use of drugs is low.

Synanon's leaders do not claim to "cure" drug addicts. They are prone to measure success by pointing to the fact that the organization now includes the membership of forty-five persons who were heroin addicts for at least ten years. Two of these were addicted for more than thirty years and spent those thirty years going in and out of prisons, jails, the U.S. Public Service Hospital, and similar institutions. The leaders have rather inadvertently used a theory of rehabilitation that implies that it is as ridiculous to try to "cure" a man of drug addiction as it is to try to "cure" him of sexual intercourse. A man can be helped to stay away from drugs, however, and this seems to be the contribution Synanon is making. In this regard, its "success" rate is higher than that of those institutions officially designated by society as places for the confinement and "reform" of drug addicts. Such a comparison is not fair, however, both because it is not known whether the subjects in Synanon are comparable to those confined in institutions, and because many official institutions do not concentrate on trying to keep addicts off drugs, being content to withdraw the drug, build up the addicts physically, strengthen vocational skills, and eliminate gaps in educational backgrounds.

We cannot be certain that it is the group relationships at Synanon, rather than something else, that is keeping addicts away from crime and drugs. However, both the times at which dropouts occur and the increasing antidrug attitudes displayed with increasing length of residence tend to substantiate Sutherland's theory of differential association and Cressey's notion that modifying social relationships is an effective supplement to the clinical handling of convicted criminals. Drug addiction is, in fact, a severe test of Sutherland's sociological theory and Cressey's sociological principles, for addicts have the double problem of criminality and the drug habit. The statistics on dropouts suggest that the group relations method of rehabilitation does not begin to have its effects until newcomers are truly integrated into the antidrug, anticrime group that is Synanon.

4. The Watchful Street

Both the selection on milieu therapy and the article by Volkman and Cressey are concerned with reforming the individual who is already set on the path of criminality. But there is also the problem of preventing criminal or delinquent behavior from arising in the first place. One part of the answer to this problem, as Jane Jacobs points out in her analysis of urban streets, may be in the physical structure of our cities and the patterns of human activity that provide controls. The argument is important because it suggests that dealing with crime can depend on a good deal more than the changing of personality traits.

Streets in cities serve many purposes besides carrying vehicles, and city sidewalks—the pedestrian parts of the streets—serve many purposes besides carrying pedestrians. These uses are bound up with circulation but are not identical with it and in their own right they are at least as basic as circulation to the proper workings of cities.

A city sidewalk by itself is nothing. It is an abstraction. It means something only in conjunction with the buildings and other uses that border it, or border other sidewalks very near it. The same might be said of streets, in the sense that they serve other purposes besides carrying wheeled traffic in their middles. Streets and their sidewalks, the main public places of a city, are its most vital organs. Think of a city and what comes to mind? Its streets. If a city's streets look interesting, the city looks interesting; if they look dull, the city looks dull.

More than that, and here we get down to the first problem, if a city's streets are safe from barbarism and fear, the city is thereby tolerably safe from barbarism and fear. When people say that a city, or a part of it, is dangerous or is a jungle what they mean primarily is that they do not feel safe on the sidewalks.

But sidewalks and those who use them are not passive beneficiaries of safety or helpless victims of danger. Sidewalks, their bordering uses, and their users, are active participants in the drama of civilization versus barbarism in cities. To keep the city safe is a fundamental task of a city's streets and its sidewalks.

This task is totally unlike any service that sidewalks and streets in little towns or true suburbs are called upon to do. Great cities are not like towns, only larger. They are not like suburbs, only denser. They differ from towns and suburbs in basic ways, and one of these is that cities are, by definition, full of strangers. To any one person, strangers are far more common in big cities than acquaintances. More common not just in places of public assembly, but more common at a man's own doorstep. Even residents who live near each other are strangers, and must be, because of the sheer number of people in small geographical compass.

The bedrock attribute of a successful city district is that a person must feel personally safe and secure on the street among all these strangers. He must not feel automatically menaced by them. A city district that fails in this respect also does badly in other ways and lays up for itself, and for its city at large, mountain on mountain of trouble.

Today barbarism has taken over many city streets, or people fear it has, which comes to much the same thing in the end. "I live in a lovely, quiet residential area," says a friend of mine who is hunting another place to live. "The only disturbing sound at night is the occasional scream of someone being mugged." It does not take many incidents of violence on a city street, or in a city district, to make people fear the streets. And as they fear them, they use them less, which makes the streets still more unsafe.

To be sure, there are people with hobgoblins in their heads, and such people will never feel safe no matter what the objective circumstances are. But this is a different matter from the fear that besets normally prudent, tolerant and cheerful people who show nothing more than common sense in refusing to venture after dark—or in a few places, by day—into streets where they may well be assaulted, unseen or unrescued until too late.

The barbarism and the real, not imagined, insecurity that gives rise to such fears cannot be tagged a problem of the slums. The problem is most serious, in fact, in genteel-looking "quiet residential areas" like that my friend was leaving.

It cannot be tagged as a problem of older parts of cities. The problem reaches its most baffling dimensions in some examples of rebuilt parts of cities, including supposedly the best examples of rebuilding, such as middle-income projects. The police precinct captain of a nationally admired project of this kind (admired by planners and lenders) has recently admonished residents not only about hanging around outdoors after dark but has urged them never to answer their doors without knowing the caller. Life here has much in common with life for the three little pigs or the seven little kids of the nursery thrillers. The problem of sidewalk and doorstep insecurity is as serious in cities which have made conscientious efforts at rebuilding as it is in those cities that have lagged. Nor is it illuminating to tag minority groups, or the poor, or the outcast with responsibility for city danger. There are immense variations in the degree of civilization and safety found among such groups and among the city areas where they live.

Some of the safest sidewalks in New York City, for example, at any time of day or night, are those along which poor people or minority groups live. And some of the most dangerous are in streets occupied by the same kinds of people. All this can also be said of other cities.

Deep and complicated social ills must lie behind delinquency and crime, in suburbs and towns as well as in great cities. This book will not go into speculation on the deeper reasons. It is sufficient, at this point, to say that if we are to maintain a city society that can diagnose and keep abreast of deeper social problems, the starting point must be, in any case, to strengthen whatever workable forces for maintaining safety and civilization do exist—in the cities we do have. To build city districts that are custom made for easy crime is idiotic. Yet that is what we do.

The first thing to understand is that the public peace—the sidewalk and street peace—of cities is not kept primarily by the police, necessary as police are. It is kept primarily by an intricate, almost unconscious, network of voluntary controls and standards among the people themselves, and enforced by the people themselves. In some city areas—older public housing projects and streets with very high population turnover are often conspicuous examples—the keeping of public sidewalk law and order is left almost entirely to the police and special guards. Such places are jungles. No amount of police can enforce civilization where the normal, casual enforcement of it has broken down.

The second thing to understand is that the problem of insecurity cannot be solved by spreading people out more thinly, trading the characteristics of cities for the characteristics of suburbs. If this could solve danger on the city streets, then Los Angeles should be a safe city because superficially Los Angeles is almost all suburban. It has virtually no districts compact enough to qualify as dense city areas. Yet Los Angeles cannot, any more than any other great city, evade the truth that, being a city, it *is* composed of strangers not all of whom are nice. Los Angeles' crime figures are flabbergasting. Among the seventeen standard metropolitan areas with populations over a million, Los Angeles stands so pre-eminent in crime that it is in a category by itself. And this is markedly true of crimes associated with personal attack, the crimes that make people fear the streets.

Los Angeles, for example, has a forcible rape rate (1958 figures) of 31.9 per 100,000 population, more than twice as high as either of the next two cities, which happen to be St. Louis and Philadelphia; three times as high as the rate of 10.1 for Chicago, and more than four times as high as the rate of 7.4 for New York.

In aggravated assault, Los Angeles has a rate of 185, compared with 149.5 for Baltimore and 139.2 for St. Louis (the two next highest), and with 90.9 for New York and 79 for Chicago.

The overall Los Angeles rate for major crimes is 2,507.6 per 100,000 people, far ahead of St. Louis and Houston, which come next with 1,634.5

and 1,541.1, and of New York and Chicago, which have rates of 1,145.3 and 943.5.

The reasons for Los Angeles' high crime rates are undoubtedly complex, and at least in part obscure. But of this we can be sure: thinning out a city does not insure safety from crime and fear of crime. This is one of the conclusions that can be drawn within individual cities too, where pseudo-suburbs or superannuated suburbs are ideally suited to rape, muggings, beatings, hold-ups and the like.

Here we come up against an all-important question about any city street: How much easy opportunity does it offer to crime? It may be that there is some absolute amount of crime in a given city, which will find an outlet somehow (I do not believe this). Whether this is so or not, different kinds of city streets garner radically different shares of barbarism and fear of barbarism.

Some city streets afford no opportunity to street barbarism. The streets of the North End of Boston are outstanding examples. They are probably as safe as any place on earth in this respect. Although most of the North End's residents are Italian or of Italian descent, the district's streets are also heavily and constantly used by people of every race and background. Some of the strangers from outside work in or close to the district; some come to shop and stroll; many, including members of minority groups who have inherited dangerous districts previously abandoned by others, make a point of cashing their paychecks in North End stores and immediately making their big weekly purchases in streets where they know they will not be parted from their money between the getting and the spending.

Frank Havey, director of the North End Union, the local settlement house, says, "I have been here in the North End twenty-eight years, and in all that time I have never heard of a single case of rape, mugging, molestation of a child or other street crime of that sort in the district. And if there had been any, I would have heard of it even if it did not reach the papers." Half a dozen times or so in the past three decades says Havey, would-be molesters have made an attempt at luring a child or, late at night, attacking a woman. In every such case the try was thwarted by passers-by, by kibitzers from windows, or shopkeepers.

Meantime, in the Elm Hill Avenue section of Roxbury, a part of inner Boston that is suburban in superficial character, street assaults and the ever present possibility of more street assaults with no kibitzers to protect the victims, induce prudent people to stay off the sidewalks at night. Not surprisingly, for this and other reasons that are related (dispiritedness and dullness), most of Roxbury has run down. It has become a place to leave.

I do not wish to single out Roxbury or its once fine Elm Hill Avenue section especially as a vulnerable area; its disabilities, and especially its Great Blight of Dullness, are all too common in other cities too. But differences like these in public safety within the same city are worth noting.

The Elm Hill Avenue section's basic troubles are not owing to a criminal or a discriminated against or a poverty-stricken population. Its troubles stem from the fact that it is physically quite unable to function safely and with related vitality as a city district.

Even within supposedly similar parts of supposedly similar places, drastic differences in public safety exist. An incident at Washington Houses, a public housing project in New York, illustrates this point. A tenants' group at this project, struggling to establish itself, held some outdoor ceremonies in mid-December 1958, and put up three Christmas trees. The chief tree, so cumbersome it was a problem to transport, erect, and trim, went into the project's inner "street," a landscaped central mall and promenade. The other two trees, each less than six feet tall and easy to carry, went on two small fringe plots at the outer corners of the project where it abuts a busy avenue and lively cross streets of the old city. The first night, the large tree and all its trimmings were stolen. The two smaller trees remained intact, lights, ornaments and all, until they were taken down at New Year's. "The place where the tree was stolen, which is *theoretically* the most safe and sheltered place in the project, is the same place that is unsafe for people too, especially children," says a social worker who had been helping the tenants' group. "People are no safer in that mall than the Christmas tree. On the other hand, the place where the other trees were safe, where the project is just one corner out of four, happens to be safe for people."

This is something everyone already knows: A well-used city street is apt to be a safe street. A deserted city street is apt to be unsafe. But how does this work, really? And what makes a city street well used or shunned? Why is the sidewalk mall in Washington Houses, which is supposed to be an attraction, shunned? Why are the sidewalks of the old city just to its west not shunned? What about streets that are busy part of the time and then empty abruptly?

A city street equipped to handle strangers, and to make a safety asset, in itself, out of the presence of strangers, as the streets of successful city neighborhoods always do, must have three main qualities:

First, there must be a clear demarcation between what is public space and what is private space. Public and private spaces cannot ooze into each other as they do typically in suburban settings or in projects.

Second, there must be eyes upon the street, eyes belonging to those we might call the natural proprietors of the street. The buildings on a street equipped to handle strangers and to insure the safety of both residents and strangers, must be oriented to the street. They cannot turn their backs or blank sides on it and leave it blind.

And third, the sidewalk must have users on it fairly continuously, both to add to the number of effective eyes on the street and to induce the people in buildings along the street to watch the sidewalks in sufficient numbers. Nobody enjoys sitting on a stoop or looking out a window at an empty street. Almost nobody does such a thing. Large numbers of people entertain themselves, off and on, by watching street activity.

In settlements that are smaller and simpler than big cities, controls on acceptable public behavior, if not on crime, seem to operate with greater or lesser success through a web of reputation, gossip, approval, disapproval and sanctions, all of which are powerful if people know each other and word travels. But a city's streets, which must control not only the behavior of the people of the city but also of visitors from suburbs and towns who want to have a big time away from the gossip and sanctions at home, have to operate by more direct, straightforward methods. It is a wonder cities have solved such an inherently difficult problem at all. And yet in many streets they do it magnificently.

It is futile to try to evade the issue of unsafe city streets by attempting to make some other features of a locality, say interior courtyards, or sheltered play spaces, safe instead. By definition again, the streets of a city must do most of the job of handling strangers for this is where strangers come and go. The streets must not only defend the city against predatory strangers, they must protect the many, many peaceable and well-meaning strangers who use them, insuring their safety too as they pass through. Moreover, no normal person can spend his life in some artificial haven, and this includes children. Everyone must use the streets.

On the surface, we seem to have here some simple aims: To try to secure streets where the public space is unequivocally public, physically unmixed with private or with nothing-at-all space, so that the area needing surveillance has clear and practicable limits; and to see that these public street spaces have eyes on them as continuously as possible.

But it is not so simple to achieve these objects, especially the latter. You can't make people use streets they have no reason to use. You can't make people watch streets they do not want to watch. Safety on the streets by surveillance and mutual policing of one another sounds grim, but in real life it is not grim. The safety of the street works best, most casually, and with least frequent taint of hostility or suspicion precisely where people are using and most enjoying the city streets voluntarily and are least conscious, normally, that they are policing.

5. Twelve Percent

The report of the President's Commission on Law Enforcement and Administration of Justice, published in 1967, gave voice to national concern with the problem of crime and also suggested some possible remedies. But plans for more effective law enforcement are of little use unless vocal public concern is translated into active, informed support. Unfortunately, the public's concern with crime often seems to be based on irrational fear rather than knowledge, and far too few people have gone from words to vigorous participation in community programs.

The Commission cannot say that the public's fear of crime is exaggerated. It is not prepared to tell people how fearful they should be; that is something each person must decide for himself. People's fears must be respected; certainly they cannot be legislated. Some people are willing to run risks that terrify others. However, it is possible to draw some general conclusions from the findings of the surveys.

The first is that the public fears most the crimes that occur least often, crimes of violence. People are much more tolerant of crimes against property, which constitute most of the crimes that are committed against persons or households or businesses. Actually, the average citizen probably suffers the greatest economic loss from crimes against business establishments and public institutions, which pass their losses on to him in the form of increased prices and taxes. Nevertheless, most shoplifters never get to court; they are released by the store managers with warnings. Most employees caught stealing are either warned or discharged, according to the reports of businesses and organizations in the Commission's survey in three cities.

Second, the fear of crimes of violence is not a simple fear of injury or death or even of all crimes of violence, but, at bottom, a fear of strangers. The personal injury that Americans risk daily from sources other than crime are enormously greater. The annual rate of all Index offenses involving either violence or the threat of violence is 1.8 per 1,000 Americans. This is minute relative to the total accidental injuries calling for medical attention or restricted activity of 1 day or more, as reported by the Public Health Service. A recent study of emergency medical care found the quality, numbers, and distribution of ambulances and other emergency

From the President's Commission on Law Enforcement and Administration of Justice, **The Challenge of Crime in a Free Society** (Washington, D.C.: U.S. Government Printing Office, 1967).

services severely deficient, and estimated that as many as 20,000 Americans die unnecessarily each year as a result of improper emergency care. The means necessary for correcting this situation are very clear and would probably yield greater immediate return in reducing death than would expenditures for reducing the incidence of crimes of violence. But a different personal significance is attached to deaths due to the willful acts of felons as compared to the incompetence or poor equipment of emergency medical personnel.

Furthermore, this chapter has noted that most murders and assaults are committed by persons known to the victim, by relatives, friends, or acquaintances. Indeed on a straight statistical basis, the closer the relationship the greater the hazard. In one sense the greatest threat to anyone is himself, since suicides are more than twice as common as homicides.

Third, this fear of strangers has greatly impoverished the lives of many Americans, especially those who live in high-crime neighborhoods in large cities. People stay behind the locked doors of their homes rather than risk walking in the streets at night. Poor people spend money on taxis because they are afraid to walk or use public transportation. Sociable people are afraid to talk to those they do not know. In short, society is to an increasing extent suffering from what economists call "opportunity costs" as the result of fear of crime. For example, administrators and officials interviewed for the Commission by the University of Michigan survey team, report that library use is decreasing because borrowers are afraid to come out at night. School officials told of parents not daring to attend PTA meetings in the evening, and park administrators pointed to unused recreation facilities. When many persons stay home, they are not availing themselves of the opportunities for pleasure and cultural enrichment offered in their communities, and they are not visiting their friends as frequently as they might. The general level of social interaction in the society is reduced.

When fear of crime becomes fear of the stranger the social order is further damaged. As the level of sociability and mutual trust is reduced, streets and public places can indeed become more dangerous. Not only will there be fewer people abroad but those who are abroad will manifest a fear of and a lack of concern for each other. The reported incidents of bystanders indifferent to cries for help are the logical consequence of a reduced sociability, mutual distrust and withdrawal.

However, the most dangerous aspect of a fear of strangers is its implication that the moral and social order of society are of doubtful trustworthiness and stability. Everyone is dependent on this order to instill in all members of society a respect for the persons and possessions of others. When it appears that there are more and more people who do not have this respect, the security that comes from living in an orderly and trustworthy society is undermined. The tendency of many people to think of crime in terms of increasing moral deterioration is an indication that they are losing their faith in their society. And so the costs of the fear of crime to the social order may ultimately be even greater than its psychological costs to individuals.

Fourth, the fear of crime may not be as strongly influenced by the actual incidence of crime as by other experiences with the crime problem generally. For example, the mass media and overly zealous or opportunistic crime fighters may play a role in raising fears of crime by associating the idea of "crime" with a few sensational and terrifying criminal acts. Past research on the mass media's connection with crime has concentrated primarily on depictions and accounts of violence in the mass media as possible causes of delinquency and crime. Little attention has thus far been given to what may be a far more direct and costly effect—the creation of distorted perceptions of the risk of crime and exaggerated fears of victimization.

The greatest danger of an exaggerated fear of crime may well reside in the tendency to use the violent crime as a stereotype for crimes in general. For example, there may be a significant interplay between violence and the mass media and the reporting of general crime figures. Publicity about total crime figures without distinguishing between the trends for property crime and those for crimes against persons may create mistaken ideas about what is actually happening. If burglaries and larcenies increase sharply while violent crimes decrease or remain stable, the total figures will follow the property crime figures, since crimes against property are more than four-fifths of the total. Yet under these conditions people may interpret the increases in terms of the dominant stereotype of crimes of violence, thus needlessly increasing their fears. They may not only restrict their activities out of an exaggerated fear of violence but may fail to protect themselves against the more probable crimes. The fact is that most people experience crime vicariously through the daily press, periodicals, novels, radio and television, and often the reported experiences of other persons. Their fear of crime may be more directly related to the quality and the amount of this vicarious experience than it is to the actual risks of victimization.

The Commission believes that there is a clear public responsibility to keep citizens fully informed of the facts about crime so that they will have facts to go on when they decide what the risks are and what kinds and amounts of precautionary measures they should take. Furthermore, without an accurate understanding of the facts, they cannot judge whether the interference with individual liberties which strong crime control measures may involve is a price worth paying. The public obligation to citizens is to provide this information regularly and accurately. And if practices for disseminating information give wrong impressions, resources should be committed to developing more accurate methods.

Finally, public concern about crime need not have only the adverse effects that have been described so far. It can be a powerful force for action. However, making it one will not be easy. The Commission's Washington survey asked people whether they had ever "gotten together with other people around here, or has any group or organization you belong to met and discussed the problem of crime or taken some sort of action to combat crime." Only about 12 percent answered affirmatively, although the question was quite broad and included any kind of group meeting or discussion. Neither did most persons believe that they as individuals could do anything about crime in their own neighborhoods. Only slightly over 17 percent thought that they could do either a lot or just something.

Most people feel that the effort to reduce crime is a responsibility of the police, the courts and perhaps other public agencies. This was even true to some extent of administrators and officials of public agencies and utilities who were interviewed in the three city precinct surveys. However, when these officials were pressed they were able to think of many ways in which their organizations might help reduce crime, such as cooperating to make law enforcement easier, donating and helping in neighborhood programs, providing more and better street lighting, creating more parks with recreational programs, furnishing more youth programs and adult education, and promoting integration of work crews and better community relations programs.

Every American can translate his concern about, or fear of, crime into positive action. Every American should.

6. Unfinished Business

There are many people who argue that the crime problem cannot be attacked in bits and pieces but requires extensive social changes, such as the elimination of slums, the creation of meaningful work, and a strengthening of the family. The prevention and control of crime, it is claimed, involves a good deal more than extra police, better prisons, or psychotherapy; we need to build a better society, in which violence, alienation, and material deprivation no longer have a place.

Paul Goodman, writing within a long tradition of dissent, describes our "missed revolutions." If there are some who say that he is being Utopian, pointing to an ideal society that cannot be achieved in reality, there are others who argue that what is possible is an open matter to be determined by experience and not by fiat.

The use of history, Benjamin Nelson used to say, is to rescue from oblivion the lost causes of the past. History is especially important when those lost causes haunt us in the present as unfinished business.

I have often spoken in this essay of the "missed revolutions that we have inherited." My idea is that it is not with impunity that fundamental social changes fail to take place at the appropriate time; the following generations are embarrassed and confused by their lack. This subject warrants a special study. Some revolutions fail to occur; most half-occur or are compromised, attaining some of their objectives and resulting in significant social changes, but giving up on others, resulting in ambiguous values in the social whole that would not have occurred if the change had been more thoroughgoing. For in general, a profound revolutionary program in any field projects a new workable kind of behavior, a new nature of man, a new whole society; just as the traditional society it tries to replace is a whole society that the revolutionists think is out of date. But a compromised revolution tends to disrupt the tradition without achieving a new social balance.

It is the argument of this book that *the accumulation of the missed and compromised revolutions of modern times, with their consequent ambiguities and social imbalances, has fallen, and must fall, most heavily on the young, making it hard to grow up.*

A man who has attained maturity and independence can pick and choose among the immense modern advances and somewhat wield them as his way of life. If he has a poor society, an adult cannot be very happy, he will not have simple goals nor achieve classical products, but he can fight and work anyway. But for children and adolescents it is indispensable to have a coherent, fairly simple and viable society to grow up into; otherwise they are confused, and some are squeezed out. Tradition has been broken, yet there is no new standard to affirm. Culture becomes eclectic, sensational, or phony. (Our present culture is all three.) A successful revolution establishes a new community. A missed revolution makes irrelevant the community that persists. And a compromised revolution tends to shatter the community that was, without an adequate substitute. But as we argued in a previous chapter, it is precisely for the young that the geographical and historical community and its patriotism are the important environment, as they draw away from their parents and until they can act on their own with fully developed powers.

In this chapter, let us collect the missed or compromised fundamental social changes that we have had occasion to mention; calling attention to what *was* achieved and what *failed* to be achieved, and the consequent confused situation which then actually confronts the youth growing up.

Let us start with the physical environment.

Technocracy. In our own century, philosophers of the new technology, like Veblen, Geddes, or Fuller, succeeded in making efficiency and know-how the chief ethical values of the folk, creating a mystique of "production," and a kind of streamlined esthetics. But they did not succeed in wresting management from the businessmen and creating their own world of a neat and transparent physical plant and a practical economics of production and distribution. The actual results have been slums of works of engineering, confused and useless overproduction, gadgetry, and new tribes of middlemen, promoters, and advertisers.

Urbanism. As Le Corbusier and Gropius urged, we have increasingly the plan and style of functional architecture; biological standards of housing; scientific study of traffic and city services; some zoning; and the construction of large-scale projects. But nowhere is realized the ideal of over-all community planning, the open green city, or the organic relation of work, living, and play. The actual results have been increasing commutation and traffic, segregated ghettos, a "functional" style little different from packaging, and the tendency to squeeze out some basic urban functions, such as recreation or schooling, to be squeezed out altogether.

Garden City. The opposite numbers, the Garden City planners after Ebenezer Howard, have achieved some planned communities protected by greenbelts. But they did not get their integrated towns, planned for industry, local commerce, and living. The result is that actual suburbs and garden cities are dormitories with a culture centering around small children, and absence of the wage earner; and such "plans" as the so-called shopping centers disrupts such village communities as there were. The movement to conserve the wilds cannot withstand the cars, so that all areas are invaded and regulated.

Let us proceed to economic and social changes.

New Deal. The Keynesian economics of the New Deal has cushioned the business cycle and maintained nearly full employment. It has not achieved its ideal of social balance between public and private works. The result is an expanding production increasingly consisting of corporation boondoggling.

Syndicalism. Industrial workers have won their unions, obtained better wages and working conditions, and affirmed the dignity of labor. But they gave up their ideal of workers' management, technical education, and concern for the utility of their labor. The result is that a vast majority couldn't care less about what they make, and the "labor movement" is losing force.

Class Struggle. The working class has achieved a striking repeal of the iron law of wages; it has won a minimum wage and social security. But the goal of an equalitarian or freely mobile society has been given up, as has the solidarity of the underprivileged. The actual result is an increasing rigidity of statuses; some of the underprivileged tending to drop out of society altogether. On the other hand, the cultural equality that has been achieved has been the degradation of the one popular culture to the lowest common denominator.

Production for Use. This socialist goal has been missed, resulting in many of the other failures here listed.

Sociology. During the past century, the sociologists have achieved their aim of dealing with mankind in its natural groups or groups with common problems, rather than as isolated individuals or a faceless mass. Social science has replaced many prejudices and ideologies of vested interests. But on the whole, social scientists have given up their aim of fundamental social change and an open-experimental method determining its goals as it went along: the pragmatist ideal of society as a laboratory for freedom and self-correcting humanity. The actual result is an emphasis on "socializing" and "belonging," with the loss of nature, culture, group solidarity and group variety, and individual excellence.

Next, political and constitutional reforms.

Democracy. The democratic revolution succeeded in extending formal self-government and opportunity to nearly everybody, regardless of birth, property, or education. But it gave up the ideal of the town meeting, with the initiative and personal involvement that alone could train people in self-government and give them practical knowledge of political issues. The actual result has been the formation of a class of politicians who govern, and who are themselves symbolic front figures.

The Republic. Correspondingly, the self-determination won by the American Revolution for the regional states, that should have made possible real political experimentation, soon gave way to a national conformity; nor has the nation as a whole conserved its resources and maintained its ideals. The result is a deadening centralism, with neither local patriotism nor national patriotism. The best people do not offer themselves for public office, and no one has the aim of serving the Republic.

Freedom of Speech. Typical is the fate of the hard-won Constitutional freedoms, such as freedom of speech. Editors and publishers have given up trying to give an effective voice to important but unpopular opinions. Anything can be printed, but the powerful interests have the big presses. Only the safe opinion is proclaimed and other opinion is swamped.

Liberalism. The liberal revolution succeeded in shaking off onerous government controls on enterprise, but it did not persist to its goal of real public wealth as the result of free enterprise and honestly informed choice on the market. The actual result is an economy dominated by monopolies, in which the earnest individual entrepreneur or inventor, who could perform a public service, is actively discouraged; and consumer demand is increasingly synthetic.

Agrarianism. Conversely, the Jeffersonian ideal of a proud and independent productive yeomanry, with natural family morals and a cooperative community spirit, did in fact energize settling the West and providing the basis for our abundance. But because it has failed to cope with technological changes and to withstand speculation, "farming as a way of life" has succumbed to cash-cropping dependent on distant markets, and is ridden with mortgages, tenancy, and hired labor. Yet it maintains a narrow rural morality and isolationist politics, is a sucker for the mass culture of Madison Avenue and Hollywood, and in the new cities (e.g., in California, where farmers have migrated) is a bulwark against genuine city culture.

Liberty. Constitutional safeguards of person were won. But despite the increasing concentration of state power and mass pressures, no effort was made to give to individuals and small groups new means easily to avail themselves of the safeguards. The result is that there is no longer the striking individuality of free men; even quiet nonconformity is hounded; and there is no asylum from coast to coast.

Fraternity. This short-lived ideal of the French Revolution, animating a whole people and uniting all classes as a community, soon gave way to a dangerous nationalism. The ideal somewhat revived as the solidarity of the working class, but this too has faded into either philanthropy or "belonging."

Brotherhood of Races. The Civil War won formal rights for Negroes, but failed to win social justice and factual democracy. The actual result has been segregation, and fear and ignorance for both whites and blacks.

Pacifism. This revolution has been entirely missed.

. . .

Let us proceed to some more general moral premises of modern times.

Reformation. The Protestant Reformation won the possibility of living religiously in the world, freed individuals from the domination of the priest, and led, indirectly, to the toleration of private conscience. But it failed to withstand the secular power; it did not cultivate the meaning of vocation as a community function; and in most sects the spirit of the churches did not spring from their living congregations but was handed down as dogma and ascetic discipline. The final result has been secularism, individualism, the subordination of human beings to a rational economic system, and churches irrelevant to practical community life. Meantime, acting merely as a negative force, the jealous sectarian conscience has driven religion out of social thought.

Modern Science. The scientific revolution associated with the name of Galileo freed thinking of superstition and academic tradition and won attention to the observation of nature. But it failed to modify and extend its method to social and moral matters, and indeed science has gotten further and further from ordinary experience. With the dominance of science and applied science in our times, the result has been a specialist class of scientists and technicians, the increasing ineptitude of the average person, a disastrous dichotomy of "neutral" facts versus "arbitrary" values, and a superstition of scientism that has put people out of touch with nature, and also has aroused a growing hostility to science.

Enlightenment. The Enlightenment unseated age-old tyrannies of state and church and won a triumph of reason over authority. But its universalism failed to survive the rising nationalisms except in special sciences and learning, and its ideal of encyclopedic reason as the passionate guide to life degenerated to the nineteenth-century hope for progress through science and learning. And we now have an internationalism without brotherhood or peace, even concealing science as a strategic weapon; and a general sentiment that the rule of reason is infinitely impractical.

Honesty. The rebellion for honest speech that we associate with Ibsen, Flaubert, etc., and also with the muckrakers broke down the hypocrisy of Victorian prudishness and of exploiting pillars of society; it reopened discussion and renovated language; and it weakened official censorship. But it failed to insist on the close relation between honest speech and corresponding action. The result has been a weakening of the obligation to act according to speech, so that, ironically, the real motives of public and private behavior are more in the dark than ever.

Popular Culture. This ideal, that we may associate in literature with the name of Sam Johnson and the Fleet Street journalists, in the plastic arts with William Morris and Ruskin, freed culture from aristocratic and snobbish patrons. It made thought and design relevant to everyday manners. But it did not succeed in establishing an immediate relation between the writer or artist and his audience. The result is that the popular culture is controlled by hucksters and promoters as though it were a saleable commodity, and our society, inundated by cultural commodities, remains uncultivated.

Finally, some reforms directly connected with children and adolescents.

No Child Labor. Children have been rescued from the exploitation and training of factories and sweat shops. But, relying on the public schools and the apprentice-training in an expanding and open economy, the reformers did not develop a philosophy of capacity and vocation. Nor, since there were many small jobs, did they face the problems of a growing boy needing to earn some money. In our days, the result is that growing youths are idle and vocationally useless, and often economically desperate; and the schools, on the contrary, become apprentice-training paid for by public money.

Compulsory Education. This gave to all children a certain equality of opportunity in an open expanding industrial society. Formal elementary discipline was sufficient when the environment was educative and provided opportunities for advancement. In our circumstances, formal literacy is less relevant, and overcrowding and official interference make individual attention and real teaching impossible; so that it could be said that the schools are as stupefying as they are educative, and compulsory education is often like jail.

Sexual Revolution. This has accomplished a freeing of animal functioning in general, has pierced repression, importantly relaxed inhibition, weakened legal and social sanctions, and diminished the strict animal-training of small children. The movement has not so much failed as that it is still in process, strongly resisted by inherited prejudices, fears, and jealousies. By and large it has not won practical freedom for older children and adolescents. The actual present result is that they are trapped by inconsistent rules, suffer because of excessive stimulation and inadequate discharge, and become preoccupied with sexual thoughts as if these were the whole of life.

Permissiveness. Children have more freedom of spontaneous behavior, and their dignity and spirit are not crushed by humiliating punishments in school and in very many homes. But this permissiveness has not extended to provide also means and conditions: Young folk might be sexually free but have no privacy; they are free to be angry, but have no asylum to escape from home, and no way to get their own money. Besides, where upbringing is permissive, it is necessary to have strong values and esteemed behavior at home and in the community, so that the child can have worthwhile goals to structure his experience; and of course it is just these that are lacking. So permissiveness often leads to anxiety and weakness instead of confidence and strength.

Progressive Education. This radical proposal, aimed at solving the dilemmas of education in the modern circumstances of industrialism and democracy, was never given a chance. It succeeded in destroying the faculty psychology in the interests of educating the whole person, and in emphasizing group experience, but failed to introduce learning-by-doing with real problems. The actual result of the gains has been to weaken the academic curriculum and foster adjustment to society as it is.

A POSTSCRIPT

In trying to understand criminal behavior and find a means for its control, there is a great temptation to come up with simple theories and simple remedies. We have no illusions, however, that this is possible, and we hope that the reader has none either. Our existing store of knowledge is painfully small, and, although we are optimistic about what will be discovered in the next several decades, in the meantime we had best avoid the strident claims of expertise *and quick solutions that are thrust upon us with too easy assurance.*

We have argued, with the voices of other men, that the definition of crime involves profoundly important and difficult value judgments, and a smug morality does not provide an answer; the search for the causes of crime must go far beyond a facile equation between individual pathology and criminal behavior; and our attempts to control and prevent crime inevitably entangle us in other social goals—most notably, the protection of civil liberties.

To a large extent, then, we finish with questions, not answers; unresolved disputes, not final verdicts; uncertainties, not a clear path to a proven cure. There are some people, undoubtedly, for whom such ambiguities are intolerable. We suspect, however, that the ability to live with these ambiguities, to exist in a state of tension with conflicting goals and a slowly receding ignorance, is a necessary element in the search for a just social order in which the "crime problem" is kept in perspective.

Index